the Outlaw Bible of
american essays

The
Outlaw Bible
of
american essays

EDITED BY

Alan Kaufman

THUNDER'S MOUTH PRESS
New York

THE OUTLAW BIBLE OF AMERICAN ESSAYS

Published by
Thunder's Mouth Press
An imprint of Avalon Publishing Group, Inc.
245 West 17th Street, 11th floor
New York, NY 10011

www.thundersmouth.com

AVALON
publishing group incorporated

Compilation copyright © 2006 by Alan Kaufman
Pages 341–343 serve as an extension of this copyright page

First printing, October 2006

Library of Congress Cataloging-in-Publication Data is available.

ISBN-10: 1-56025-935-3
ISBN-13: 978-1-56025-935-0

9 8 7 6 5 4 3 2 1

Book design by Simon M. Sullivan

Printed in the United States of America
Distributed by Publishers Group West

For Joseph Herlisy, Silas Paine, John Ortley Lane and Kevin J.Ryan: Outlaws to the bone.

And to some friends who dare to live the life: Mike & Marcella Gates, Lewis & Elizabeth Rutherford, David Newman, Terese Taylor, Steve Gardner, Bill Wright, Mike Kelleher, Scott (Spot) Marshall, Carmen Rodrigues, Ralph & Izzy Spite, Lauren Volper, Dorka Keehn, Pauli Grey, Kristen Kadner, and Tim Wicks—Blake smiles upon you all.

contents

ALAN KAUFMAN

Introduction

". . . and the rule is no crap. There is to be no crap."
— Midnight Cowboy *by James Leo Herlihy*

WITH THIS BOOK I CONCLUDE my roundup of American outlaw literary culture: an anthological trilogy that includes two previously published volumes, *The Outlaw Bible of American Poetry* and *The Outlaw Bible of American Literature*.

In the first volume, spanning the period from the Second World War to the present, I assembled, with assistance from S. A. Griffin, the poets of the underground scene, some of them completely forgotten or simply unknown. In the second book, which I coedited with Barney Rosset and Neil Ortenberg, I ingathered countercultural prose voices of the past half century.

For this volume, I recruit a set of incendiaries who expand on themes that emerged from the first two books: the betrayed American Dream, personal and artistic freedom, sexual daring, the struggle for racial and gender equality, revolutionary politics, violence and death; all are explored here in depth.

The *Outlaw Bible* trilogy is intended to transmit to today's rebels—and also tomorrow's—an outsider canon of unsparing inquiry and revolt that has rumbled at the heart of modern American letters and identity since World War II, when Auschwitz and Hiroshima changed forever our idea of what it means to be human. The spirit of it hearkens back to the Great Awakening of street sensibility that incited early colonialists to erupt in the American Revolution.

It is a discourse whose fullest implications have been denied, ignored, and even, at times, ruthlessly suppressed by a capitalist police state bent upon preserving, at all costs, through legal or extralegal means, a politically safe and financially profitable status quo of public subservience.

Decades after facing a world of death camps and nuclear devastation, America's business, at home and abroad, still remains business. The images of naked Jewish corpses in pits, and of radioactive Japanese kids with burned faces sliding off, left us after World War II but temporarily fazed.

1

The murders of Malcolm, Martin, Medgar, John, and Bobby, and the madness of Vietnam, Selma, Montgomery, Kent State, Chile, and El Salvador followed relentlessly. Even 9/11 did not really set us back for long. We continue to do business as though it were a war, and to wage war as though it were a business.

In America today this legacy proceeds unimpeded, as we legislate against gays precisely as once the Nazis did, with new versions of the Nuremberg Laws, forbidding them the most fundamental rights. We hunt immigrants like fugitives, even as we hire them without benefits to perform our most degrading tasks. We whisk away national security "suspects" to secret domestic prisons and release them on the streets months later, shocked and broken. We torture; it is now policy. We invade and bomb without good cause. We butcher innocent creatures in abattoirs reminiscent of death camps, yet hunger in America is on the rise. We are governed by a president who steals elections, wages futile wars, spies on his citizens, and rules without reference to the Constitution. Orwell's *1984* is not merely upon us: it is already old hat.

Set against the sterile, creeping horror of our media-sickened, death-denying (and also death-dealing) way of life, the *Outlaw* trilogy illuminates the hopeful struggle by some to recover or else introduce—through crazy courage, shameless openness, and limitless passion—some other wilder, freer, and yes, also, at times, kinder version of America.

This vision is best summed up by Jack Kerouac, who described it perfectly in *On The Road*:

> . . . all that raw land that rolls in one unbelievable huge bulge
> over to the West Coast, and all that road going, all the people
> dreaming in the immensity of it, and in Iowa I know by now the
> children must be crying in the land where they let the children
> cry, and tonight the stars'll be out, don't you know that God is
> Pooh Bear? the evening star must be drooping and shedding her
> sparkler dims on the prairie, which is just before the coming of
> complete night that blesses the earth, darkens all the rivers, cups
> the peaks and folds the final shore in, and nobody, nobody
> knows what's going to happen . . .

This is a poetry of unbridled faith in some essential human innocence, despite the dwarfed and dirty image of humanity pedaled by the corporations. It is something we can still sense and search for, like Neal Cassady's quest for his father. It is the America of Mark Twain and John Coltrane alike, regardless of those spoilers, Bin Laden and Bush. Melville and Whitman saw it, knew of it, as did Jackson Pollock, Thelonius Monk, and Kenneth Patchen. You can hear it in the poem-songs of Bob Dylan and Woody Guthrie, Bruce Springsteen, Leonard Cohen, and Tom Waits. It is alive still today.

But it exists largely in the lonely, broken imaginations of poets and rev-olutionaries, of runaway young bohos and artistic visionaries, asleep in their cardboard box beds outside Greyhound bus stations or else burning light to dawn in ugly rooms as they pour out their last ounce of courage into poems, manifestos, novels, manuscripts, and songs that no one might ever read or believe in, because they're too radically on the edge.

And to redeem this idea of America may take more then writing hon-estly and well. It may need outright political and social struggle en masse by all of us. For it is an idea that has, since Kerouac's time, been increasingly buried under corporate pyramids fed with the fattened bodies of wage-slaves, young and old alike, male and female, whole families even: entombed by mall cement and mind-trapped by market trickery and polit-ical snake-oil. In this spiritual and material void, while the American soul struggles furiously for its very life, the forces of reaction grow evermore entrenched and at times appear to be immutable facts, as much as the air we breathe.

But they are not immutable. Evil can be overthrown. Each essay in this book—like the works in the previous two volumes—is a refusal to accept its immutability and is an encouragement to break wrongful laws, strike blows against this growing empire of despair, live your vision boldly—and in so doing to affirm our nation's first and most defining task as nothing less than the defense of personal and communal freedom and protection of the indi-vidual's right to difference, no matter what the cost.

If this trilogy reveals an essentially religious impulse, the attempt to fashion from controversial texts a new kind of bible—an Outlaw Bible of American Revolt—with its face set defiantly against what the poet Jack Hirschman has called in a recent interview "the dopey clown show of teeming loneliness," then so be it. As Walt Whitman wrote, "We consider bibles and religions divine—I do not say that they are not divine; I say that they have all grown out of you and may grow out of you still: it is not they who give life—it is you who give the life."

Here then, is some of the life given in this book:

From behind prison walls, from out of the shocking eye of the American inferno, the pyramid's molten core, is Robert Beck's life recapped in explosive, poisonous detail—his downfall, first as a pimp, and then as a brutalized convict, a catastrophe that transformed him into the bestselling author known as Iceberg Slim.

Here is Hubert Selby Jr. on his struggle to write despite a mind addled with addiction and a body perpetually near death.

Here is the San Francisco poet laureate and full-time street revolutionary Jack Hirschman on the war of art and literature against the air-conditioned capitalist nightmare.

Here is Tennessee Williams on America's betrayal of the success-anointed artist; Sue Coe on the gruesome slaughter of innocent creatures; Allen Ginsberg on the tormented quest to write *HOWL*; and William Burroughs on the State's ploys to seize our minds.

In these pages, you'll stand with Eldridge Cleaver on the steps of *Ramparts* magazine as Black Panther Huey Newton faces down armed cops with a shotgun in his hands; pass days and nights with Michelle Tea at Tranny Camp against the backdrop of the Republican siege of Gays; issue communiqués from the front lines of the revolution with White Panther founder John Sinclair; and with Annie Sprinkle apply the fearsome lash to quivering, naked butts at the shame-free Hellfire Club.

Here are Kurt Vonnegut on obscenity, Ray Charles on women, Brenda Knight on lady Beats, Scarlot Harlot on the rights of prostitutes, and Paul Simon with Miriam Makeba on World music. And here are relative newcomers like Timothy "Speed" Levitch, James Sullivan, Fly, and Erik La Prade alongside such underground legends as Paul Krassner, Dotson Rader, Sparrow, Eileen Myles, Bob Holman, Susie Bright, David Meltzer, Ben Fong-Torres, V. Vale, and even a weigh-in from the outlaw academic bell hooks.

My take on what constitutes an essay follows closely that of Montaigne, who invented the genre: an essay is anything you say it is. And so in this volume one will find essays produced in every imaginable form. Montaigne would have approved.

I could never have produced these anthologies had I lived in any place other than the Bay Area, for San Francisco, I'm proud to say, is not the U.S.A. Here is the birthing source of most of the great cultural and political awakenings that have rocked America. Here the resonance of historic rebellions, from the Wobblies to the Beats to the student movement to the Panthers, the Summer of Love Hippies, and even Punk yet echo, no matter how faintly, in the grim studded leather avenues of Oakland and in the tie-dyed streets of Berkeley and in the graffiti-scrawled side streets of Frisco's South of Market.

A new revolt brews, building orgasmic steam. To find it, you must listen carefully for its tremors in the neon alleys of the Tenderloin and eavesdrop on the storefronts of the Mission, where rebel poets and vagabond painters and politicos slouch in torn armchairs, talking fire.

It is in live music by great unknowns rattling the walls of dingy tenements and walkups in the Lower Haight.

You can sense it when the skies turn royal blue and the Hell's Angels roar on chopped hogs through Haight-Ashbury and shirtless bandmates with braided hair set up outdoor mikes and speakers in the nearby grassy Panhandle and wail electric to small handfuls of young beautiful people with, yes, real flowers in their hair.

Everywhere, I see nascent Panthers and Beats and Hippies and Weathermen and Punks—reincarnated anew as their very own as yet unnamed thing—and even now, as I write these words, young outlaws conspire— through poetry, novels, tagging, street theater, 'zines, alternative commerce, art, music, trainhopping, communal living, sobriety, body manipulation, spiritual practices, political street action, sexual and gender experimentation, and a sheer unflinching embrace of the high-wire unknown—to defeat the murderous system, that seeks to crush their souls and annihilate their hearts.

Their counterparts exist everywhere, too, in growing numbers, in town and city, throughout the United States. Born of disillusionment with the lies of corporate life, angry at being ruled by a fascist government, they are refugees seeking escape from minimum-wage jobs and a co-opted counterculture. These freedom riders of the new millennium comprise a vast network of committed creatives living alternative lifestyles. The artist Fly has fashioned a kind of hand-drawn national portrait gallery of some of these rebels, a few of which are reprinted here in *The Outlaw Bible of American Essays*. Their very existence defies the media's mental carpet-bombing campaign to portray today's young as shallow, unimaginative, and lost. In Fly's "Peops" I see only new Eldridge Cleavers and Patti Smiths, Jimi Hendrixes, Jack Kerouacs, Allen Ginsbergs, Grace Slicks, and Abbie Hoffmans. But they are doing it on their own terms.

We are all outlaws in the eyes of America. And so are you, whoever you are. Turn off your TV, rip out your iPod, slam shut that anesthetizing laptop, put your cell phone ringer on permanent "off" and step outside into the street. Because it's in the street that all real revolutions thrive.

And see there now, like figures in a dream, skateboarding by or on stripped-down bicycles with raised forks, men and women with full-sleeve tattoos, flying past, hair free in the wind. Now go visit them in the cafés raging at open mikes and in the storefront galleries hanging outrageous subversive art and over there in the alleys, tagging Burroughs-like secret viral codes of spray-painted outrage on the oozing walls of this crumbling empire, and if you lift your head just a bit you'll hear, above the traffic, the distant strains of their forward-dreaming Stratocasters and Fenders pronouncing liberation—yours and mine and everyone's—on the new spring breeze. And then come on, Outlaw, say "fuck you" to the system and join our revolution.

June 6, 2006
San Francisco, California

ICEBERG SLIM (ROBERT BECK)

From a Steel Box to a Wicked Young Girl

I WANT TO SAY AT the outset that I have become ill, insane as an inmate of a torture chamber behind America's fake facade of justice and democracy. But I am not as ill as I was, and I am getting better all the time. And also, I want to make clear that my reason for starting these notes at a point of personal anguish and suffering is that these experiences marked the end of a corrupt pimp life and were the prelude to a still mauled but constructive new life. I am not "playing the con" for sympathy.

In the cold-blooded academy of ghetto streets I was taught early that suffering is inevitable and necessary for an aspiring pimp, pickpocket, or con man and even just a nigger compelled to become a four-way whore for the Establishment. I learned also that sympathy is a counterfeit emotion for suckers that is usually offered with a crooked con grin of amused contempt and rejected with a spittled snarl.

Within the moldering walls of Chicago's House of Correction, in one of its ancient cellhouses, is a row of steel punishment cubicles where rule-breaking inmates spend at most several days. In 1960 I was locked in one of the steel boxes for ten months. I owed the joint an unserved part of a sentence from which I had vanished thirteen years before like a wisp of black smoke and without the usual damage to joint fixtures or guards' skulls. And apparently the sweet joker who ordered me stuffed into the steel box to commit suicide or go mad (when I was returned to the joint on escape charges) felt he owed vengeance on me to his long-ago fellow clique of torturers and grafters who must have suffered a shit storm of consternation and rage when nigger me bypassed their booming instant release service and hadn't bought out, but thought out.

But that second mob of debonair demons sure butchered off a hunk of my mental ass. For even now, a new life and a decade later, I will lay odds that until the grave the images and sounds of that violent, gibbering year will stomp and shudder my mind.

One instance, among many: I am in a pleasant mood when I hear through an open window the profane chanting of teenagers playing a merry game of ghetto dozens (*dozens*—the denigration of another's parents or ancestors) that explode in a montage of pain, bright as flame, that shocks my brain. Again for the thousandth time I see and hear the likable little black con in the steel box next to mine, my only buddy, suddenly chanting freaky lyrics of a crazy frightening song about how God is a double-crossing cocksucker and how he is going to sodomize and murder his crippled bitch mama.

I cry out like a scalded child, leap off my straw mattress, and stand on trembly legs peering into Shorty's cubicle through a ragged break in the weld of the sheet steel wall. He's buck naked, and his soft black baby face is twisted hard and hideously old as he stands slobbery with his hands flying like frenzied bats up and down his long stiff penis.

I have the vague hope that he's "gaming," playing the con, for the heartless white folks for some personal benefit or advantage. But there's a chilling realism, a perfection about Shorty's awful performance, so I rib him gently.

"Buddy, put your pants on and stop that chump jeffing. (*Jeffing*—playing or employing a low grade of con based on one's blackness and the projection of the contemptible "Sambo" or "Rastus" image.) Instead of a hospital broad tucking you between white sheets, the ass kickers will show any minute now. Dummy up for me, pal. Huh? I like you and I got a weak belly."

Shorty gives me zero response, and his walling eyes are like coals of white fire. I feel a jolt of panic in my chest and a terrifying fluttery quaking inside my skull.

And because I know that madness can be catching, I get stupid and scream, "You little jive ass, you're suppose to be a player. Remember? What you gonna do, let these dirty white folks crack you up?"

But he's so pitiful, I go soft and plead, "Shorty, get your head together. Please pal, listen to me!"

I beg him until I stink of emotion sweat and my voice fades to a squealy whisper. But Shorty doesn't listen for the pathetic reason that he can't hear me or anything else except his private hellish drumbeat.

The guards come soon to take Shorty away forever, and he yelps and whimpers like a puppy under their fists and feet. I quiver, and my teeth slash into my bottom lip with every thud. And as Shorty is dragged away, I sink to the concrete floor and roll myself into a fetal ball against a frightening chaos of pulsing green-streaked puffy bladders that whirl madly in terrible near collision on a shuddery screen inside my head. I feel great anguish and terror as if the berserk missiles are really sections of myself facing bloody destruction.

The tragedy of Shorty and its recurring long-range misery for me is but one "House" horror among many that haunt my new life.

From a Steel Box to a Wicked Young Girl

A day or so before my expected legal release date from the "House," I was taken from my steel box to an interview with a charmer who told me with a choreographed Billy Graham–type smile that a new computation of my time served and owed left me in debt to the joint for two additional months. I had spent the two months in county jail where I had been taken after Captain Churchill, a "House" bloodhound, backed by city police, crashed my pad and cracked me on an ancient fugitive warrant for the escape from the "House."

I had expected the attempt to steal from me the two months served in county jail. I stood battered but tall before the desk of the head Nazi and bombed the freakish grin off his fat face with the recital of an affidavit I had composed and memorized. Having no legal training, I could only sense its validity intuitively.

My position was that Captain Churchill, a "House" official, had arrested me. I was from the instant of that arrest legally in the custody of the "House," and even in the event that Captain Churchill had somehow managed to jail me on as unlikely a place as the moon for two months, I technically would have been serving "House" time. I closed my argument with a flexing of fake muscle based on the misfortune of a "House" guard who had furnished grist for recent newspaper headlines. He was then under indictment for selling and delivering a hacksaw blade to a group of half corpses in the steel caskets down the way from mine.

So for a dramatic flexing of that personal muscle, I hunched my wasted frame forward and arrogantly glued my palms to the mirrorlike top of the Nazi's desk. I flinched back from a remarkable likeness of the wolfman staring up at me and switched my eyes to the fat red face before me. I told it in that low, disarming tone of voice used by sneaky cops just before they stomp or kick you into insensibility that the notorious guard under indictment had delivered, to a friend of mine on the outside, several pieces of explosive and embarrassing (for the Nazi and his City Hall bosses) mail.

His face turned from red to white to blue, and I remembered the rumors about his faulty pump. I stood there grinning and watched him choking and gasping for air. I went on to assure him that the letter contained the names of racketeering guards and an exposé of corruption within the joint that perhaps even he was not aware of. And I assured him that my friend would make public the contents of the letters if I did not get my legal release date.

I secretly hoped that convict me and my threats might have triggered a fatal attack. My emotions made of that pulse-leaping moment a monument of vengeance, an event that could not have been excelled except by the exquisite pleasure of blowing out his diseased brains. And for the first time since I'd been caged in the steel box, I felt like a human being—like a man.

He seemed to be strangling as I smiled at him and slipped out the door to the escort guard waiting in the corridor for me. I paced the steel box in an agony of suspense: Was the torturer dead? Then panic and despair: I couldn't survive in the box for those extra two months! Wouldn't the muscle of my bluff and my chance for a legal release date die with him?

Later that afternoon, the cellhouse vibrated with the sudden thunder of profane raillery and the feet of shop cons going to their cells on the tiers above me. I tuned my ears up high, but no gleeful announcement of the head keeper's death filtered down through the bedlam of voices and epidemic farting.

He had survived, and the chances were that I would escape the steel box within forty-eight hours. But suddenly I was terrified at the prospect of freedom. Almost immediately I realized why. I was caught in the nightmare bind that an older pimp faces after the age of thirty-five. He is then prone to many setbacks and disasters. Any one of them can put him on his uppers and without the basic gaudy bait, like an out-of-sight car, psychedelic wardrobe, the diamonds necessary to hook and enslave a fresh stable of humping young whores.

I still owned a portion of the mind of a young whore. But my bottom or main whore of many years had delivered my car, jewelry, clothes, and other vital pimp flash to an obscure but younger, fresher monster than I. The young mudkicker had written me frequently and she had regularly sent me small money orders. She had left a Montana bordello to run afoul of a spermy gambler who mined her commercial curves and blew away my heady dreams of mountainous greenbacks by blasting a squealer into her belly.

And now her sobby letters indicated that she was petulantly waiting for me, her favorite field marshal of cunt huckstering, to liberate her from her slum pad and her unwanted motherhood.

But she didn't know I'd had the jolting insight that I had been a sucker, conned by my own velvet bullshit, which the whores had bought for a generation, about the magnificence of the pimp game. She didn't know I was determined not to join that contemptible group of aging pimps I had seen through the years and pitied as they went their pathetic way with a wild dream of new glory and a big fast stable of young freak mudkickers.

Young whores give an old pimp down on his luck merciless treatment. They flirt with him, play on him, give the corrupt old dreamer hope and then viciously poke fun at him as they coldly reject him. No, I was not going back to become one of them. And I was just as determined not to become a suicidal stickup artist or other "heavy" hustler.

But how was I going to make it out there in the free world with no training except in the art of pimping? I vowed there in the box to kill myself before I became like "Dandy" Sammy. He had been a boss pimp whom I had idolized as a boy when I was getting street poisoned.

One dazzling summer afternoon in Cleveland, at the peak of my pimphood, I was confronted on the sidewalk outside my hotel by an old, stooped, black man. He clutched a shoeshine box and he stank of the vomit encrusting his ragged shirtfront. His pitch was a poem of pathos.

I declined a shine, but the seamed ruin of his face nudged a ghost inside my skull. Almost mechanically I gave him a twenty-dollar bill and went past him. His face haunted me across a dozen states and cities.

Six months later I was shooting "H" in a fellow pimp's pad. An old whore got dreamy-eyed and cracked about how much bread she had made for Dandy Sammy and what a helluva pimp he had been. And then suddenly I knew who the filthy old bum with the shoeshine box had been.

Now I waited in a steel box with compounded misery, Mama was dying of an incurable disease out in California, and the guilt I felt for my neglect of her through the years was crushing. Mama's friends had sent me more than enough money for the trip to California. I had promised Mama I would come to her upon my release.

I got my legal release date and stood weakly outside the joint, blinking in the April sun. I was a confused, wasted shadow of myself—unsure of in what direction lay the Southside. I chose a direction and found freedom from the box so intoxicating that I walked miles before my legs got rubbery. I staggered into a greasy spoon on the Southside and gulped down a bowl of gumbo. Peeping at my gruesome reflection in the chrome napkin holder, I wondered how my cute young whore would react to a face as wrecked as mine.

I went to a barber shop on Forty-third Street and got a shave and mud massage with scalding towels galore. I relaxed beneath the searing steam and tried to piece together exit con for the girl. I had expected the barber to perform a minor miracle, but his mirror told me I looked like my own grandpaw.

I walked toward the El station in my still blurry state of mind and stupidly decided I wouldn't go to the girl's kitchenette pad and display my ruin. Perhaps I was afraid that my sick pimp brain couldn't cope with the certain temptation face-to-face to peddle her plush pussy. I would catch

From a Steel Box to a Wicked Young Girl

the first plane or train leaving Chicago and send her a nice creamy letter from Los Angeles.

Then it hit me! The girl's trip to employment in Montana was still within the white slave statute of limitations. I stopped and leaned weakly against a lamppost. I realized that I would be asking for a bit in the federal joint if I split from the girl in a way to leave her hostile.

I was one of the dozen or so black pimps the FBI kept constant tabs on to nail on a white slave beef. Their deadly method was to swoop down on an angry girl, usually when she was facing a jail term for prostitution, and offer her freedom if she would sign a criminal complaint against the pimp who'd left her raw and vengeful.

I'd been shipped off once to a federal pen because I'd been careless and cut a girl loose in the rough. The greatest fear a seasoned pimp has is that some salty whore he has split from will sign a paper offered by an eager FBI agent stipulating she was sent across state lines to hustle.

It was early afternoon when I went through the foyer of the tenement building and spotted her at the end of the first-floor hallway. She was holding the infant in her arms and laughing gaily with an ebony skeleton who was jiggling inside an orange-print tent and popping her fingers to the music and lyrics of the "Madison"—a then current dance craze.

I walked to within three feet of them before my girl saw me. For a moment her tan face was a cool, indifferent blank. And then, in a series of lightning changes, it twisted with recognition from wincing shock at my ghastly ruin, to puckered-mouth pity, to the fraud of neon-eyed, squealy-mouthed ecstasy. I felt violence bubbling inside my skull, but I managed a grotesque grin and took the tiny infant in my arms. I heard the skeleton giggle derisively and dance away as I lowered my mouth to the curvy lips of my one and only (and last) whore.

I felt that old hot writhing of her lips and my tongue was instantly flogged by the wet whip lashing forth with its spray of honey. I began to wonder about how tough the exit from her life could possibly be.

I followed her into the furnished dungeon and sat in a rickety rocker beside a half-open, soot-streaked window. I pretended to be fascinated by the scabrous view of the garbage-strewn alley as I frantically tried to frame exit dialogue that wouldn't get me crossed into a long bit in a federal joint.

All of the countless whores I have known and those I have controlled revealed a hunger for notoriety and for punishment, psychic or physical or both. The phony glamour and cruelty of the pimp fill these needs and are the magnets that attract and hold the whore to the pimp.

From a Steel Box to a Wicked Young Girl

Since I was aware of these things, my strategy to cop a heel smoothly from the young whore was obvious. I had to convince her of my inability to handle her affairs and to blaze again in pimp glory. I was going to ignore her freakish yen for the punishment ritual of "kiss, kick" that is the pimp's trade.

I had to come on with low-voltage, square-world dialogue and saccharine sweetness. I couldn't quit her because of the "white slave" threat, and I had to be certain that she quit me not in anger but in pity.

I held the gambler's squealer and tuned out the girl's rundown on the yoyo affairs of pimps and whores we knew until twilight.

After we had eaten a soul food supper and the baby was asleep, she lay in my arms and beat me to the nitty-gritty by peevishly saying, "You haven't been rapping much, and the little you've rapped sounded 'off the wall' like a chump trick. You salty 'cause I had that sucker's baby?"

I playfully spanked her behind and said, "Sweet puppy, accidents happen to a genius, so how can I be salty with you about the kid? She's beautiful. It's just going to take a little time to come to myself after what the white folks did to me in that steel box. And I'm confused like a sucker fresh from the sticks."

She said icily, "I can dig it. But what the hell about the game and are you going to keep me in this lousy pad forever? I'm the only bitch that stayed in your corner when you went to the joint. Don't forget that."

I kissed the brown skin bomb from belly button to earlobe and said sweetly, "Baby Angel, I'm hip you're my star, but my head is really bad. I'm ashamed to tell you how bad. I don't see how my foggy head can put together a stable of girls and control it. And besides it wouldn't be right for a beautiful young girl like you to hump her heart out to get the playing front for a washed-out old nigger pimp like me. And Angel, what about the poor little kid? She needs her mama all the time, and you need a man with ideas or with a job. My brain is dead, and I'm too sick to work. Maybe I should split the scene so some fast young stud can come in and take care of your business. It's up to you, Baby Angel, you call the shots. Like I told you, I'm dead upstairs."

She stiffened in my arms and was silent for a long moment.

Finally she raised herself on an elbow and stared into my eyes and said quietly, "For real, I can call the shots?"

I nodded and she sprang to her feet. She slipped into a kimono, went to her purse on the dresser, and dashed out the door. I heard a coin clinking into the phone in the hall.

I got up and stuck my ear against the door. I heard her placing a collect long distance call to a whorehouse in northern Michigan. The sudden racket of missile warfare between a shouting couple across the hall blotted out the girl's voice.

I was sitting on the side of the lumpy bed, faking my cool, when she joyously pranced in and screeched out the numbing news. It was bad, way out bad for me and Mama on her deathbed out in California. The establishment in Michigan would have an opening for her three-way talent at the end of the week. She went into a detailed rundown on how to feed, bathe, burp, and diaper the gambler's squealer while she was away nobly flatbacking our escape from the kitchenette dungeon.

There was at the time a very deep reason or fear that overrode the obvious ones why I was not aching to help this poor frustrated mother to employment in the Michigan flesh factory. Several years before, an overconfident pimp acquaintance of mine had sent his one and only whore to the Michigan spot under consideration directly that she healed from the dropping of twin boys.

I visited mama pimp at his pad and pointed out that the town was crawling with shit-talking, whore-starved young studs, and that a dizzy young hot money tree like his was certain to be chopped down by a new master under the strain of whorehouse boredom and loneliness. He sneered and went into the usual novice pimp monologue about how "tight" he had his woman and the power of his "game."

He was surprised that I wasn't aware of the trump he held in the twins to bind his girl to him forever. He was an arrogant ass, so I made no effort to "pull his coat" to the street-tested truth that while whores simpered their love and loyalty, they were really pressure-shocked robots who prayed for the pimp's destruction and often dumped babies in alleys like garbage.

Within a month the Michigan mudkicker found her new master and the naïve young pimp was stuck with a brace of howling crumb crushers. But fortunately for the twins, the pimp's mother found them adorable and took them over.

And now, in the funky autumn of my life, I was apparently being set up for mamahood. What with the white slave thing still pulsing, it was a treacherous and explosive situation with a five-day fuse. I considered extreme strategy as I lay beside her in midnight misery.

I decided to play the role of rapidly worsening senility. "What is usually most disgustingly flawful about the senile?" I asked myself. "No control of the plumbing, of course," I answered.

I scooted back from the girl's sleeping form and shortly managed a stout stream that momentarily made of her a peninsula. But she slept on, wearing on her lovely face the last beatific (or any other) smile I was to witness. Soon, above the din of erotic rats squeaking their rodent rapture within the dungeon walls, I joined my whore madonna in pungent slumber.

Next morning she was curly-lipped furious and my slack-jaw idiocy augmented by even looser bowels had by nightfall inspired her to masterworks of creative profanity. She roughly diapered me on the greasy couch (my new bed) with a mildewed bath towel and she literally reeled away in disgust when I gurgled like a big black happy baby.

Much later I heard her tiptoe to the hall phone and repeatedly call numbers and ask for "Cat Daddy," an ancient pimp with enormous light-gray eyes and a penchant for young whores. I was praying that they made a contract together, because a whore almost never sends her exiting pimp to the penitentiary when her new pimp is on the scene to witness her treachery.

The next day, when the girl was out with the baby, I went to the corner drugstore and talked to Mama in California. We really cried more than talked, but I felt happy that she was still alive as I walked back to the dungeon. I was a hundred yards from the building when I saw the girl, with the squealer in arms, alight from Cat Daddy's orchid-hued spaceship. I stopped and sat down on a stoop. She stood outside the car and for a minute and a half she dipped and nodded her head toward the gesticulating silhouette inside. I suddenly felt a weird combination of joy and loss for I realized that she was giving Cat Daddy the classic "yes" response a young whore plays out for her new pimp.

I sat on the stoop for over an hour after she had gone in. When I went in, she pulled me down beside her on the bed and went into her thing. She told me in a pleasant voice that she felt very sorry that my illness had forced her to get herself and the baby a sponsor. She was moving soon, like within twenty-four hours, into a groovy pad furnished by the sponsor. But she was awfully worried about me, and perhaps I would be smart to run a game for care on one of the County institutions until our luck changed.

I strangled my wild joy (and a pang of loss) behind a blank mask and mumbled, "Baby daughter, I'm going to my Mama. She knows better than anybody how to nurse me back to the pink. And Angel Dumpling, as soon as I get myself and my game together I'll write you at that bar on Forty-seventh Street and send for you and my baby girl."

Later I lay sleepless in the stifling room, watching her sleeping. Her magnificent body was nude except for wisps of whorehouse costume that seemed ready to burst against the buxom stress of her honey toned curves and fat jet bush gleaming through the peach gauze.

I remembered the fast stacks of greenbacks, the icy, goose-pimpling, hot-sweet torture of that freak tongue, and the exquisite grab of that incredibly heavy-lipped cunt in the giddy beginning when her sick whore's skull was bewitched by my poisonous pimp charisma. My erection was sucker swift and rock hard, but as I started off the couch toward her, it collapsed. I suddenly realized that I had lost all power over her and therefore in her cold-blooded whore judgment I was just another customer, a chump John. I turned my face to the wall and worried until dawn about my moves and the wisdom of willfully blowing off a young freak whore with mileage galore left to hump away.

I was fully dressed, standing by the side of the bed looking down on her, when she awoke and cringed away. I smiled and flapped good-bye with my fingers like a child. Her lips mutely formed "good luck," and I went quickly away. In the cab on the way to the airport, I felt a stab of regret that I was leaving her forever back there. But then immediately the pain was gone in the great relief of my smooth exit from her and the terrible emptiness of the pimp game. And it was good to realize that no longer would I brutalize and exploit black women.

From a Steel Box to a Wicked Young Girl

Why I Continue to Write

I STARTED WRITING BECAUSE I wanted to do something with my life before I died. I still do.

I went into the hospital in 1946, with advanced tuberculosis, and altogether I spent three and a half years in the hospital. By the time I got out, I had had 10 ribs removed, one lung collapsed, a piece of the other one removed, and there were some severe complications from an experimental drug that was used to keep me alive. During these years I was given up for dead several times. One doctor told me that I could not live, I just didn't have enough lung capacity, and I should just go home and sit quietly and I would soon be dead. Now, I am blessed with a rotten attitude, and my response to statements of this nature is: Fuck you, no one tells me what to do!

Anyway, I was sitting at home and had a profound experience. I experienced, in all of my Being, that someday I was going to die, and it wouldn't be like it had been happening, almost dying but somehow staying alive, but I would just die! And two things would happen right before I died: I would regret my entire life; I would want to live it over again. This terrified me. The thought that I would live my entire life, look at it and realize I blew it forced me to do something with my life. This did not make me a writer, but provided the incentive to discover that I am a writer.

I wrote every night after work, struggling to learn how to write, and at the end of six years, *Last Exit to Brooklyn* was finished. In 1964, thanks to Barney Rosset and others at Grove Press, *Last Exit* became a huge success. There were interviews, articles, photographs, all manner of publicity (positive and negative), and it was all very intimidating. What was frightening was the responsibility. I was unaware of this at the time, but in retrospect I can see that it was relatively easy to write when no one knew I was alive. The world had no expectations. But when the world is watching you, and you believe in your heart that you are really worthless and someday they will find out, the pressure is unbearable. I simply withdrew into a shell and didn't write for six years.

And then I began writing again. Since *Last Exit* I have published five books, and my life has gone through many changes. In 1988, the movie version of *Last Exit* once again brought a lot of attention. This was followed by more obscurity, broken occasionally by my association with Henry Rollins. The strange thing about all this is that I am still here, and periodically I publish another book.

Unfortunately, a great deal of my energy is expended in just staying alive, which doesn't leave much for the other things. Yet I do keep writing whenever possible. Writing, like any art, is a continuing process of discovering the infinite possibilities of Life. A blank piece of paper can be terrifying. It can also be exciting when ideas, images, and sounds come together and sing off the page. For me there is no other experience like it. When I just touch the keyboard, a part of me comes to life that at one time I did not know existed.

Being an artist doesn't take much, just everything you got. Which means, of course, that as the process is giving you life, it is also bringing you closer to death. But it's no big deal. They are one and the same and cannot be avoided or denied. So when I totally embrace this process, this life/death, and abandon myself to it, I transcend all this meaningless gibberish and hang out with the gods. It seems to me that that is worth the price of admission.

JACK HIRSCHMAN

Culture and Struggle

DUMPSTERS, ALLEYS LITTERED WITH WHAT'S been discarded, including human crumples, panhandlers at corners or along walls scribbled with graffiti, hungry men and women on food lines, public suffering misery waste shame dregs garbage of porn and drugs and drink, the lost job, broken home,

can't sell soul, one big hole, feel like a mole, down in the depths or on the lam standing still in the Tenderloin of an inner-city everywhere now.

Such images increasing in replication represent the fate of more and more people in this land, in a time when technological advancement on a global scale is creating merciless conditions wherein millions and millions of people will be, if they are not already, economically and then physically holocausted,

while the profound truth uttered by the Native American Wassaja—"We are hoodwinked, duped more and more each year; we are made to feel that we are free and we are not"—throbs in our being.

Everything's being driven backwards to the wrong Right, not to right the wrongs but deeper into a corporate state whose media-evil snares and traps are thick with decay, info-terrorism, more doubletalk than hands could shake ten fingers at; and bodies and souls everywhere are lowered into vats of diminishing wages, all watched over by massively growing police-brutal state apparatuses.

It's a system of corporate profiteers, haywire stockmarket-mongers, and thugs of all sorts feeding on us poor people, and we want that system brought down once and for all.

We know it's in the deep shit of its own decay and has been rotting amid its desperate half-assed triumphs for more than two generations. We want to help, as cultural consciences, finish off its carcass, which has been stinking up humanity for as long as most of us remember.

And transform it into something authentically new and young and fresh and appealing:

we want the way money is amassed and distributed and thought about changed,

and the way the poor, the homeless, and immigrants are dealt with changed,

and we want rule by private property and the lie of "free enterprise" changed.

The "We" I've been talking from is really These States, composed of all those who daily feel the bite and bark of a dogging capitalist/imperialist system, including those who are not only aware that genocide, economic or otherwise, is at its core but who are actively engaged in the fight against that genocide

who either must fight or physically die; that is,

must break into buildings or die in the cold,

must answer every charge of welfare fraud with a rally for people's justice,

must straighten the twisted information that immigrants are the enemies of workers here, or that the young rather than the banks and the corporations are the thieves and addicted monsters,

must broadcast over airwaves liberated by takeovers (just as with abandoned buildings) because only corporate wealth has claim to widespread kilowatt power,

must graffiti because there's no unbought place where writing, drawing, and the protest-cry weigh the same and, by their very existence, attack private property.

And underlying all these "musts" are the will and desire to change history, and the belief that the people of this new class can do precisely that.

We don't see a difference between poetry, prose, graphic arts, song, music, etc., on this terrain horizoning with the construction of tomorrows. Separating these genres is another kind of division the ruling-class enslavers have washed many a brain with.

We know their intelligentsia is all bullshit fake aesthetic segregations.

We know because, at the heart of this seminal and budding poor-people's struggle is a propagandance inclusive of all the arts.

Moreover, and despite the attempts on the part of the cowardly ruling-class intelligentsia to palm off the revolutionary story as nothing but a "humanistic" one accommodatable by the corporate academy,

we know that we are all in possession of a modern classical tradition, including everything from the Internationale to Native chants, as well as union and slave songs en route to collective affirmations and liberation, respectively;

a revolutionary tradition including the poems of Blake, Whitman's great majesties, abolitionist narratives, and the writings of Frederick Douglass, the poems of Hopkins ("I look forward to nothing more than the communist revolution," 1871), the great active meditations and strategies on the end of war and hunger that are the center of the writings of Marx and Engels;

and then, in our own century, the works of Mayakovsky, London, Lorca, Brecht, Sinclair, Neruda, Hill, Vallejo, Roumain, Hughes, Parker, Dalton, Monk, Castillo, Pasolini, Eluard, Hikmet, Aragon, Laraque, Darwish, Baraka, Adnan, Gramsci, Benet, Scotellaro, Heartfield;

and Robeson, Luxemburg, Rivera, Lenin, Siquieros, Orozco, Pollock, Lowenfels, Benjamin, Lourde, Ho Chi Minh, Rugama, Quemain, Stephan-Alexis;

and the hundreds, no, thousands of poets—man, woman and child—as well as artists, musicians, dancers, in collectives or theater companies or struggling forward in their creative solitudes, believing in and fighting for the total liberation of humanity from its chains, over and above the walls of the narrow one-celled alienation, isolation and imprisonment which the capitalist world visits upon us all.

It's to this revolutionary and progressive cultural tradition, which all poets and artists intuitively recognize as related to the working class, the working poor, and the new class of the permanently unemployed, the homeless, the criminalized, and those economically abused by the whiplash of electronic means of production in the hands of the capitalists,

that my own work has specifically united itself for more than twenty years. It's a tradition that's engaged the energies of my poems (because in fact it *creates* the energies of my poems), as well as of my translations of revolutionaries from other lands; my verbo-visual "talking leaves"; my painted books and larger paintings; agitprop journalistic articles; the editing of different anthologies relative to the struggle; the "printing" of poems "in the journal between the ears" on the streets, in the name of revolutionary communication; and the works done for cultural brigades like the Roque Dalton Cultural Brigade, the Jacques Roumain Cultural Brigade; in addition to the Union of Left Writers, the Coalition of Writers' Organizations, the Communist Labor Party, and the League of Revolutionaries for a New America.

This revolutionary tradition, which came into existence about 150 years ago—a young tradition! a vibrant tradition!—continues to expose the rats of capitalism for the garbage they are, and the system itself for the null and void it is, while affirming, re-affirming, and ever-affirming the struggles and victories (however small, however large) of the poor and exploited.

And it's because we especially defend and affirm the poorest sectors of society, those who are most vulnerable, the good and beautiful Truth of revolutionary potential cuts through the current habits and trends of intellectual adherences to Nothingness.

We are never decorators of Nothing. Nor do we pretend we are the avant-garde while actually engaging in backbiting competition—a mirror of capitalist relations—for what comes down to: Bux.

Our rage, a rage for change, is, in part, yes, because we are poor; but it is mainly because others are, and in misery and oppression.

At the heart of it all, why else does a poet write?

We furthermore say that we *know* the enemy and it is not ourselves. It is rather a system of daily and grinding economic and social squalors, commodifications, degradations, and losses of dignity.

That's why poem, painting, music, etc., all are so very necessary. And why we remember, in the immediate now and for the future, the resonating affirmations of, say, Whitman, those expanses of generosity and mimpathy which he dreamed for us and which we know the system we live in the trap of has fogged and trashed, via the profit-murder it executes us with, every living moment;

but whose expanses of inner feeling and whose vision of These States not as a corporate monstrosity and prison of prisons, but as a mass process of compassion collectively unfolding as a people of diverse ingenuities and loves

we continue to recognize and reverence

because in fact it's in its budding form, that revolutionary flowering, even amid the general and specific rots of the day,

and we aim to help it blossom forth.

Our society is already luminously informed by a diversity of expressions come from Native, African-American, Latino, Caribbean, Asian, Middle-Eastern, African, Pacific Island and European cultures all comprising the multinational working class.

Many of these cultural expressions emerged in the wake of the important Civil Rights movement, which spread nationally from the South during the Sixties. Because the African-American struggle for freedom from slavery is so important, African-American liberty—its ironies, bitternesses and failures in the midst of achievements—is very fresh, very raw with them, one of the reasons why their musics (from slave-song to gospel to scat; from jazz to bop to R&B to rock and roll, and progressive and experimental music extending from jazz, and rap), because they arise out of the direct struggles for survival and "dreams deferred," are the sounds and melodies of a living and continually oppressed and vulnerable people, the measures of *all* the people; because African-Americans are the ones the system of capitalism most derogates and uses to terrorize and control the rest of the population.

Culture and Struggle

And it's precisely because the other poor peoples know—even if unconsciously—that the Black struggles have been able to galvanize struggles for cultural autonomy on the part of others within the "Rainbow" of the States.

And also because, long before the fight against slavery in the South (go back to the riots in New York City in 1642), Blacks refused to accept the system—in essence, capitalism—knowing its roots lay in human slavery and the turning of people into things, we have been witnesses to an ever-manifesting resistance that has inspired cultural and social motions throughout our century.

For example, jazz has been a popular expression on an international level since World War I—this nation's most distinctive and enduring popular art form. Its influence, say, on the Beat movement (see the works of Kerouac, the poems of Bob Kaufman, the opening lines of both "Howl" and "Kaddish" by Ginsberg) has been central. And in response to a question relating to his important "Projective Verse" essay, Charles Olson remarked that the new experimental field-prosody he was espousing was "all Charlie Parker." Such words actually mimicked those of Robert Creeley, who had written them in a letter to Olson years earlier; but, in fact, Parker, and especially Thelonius Monk, *did* relate to Olson's "Projective" suggestion to poets to use a typewriter as a piano (Monk is perhaps the most literary and dialectical of modern jazz composers). And it is a fact that the "opening of the field" of the page of poetry, which came to full fruition in the Fifties and Sixties and continues today as among the most exciting aspects of poetic composition, is rooted in jazz experiments emerging from the Harlem Renaissance as *they* merged with other cultural forms—abstract expressionist painting, for example—that served as explosive preludes to the monumental composition that was the Civil Rights movement itself.

And today, spoken writing like gangsta and other Rap, manifesting out of authentic situations of poverty, exclusion and institutionalized racism, presents the protest of a constructive nihilism and beats on the drum of and for YouthYouthYouth, as if a rhythmic, oral, African or Haitian voodoo communications system were passing important signals through the computerized night.

In the United States of poetry today, certain Rap lyrics contain the most vivid attacks on the private-property system by revealing and satirizing the nihilism inherent in the money-madness and the hatred of everything—self, other, and world—that is the plight of so many young people in this land.

In Rap, moreover, such an intricate rhyming—often spontaneously composed—has not appeared in serious poetry since the Russian poems of

Vladimir Mayakovsky, the great poet of the Bolshevik Revolution and the first street poet of the Twentieth Century.

And don't think the powers-that-be want Mayakovsky's lyrics out there any more than they do those of Rap. In fact, in the recent Penguin edition of 20th Century Russian literature, get this—Mayakovsky is excluded, as if the greatest poet of the Soviet period simply no longer existed (indeed, to date, only about half of his collected works have been translated into American English)!

And it's precisely that kind of annihilating exclusion—meant to deny the very existence of an important historical phenomenon—that Rap artists are experiencing as well, not simply as a censorship, but as an as/if Rap didn't really exist at all (a condition African-Americans well know on the ontological plane);

and that would be an incredible loss because, if really seen and understood in motion on the streets and in the parks of this land (not simply as something "star-studded" in a one- or two-man teevee gig), Rap represents a genuine breakthrough in oral co-operation and collectivity,

one rapper "passing" meaning and rhythm to another; the other, to another, with variations in lyric and rhythm both; until the dovetailing and ricocheting raps and the built-up strophes of meaning given out by each rapper after a while assume the anonymity of real process, genuine social statement and authentic communal participation.

Precisely, of course, what the system has to control or destroy, lest it grow as a model of organized culture in action, that is, Revolutionary Culture.

Graffiti (which the system also detests and outlaws, just as it detests and outlaws any cultural form whose social rage and ingenuity are difficult to commodity completely), like Rap, also has its toilet-door, obscene and scatological dimension,

but also and likewise: revolutionary slogans; sheer energetic ecstasies of code-tagging and letter shape; and, above and within all, a dynamic "possessing" (in the sense of taking over) of private property and making it public through an act of alphabetic or logographic affirmative/defacement.

Something of the same elements go on in Rap, which gives the illusion—if it doesn't present itself as the fact—that it is "written" spontaneously and off the top of one's head, with a drummy, possessive and grabbing beat, and a social message included within it.

Both Rap and Graffiti are part of the contemporary Projective arts involving youthful participation in a growing—sporadically and seminally but very definitely—new-class consciousness.

Both are victims of censorship and whitewash. Both are textured as outlaw and guerrilla art forms. And both are cultural weapons in the development of the poor-people's movement.

A third important and courageous weapon is exercised by a small but growing brigade of airwave liberators, those who set up microtransmitters and fight the corporate state and its FCC apparatus by freeing airwaves for the people. They might be broadcasting about police terror and brutality from and to a poor housing project in Springfield, Illinois; reading an attack on San Francisco's mayor for his Matrix program's criminalizing of the poor; reading a communiqué from the Mayan guerrillas fighting the NAFTA governments of Mexico and Washington, D.C.; or they might be calling for—and not simply announcing the results of—a demonstration or protest march.

These techno guerrillas are on the cutting edge of the cultural front at a time when there's been a deepening of police-state tactics with respect to the poor; when the ruling class and its media jackals are everywhere broadcasting crime-terror-mayhem-rape in order to keep sowing divisiveness and terror among the people.

As such, the radio liberators are taking back technological space/time, the relativity robbed by the capitalists, and putting it back into the hands and ears of those to whom it really belongs.

I've mentioned the importance of the poor people's struggles as they extend from the Civil Rights Movement. But there is an equally important resistance that the poor can always make contact with in this land, and that is the resistance of the Native peoples.

We know the names, like Geronimo and Crazy Horse, Wounded Knee, Sequoyah, and Sarah Winnemucca. We know likewise of a continuous colonization that has been staked out by the imperialists across the Native territories.

But what is most important, culturally, as far as the Native dimension is concerned, is that the revolutionary future we foresee when the poor and exploited and oppressed peoples of this land come together and organize to finally have done with the thieving system that is currently and viciously in place—that revolutionary future will be one in which the new means of production, the computers and media and other technological advancements, will not serve as profit-Frankensteins but as instruments to further a non-mercenary progress for all the people so that they no longer are hungry or homeless or divided one from another.

It will be a co-operative society, with authentic sharing and reciprocity, reverberant to the historically recent and still existing peoples of this continent, who exploited neither each other nor the living creatures around them.

Toward that future, our responsibility as poets and painters and musicians and dancers, all interfacing and opening out, ought to be to "present the present" as irrefutably a part of the revolutionary process and beacon toward that time—with new poems, songs, dreams, yearning and inspirations—when all our individual selves are massed to finally spring humanity from its prison.

The Catastrophe of Success

THIS WINTER MARKED THE THIRD anniversary of the Chicago opening of "The Glass Menagerie," an event that terminated one part of my life and began another about as different in all external circumstances as could well be imagined. I was snatched out of virtual oblivion and thrust into sudden prominence, and from the precarious tenancy of furnished rooms about the country I was removed to a suite in a first-class Manhattan hotel. My experience was not unique. Success has often come that abruptly into the lives of Americans. The Cinderella story is our favorite national myth, the cornerstone of the film industry if not of the Democracy itself. I have seen it enacted on the screen so often that I was now inclined to yawn at it, not with disbelief but with an attitude of Who Cares! Anyone with such beautiful teeth and hair as the screen protagonist of such a story was bound to have a good time one way or another, and you could bet your bottom dollar and all the tea in China that that one would not be caught dead or alive at any meeting involving a social conscience.

No, my experience was not exceptional, but neither was it quite ordinary, and if you are willing to accept the somewhat eclectic proposition that I had not been writing with such an experience in mind—and many people are not willing to believe that a playwright is interested in anything but popular success—there may be some point in comparing the two estates.

The sort of life that I had had previous to this popular success was one that required endurance, a life of clawing and scratching along a sheer surface and holding on tight with raw fingers to every inch of rock higher than the one caught hold of before, but it was a good life because it was the sort of life for which the human organism is created.

I was not aware of how much vital energy had gone into this struggle until the struggle was removed. I was out on a level plateau with my arms still thrashing and my lungs still grabbing at air that no longer resisted. This was security at last.

I sat down and looked about me and was suddenly very depressed. I thought to myself, this is just a period of adjustment. Tomorrow morning I will wake up in this first-class hotel suite above the discreet hum of an East Side boulevard and I will appreciate its elegance and luxuriate in its comforts and know that I have arrived at our American plan of Olympus. Tomorrow morning when I look at the green satin sofa I will fall in love with it. It is only temporarily that the green satin looks like slime on stagnant water.

But in the morning the inoffensive little sofa looked more revolting than the night before, and I was already getting too fat for the $125 suit which a fashionable acquaintance had selected for me. In the suite things began to break accidentally. An arm came off the sofa. Cigarette burns appeared on the polished surface of the furniture. Windows were left open and a rainstorm flooded the suite. But the maid always put it straight and the patience of the management was inexhaustible. Late parties could not offend them seriously. Nothing short of a demolition bomb seemed to bother my neighbors.

I lived on room service. But in this, too, there was a disenchantment. Some time between the moment when I ordered dinner over the phone and when it was rolled into my living room like a corpse on a rubber-wheeled table, I lost all interest in it. Once I ordered a sirloin steak and a chocolate sundae, but everything was so cunningly disguised on the table that I mistook the chocolate sauce for gravy and poured it over the sirloin steak.

Of course all this was the more trivial aspect of a spiritual dislocation that began to manifest itself in far more disturbing ways. I soon found myself becoming indifferent to people. A well of cynicism rose in me. Conversations all sounded as if they had been recorded years ago and were being played back on a turntable. Sincerity and kindliness seemed to have gone out of my friends' voices. I suspected them of hypocrisy. I stopped calling them, stopped seeing them. I was impatient of what I took to be inane flattery.

I got so sick of hearing people say, "I loved your play!" that I could not say "thank you" any more. I choked on the words and turned rudely away from the usually sincere person. I no longer felt any pride in the play itself but began to dislike it, probably because I felt too lifeless inside ever to create another. I was walking around dead in my shoes and I knew it, but there were no friends I knew or trusted sufficiently, at that time, to take them aside and tell them what was the matter.

This curious condition persisted about three months, till late spring, when I decided to have another eye operation mainly because of the excuse it gave me to withdraw from the world behind a gauze mask. It was my fourth eye operation, and perhaps I should explain that I had been afflicted for about five years with a cataract on my left eye which required a series of needling operations and finally an operation on the muscle of the eye. (The eye is still in my head. So much for that.)

Well, the gauze mask served a purpose. While I was resting in the hospital, the friends whom I had neglected or affronted in one way or another began to call on me and now that I was in pain and darkness, their voices seemed to have changed, or rather that unpleasant mutation which I had suspected earlier in the season had now disappeared and they sounded now as they had used to sound in the lamented days of my obscurity. Once more they were sincere and kindly voices with the ring of truth in them and that quality of understanding for which I had originally sought them out.

As far as my physical vision was concerned, this last operation was only relatively successful (although it left me with an apparently clear black pupil in the right position, or nearly so) but in another, figurative way, it had served a much deeper purpose.

When the gauze mask was removed, I found myself in a readjusted world. I checked out of the handsome suite at the first-class hotel, packed my papers and a few incidental belongings, and left for Mexico, an elemental country where you can quickly forget the false dignities and conceits imposed by success, a country where vagrants innocent as children curl up to sleep on the pavements and human voices, especially when their language is not familiar to the ear, are soft as birds'. My public self, that artifice of mirrors, did not exist here, and so my natural being was resumed.

Then, as a final act of restoration, I settled for a while at Chapala to work on a play called "The Poker Night," which later became "A Streetcar Named Desire." It is only in his work that an artist can find reality and satisfaction, for the actual world is less intense than the world of his invention, and consequently his life, without recourse to violent disorder, does not seem very substantial. The right condition for him is that in which his work is not only convenient but unavoidable.

For me a convenient place to work is a remote place among strangers where there is good swimming. But life should require a certain minimal effort. You should not have too many people waiting on you, you should have to do most things for yourself. Hotel service is embarrassing. Maids, waiters, bellhops, porters and so forth are the most embarrassing people in the world for they continually remind you of inequities which we accept as the proper thing. The sight of an ancient woman gasping and wheezing as she drags a heavy pail of water down a hotel corridor to mop up the mess of some drunken overprivileged guest is one that sickens and weighs upon the heart and withers it with shame for this world in which it is not only tolerated but regarded as proof positive that the wheels of Democracy are functioning as they should without interference from above or below. Nobody should have to clean up anybody else's mess in this world. It is terribly bad for both parties, but probably worse for the one receiving the service.

I have been corrupted as much as anyone else by the vast number of menial services which our society has grown to expect and depend on. We should do for ourselves or let the machines do for us, the glorious technology that is supposed to be the new light of the world. We are like a man who has bought a great amount of equipment for a camping trip, who has the canoe and the tent and the fishing lines and the axe and the guns, the mackinaw and the blankets, but who now, when all the preparations and the provisions are piled expertly together, is suddenly too timid to set out on the journey but remains where he was yesterday and the day before and the day before that, looking suspiciously through white lace curtains at the clear sky he distrusts. Our great technology is a God-given chance for adventure and for progress which we are afraid to attempt. Our ideas and our ideals remain exactly what they were and where they were three centuries ago. No. I beg your pardon. It is no longer safe for a man even to declare them!

This is a long excursion from a small theme into a large one which I did not intend to make, so let me go back to what I was saying before.

This is an oversimplification. One does not escape that easily from the seduction of an effete way of life. You cannot arbitrarily say to yourself: I will now continue my life as it was before this thing, Success, happened to me. But once you fully apprehend the vacuity of a life without struggle you are equipped with the basic means of salvation. Once you know this is true, that the heart of man, his body and his brain are forged in a white-hot furnace for the purpose of conflict (the struggle of creation) and that with the conflict removed, the man is a sword cutting daisies, that not privation but luxury is the wolf at the door and that the fangs of this wolf are all the little vanities and conceits and laxities that Success is heir to—why, then with this knowledge you are at least in a position of knowing where danger lies.

You know, then, that the public Somebody you are when you "have a name" is a fiction created with mirrors and that the only somebody worth being is the solitary and unseen you that existed from your first breath and which is the sum of your actions and so is constantly in a state of becoming under your own violation—and knowing these things, you can even survive the catastrophe of Success!

The Catastrophe of Success

It is never altogether too late, unless you embrace the Bitch Goddess, as William James called her, with both arms and find in her smothering caresses exactly what the homesick little boy in you always wanted, absolute protection and utter effortlessness. Security is a kind of death, I think, and it can come to you in a storm of royalty checks beside a kidney-shaped pool in Beverly Hills or anywhere at all that is removed from the conditions that made you an artist, if that's what you are or were or intended to be. Ask anyone who has experienced the kind of success I am talking about—What good is it? Perhaps to get an honest answer you will have to give him a shot of truth serum, but the word he will finally groan is unprintable in genteel publications.

Then what is good? The obsessive interest in human affairs, plus a certain amount of compassion and moral conviction, that first made the experience of living something that must be translated into pigment or music or bodily movement or poetry or prose or anything that's dynamic and expressive—that's what's good for you if you're at all serious in your aims. William Saroyan wrote a great play on this theme, that purity of heart is the one success worth having. "In the time of your life—live!" That time is short and it doesn't return again. It is slipping away while I write this and while you read it, and the monosyllable of the clock is Loss, loss, loss, unless you devote your heart to its opposition.

Everyday Barf

I DON'T MIND TODAY, BUT the everyday makes me barf. There's no such thing. Puking would put something on the sidewalk of the everyday so it could begin to be now. And what do we think about writing now. I was asked to write a political sestina for some website and once I did, they sent it back all numbered and pointing out I had not done it correctly. Not only had I not gotten correctly to the envoi, but harrumph I had also done something with the six words, something bad. I had never written a sestina before and I was fairly proud of it. We had a few pissy exchanges, and finally I was declared hateful by this guy because I suggested he was conservative and even censorious. It strikes me that form has a real engagement with content and might even want to get a little sleazy with the content and suggest it stop early or go too far. How can you stop form from wanting to do that. I wrote my sestina on a boat. I was living in P-town this summer in Mimi's house, where she often pointed out that Charles had also lived with his family. Each time I left that house to go to New York or California I took a quick boat and this one time it was the week of the RNC and I thought well I'll write the fucking sestina on the way to the reading in New York. It's a political reading, so I'm thinking that way. The boat bucked and rocked. I thought the poem was incredibly boring, the words forced but for some reason I had nothing better to do I kept plodding along, peeking at my scheme. I was teaching a workshop that week at FAWC; do you know what FAWC is.

In New York I was standing outside of Fox with a group of activists and we were screaming get the Fox out of here. Get—the—Fox out of here. Then we would go: O-Reil-ly. O-Rei-ly. This Bronx cheer made me a little nervous. Certainly O'Reilly's a conservative prick but are they laughing at him being Irish. Are they invoking some working class dialect, some familiarity or something because of the sound of his name. I have never watched this guy. Does he play the regular guy? What's his voice like? Who are the activists who have written the cheer. I was glad when they got back to the Fox one. Get the Fox out of here!

The experience of arriving at an activist event you've only read about—chosen from the calendar of them. Maybe standing with your friends. Holding a hot pink unemployment sheet. Standing in Union Sq. Park knowing that a line of you reaches to Wall Street and up to Penn Station. Just being an arm in a performance piece. Just being a voice, like being in some weeklong workshop all over New York against the republican party, and you can just kind of dip in. When O'Reilly got in trouble recently I thought about standing outside his job yelling his name. I mean I didn't feel bad or anything but I felt an interesting echo, like whatever discomfort I felt in taking part in the group sounding of his name, my doubts now slammed up against a solid scandal and the screaming now felt good.

The boat jogged my poem and I got to New York and read it in a large room and it was hot and I felt like I had done my poet job. I sat back down with Jordana and she nodded and squeezed my arm. "You did good." I took the boat again a few weeks later. I was feeling a little sad this time since I had been trying to get my mother who lives in Massachusetts to come back with me to P-town, but maybe I really didn't want that, and she didn't know if she wanted that either, but somehow I now felt I had failed. The boat bucked and waved. The boat was rocking so badly that finally no one was allowed to be out on the deck. They had to come in. I saw a girl out there in a hood with her boyfriend. Maybe her hood was gold. I had one of those. I used to wear it under a tweed suitjacket. Maybe <u>his</u> sweatshirt was gold. Was it raining. It was stormy. It was almost too stormy for people to ride boats. And the man next to me began puking. Urp, he went. Splatter, right into a paper bag. I think he was a fag. He was with his lover. Wha Wha Wha. He gagged. The woman next to me & I looked slightly at each other. This is gross. She was sitting with a man, but she chose me to share the feeling with. We were disgusted. Maybe a little bit scared. I didn't want to puke. Not like this. No place. I never want to puke. Hate puking. Haven't puked for years. Then behind me a woman began. Really gagging her ass off. Heaving. Again, and again. Little coughs of puke. Getting it together. Puking again. We were sick. The whole bunch of us were rocking with the gags, praying to fucking god we wouldn't start puking our guts out too. You could also smell the stuff. And the rain splashing against the glass windows of the boat. The boat tipping, aiming up. Have you noticed how tipping is in the news. For a while things were spiking, they were ramping up and now they're tipping. That's the word we like, it's what we see and I saw the boat rolling and tipping. Barf. It seemed my mother wouldn't have enjoyed this trip. She's 83. How would she receive a boat full of puking adults. I think she would have gotten up and moved. She wouldn't have just sat there. I began to think I had done the right thing by not getting her on this boat with me. I wasn't so wrong. Opened my notebook and started celebrating that fact. What fact? My séance. My sitting here on my ass on the boat in the middle of all these people puking. You think of kids, I always heard that kids in you know like first grade have this serial puking. I hear it as a story in families too. Suddenly each kid one after another started puking their guts out. Mom and Dad mopping up, occasionally lowering their own heads into the toilet. Blah. Adults do it too. I imagine my relatives coming over from Europe puking on the floor of the boat in between fucks and bites of their jerky. Bites of their belts or their shoes. Whatever they ate. Sucking on the tittie. Whatever. Within this primal scene I wrote my mother a poem. The puking I do. This. Dear Mom. Blah. My whole life shooting all over the windows of the boat. Dear Mom Blah. The stuff streaming word by word across the lines down the page of my notebook. A black and white composition notebook. One of those spray theme covers with a nice rectangle of ownership saying who I am. Eileen. This is my book. Dear Mom. I stopped apologizing for not bringing her. I understood she would have gotten sick. There was a logic. Perhaps I'll read the poem. I think I shared my fear of dying with my mother. There's a kind of dying that lives in my family. An accidental clown death. My father died like that. Fell off the roof. Splat. I think I had just been robbed in Los Angeles. I had been at the delightful Pho café and in a crowd of art people standing around rubbing their bellies satisfied while this other crowd popped my trunk and stole my computer and all my clothes including my new digital camera I hadn't figured out yet. Utterly gone. Me standing in my camera telling a joke. So my trunk's wide open like a complete asshole. Nobody noticed this happened except me. I was poking my head out the door of the restaurant and there's my trunk wide open. I'm not upset. I'm numb. I'm a little destroyed. I got my notebook, I continued my dinner with Simon. Later that night I went to Judith's where I was staying and though she told me she lived upstairs the downstairs door was open and I walked right in. It looked wrong; the art, something. Suddenly this guy is coming towards me, scared. Scared like he would pick up a gun and shoot me he was so scared. Dear Mom, not only have I drowned today, but I was robbed and then I was shot. Bad luck. Second generation clown death. All these thoughts are teeming as people around me are going whaa. It hasn't stopped. It's normalized. Once my girlfriend moved to Paris, like 1986, and I took her to the airport. Then I got on the train I think, and went home. It was a big deal but I wasn't upset. I walked into the bathroom and began shitting and puking at once. I felt like a worm. Like there was no difference between me—and anything. It was just this force flowing through me. Loss. I must be feeling bad I thought, sitting on the can leaning into the sink. What must I be feeling. She had wanted to go to Acme, a restaurant on Jones St. What did we eat. Chicken fried steak. Maybe that's what it was. I start telling my mother about the kids outside the window. Oh I get it—that was <u>before</u> the puking began. In fact I guess I was writing my poem through the puking. I even remember trying to read. There was this great book Chronophobia which was about time. Like what's not, right. I can barely tell you what it was about yet I feel all these systems kicking in. Like when you hear your computer shift. This book was just so right. People driving in cars on unborn highways, people blowing things up in deserts. A woman Bridget Riley going to see a collector who turned her work into a dress. I thought you'd like it, he said. She got blamed for Op Art which they continually tried to link to her being some kind of Irish domestic servant, and she responded by negating her sex. Feminism was splashing up around her like vomit and obviously that's the problem. I remember in junior high we would walk across the street to the high school to get our lunch. One kid would hold the door open for hundreds of others and that kid would announce every day what it was. He said, vomit. The door was reddish kind of clay colored. He stood on a cement block and it made him taller than us while he held the door. I remember thinking oh vomit for lunch. I didn't know what that was. We would "throw up" when I was a kid, that's what we did at home and maybe around 6th grade the word <u>puke</u> came in. This is like 1961. I sat down at the lunch table with my orange tray. On the plate was a pile of little brown meatballs in a light brown gravy. In retrospect I guess it was Swedish meatballs. I think that would be its name. I ate the little meatballs. They were not bad. We got back to class, and the nun asked us what we had had for lunch and I said <u>vomit</u> quickly, feeling smart at once. A new swedish word. I remember standing out in the hall that afternoon, being punished, remembering the raucous sound of the classroom laughter. Even I joined in, feeling entirely out of control, humiliated, but the enormous release that the one word had triggered still made me snort and gag with pleasure. Alone. It wasn't so bad to be totally wrong if you just didn't know and it was so much fun. There was something Bob Dylan didn't know and I can't remember what it was. It was about moving. I totally devoured that book, his autobiography. Amra asked me what I had been seeing lately. Like what was my art month. It was the show at the Hammer, I liked that painting show, the Undiscovered Country. I suppose I liked the title more than the show. The idea of a painting show being named after death seems just brilliant. I mean it's so fucking coy. Is painting really so far away. To who? It's just a crazy idea, but Shakespeare's line is so damn good that you can hang anything on it and it works. Bob Dylan said if you write while you're moving, it's good. The painting becomes really alive in the land of dead words. In the dream of death. Death is so great because it's the attachment you can never open. I mean you can force it open, but is that really yours. I saw Tarnation and I'm not sure what I think. Who could not love that kid doing drag at twelve or thirteen. Who was not scared for that kid. But the whole story was not a good idea. I hate the whole story. I hate it with a passion. Which is why I loved Bob Dylan's book. I had been prepared by another idea I had about him. Jordana gave me Positively Fourth Street, this other Bob Dylan book and I thought why do you think I care about that but this summer in P-town I simply read one book after another that she gave me. It's hard to live with someone *and* read the books they give you. You'd rather ask them why they gave it to you and be done with it. Though in their absence you read. I'm wondering now—what did she mean? Bob Dylan used to tear pictures out of magazines and arrange them on the floor and then kneel over them with his guitar and write songs. It seems so perfect. Now that I think about it it seems like jerking off. I'm not sure if it's jerking off like a man. It might be jerking off like a woman. In his own book Chronicles, Bob describes coming to New York and hanging out and singing his songs. I mean he was singing other people's songs for a while. I think his first song he pretended it was somebody else's and he slipped it in with theirs. He loved Woody Guthrie and he went to see him every day in the hospital when Woody was dying. It seems like a man thing to do, to visit the great guy dying. I really don't know who the great woman is, so where would I go. My mother would always try and make us look at the sky. Look at that sunset Eileen. It made you really want to look away. It just ruined it for me. It was all about her. And that's what I saw when I looked out the window that day. All these words were living. The boat was rocking and the people were puking and it was her gift to me. So I say what our president said when he was told how great it was to have god in the white house. He said thank you. He thanked them for how beautiful they were. It was good to be here.

ALLEN GINSBERG

Notes Written on Finally Recording Howl

BY 1955 I WROTE POETRY adapted from prose seeds, journals, scratchings, arranged by phrasing or breath groups into little short-line patterns according to ideas of measure of American speech I'd picked up from William Carlos Williams' imagist preoccupations. I suddenly turned aside in San Francisco, unemployment compensation leisure, to follow my romantic inspiration—Hebraic-Melvillean bardic breath. I thought I wouldn't write a *poem*, but just write what I wanted to without fear, let my imagination go, open secrecy, and scribble magic lines from my real mind—sum up my life—something I wouldn't be able to show anybody, writ for my own soul's ear and a few other golden ears. So the first line of *Howl*, "I saw the best minds etc.," the whole first section typed out madly in one afternoon, a tragic custard-pie comedy of wild phrasing, meaningless images for the beauty of abstract poetry of mind running along making awkward combinations like Charlie Chaplin's walk, long saxophone-like chorus lines I knew Kerouac would hear *sound* of—taking off from his own inspired prose line, really a new poetry.

I depended on the word "who" to keep the beat, a base to keep measure, return to and take off from again onto another streak of invention: "who lit cigarettes in boxcars boxcars boxcars," continuing to prophesy what I really knew despite the drear consciousness of the world: "who were visionary Indian angels." Have I really been attacked for this sort of joy? So the poem got awesome, I went on to what my imagination believed true to eternity (for I'd had a beatific illumination years before during which I'd heard Blake's ancient voice and saw the universe unfold in my brain) and what my memory could reconstitute of the data of celestial experiences.

But how sustain a long line in poetry (lest it lapse into prosaic)? It's natural inspiration of the moment that keeps it moving, disparate thinks put down together, shorthand notations of visual imagery, juxtapositions of hydrogen jukebox—abstract *haikus* sustain the mystery and put iron poetry back into the line: the last line of *Sunflower Sutra* is the extreme, one stream of single word associations, summing up. Mind is shapely, art is shapely. Meaning mind practiced in spontaneity invents forms in its own image and gets to last thoughts. Loose ghosts wailing for body try to invade the bodies of living men. I hear ghostly academies in limbo screeching about form.

Ideally each line of *Howl* is a single breath unit. My breath is long—that's the measure, one physical-mental inspiration of thought contained in the elastic of a breath. It probably bugs Williams now, but it's a natural consequence, my own heightened conversation, not cooler average-daily-talk short breath. I get to mouth more madly this way.

So these poems are a series of experiments with the formal organization of the long line. Explanations follow. I realized at the time that Whitman's form had rarely been further explored (improved on even) in the U.S.—Whitman always a mountain too vast to be seen. Everybody assumes (with Pound?) (except [Robinson] Jeffers) that his line is a big freakish uncontrollable necessary prosaic goof. No attempt's been made to use it in the light of early-twentieth-century organization of new speech-rhythm prosody to *build up* large organic structures.

I had an apartment on Nob Hill, got high on peyote, and saw an image of the robot skullface of Moloch in the upper stories of a big hotel glaring into my window; got high weeks later again, the visage was still there in red smoky downtown metropolis, I wandered down Powell street muttering, "Moloch Moloch" all night and wrote *Howl II* nearly intact in cafeteria at foot of Drake Hotel, deep in the hellish vale. Here the long line is used as a stanza form broken into exclamatory units punctuated by a base repetition, Moloch.

The rhythmic paradigm for Part III was conceived and half-written same day as the beginning of *Howl*; I went back later and filled it out. Part I, a lament for the Lamb in America with instances of remarkable lamblike youths; Part II names the monster of mental consciousness that preys on the Lamb; Part III a litany of affirmation of the Lamb in its glory: "O starry spangled shock of Mercy." The structure of Part III, pyramidal, with a graduated longer response to the fixed base.

I remembered the archetypal rhythm of Holy Holy Holy weeping in a bus on Kearny Street, and wrote most of it down in notebook there. That exhausted this set of experiments with a fixed base. I set it as *Footnote to Howl* because it was an extra variation of the form of Part II. (Several variations on these forms, including stanzas of graduated litanies followed by fugues, will be seen in *Kaddish*.)

A lot of these forms developed out of an extreme rhapsodic wail I once heard in a madhouse. Later I wondered if short, quiet, lyrical poems could be written using the long line. *A Strange New Cottage in*

Berkeley and *A Supermarket in California* (written same day) fell in place later that year. Not purposely, I simply followed my angel in the course of compositions.

What if I just simply wrote, in long units and broken short lines, spontaneously noting prosaic realities mixed with emotional upsurges, solitaries? *Transcription of Organ Music* (sensual data), strange writing which passes from prose to poetry and back, like the mind.

What about poem with rhythmic buildup power equal to *Howl* without use of repetitive base to sustain it? *The Sunflower Sutra* (composition time twenty minutes, me at desk scribbling, Kerouac at cottage door waiting for me to finish so we could go off somewhere to party) did that, it surprised me, one long who.

Next what happens if you mix long and short lines, single breath remaining the rule of measure? I didn't trust free flight yet, so went back to fixed base to sustain the flow, *America*. After that, a regular formal type long poem in parts, short and long breaths mixed at random, no fixed base, sum of earlier experiments—*In the Baggage Room at Greyhound. In Back of the Real* shows what I was doing with short lines (see sentence above) before I accidentally wrote *Howl*.

Later I tried for a strong rhythm built up using free, short, syncopated lines, *Europe! Europe!* a prophecy written in Paris.

Last, the Proem to *Kaddish* (NY 1959 work)—finally, completely free composition, the long line breaking up within itself into short staccato breath units—notations of one spontaneous phrase after another linked within the line by dashes mostly: the long line now perhaps a variable stanzaic unit, measuring groups of related ideas, grouping them—a method of notation. Ending with a hymn in rhythm similar to the synagogue death lament. Passing into dactylic? says Williams? Perhaps not: at least the ear hears itself in Promethean natural measure, not in mechanical count of accent.

All these poems are recorded now as best I can, though with scared love, imperfect to an angelic trumpet in mind. I have quit reading in front of live audiences for a while. I began in obscurity to communicate a live poetry; it's become more a trap and duty than the spontaneous ball it was first.

A word on the Academies: poetry has been attacked by an ignorant and frightened bunch of bores who don't understand how it's made, and the trouble with these creeps is they wouldn't know poetry if it came up and buggered them in broad daylight.

A word on the Politicians: my poetry is angelic ravings and has nothing to do with dull materialistic vagaries about who should shoot who. The secrets of individual imagination—which are transconceptual and non-verbal—I mean unconditioned spirit—are not for sale to this consciousness, are no use to this world, except perhaps to make it shut its trap and listen to the music of the spheres. Who denies the music of the spheres denies poetry, denies man, and spits on Blake, Shelley, Christ, and Buddha. Meanwhile, have a ball. The universe is a new flower. America will be discovered. Who wants a war against roses will have it. Fate tells big lies, and the gay creator dances on his own body in eternity.

AUTHOR'S NOTE:
Need comment on end—This provocative, even inflammatory peroration seems to have offended a number of straight poets and was oft quoted, a declaration of absolute poetic purpose that the critic Richard Howard still remembered decades later, taking exception to my insistence of "unconditioned Spirit." This aggression may have exacerbated the Battle of Anthologies between Open Form and Closed Form poets. An incendiary tract, aimed at both Marxist and CIA Capitalist (*Encounter*) Critics, as well as bourgeois judgmental sociologists, Norman Podhoretz probably in mind.

Notes Written on Finally Recording Howl

Wall Street:
The Story of What Happened to Our Intimacy

Did you ever feel like you've been cheated?!
—*Johnny Rotten*

*I look forward to the day when our lives won't be printed on
dollar bills!*
—*Clifford Odets*

THE MYTHOLOGICAL GESTURE THAT GAVE birth to this land was not as
mystical as a lady of the lakes emanating from the waters with Excalibur or
as romantic as a dare between two brothers and seven hills. The mythological gesture that gave birth to this land was a **transaction**.

A transaction is the most mediocre form of human intercourse. It is an
exchange of mutual fictions rather than of true feeling. It is a way for two
people to take at the same time, together. *There is more human interaction
in murder than there is in a transaction.*

THE **TRANSACTION**—THE MOST MEDIOCRE FORM OF HUMAN INTERCOURSE.

A transaction is bad sex happening all over the city, all day, everywhere. The
gesture emanates simultaneously from our fear and our need for each other.
While handing someone a dollar bill, we are necessarily entering his personal space but keeping ourselves at arm's distance.

There is so much uninspired *sex in the city*, it keeps me up at night.
Just as Natasha-Ignoring-Simone does.

We all need a hug and we even want to get close to each other, but we
are afraid of each other. The transaction develops from this contradiction.
Anyone is invited into our immediate periphery as long as they have a constructive, profitable reason to be there.

Therefore, to be profitable is to be good at *not* giving.

*The **transaction** is the gesture at the beginning of the mythological tale* *called "New York City."* **Peter Minuit**, a German representing Dutch interests, purchased the island from a passing Native American tribe in 1624. The deal was a fiction. The Native Americans accepting the barter were just visitors themselves. What was actually transacted were chickens and dry goods and red wheelbarrows. The Native Americans probably walked away from the encounter talking about the strange, generous man who had just been washed ashore and given them all these great things.

The original sexual intercourse that gives birth to the idea of Nieuw Amsterdam is uninspired sex between men who did not speak the same language, linguistically or spiritually. New York City, likewise, was created to be a great escape from sharing.

Wall Street was a wall built officially by the original European settlers of this island to protect themselves from the English who were to the north in Massachusetts. Subliminally, the wall was built to protect them from the boundless possibilities of an unlabeled continent laid out before them.

IN THE FACE OF BOUNDLESSNESS, HUMAN BEINGS HAVE A TENDENCY TO BUILD WALLS.

Wall Street is still a wall. The wooden barricade of the seventeenth century was torn down long ago and used by the British for firewood, but the consciousness that gives Wall Street meaning is a colossal fortress built between ourselves and our hearts.

MONEY IS OUR ONGOING ATTEMPT TO REPLACE *intimacy,* and therefore money is our painful lesson plan teaching us that there is no replacement for intimacy.

Welcome to Wall Street!

WE BEGIN AT PETER MINUIT PLAZA IN FRONT OF THE STATEN ISLAND FERRY TERMINAL:

Behind us, stretching along the water, is the **Staten Island Ferry Terminal**, green with oxidation. During the 1890s, there were more than one hundred ferryboats launching in a hundred different directions from Manhattan Island. The Staten Island Ferry, the most famous of the few still sailing, is a twenty-five-minute, free oceanic journey. It is a far faster and easier-going way to view the Statue of Liberty than the "Liberty Ferry" that sails directly to the statue. (**See "A Tour of the Statue of Liberty: Stay Free"**).

On an evening tour, I stood with a Dutch woman on the Staten Island

Ferry as we sailed toward Manhattan. The sky and the city together formed a living El Greco painting, and the view from the boat seemed unlikely, and as we got closer to the shore, it seemed impossible. The Dutch lady asked me, "Why all the lights? Why don't they turn off the lights if no one is in the buildings?" I replied, "Because **New York City is a movie star**. It's posing."

The rational Dutch lady looked at me, confused. I cackled. Together, we were a complete manifestation of all the primary ingredients that gave birth to this phantasm before us.

Through the trees, across **Battery Park**, one can still stare out to the succulent spot, in the middle of the watery New York Harbor, where the great cruiser **Verrazano** stood sometime in 1524, as he put it, "at the mouth of a great river, between two hills."

This incredible harbor with its direct, flowing entrance into the Atlantic Ocean is what initially brought the polite marauders we call "Europeans" to this place. The island itself was a giant rock and a ridiculous place to live. Here we are standing on landfill. **This patch of land is not historically accurate** from *the point of view of the glaciers* who, in their last melting breath, sculpted this island in a passionate attempt to leave their imprint on the world.

The radically curved skyscraper in front of us, **17 State Street**, echoes the original shoreline of the island when it was purely a remnant left behind by the **Ice Age**.

If you ever get really depressed and feel surrounded by seemingly unsolvable problems, remember that we are all living between two ice ages. This thought has saved my life on a couple of occasions.

The **Seton House** is the Georgian house sitting next to 17 State Street. It is the only survivor of a row of Georgian mansions that skirted this original edge of the city, overlooking the harbor. This house was spared because it was the residence of the first American-born saint, **Elizabeth Ann Seton.**

The Staten Island Ferry boat was invented by a dynamic flesh experiment in survivalism called Cornelius Vanderbilt. The Vanderbilt family was an upper-middle-class family living on Staten Island at the beginning of the nineteenth century. According to legend, the fifteen-year-old Cornelius asked his mother for a hundred-dollar loan to buy a few wooden rafts for the purpose of transporting his friends and relatives between Staten Island and Manhattan. He returned to her a month later with a thousand dollars in profit.

By the time Vanderbilt is eighteen, he has a fleet of schooners that are fast enough to outrun the British ships during their siege of New York in 1812, making him the major food and provisions provider for the entire city during that time. He also uses the ships' dexterity to encroach upon the highly profitable trade of mussels and clams in Maryland, Virginia, and New York. At the age of twenty-five, having already invented three different fortunes, Vanderbilt focuses his concentration on railroads. His **New York Central Railroad Company** becomes the rail company that turns the entire eastern seaboard of the United States into a cute primrose path to paradise. *Paradise is 42nd Street and Park Avenue.* Inadvertently, Cornelius Vanderbilt gives birth to Midtown Manhattan by making the small depot on 42nd Street his railroad's hub. **(See "The Midtown Rush-Hour Tour.")**

The most important fact about Cornelius Vanderbilt is that he was a bad father. He was one of the wealthiest self-made men in the world and yet he still felt the need to compete with his children. He believed he could absolve his sins of violence against life with cold, hard cash. His fortune was a surrogate for all the human relationships he missed out on. His incredible resume is actually a list of excuses as to why he never had time to sit in his living room. His empire and his board meetings: all of it was an elaborate escape from intimacy.

Cornelius Vanderbilt—not a good father.

Capitalism, a giant crib, does not reward those who pursue the fullest amplifications of self, it rewards those who have given up that pursuit to meekly settle down with visions of themselves as mediocre children taught to dream. Fathers can disown sons if the sons turn out to be bad investments. Love is having everyone's goals in alignment. **(Refer to *Death of a Salesman* by Arthur Miller.)**

The entire idea of an economy was developed by those using money for identity. An economy is a society's method of containing its people in every facet of their lives except for sex and faith. It is **THE ONGOING STRATEGY HATCHED BY THE OLDER GENERATION to subjugate the younger generation.** Economy exists for the sole purpose of keeping us from staring into each other's eyes.

A capitalistic economy, a libertarian economy, a Keynesian economy, an economy of the invisible hand, and a communist economy all insist, without ever stating it, that our contributions to them are more important than our contributions to each other.

We are standing at the base of **Water Street,** so called because this area where we stand was originally water. As we float down **Water Street**, the **Brooklyn Bridge** is off to our right, starboard. **John Augustus Roebling**, the visionary and architect of this bridge, went insane when he saw it actualized. His story, mythological, is the same as Doctor Frankenstein's. His creation thrilled him in dreams and terrified him in oxygen.

Completed in 1883, many men died during the construction of this bridge and felt justified dying in its name. This is because the bridge, much more than a bridge in their eyes, is the symbolic consummation of manifest destiny—the American usurpation of the North American continent. Therefore, **the bridge can also be called a GRAVESTONE.**

I highly recommend walking across the Brooklyn Bridge. The bridge is very collapsible in the imagination, and even more so when actually underneath your feet. In the early days of the bridge's career, many people were trampled to death while crossing it. **Large pedestrian crowds would feel the vibrations undulating in the bridge's suspension and would unanimously panic.** Assuming the bridge was collapsing, the crowds would run off in disorganized hordes, trampling each other to death.

No one dared observe that the crowd's reaction to its deadly feelings of imbalance was, from the bridge's point of view, a contribution to its ongoing perfect balance. This dance between balance and imbalance is a part of every rush hour, but these were the truest rush hours New York City has ever known.

Once I had a couch-surfing sleepover on the large, manly couch of **Norman Mailer** in his amazing pad in Brooklyn Heights. (The invitation came from Mailer's son, **Steven,** a lovely man and a marvelous actor. Norman never knew I was there.) The raised ceiling of the apartment had tall walls cascading with hammocks and platforms, rope and ladders. I had never been in an apartment that felt so much like a tall ship. From each platform of the place, a new view of the Brooklyn Bridge and the harbor awaited.

Tossing and turning in the thick linen while my head rested on a toughened, manly pillow, I noticed a large hardcover book—the fortieth anniversary issue of *Playboy,* a limited edition that contained a celebratory abridged photographic history of all the playmates who had ever posed nude for the magazine. On the inside of the cover, **Hugh Hefner** had written in large magic-marker hieroglyphics, "Norm—It's been a great forty years . . . Love, Hef."

I stared at the photographs of nude women from my favorite decade of centerfolds—the 1950s—and I realized another truthful life lesson while staring between a certain woman's thighs from 1955. There is more history of New York City in a *Playboy* centerfold than in the entire *Encyclopedia of New York* or any other academic study of the place. The *Playboy* centerfold is an autobiography of our heartbeats and our genitals. *The Encyclopedia of New York* is written by our brains to build a better tomorrow for our self-doubt. In my analogy, I didn't mean to exclude womankind or their own rebellions against alphabetizing, but you can understand—I was on Norman Mailer's couch.

We coast farther up Water Street until we see **Broad Street** experiencing its genesis on our left. Take a left onto Broad Street. Broad Street was the original canal flowing from the East River through the Nieuw Amsterdam trading post. This is why Broad Street is much wider than the other more claustrophobic streets of Nieuw Amsterdam around us.

In mythology, water represents the unconscious. Mythology's view of Broad Street, therefore, would be as an elongated unconsciousness paved over. Broad Street is, in mythological terms, repression. Feel the repression under your feet. *Tread carefully along the sidewalk and see if you can feel the repressed unconsciousness of this place thumping from below,* then take note of the yellow building on our right. This is **Fraunces Tavern.**

Fraunces Tavern was the James Delancey house, and it became Fraunces's tavern in 1757. Fraunces eventually became George Washington's personal chief steward. The original Continental Congress was founded inside the tavern, and George Washington said his farewell to the officers in his army here. This is a reconstruction of the original structure which burned many times in several different fires throughout the nineteenth century. The reconstruction was executed by "The Sons of the Revolution of New York State" and their agenda.

Today, **FRAUNCES TAVERN** is a museum and a restaurant.

When one peruses the modern incarnation of Fraunces Tavern, one realizes that reconstruction has an aftertaste that is similar to mouthwash. It is a clean, polite study of carnage and despair that results in pristine nostalgia and vague philanthropy. Most attempts to re-create history fail to understand that history is not a documentation as much as it is a sensation. When I visited the Holocaust Museum in Washington, D.C., I felt totally safe and secure, and I passed through without one insult, without one threat made on my life. **WHEN I VISIT ELLIS ISLAND TODAY, I FEEL THE AIR-CONDITIONING MUCH MORE THAN THE POSSIBILITY OF BEING DENIED ENTRY TO THE UNITED STATES BECAUSE I HAVE GOUT.**

Go inside to the new bar in Fraunces Tavern, get a round of drinks, and toast to the fact that all reconstruction is taxidermy. Toast to this place, another attempt historians have made to exclude, and therefore absolve, themselves from history. History is not something to be documented. It is something to be felt. How does it feel to me? *History is fifteen thousand years of neurotic disequilibrium breathing on the back of my neck.*

Walk steadily up Broad Street. Note the narrow streets all around you. Claustrophobic in feeling, many of these Lower Manhattan streets will never see sunlight again. These are the oldest streets of Manhattan Island. These streets were designed by the Dutch of the early seventeenth century. Welcome to Nieuw Amsterdam.

As we cross **Pearl Street,** feel the presence of New York City's first **printing press,** the mascot of modern European civilization, which sat at **81 Pearl Street.** As we cross over **South William Street,** listen for the Hebraic and Ladino prayers still floating in the wind as they emanate from New York City's first synagogue, which stood at **26 South William Street.** The synagogue was built in 1730 and was engulfed, along with six hundred other buildings in this area, by the great fire of 1835.

The fire of 1835 happened in mid-December during freezing temperatures and a blowing gale. The water from the firemen's hoses froze before even reaching the fire. One of the major fires of early American history, it wiped out most of the original Nieuw Amsterdam architecture and led to the utilization of cast iron and other new materials by builders of the city anxious to build nonflammable buildings. (**For more on this, refer to "A Tour of SoHo, or How to Render Sexual Frustration Obsolete."**)

As we cross over **Beaver Street,** taste some of the great food of past generations served in **Delmonico's,** the original premier restaurant of New York, founded in 1827. It was also the site of some of New York's original premier gossip.

As we move farther north, let us take a moment to view the tiny street called **Exchange Place**, not as a street but as an art installation. In the context of this neighborhood, the name of this street is a reference to money trading. Viewed as an enormous, autonomous sculpture, Exchange Place is a series of sexual longings exchanged but not shared between a vast variety of shafts and concave angles. There are complicated sexual postures formed between these gigantic shapes, but no consummation. The skyscrapers attain their altitude due to wanton lust. The human beings moving around this living sculpture that takes up an entire city block do their own version of exchanging instead of sharing, thus echoing the vast shapes that dwarf them.

Wall Street: The Story of What Happened to Our Intimacy

This sculpture is here as a reminder that THE MAIN THING THAT COMES FROM REPLACING *intimacy* WITH MONEY is THAT NO ONE *gets laid.*

The neoclassical edifice facing Exchange Place and sitting on a slight curvature of the street line is the **New York Stock Exchange.**

This is the landmark of pulling in and out of stocks. This is the world where an ideal day is a day spent buying low and selling high. This is a place where nonparticipatory attitudes and general hesitations about living life are actively convincing themselves that they have a purpose. This is the embodiment of cynicism.

CYNICISM is a nonparticipatory LETHARGY aimed at our afternoons. Just as a good stockbroker knows how to pull out in time for downward slopes in a stock, a good cynic knows how to pull out of an afternoon, meekly running from circumstances not going his or her way. Cynicism is the effective use of noncommunication with the world, which leads to the effective use of noncommunication with our fellow human beings, which is capitalism.

Anti-**Cruise** views an **afternoon** as something to be utilized and/or contained in the name of **self-preservation** and **self-promotion.** The anti-Cruise participates in an afternoon only if there is practical necessity or if the events and emotions involved are very favorable. The anti-Cruise attends a party only for the political reasons of making an appearance, never to actually party.

The CRUISE *is here to completely EMBRACE the world.* The Cruise views any afternoon as a masterpiece of art and a daily opportunity to fall in love with the world. The Cruise is here to participate in every afternoon regardless of the results: ascension or demolition.

The Stock Exchange is open to the public on weekdays for free tours during business hours. There is a small museum exhibition one passes through before reaching the soundproof booth that hangs over the main room. *The abridged history of the exchange inadvertently proves for all time that MATERIALISM IS THE UTILIZATION of the FEAR OF OTHER PEOPLE'S OPINIONS.*

Once inside the soundproof booth, one looks down upon a giant playpen filled with children dressed up in different costumes playing a game that involves frantic gesturing, screaming, and jumping up and down. Even though the booth is soundproof, one can still hear the children's collective air of self-importance. The Stock Exchange and all who monitor it are addicted to their own suspense. "A bear market" and "a bull market": two opposites thriving off each other. The whole operation would crumble and become a forgotten ruin if it did not mirror a casino. If it were only a place to make money or exclusively a place to lose money, there would be no drama.

In front of the Stock Exchange is the **buttonwood tree.** It was under this tree, in 1792, that the first meeting of brokers took place, and today, this buttonwood tree still stands in front of the Stock Exchange, ceremoniously facing Wall Street. WHEN COMMERCE ENTERED THIS THIN STREET IN FRONT OF US CALLED "WALL STREET," ALL THE CURRENCIES OF THE WORLD DISCOVERED THE SAME GOD.

Take a moment with this sad, sickly sapling reaching out for sunlight through the wrought-iron cage in which it is incarcerated. A steel grate lies over its root system. There are usually miscellaneous scraps of garbage piled around the tree's base. It is less a tree than it is a symbol. *The tree is a piece of **nature**, shot and **stuffed** and **hung** over a god's fireplace.*

It is clear where this intersection's priorities lie when one compares the size of the Stock Exchange's façade to nature's representative here. With this vision, the city is exhibiting how much more seriously we take our illusions than we do our reality.

The **Buttonwood Tree** in front of the **Stock Exchange**—less a *tree,* more a *symbolic gesture.*

Perception is a dogmatic gesture. For instance, I can point to the statue across the street from the Stock Exchange, kitty-corner from the buttonwood tree, and tell you that it is a portrayal of **George Washington** taking the oath of office as the first president of the United States. This statue will now take on a significance and a symbolism for you that is, perhaps, unstoppable.

Now take a deep breath and close your eyes for a solid moment of centrality that emanates from within. When we reopen our eyes and view this statue again, let us try to view it with complete objectivity, bereft of any specific ideological accoutrement or national pride. Open your eyes. What do you see? There is a large man in eighteenth-century garb with an expression of need on his face. He is not smiling. He has one hand resting on air, the palm facing the Earth. His other hand is being held out, and this hand being held out is half clenched.

George Washington is hoping someone will hold his hand. He is standing here, in bronze, among throngs of people, waiting for someone to reach out and hold his hand.

Wall Street: The Story of What Happened to Our Intimacy

Let us close our eyes and breathe again, reopen them, and this time view the statue as George Washington, the first president of the United States, waiting for someone to hold his hand. This statue is the most profound encapsulation of American history I have ever seen.

The statue is an example of history being felt by someone more than history being documented. It was sculpted by **John Quincy Ward** and by the vibrations of early American history—that incredible drama, dancing around this corner right now.

The building behind George Washington is the **Federal Hall National Memorial,** built in 1842 as the U.S. Custom House to replace the second City Hall. It was in that building that **Peter Zenger,** an early-eighteenth-century journalist, was tried for sedition after printing mockeries in a local publication about an English government official. Zenger's acquittal planted the seeds of a "free press" in the collective unconscious. *THE RIGHT TO exhibit our opinions IS ONLY RESTRICTED NOW BY OUR OWN self-censorship.*

Here, at the corner of Wall Street and Broad, in 1765, the **Stamp Act Congress** met and drafted a declaration of rights and a list of grievances. This was the first formal congregation of American colonists to stand together in a room and use the phrase "Taxation without representation." These were the words that would spark the war with England.

Here, at the corner of Wall Street and Broad, on July 18, 1776, the **Declaration of Independence** was read aloud. The Declaration has become one of history's great guidelines on how to theorize a miracle. America is an endeavor trying not only to declare itself but also to experience itself. American tourists prefer to ride sightseeing buses through New York because **THERE IS TOO MUCH AMERICA HERE** and it is easier to deal with if it is all a blur.

New York City was occupied by the British for seven out of the eight years of the American Revolutionary War, and the building that stood on this corner was their headquarters throughout the entire occupation. After the war, the **Northwest Ordinance** was passed by the **Second Continental Congress** from this corner. This was the Americans' first attempt to create a country with a centralized government. The democracy they eventually craft on this corner has now outlived even the Athenian democracy.

Pierre L'Enfant, the designer of Washington, D.C., and Indianapolis, Indiana, renovated the second City Hall building in 1789. When he finished the remodeling, the building that once stood on this corner became the capitol of the United States. Here, on the corner of Wall Street and Broad, the same Congress that now meets in Washington, D.C., met for the first time on March 4, 1789. As its first official act, Congress counted the electoral ballots for the first presidential election and noted the unanimous vote for George Washington as the president of the brand-new country.

On Wall Street and Broad, on April 30, 1789, shortly before the fall of the Bastille in Paris, George Washington took his oath of office. He has been standing here ever since waiting for someone to hold his hand.

When I worked on the double-decker tour bus, my vehicular lover and the erogenous center of my postadolescent life, we used to turn on this corner every single tour. Three or four or five times a day, I would point to this George Washington monument and feel the entire bus sway to the left as *passengers from all over the world LEANED OVER THE SIDE OF THE BUS to see exactly where he stood as he took his oath.* **They were leaning into a lie.**

Why do we yearn to know exactly where George Washington stood? **Isn't historical accuracy just our memories becoming totalitarian on us?**

The study of history is often trying to convince us that there was only one story. We know that any anecdote has as many versions as people who witnessed it.

George Washington had no better idea why he was here than we do, and he was just as confused as we are. His most heroic moments happened on the nights he apologized to Martha for gawking at her girlfriends. *All the historical anecdotes of early American history that danced across this corner were extensions of George Washington's NEED FOR A HUG.*

Directly across the street from George Washington's statue is the **J. P. Morgan Guaranty Building.** On the Wall Street side, in the wall of bright, white limestone, one can still see pockmarks from the anarchist bomb that exploded here in 1920. It is still presumed that the anarchists attacked J. P. Morgan's headquarters because they deemed him one of the significant ingredients of World War One.

Let's walk north, past George Washington's statue up the tiny street called **Nassau Street.** As we cross Wall Street, look off to the right. This is the full extent of this infamous street. Narrow—it was originally designed for horse carriages. About five or six blocks long with enormous buildings crammed together, *Wall Street is what* **Brunelleschi,** *the Renaissance* **architect** *who discovered perspective, envisioned as he* **breathed his last breath.** From this corner, we are viewing the final breathless vision of that visionary.

Nassau Street is named after the royal family of the Netherlands and is an example of how some of the streets of Lower Manhattan still have their original Dutch names. Dutch, as a language, would leave its mark on American English in important places. The word "yacht," for instance, and the word "cookie." The British say "biscuit." *If it weren't for the slight Dutch imperialism that went down on these streets, it is possible that* **Cookie Monster** *would have been chasing down biscuits his whole life.*

The next corner is **Pine Street,** and to the left is the enormous glass-and-aluminum **Chase Manhattan Bank Building,** approximately sixty stories high. The building houses the world's largest bank vault. It is five floors below ground and holds billions of dollars in "securities" and a few million dollars of actual cash. The building rings with bigness. Big money, big plaza, big people with big ideas on the topics of themselves and their place in the world. The whole bank is named after **Salmon Chase,** who founded the current national banking system and its currency as secretary of the treasury under Abraham Lincoln.

But perhaps biggest of all, bigger than the personalities and even the building itself, bigger than the billions of "securities" hanging out in the vault, and even bigger than those securities' feelings of security, are the French businessman-turned-sculptor Jean Dubuffet's sculptural sixty-foot magic mushrooms sprouting out of the Chase Manhattan Plaza.

The simple visual truth lies before us as we stand on this astonishing monumental Financial District plaza—we are standing in the shadow of enormous **mushrooms.**

The Mayans called the mushroom *"FLESH OF THE GODS."* Their calendar, divided into five epochs, ends altogether on December 22, 2012. We are living in the time they termed the final epoch of human life on this planet. If we could return to Chichén Itzá and stand with the Mayans of two thousand years ago, and explain to them that we are actually alive on a city plaza in the middle of New York City in the last moments of their fifth epoch, their reply, translated from the Mayan, would sound like this: "Wow!"

Mushrooms are a tour guide in the landmark of irrationality. They are emissaries of the Earth guiding us across the incomprehensible, across the cliffsides of beyond belief.

Stand with me on this city plaza and watch the businessmen and other associates of commerce, dressed up in their appropriate wardrobes, pass back and forth, ignoring the sixty-foot mushrooms.

The **mushrooms** *have come here to the* **Financial District** *because it is a place of* **NO SURRENDER.**

It is a place where success is a measurement of the effective use of one's selfishness instead of the effective use of one's selflessness. This is a symptom of sullenness and of taking life too seriously. This leads to the attitude that everyone is here to protect us from ourselves. The mushrooms turn these tormented illusions into Silly Putty.

For now, the **giant MUSHROOMS** *stand here silently watching people lose sight of the fact that* **reality is an u n f o l d i n g miracle** *as they commit themselves to competitive behavior.*

Competition is the act of seeking an exit from your life. It is to be building a self with builders other than self. It is spending the day focusing attention on the opinions and actions of everyone else instead of concentrating on one's own struggle.

The entire idea of a **business** is to create a scheme where we feel justified in avoiding our own struggle. There we have bosses whose problems are considered more important than our own all day, every day. If "successful," we then become bosses who can delineate our struggle to the next generation.

As we walk away from the Chase Manhattan Plaza toward Broadway, turn around and view the giant mushrooms and the pedestrians from a distance. The entire vision of tiny people wrapped up in their own dramas while being dwarfed by huge mushrooms is a microcosmic diorama of what is going on worldwide right now. According to prophets, gurus, the high-minded and courageous, and shamans, this planet has just now exited the two-thousand-year astrological alignment called the Age of Pisces and is now entering the **Age of Aquarius.** *It is time for us to give ourselves to the* **UNKNOWN,** *instead of expending all of our* **life energy** *demanding that* **we know.**

When we return to **Broadway,** take a left. At the corner of Wall and Broadway is the large brown church called **Trinity Church.** Trinity Church is actually the third church on this site. The church was originally chartered by King William III in 1697. Queen Anne granted the land in 1705, and this version was constructed in 1846. Queen Elizabeth, when she visited New York in the twentieth century, stopped by Trinity Church and a plaque on the floor at the entrance of the church commemorates that Anglican landmark in time. In its initial incarnation, Trinity Church was the tallest structure of New York City's skyline.

Trinity Church's cemetery is a hall of fame. The hedge stones, older than the current church standing among them, crumble with mystery, early

American genius and its insanity: **Robert Fulton,** inventor of the steamboat; **Albert Gallatin,** secretary of the treasury under Thomas Jefferson; **William Bradford,** the curator of the first printing press in America; **Captain James Lawrence,** a naval commander victorious in the permanent seas of vivacity when he spoke his dying command, "Don't give up the ship!" The Gothic spire that looks like the top of a buried church is a memorial to soldiers of the American Revolution who died as prisoners on Liberty Street.

Alexander Hamilton, secretary of the treasury under George Washington, co-author of the *Federalist* papers, and one of the founding fathers of the United States of America, is buried next to his wife, **Eliza,** on the south side of the burial grounds. Hamilton, as a New Yorker, knew that Thomas Jefferson's Virginian vision of America as an agrarian nation was off. He knew America was destined to be a manufacturing nation. He founded the **Bank of New York** in 1784, the oldest commercial bank in the United States. The bank's current headquarters is on the corner of Wall Street and William Street.

Today, **Alexander Hamilton's grave** *sits proudly next to a* **shoe outlet.** This simple fact is proof that he was right.

Hamilton was killed in a pistol duel that occurred between him and **Aaron Burr** in Weehawken, New Jersey, in 1804. Burr, described by Abigail Adams as "the most insidious man of his generation," had founded the second major bank of the city, called the **Manhattan Company.** Their duel was actually a duel between banks, and **the founding father's death was a heroic example of a CLASSIC CORPORATE TAKEOVER.**

Outside the gate of Trinity Church, we proceed down Broadway, considered to be one of the longest roads of the world. We are descending toward its absolute genesis.

At **39 Broadway,** note the small plaque that marks this address as the second White House of American history. This is where George Washington lived for six months in his first term as president of the United States. Though the house is long erased and replaced by a large commercial building, the cool energy of Washington's late-night contemplations still pervades.

At **26 Broadway** is the former **Standard Oil Building,** the corporate headquarters of John D. Rockefeller's Standard Oil Company. Rockefeller's famous quip **"Do unto others before they do it to you"** could be the epitaph inscripted across our intimacy's gravestone.

At **25 Broadway** is the former **Cunard Building.** Cunard was/is the major ocean-liner company, whose first voyage between New York and

England happened in 1840. The entire architecture is a vibratory reminiscence and a tactile ornament from the days when people would take stylish
weeklong journeys across the Atlantic Ocean. Ships filled with piles of
steaks, vats of wine, and fine delicacies would sail on the open seas as
women's breasts in evening gowns swayed first port side then starboard side.
The Renaissance façade suddenly sprouts a colonnade, the interior nautical
vestibule flowing with the rhythm of an ocean, and flows into a great hall
where the climax of an ocean liner vaults into revelries of great aquatic
cruisers.

*I often stand outside this building thinking of **Magellan.*** I completely
identify with him. The major decision of his life was whether to go with or
against the wind.

MAGELLAN—the *major decision of a discoverer's life is whether to go*
WITH *or* **AGAINST** *the* **WIND.**

The oval-shaped park currently crowned by the statue of an enormous,
charging bull is **Bowling Green Park.** This was, as we learned earlier, New
York City's first park. In 1771, a statue of King George III of England was
erected in Bowling Green and stood where the central fountain currently
flows, quietly associating with the mythological metaphoric meaning of
water as the unconscious. After the public reading of the Declaration of
Independence on July 18, 1776, angry colonists rampaged through the streets
and had a fun carnage with the King George statue. (**For more about
Bowling Green Park, refer to "A Tour of the Statue of Liberty: Stay Free!"**)

The ornate **U.S. Custom House** designed by **Cass Gilbert** stands
behind the Bowling Green oval. Today it is the **National Museum of the
American Indian.** The alive beaux arts architecture of the building, once
committed to the commercial responsibilities of a busy trading harbor, now
houses a monumental collection of Native American art.

The entire complex is a bizarre extended thought, extending from the
initial awkward handshake that took place between Peter Minuit and his
Reckagawawanc counterpart.

As we look around the corner of the U.S. Custom House, down State
Street, we will see the Peter Minuit Plaza, where we began this possibility
for intimacy in a landscape built to protect us from it.

*We have completed one big circle. A circle of worries leading to **further
worrying, a circle of achievements that have never achieved enough—
in other words,** THE "AMERICAN DREAM."*

At the end of the circle, let us put aside Wall Street consciousness and see beyond the American dream just for a moment and recognize that the only thing we ever truly pay for in this world is a lack of generosity.

Intimacy is a direct experience. It is not a theory, it is not something to be documented, it cannot be photographed; intimacy must be felt. The ability to share our feelings with other people begins with us actually feeling the feeling.

Now, experience a moment of true intimacy.

Draw a picture of yourself.

BARNEY ROSSET

Letter Home

(Written shortly before embarking from Karachi, India)

November 19, 1945
Kalaikunda, India

THE POLITICAL SITUATION ALL OVER the world, but particularly in the Far East, is pretty discouraging, because the Americans, British, and French seem to have taken up the same policies that the Japanese and Germans left off with. It seems pretty clear to me that the failure of the British to get out of India and their fighting in Indonesia is a direct contradiction to all their high-sounding war aims and radical change in party. They have no more right to rule India than the Chinese do, and it would be impossible to make a bigger mess of things than they have. Right here in India they have men like Nehru who are among the greatest in the world. Their help to the Dutch, who want to get back their ill-gotten possessions, is also disgusting. The same goes for the French in Indo-China. The people there were persecuted and exploited by the French for years, and I think that they would rather have the Japanese than the French rule them, and with good cause.

Where we are dead wrong is in our policy with China. The Central Government in China is the biggest bunch of grafters and crooks I have ever seen. Chiang Kai-shek is nothing but a fascist in my estimation, and *never* fought the Japanese throughout the war, whereas the Chinese communists fought continuously without our help, killed Japanese, and at the same time raised the living standards of the people. So what do we do, we arm the Central Government to fight the communists. The least we could have done would have been to have kept our hands off and let them fight it out, and if we had, the communists would have won hands down, because the morale on their side is incomparably higher. The Central Government troops want no part of fighting, and I have no doubt that they may not do it anyway. The Russians only helped the Central Government during the war, but I have heard it said that after the Russians captured Manchuria and then pulled out of there they left the

Japanese equipment behind, giving it to nobody, but just letting it lie where they found it. Then the communists came in and grabbed it. That sounds almost too good to be true. The communists are incredibly ingenious with equipment and they can use anything or make anything, as I have seen. They made rifles and pistols by hand, and I saw the weapons, too. And with them they killed more Japanese than the Central Government troops did with American equipment, which they hardly used in front lines anyway. At the front they used the old stuff and the poorest soldiers. I saw them using old Russian artillery and ten-year-old ammunition, while in the rear areas they have the new American stuff.

It is a very sad fact that the average American left China hating the Chinese because he considered them to be all crooks, fools, and cowards, which actually was not the case by a long shot. He got that impression from Central Government tactics and methods because that is all he saw.

In Kunming, the biggest black market you can imagine flourished. You could buy any piece of American equipment if you had enough money—food, clothes, carbines, pistols, jeeps, gasoline, anything. High Chinese officials were implicated and the American Criminal Investigation Department was licked because they could not investigate Chinese, only Americans, so all they ever caught was the small fry. Important Chinese civilians and military men lived like kings, with new cars, beautiful homes, and the best of everything. In Yenan there was *no* black market whatsoever. The highest-ranking communist generals lived *exactly* like the rank and file of the soldiers. That is just one illustration of the caliber of the men in the two governments. I don't say these things as guesses but as things I know. Articles talking about cruelty and lack of democracy in the communist area amuse me. You have no conception in the States of how people live in China. In the Central Government areas, they would just as soon shoot a man as look at him. Every day they led people out to be shot. General Dai Li headed a Gestapo system, and a main function of that system was to spy on Americans. The Chinese government furnished interpreters to the American army. These interpreters were all officers in the Chinese army and they all attended a school for spy work before going on the job. They made regular reports to HQ on all conversations and all actions of Americans. The Chinese government did not want Americans in China, only their equipment. The American government is making a big mistake in supporting the Central Government because the other group would build China up much faster and make a much better customer for us than the bunch of thieves in power now ever will.

If the Americans, Dutch, British, and French persist in this attempt to rule other peoples in the world, which they have no right to do, then we are headed in a straight line for the third world war, because these people won't stand for it. If it had not been for Gandhi in India, I feel sure the Indians would have killed countless thousands of English, but his leadership in nonviolence has saved a lot of lives. In return, the British put him in prison. Just as the Irish and Americans broke away from the English, these people here will, too, and if the British don't let them go peacefully, they will just have to kill all the English. Eighty million can't rule four hundred million forever. These people are not stupid; they just don't have the materiél, but that never stopped anybody permanently before. It is quite lucky the Japanese never reached India, because if they had, they would have found a lot of sympathizers here to help them, just like the Germans found in Ireland.

A Hollywood-Style Tough:
The 1950s and the Fabrication of the Teenager

ROBERT MITCHUM WAS A BUDDING MOVIE star in the late 1940s, a cool customer with a thick chest and a stony, heavy-lidded gaze that telegraphed his trademark contempt. Born in 1917 in Bridgeport, Connecticut, he drifted through his teen years, once escaping from a Georgia chain gang while serving a short sentence for vagrancy. As a young man he landed in Southern California, where he discovered acting in an amateur theater company in Long Beach. It seemed like a much easier way to make a living than hauling loads on the docks.

During World War II Mitchum was cast in two dozen quickie pictures, mostly boilerplate war dramas, with an occasional detour into Westerns. By the time he drew a Best Supporting Actor nomination in 1945 for his work as Lt. Bill Walker in *The Story of G.I. Joe,* he had earned a reputation among gossip columnists as a loose cannon. He was "Hollywood's Bad Boy," a combustible celebrity always good for some ink. The rap was cemented in mid-1948, when Mitchum was arrested with three others at a private home for possession of narcotics. Ironically, on the morning of the incident he had been scheduled to address a group of students for National Youth Day on the subject of juvenile delinquency—presumably, how to avoid it—at Los Angeles City Hall at the mayor's request. Mitchum had canceled.

The actor a friend, and two female acquaintances were raided by police that night as they sat smoking marijuana in a Laurel Canyon bungalow where the women were staying. In 1948, smoking "tea" was still considered an exotic transgression, an unfathomable act to many ordinary Americans. Mitchum and his sidekick, Robin "Danny" Ford, a bartender trying to break into the real estate business, were photographed in the custody of the L.A.P.D., wearing the all-denim uniform of the county jail. With his shirt unbuttoned to the navel and a defiant smirk on his face, Mitchum tipped back in his chair, flouting the scandal. Ever the wiseguy, he gave his occupation as "former" actor and joked to the press, "I'm sorry if my new look doesn't appeal to you. It doesn't appeal to me either."

But the look of denim was starting to appeal to more restless young men and women. Dungarees, still the occupational clothing of many respectable professions (rancher, fireman, lumberjack), were beginning to take on an aura of disrepute. For some, they were simply an extension of childhood. Men who were boys in the 1920s or '30s, whose mothers bought them blue jeans through catalogs featuring illustrations of little buckaroos, began wearing them into adulthood. It was one way of announcing their aversion to the responsibilities of maturity. In Hollywood, the Western genre featured an increasing number of rough characters in denim pants and jackets, with the good guys and bad often occupying the same vast territory beyond polite society.

As Mitchum's prison photo attested, the use of denim was also widespread in the correctional system. Durable, low-maintenance and machine-washable, the fabric is ideally suited to prison life. When Charlie Chaplin is incarcerated on suspicion of communist sympathies in *Modern Times* (1936), he and some bullying fellow inmates bumble through the slapstick of a botched jailbreak in boxy prison blues. For real-life detainees, the outfit could be demoralizing, just as it had been for slaves in the south. During the Depression, with government money sometimes too scarce to buy prison uniforms, many vagrants wore their own clothes behind bars. In Nazi Germany, denim was considered lowly enough for the concentration camps. One Dachau survivor described the terrible conditions there: "Our prison clothes were a heavy, coarse denim. They would freeze when they got wet. We were not issued hats, gloves, or underwear."

Denim is still common in many prisons as an alternative to jailbird stripes and orange jumpsuits. In Oregon, a small company called Prison Blues makes denim workwear using paid prison labor. As part of a progressive inmate work program, state prisoners have been making their own jeans, workshirts, and yard coats since 1989. Prison Blues was founded in 1997 when an Oregon ballot measure cleared the way for private-sector partnerships with the state's Department of Corrections. An early attempt to market the product with inmates drew some negative publicity, prompting Prison Blues to recast itself as American-made clothing for loggers and other reputable workingmen.

"The public wasn't too thrilled, to be honest," says John Borchert, the company's head of marketing. "They didn't want their kids to think that prisoners were cool."

There has always been a class distinction apparent in wearing denim. By the 1940s, however, the material was becoming a personal choice, not just an institutional obligation. For the first time it could be seen as a fashion. More

A Hollywood-Style Tough: The 1950s and the Fabrication of the Teenager

accurately, young people wearing dungarees were making an *anti*–fashion statement as they imagined a kinship with the country's dispossessed—hobos, hardened criminals, and the heroic loners of the mythic west. A new cultural tug of war was taking place over the widening generation gap.

As with many culture clashes, both sides fell easily into their prescribed roles. Confronted with the grim realities of the Depression and atomic bombs, some students began to adopt a surly sort of fatalism. At the same time, the post-war sense of relief was evolving into a newfound sense of entitlement. Cars were no longer just the playthings of the wealthy, and ready access to them gave high schoolers and young adults an unprecedented mobility. For the first time, money earned from after-school jobs was not expected to be turned over to mom and dad but could be spent on records, clothing, and recreation. School administrators, fearing a loss of control, isolated dungarees as a sign of unrest and swiftly set prohibitions against them. The school system of Buffalo, New York, was one of many that banned jeans in its high schools. "These students are portraying what we consider bad taste in school attire and behavior," one schoolmarmish figure tells the camera in an instructional film typical of the period. Modeling for the narrator is a nervy high school couple wearing dungarees, the girl in ankle bracelets and drop earrings and the boy in a black jacket, his shirt open at the collar.

Denim mills and jeans makers struggled against that perception. North Carolina's Erwin Mills, for instance, promoted its "Bluserge" denim in trade magazine ads of the mid-1950s, touting the company's "Clean Jeans for Teens" initiative, dungarees sold three to a hanger and targeted for mothers buried knee-deep in laundry. The accompanying illustration featured a smiling, well-scrubbed young man with schoolbooks slung over his shoulder, wearing a V-necked sweater, a tie, a pair of penny loafers, and crisp denim trousers.

But many parents saw jeans as the clothing of a much less wholesome kind of boy. "If you want to know the good boys from the bad boys, you can tell just by looking at them," as one Levi Strauss & Co. executive put it, describing the brand's sudden image problem. As early as 1949, the company felt compelled to defend its product with advertising—"Denim: Right for School." "It was a battle for my dad to overcome the initial negative images," says Levi Strauss & Co. chairman Bob Haas. "We were working against the stereotype in the newspaper business at that time against jeans, and specifically the Levi's brand, as shorthand for an outlier, a rogue, a criminal."

A Hollywood-Style Tough: The 1950s and the Fabrication of the Teenager

Haas's father, Walter Haas Jr., joined the company in 1939 after attending business school at Harvard. After folding its old wholesale division, in 1948 Levi Strauss & Co. reached a goal long sought by Walter Haas Sr. when it achieved a net profit of $1 million for the first time. Even so, Walter Jr. was planning an overhaul. Recognizing the economic might of the postwar baby boom—*Life* magazine would soon report that young people were a $10-billion-a-year industry, "a billion more than the total sales of GM"—the heir apparent shifted the company's focus from Western wear toward the suburban youth market. Despite some initial resistance among elder executives, the move paid off handsomely. By the end of the 1950s, just a decade after Walter Sr.'s dream million-dollar profit, total annual LS&Co. sales had nearly tripled to $46 million, with a $2.5 million profit margin. Walter Haas Jr. was elected company president in 1958, with his younger brother, Peter, named executive vice president.

But the Levi's brand, like the rest of the denim industry, was not immune to growing pains. The makers of chinos and other competing garments appealed to parents not to dress their sons and daughters in denim. The American Institute of Men's and Boys' Wear, representing a coalition of ready-to-wear manufacturers, helped promote the movement against dungarees in schools. And the president of the Amalgamated Clothing Workers of America laid the blame for the blue jeans trend squarely at the blue suede shoes of a fast-rising rock 'n' roll star. His name was Elvis Presley.

The irony was that Presley himself was not especially fond of denim clothing. It reminded him of his working-class childhood. He even preferred not to wear shades of brown, because they too reminded him of workwear. But Elvis Presley Jeans were one of the earliest items of Elvis-related merchandising. They went on the market in 1956, when the singer-actor from Tupelo was in the Top Twenty almost continuously with songs including "Heartbreak Hotel," "Don't Be Cruel," and "Love Me Tender." The following year Presley wore a thick-stitched black denim jacket and jeans with a striped black-and-white shirt for the famous title dance number of his third movie, *Jailhouse Rock*, for which he was billed as the "Rebel of Song." The exuberant (if exceedingly hokey) sequence features Elvis and his fellow inmates scampering over a set styled to look like a two-tiered cell-block. Upon the film's release, black jeans became the rage of the season. Presley, who would often be cast as a guileless Li'l Abner type, here played a brooder with some genuinely unsavory qualities. Vince Everett, serving time for manslaughter, wears prison blues when he's not singing and dancing in the pen. After getting whipped for punching a guard, he staggers back to his cell with his denim jacket draped over his bare shoulders.

Other Presley roles would call for denim, such as Deke Rivers, the gas station attendant who becomes a pop star in *Loving You* (1957), or Toby Kwimper, the idiot-savant son of a family stranded in Florida in the 1962 comedy *Follow That Dream*. But Elvis, despite the allegations of the Amalgamated Clothing Workers of America, was not the idol most blameworthy for promoting a lower standard of dress among American teenagers. That notoriety belonged in large part to the two enduring figures of male Method acting of the 1950s, Marlon Brando and James Dean.

Brando in particular instinctively understood the feral message that jeans were capable of transmitting. Working in theater in New York in the late 1940s, years before his iconic role in the biker melodrama *The Wild One*, the young actor dressed just as he had in high school in suburban Illinois. "He knew what he had by way of allure," wrote his biographer, Peter Manso, "and would appear at the Russian Tea Room in Levi's and a white dress shirt that was visibly ripped, once with the collar torn off." Later, one playwright was astonished by the actor's "Bowery bum" attire, which included a pair of jeans carelessly belted with a length of clothesline.

Brando's first major breakthrough came with the 1947 Broadway production of Tennessee Williams's *A Streetcar Named Desire*. For the smoldering role of Stanley Kowalski, costume designer Lucinda Ballard drew her inspiration from a crew of ditchdiggers working in Midtown Manhattan. "Their clothes were so dirty that they had stuck to their bodies," she recalled. "It was sweat, of course, but they looked like statues. I thought, 'That's the look I want . . . the look of animalness.'" It was an appearance that suited Brando's brute physicality well. Ballard started with the T-shirt, still considered scandalous when worn without an overshirt. She fitted the actor very tightly, dying the T-shirts a faint red and tearing them at the shoulder.

Brando's blue jeans were similarly snug. Ballard, Manso suggested, "invented the first pair of fitted blue jeans, changing forever not just the face of theater but American fashion. 'I thought of them as though they were garments in the time of the Regency in France,' she said, 'which meant fitting the Levi's wet, pinning them tight. I had seven pair and I washed them in a washing machine for twenty-four hours.'" After tailoring, during which Brando insisted on wearing no underwear, he leaped gleefully around the fitting room. "This is it!" he shouted. "This is what I've always wanted!"

A Hollywood-Style Tough: The 1950s and the Fabrication of the Teenager

Ballard had removed the inside pockets from the test pair, and the actor implored her to make the same alteration to the rest of the pants. "I think that Stanley would have liked to push his hands in his pockets and feel himself," he told her. Clearly, he had a grasp of the character.

Kowalski was a prototype for a new American caveman, furious with inarticulate passion, insatiable, bluntly sexual. He wasn't sure what he wanted, but he knew how to get it. "Guess I'm gonna strike you as being the unrefined type, hah?" Stanley challenges his wife's fragile sister, Blanche Dubois, when they meet. For the film version of *Streetcar*, which came out in 1951, with Ballard again in charge of wardrobe, Brando wore a more nondescript style of trousers. But two years later the actor gave Levi Strauss & Co. the best unsolicited publicity a business could imagine when he and his fellow motorcyclists wore the company's trademark 501s throughout *The Wild One*, a hopped-up set piece loosely based on the real-life 1947 "invasion" of tiny Hollister, California, by a group of rowdy bikers.

The movie, directed by Laszlo Benedek, greatly exaggerated the clash between the quiet townspeople and their boorish guests. The incident, which the town of Hollister (the self-proclaimed "Birthplace of the American Biker") still commemorates with yearly festivals, was laden with polarizing hysterics similar to other genre movies of the time, movies about alien invasions and the Red Scare. Outfitted in leather and denim, the members of Brando's Black Rebels Motorcycle Club speak in the exaggerated hepcat slang that would soon be identified with the cartoon image of another subset of undesirables, the beatniks. When the sheriff's daughter, the soda fountain girl who finds herself oddly attracted to Brando's Johnny Strabler, asks whether the bikers go picnicking when they're on an outing, he grimaces at her naïveté. "A picnic? Man, you are too square. You don't go any one special place. That's cornball style. You just *go*," he says, snapping his fingers.

The Wild One is no masterpiece, but it certainly made loutish behavior look like a lot of fun. Brando set the tone for future generations of aimless young Americans when a local girl, dancing to a jukebox with one of his accomplices, teases him for his sullen reserve. "Hey Johnny," she asks, "what are you rebelling against?"

"Whaddya got?" Brando replies, delivering the film's celebrated punch line. For the children of the radical 1960s, that simple rejoinder would be remembered as the first political gesture of their youth.

Taunting Brando's stoic Strabler with a drunken grin on his face, Lee Marvin nearly stole the movie as the incorrigible Chino, a piratic character loosely based on the real-life biker "Wino" Willie Forkner. Forkner was a former World War II paratrooper who had led a small contingent from the Los Angeles chapter of a gang called the Boozefighters into Hollister for the Fourth of July weekend in 1947, when the area held its annual motorcycle "scrambles." The bikers' weekend-long binge and their misbehavior—one rode his motorcycle into a barroom and left it there for the duration—was first reported in the *San Francisco Chronicle*. A few weeks later, *Life* magazine ran a photo of Don Middleton, a nineteen-year-old biker with an ample beer belly. Arriving in Hollister the day after the rally ended, the photographer improvised. He made a pile of discarded bottles and asked Middleton to pose, pie-eyed and disheveled, on his bike. The reenactment crystallized a vigilance movement against the perceived menace of marauding biker gangs and it helped create the cultural climate—of both the alarmed parents and their excitable youth—that would incite the clamor over *The Wild One*.

The din crossed oceans. In England, authorities banned the film for more than a decade. The prohibition, of course, led to a hunger among young people to see the movie, enhancing its cult status. In the movie, the Boozefighters' gang name was fictionalized as the Beetles, inspiring a certain rock 'n' roll group which would emerge in Liverpool a handful of years after the American release of *The Wild One*.

Years later, Forkner told the *Chronicle* that he and his contemporaries were mostly veterans who felt underappreciated for their service. "We were rebelling against the establishment, for Chrissakes," said Forkner, who died in 1997. "You go fight a goddamn war, and the minute you get back and take off the uniform and put on Levi's and leather jackets, they call you an asshole."

Some elders undoubtedly had a name or two for James Dean, the melancholy young actor who made a habit of playing resentful offspring. Before his premature death in a 1955 car crash, Dean ensured his lasting fame in a role that had once been reserved for Brando. In 1955's *Rebel Without a Cause*, named for the psychoanalyst's book that inspired the screenplay, Dean's Jim Stark is a misanthropic high schooler tormented by his parents' marital strife and his family's middle-class affectations. At the helm of *Rebel* was Nicholas Ray, the mercurial conjuror of disaffection who had directed Mitchum in *The Lusty Men* and Humphrey Bogart in *In a Lonely Place*. Jim Backus, who played Frank Stark, Dean's ineffectual father, once said that he thought the movie was going to be "a routine program picture . . . a sort of *Ozzie and Harriet* with venom" until the cast and crew began to gauge the extent of the excitement surrounding their fast-rising star.

At first set to be shot in black-and-white, *Rebel* became a priority for Warner Bros. as the raves rolled in for Dean's debut performance in *East of Eden*, John Steinbeck's updated version of the story of Cain and Abel. That film, released earlier in 1955, was directed by Elia Kazan, Brando's mentor in *Streetcar* and *On the Waterfront*. Of Dean's Cal Trask, Kazan once explained, "Everything this kid does should be delightfully anarchistic, odd, original, imaginatively eccentric, and full of longing. He is the unexpected personified." "I don't want any kind of love anymore," Dean tells his father in *Eden*, establishing the unglued persona that would characterize all three of his major roles. "Doesn't pay off."

In *Rebel*, *The Wild One*, and hundreds of similar wayward-youth melodramas of the era, Dean, Brando, and their long list of imitators helped define the concept of the generation gap, as many teens and young adults of the 1950s rejected the world their parents tried to make for them. "You live here, don't you?" Stark, the new kid in town in *Rebel*, asks his neighbor, Judy, played by sixteen-year-old Natalie Wood. "Who lives?" she replies wearily.

Cast as the "rebel," Dean actually plays a sensitive boy forced to confront the real juvenile delinquents of his new school. The actors playing gang members were coached by Frank Mazzola, real-life leader of the Athenians, a Hollywood youth gang, who was given a role in the movie and made a technical adviser. Based on Mazzola's instructions, the cast went through more than four hundred pairs of Levi's scuffed up just so by the wardrobe department. In the stage-setting knife fight outside the planetarium with Buzz, a thuggish ringleader in leather jacket and Levi's (played by Corey Allen), Dean is actually dressed in slacks and a sportcoat. Only when he accepts a challenge to a game of "chicken," driving stolen cars to the brink of a cliff, does he change into his jeans—which have been sometimes identified as Lee, not Levi's, and were a point of contention between the two rivals.

In the film's lasting image, the actor wears a red windbreaker over his t-shirt and jeans. A sympathetic, complex character amid a gang of one-dimensional hooligans, Stark's raw emotion and his disgust with the example his parents have set were an indictment of the modern family, consumer culture, and misplaced moralism. "You're tearing me apart!" he bellows drunkenly at his parents.

"His defiant stoop and despondent gaze, his hesitant mumble and tentative plea for love canonized a new characteristic of saintliness—simply being misunderstood," wrote one of Dean's many biographers. That pose, struck in a well-worn pair of jeans, would be a perverse badge of honor for generations to come.

Vladimir Nabokov's Lolita wasn't just, like Dean, a product of postwar America. She *was* postwar America.

"She used to visit me in her dear dirty blue jeans, smelling of orchards in nymphetland; awkward and fey, and dimly depraved, the lower buttons of her shirt unfastened," as her tormented pursuer, Humbert Humbert, recalled. If with 1955's *Lolita* Nabokov exquisitely satirized the inappropriate love of Old World intellectuals for the vulgar charms of America—that vacuous, uncultured playground still dithering through its formative years—then the title character was aptly appointed. Barefoot in blue jeans, "her toenails showing remnants of cherry-red polish," she drove Humbert to a pitiable frenzy. The motels and shopping plazas that define their cross-country excursion are the consummate low-culture backdrops for Lolita's jeans, sneakers, and lollipops. It's not just the girl Humbert falls for, against his better judgment.

In the movie theaters, men of all ages fell for an aspiring starlet named Marilyn Monroe, who wore rolled-up blue jeans and tennis shoes in her first A-list role, as Peggy in Fritz Lang's 1952 drama *Clash by Night*. Appearing as a tomboyish Rosie type who punches the clock in a cannery, in her first scene she flirts playfully with her budding boyfriend, Joe (Keith Andes), jamming her thumbs in the front pockets of her jeans as she dares him to get physical with her. "Just let me see any man try," she taunts. Later, in the film's most famous scene, Peggy and Joe run onto the beach after a swim. When she complains about having water in her ear, he picks her up by the ankles, forcing her to stand on her hands. Laughing, she pulls her jeans up over her bikini bottom, and the two race barefoot into the open-air barroom nearby.

Though she could be Hollywood's most elegant figure, a big part of Monroe's appeal was her casual demeanor, her disregard for her own beauty. Blue jeans were a recurring costume in her short career, from the J. C. Penney brand she wore in 1954's *River of No Return* (opposite Mitchum) to her Levi's and Lee Storm Rider jacket in the 1961 wild-horses drama *The Misfits*, the last completed picture for both Monroe and Clark Gable. Blue jeans also played a role in *Bus Stop*, one of the actress's most beloved movies, in which she portrayed a saloon singer pursued by a rodeo cowboy. Lee Jeans was an underwriter of the picture.

Monroe was classically American, declared the great French photographer Henri Cartier-Bresson upon a visit to the Nevada set of *The Misfits*. "One has to be very local to be universal," he said. She seemed to delight in the ordinariness of her wardrobe. The Foremost brand jeans that Monroe wore with a men's-style shirt on the runaway raft in *River of No Return* cost $2.29 a pair in Penney's department stores at the time of the movie's release. Predictably, however, the value of Marilyn's costumes has risen just a bit. In 1999, the designer Tommy Hilfiger paid $37,000 at a Christie's auction for three pairs of her jeans from *River of No Return*. He hung one in his office, and gave another to the pop star Britney Spears.

It's no accident that the dominant images of Brando, Dean, and Monroe still picture them in jeans. These actors were something new. They were complicated—tender and volatile and wry. They encouraged more than one generation of teens to remain true to their own complicated natures. The hard-and-fast rules of gender were no longer so hard and fast. Girls became more assertive; boys fumbled for ways to express themselves.

"I was a fat band boy who didn't wear cool jeans," wrote former president Bill Clinton of his 1950s childhood in his autobiography, *My Life*. With the movies, the pop charts, magazines, and other media cultivating (and helping to define) youth culture, for perhaps the first time kids around the country were uniformly aware of what constituted coolness and what did not. "The trouble with teenagers began when some smart salesman made a group of them in order to sell bobby sox," complained *PTA Magazine* in 1956. A year later *Cosmopolitan* asked the half-serious question, "Are Teenagers Taking Over?" The country, the magazine suggested, was facing "a vast, determined band of blue-jeaned storm troopers, forcing us to do exactly as they dictate."

For Aggie Guerard Rodgers and her high school crowd in Fresno, California, there was only one true cult figure, and that was James Dean. "I kept a scrapbook on Dean," Rodgers recalls. "We were all obsessed with him." Many of the boys in her school in the early 1960s grew up emulating the deceased star, and she grew up watching the boys. She was a good girl hopelessly smitten with the guys who were up to no good, cruising the hometown boulevards in their custom deuce coupes and '55 Chevys.

"Guys that dragged the Main in the [San Joaquin] Valley all worked on their cars," Rodgers says. "They were mechanics. They didn't have anything else to do—they didn't go to college. So their jeans were always really dirty. No one washed them. They were thick with grease. They were so stiff, you could stand them up in the corner." For the sake of the girls, the guys made a point to change into clean shirts to go with their grubby jeans. Some of them wore their jeans in the street-smart style of the time, with the belt loops razored off and the waistband folded down. "It was not cool to wear a belt," Rodgers says flatly.

Not surprisingly, given her extraordinary attention to detail, she went into costume design. As luck would have it, her first interview in film turned out to be for a movie called *American Graffiti*. Set in the early 1960s in Modesto, California—just up the highway from Fresno—the movie, released in 1973, was a bittersweet look back at school days among the preppies and hot-rodders of the 1950s and early '60s. It was precisely the time and place in which Rodgers grew up. The first-time director of *American Graffiti*, George Lucas, timed his debut perfectly to coincide with a growing nostalgia for the fifties, and the movie's success launched him on a rather lucrative Hollywood career. As for Rodgers, the break led to a fruitful film career of her own. She went on to design costumes for Lucas's *Star Wars: Episode VI—Return of the Jedi*, 1985's *The Color Purple* (for which she received an Academy Award nomination) and, most recently, the film adaptation of Jonathan Larsen's Broadway sensation about modern bohemia, *Rent*.

For *American Graffiti*, Rodgers dressed two characters in denim, the very Dean-like grease monkey John Milner (played by Paul LeMat) and nebbishy Toad (Charlie Martin Smith), who desperately wants to be one of the cool guys. "Toad's pants hang the way kids' pants hang now, strangely enough," she says. "They were thick and wide in the leg, and all bunched up around the feet." The main characters, matriculating Steve Bolander (Ron Howard) and his conflicted buddy Curt Henderson (Richard Dreyfuss), are plaid-shirts-and-chinos types. These were the kids who probably grew up changing into their "playclothes"—their dungarees—after school. Howard, of course, would go on to play a very similar character in the long-running sitcom *Happy Days*. His Richie Cunningham was the quintessential freckle-faced, well-groomed American boy, a congenial counterpart to the Brylcreemed, jeans-and-T-shirt role-playing of Arthur Fonzarelli (Henry Winkler). Always armored in his leather jacket, astride his motorcycle, "The Fonz" was the pop apogee of the terminally hip archetype first shaped by Dean, Brando, Presley, and their imitators.

If Dean was a dream lover for an American girl like Aggie Rodgers, Brando and Presley helped sell postwar American attitude to young men overseas. In England, still photos from the forbidden *Wild One* provided some behavioral clues for a generation of rockabilly cats. The British rockabillies, later called rockers, borrowed their initial style from Presley. Arriving in the wake of the so-called Teddy Boys—the Edwardian-revival dandies of the 1950s who dressed in drape jackets, drainpipe trousers, and string ties—the rockers first hit the streets in pegged pants, spread-collar shirts, and two-tone shoes. They quickly revised their wardrobes, however, adopting the quasi-military gang look of *The Wild One*. Many of the former Teddy Boys became de facto rockers, joining the biker fraternity. Elvis's jarring appearance in *Jailhouse Rock* further refined the image. "The contrast with his sleek white suit and spotless white shoes of 1956 is absolute," wrote the British culture critic Ted Polhemus. "But somehow this was appropriate and logical: having demonstrated that he was no longer a truck driver, he is free to remind us of his roots."

Elvis may have sufficiently outgrown his roots to revisit them, but for some country boys there was little choice. For Johnny Cash's first public performance with his group, the Tennessee Two, he set a dress code of black shirts and blue jeans. "We were a band, and we thought we ought to look like one," Cash wrote in his 1998 autobiography. "Unfortunately none of us had any clothes a 'real' band would wear—I didn't own a suit, or even a tie—but each of us did have a black shirt and a pair of blue jeans. So that became our band outfit." But his mother despised the look, and she quickly sewed some stageworthy outfits for the threesome.

In *Lolita*, set in the late 1940s, Humbert finds himself improbably immersed in the pop fantasy world of his muse. "The Lord knows how many nickels I fed to the gorgeous music boxes that came with every meal we had!" he moans. "I still hear the nasal voices of those invisibles serenading her, people with names like Sammy and Jo and Eddy and Tony and Peggy and Guy and Patty and Rex." In the real world of American teens, pop idols and their songwriters were acutely attuned to the audience. The period was full of songs about sweethearts in denim, from crooner Eddie Fisher trying his hand at rock 'n' roll with "Dungaree Doll" to the Baton Rouge heartthrob Jimmy Clanton, who had one of his biggest hits with Neil Sedaka's dreamy "Venus in Blue Jeans"—"She's Venus in blue jeans, Mona Lisa with a ponytail."

The songwriting team of Jerry Leiber and Mike Stoller, who got their start writing R&B songs for black acts, broke into the pop mainstream with the melodramatic premature-death yarn "Black Denim Trousers and Motorcycle Boots." In the song, a "motorsickle"-riding bad boy in a leather jacket "with an eagle on the back" ignores his girlfriend's pleas not to ride, dying in a collision with a "screamin' diesel" locomotive. The original recording, featuring a Los Angeles vocal trio called the Cheers (whose members included future TV personality Bert Convy), entered the Top Ten in late 1955. Other versions included a follow-up chart hit by the Western-style baritone bandleader Vaughn Monroe ("The Voice with Hair on Its Chest") and a suitably frenetic French translation ("L'Homme à la Moto") by "The Little Sparrow," Edith Piaf.

Teen recklessness was the topic of the day. "Why do you kids live like there's a war on?" pleads Doc, the fatherly candy shop owner, just before the fatal shooting in *West Side Story*. The rival Jets and Sharks are lithe street kids whose confrontations are a lusty kind of ballet performed in various shades of tight, straight-legged jeans and work pants. In the climactic sequence of the 1961 film version, Tony (Richard Beymer) dies with his jeans on in the arms of his forbidden lover, Maria (Natalie Wood). To their elders, restlessness, dissatisfaction, and misdirected violence were adding up to an alarming trend among the young. Given that such social concerns were also a surefire source of free publicity, by the end of the 1950s Hollywood had become a virtual assembly line for the production of the so-called "teensploitation" movies.

Many of these movies featured slick-talking, finger-popping caricatures of the Beat generation, the demonized literary movement. "Jack Kerouac was responsible for selling a million pairs of jeans with *On the Road*," Kerouac's cantankerous, shabby-suited colleague William Burroughs once remarked, not without some derision. *On the Road*, published in 1957, did in fact generate great word-of-mouth for the peripatetic, experience-seeking lifestyle—what Kerouac called the "rucksack revolution"—that was emerging among the postwar generation. And jeans, wearable every day regardless of the availability of a washing machine, were the ideal clothing for their lifestyle. Kerouac's literary circle, oddly enough, was not especially partial to jeans (although Allen Ginsberg did wear cuffed Wranglers in the experimental Beat film *Pull My Daisy*). Kerouac's own image was featured long after his death in a famous 1990s ad campaign for Gap, in which various hip figures were pictured wearing khakis—Ginsberg, Miles Davis, Pablo Picasso, even James Dean.

Another Dean, Kerouac's fictional Dean Moriarty, the impetuous protagonist of *On the Road*, was drawn from the actual escapades of Kerouac's friend Neal Cassady, who maniacally crisscrossed the country, often in stolen cars and later at the wheel of the Merry Pranksters' psychedelic bus. "What got Kerouac and Ginsberg about Cassady," said another Beat figure, the poet Gary Snyder, "was the energy of the archetypal West, the energy of the frontier, still coming down. Cassady is the cowboy crashing." And he dressed the part. Cassady's widow, Carolyn, once said that she never knew her husband to wear anything but blue jeans, and Dean Moriarty follows suit. "Dean was wearing washed-out tight Levi's and a T-shirt and looked suddenly like a real Denver character again," Kerouac wrote.

For polite society, the look of the "real Denver character" was a badge of dishonor. "All the children in the world have gotten too big for their britches," wails a mother in *Blue Denim*, a 1959 screen production of the Broadway play of the same name, co-written by William Noble and James Leo Herlihy (who went on to write *Midnight Cowboy*). Played by the young actor Brandon de Wilde (*Shane, Hud*), Arthur Bartley is a decent young man in rolled up "levis" (as the script indicates) who steals from his parents to pay for an abortion for his girlfriend, Janet (Carol Lynley). His budding sexuality panics him. "I'm trouble, Jan," he warns her, refusing an embrace. "I'm just this crazy goddamn body!" De Wilde was destined for an early death at age thirty. Like Dean, he died on the road in a car accident.

For some pop stars, too, tragedy would prove to be more than just a storytelling ploy. Gene Vincent, who wore a steel brace following a motorcycle accident in 1952, named his first album *Blue Jean Bop*, after his song of the same name. He met young Eddie Cochran, three years his junior, on the set of the 1956 rock 'n' roll movie *The Girl Can't Help It*, where Vincent and his Blue Caps performed their first and biggest hit, "Be-Bop-a-Lula." The burbling opening lines of Cochran's 1959 hit, "C'mon Everybody," identified him as an authentic member of the teen crowd he was singing to: "Well, c'mon everybody and let's get together tonight / I got some money in my jeans, and I'm really gonna spend it right."

Touring England with Vincent in 1960, Cochran decided to fly home to America over the Easter weekend to honor a scheduled recording date. En route to London from Bristol, the car carrying Vincent, Cochran, and Cochran's girlfriend, Sharon Sheeley, blew a tire, and the driver crashed into a lamppost. Sheeley fractured her pelvis; Vincent reinjured his leg and suffered multiple broken bones. Cochran, who was thrown through the windshield, died the following day of massive head injuries. He was twenty-one years old. Vincent eventually succumbed to an alcohol problem, dying eleven years later of a bleeding ulcer at age thirty-six.

Sheeley, a songwriter whose very first effort, "Poor Little Fool," was a number-one hit for Ricky Nelson, lived long enough to see her brief relationship with Cochran romanticized in a 1988 Levi's ad in the U.K. As she told it, despite writing a song for Eddie, dyeing her hair blond, and spending money on expensive dresses, Sheeley was unable to attract much attention from the singer, with whom she had grown infatuated. Though she was invited to Cochran's 1958 New Year's Eve party at a New York hotel, she was disappointed that Cochran himself hadn't bothered to call—he sent word through their mutual manager. In a pique, Sheeley scrubbed off her makeup and yanked on a sweatshirt, tennis shoes, and a pair of Levi's before heading out to the party. That finally got the young rocker's attention, and their whirlwind affair began that night. "Are you in love with me, Charlie Brown?" he supposedly asked her. "You better be, 'cause I'm in love with you."

Storybook legends in the making, there was a whiff of fatalism about the rockers. Sometimes called "coffee-bar cowboys" in the U.K., the rockers resented authority in much the same way the renegades of the Wild West did. Their defiance masked their sensitivity but it also ensured they'd be judged exactly as they took pains to portray themselves, as potential troublemakers.

Before they were introduced to the world in their matching lapel-less Pierre Cardin suits, a scrappy group of Liverpudlian rock 'n' rollers calling themselves the Beatles apprenticed on Hamburg's seedy Reeperbahn wearing biker gear. Stu Sutcliffe, the band's momentary, ill-fated bassist, was a Dean acolyte, and he gave the group much of its early visual style. His German art-school girlfriend, a photographer and fashionable-in-black existentialist named Astrid Kirchherr, helped with the streetwise makeover. "They look beat-up and depraved in the nicest possible way," wrote one female pop columnist in London on the eve of the Beatles' breakthrough, not long after Sutcliffe's premature death. In the spring of 1963, just prior to the ascent of their first number-one-charting U.K. single, "From Me to You," the Beatles took part in a photo session in their hometown, Liverpool. They were modeling the jeans of Lybro, a local workwear institution. The photos were used as guidelines for a company brochure in which the rising stars were rendered as line drawings. It was reportedly the only time the Beatles officially endorsed a product during their years together.

In May 1964, fights erupted in several British seaside resort towns between local rockers and much larger crowds of visiting mods, or modernists, the new wave of fashionable, scooter-riding young men who were buying into Carnaby Street hip. For the mods, the rockers were an outdated joke. In the most notorious of the skirmishes, some of which resulted in stabbings, two rockers were forced to jump off a seawall to the beach fifteen feet below. (The incidents would become the subject of the Who's 1973 rock opera *Quadrophenia*.) Reporting by the British press suggested that the rivalry was a simple matter of stylistic differences. That view, according to the critic Polhemus, lacks nuance: "In our age, style has become a language with the power to convey deeply rooted, complex attitudes and beliefs," he wrote. Class conflict was inherent in the two groups' contrasting wardrobes— "scruffy leather and jeans versus pristine casualwear and sharply pressed suits"—but the battles may also have signaled the mods' rejection of parochialism in favor of a newfound worldliness. They prided themselves on their Continental tastes and their appreciation for black American soul music and the imported rhythms of London's West Indian immigrants. Also, as Polhemus noted, the mod-rocker confrontations suggested a cultural upheaval over "changing definitions of masculinity."

While the mods were exhibiting a fussiness over clothing traditionally associated with women, some gay men in London were gravitating toward the "butch" look of the rockers. Vacationing in France, the owner of a trend-setting Carnaby Street boutique called Vince Man's Shop, observed young people wearing all-black outfits—shirts, sweaters, and jeans. He brought the look back with him to England, and it "went like a bomb," said the owner, Bill Green. "People said the stuff was so outrageous that it would only appeal and sell to the rather sort of eccentric Chelsea set or theatrical way-out types"—in other words, gay men. One scenester noted what most others had not yet openly acknowledged. "The gay crowd took to jeans," he said, "because of the closeness and tightness of them, which showed up all of the essential parts."

Both onscreen and off, jeans were becoming a self-conscious kind of costume, and the effect was increasingly campy. To be a mechanic or a rancher was one thing. To dress like one, as Dean and Brando did, was just that—playing dress-up. Not for another decade or more would denim work wear become sufficiently prevalent as recreational clothes to reclaim the ordinariness of its origins.

Denim did have some unlikely celebrity champions, wholesome favorites such as Ozzie and Harriet Nelson and Lucy and Ricky Ricardo, famous television (and real-life) couples who were photographed in crisp blue jeans. Bing Crosby, the fatherly singer and actor whose career reached back to the 1920s, became a lifelong friend of the Levi Strauss & Co. family following an incident that occurred in 1951. Crosby and a hunting buddy were on vacation in Canada when they tried to check in to a Vancouver hotel. Unrecognized, they were refused service: they were wearing Levi's jeans and jackets. (A bellman eventually identified Crosby, and the two travelers were accommodated.) Upon hearing of the mix-up through one of Crosby's Bay Area neighbors, Levi's had a denim tuxedo jacket custom-made for the entertainer. Sewn into the inside lining was a panel that read, "Notice to hotel men everywhere. This label entitles the wearer to be duly received and registered with cordial hospitality at any time and under any conditions." The jacket was presented to him at the 1951 Silver State Stampede in Elko, Nevada, for which the singer was serving as honorary mayor.

Despite the Crosby episode in Canada, by the 1950s jeans were acknowledged around the world as an American icon. During World War II, American soldiers had worn their jeans on leave in France, Italy, Germany, and Japan, generating international demand among the young. Whatever impact the soldiers had, jeans were still considered a sign of crudeness. In the melancholy French musical *The Umbrellas of Cherbourg*, set in 1957, Catherine Deneuve's young Genevieve falls deeply in love with Nino Castelnuovo's Guy Fourcher, an auto mechanic in greasy jeans. He is, of course, not good enough for her.

He was "the picture of a Hollywood-style 'tough' wearing blue jeans, leather jacket, cowboy boots, and sideburns." That's how *U.S. News & World Report* described Charlie Starkweather when the scrawny nineteen-year-old was arrested after his killing spree across Nebraska and Wyoming in 1958.

Were blue jeans really the clothes of delinquents, or were delinquents just partial to blue jeans? It was a conundrum that frankly panicked the workwear industry.

"At one point, every perp was wearing blue jeans," says Norman Karr, a lifelong promotions man who worked closely with the denim industry. In 1956, responding to a dampening of blue jeans sales ascribed to anxieties over juvenile delinquency, a coalition of textile companies sponsored the formation of the Denim Council, an organization dedicated to putting schoolchildren "back in blue jeans through a concerted national public relations, advertising, and promotional effort." Appealing to mothers, the group's public relations associates encouraged fashion designers to create new denim lines for women, and they arranged "jean queen" beauty contests with retailers around the country. When the Kennedy administration formed the Peace Corps in 1961, the Denim Council outfitted the corps' first two hundred volunteers in blue jeans, securing invaluable publicity that would pay off in subtle ways for years to come.

A Hollywood-Style Tough: The 1950s and the Fabrication of the Teenager

Jeans manufacturers were experiencing a strange paradox of the American marketplace. They had a daunting image problem, yet it was precisely that image problem that gave the product its desirability among the target audience. Anti-fashion, as the critic Anne Hollander has written, "has often simply been the next fashion."

"The last thing you can do with a teenager is tell him he can't wear something. As soon as you do, it becomes very important in his life," says Karr, who worked with the Denim Council and its successor, Jeanswear Communications, beginning in the 1970s. Like mind-altering substances, premarital sex, or banned books, jeans were increasingly coveted *because* they were prohibited. It made for some uncomfortable dilemmas for industry fathers, many of whom were fathers at home, too.

After the temporary dip in the mid-1950s, sales escalated. "There was no way to plan for the kind of growth we were experiencing," Peter Haas told Levi's biographer Ed Cray. "Every time we'd make up a plan, it would be obsolete." In the three years from 1963 to 1966, Levi Strauss & Co. doubled its annual sales to $152 million.

"It seemed impossible to me that we could sell more and more pants," said Walter Haas Sr.

Up Against the Wall!

FUCK GRAYSON KIRK was scrawled above the urinal in the downstairs men's room of Mathematics, a liberated building at Columbia occupied by two hundred SDS [Students for a Democratic Society]-led students, former hippies, former left-liberals, the formerly apolitical, uninvolved, apathetic, safe. I studied the graffito, trying to take my mind off the fact that I was urinating in a liberated bathroom four feet from where two Barnard freshmen were washing up. They were on the Food Committee, breakfast corps. It was six o'clock Sunday morning. We had held the building two days. This was our third morning. I needed a bath and a shave and a Bloody Mary, in that order.

I stood, it seemed for hours, cock in hand, erect, leaning tightly against the cold wall of the urinal, wishing the girls would leave. All week, and I had never learned the revolutionary art of sharing bathrooms with women. I stood planted to the tile, ignoring the girls' giggling, staring dumbly at the wall. What if they *never* leave, I thought, I'll be stuck here like the madman in *Marat/Sade*, hard cock permanently erect, while they wash and wash and wash . . .

Sunday morning. I was hung over. The night before I had attended a long meeting in the main lounge, chaired by Tom Hayden, where we had argued about negotiations with the administration and the faculty. Around midnight I had gone up to the fourth floor and found Brian and Frank and Dave—he wearing a white cardigan the police would leave stained with his young blood—sitting inside a faculty office, the lights off, drinking the scotch and beer they had brought into the commune before it went dry. Saturday night. We climbed into the attic of Math. We opened the window in the roof—you could see the stars that night, the air was cool and smelled of fish and of the sea—and Frank, his green eyes catching the light, sat under the bare bulb, with the three of us seated around him drinking, and quoted poetry by heart—his own, Ginsberg's, and Dylan Thomas's.

Six hours later, Sunday morning, the bathroom and the giggling freshmen. FUCK GRAYSON KIRK.

I went into the main floor lounge in search of coffee. My headache was growing. It would take three hours to kill it. It rumbled through the room making me literally lust after a shot of Pepto-Bismol. I hurt. Most of the students were still sleeping, but a few were beginning to get up, taking their blankets off the floor, moving toward the bathrooms, waking up. I leaned against the counter, found the coffee, heated the water, looked over the room. Before we took Math, the lounge had been part of the library. Now the furniture was serving as barricades before the front doors and tunnels, the library shelving was nailed against the windows, and the place—for one brief week—was being used humanly by the young.

I took the coffee and climbed two flights of stairs, maneuvering over fire hoses uncoiled down the steps, squeezing past piles of chairs waiting to be sent tumbling down when the first cop came, past little cardboard trays of Vaseline and mounds of plastic bags to be used against police gas.

In the dining room lounge. In a thick, soft chair. Asleep.

"You look drunk," Roger said, shaking me awake, looking charitably at my red eyes, my shaking hands. "You shouldn't drink so much, not when you're part of a revolutionary situation." Defensively I tried out my look of startled innocence on him, eyebrows raised, mouth dropped in surprise.

"Me? Drunk? Roger, I've never been drunk in my life!" I said, sounding drunk. He mumbled something about bourgeois decadence. It was half past six. I smiled up at him, my head swimming, looking rather bleary-eyed at his homely face. Roger is not the sight one likes to see in the morning after a hard night, sleepless, for Roger has, at twenty-one, the face of a tired failure, a revolutionary whom no one, not even his Detroit mother, took seriously. Until that week. That face! Hanging jowls, the muscles already weakened, the cheeks collapsing toward the nose, the entire face caving in on itself. Early. To say Roger looks like a bloodhound is to be kind. A paper bag Roger should wear over his head, especially at six thirty in the morning when you face another day inside a liberated building and your mind has to screw itself up to the task of revolutionary plotting with young yet desperate sophomores.

Roger sat down in the seat next to me and opened a paper sack, took out an orange, and began peeling it. I could *smell* the paper bag, last night's peanut butter sandwiches inside, three oranges, the bottom of the bag stained wet with jelly droppings. For *this* we took five buildings and held Dean Coleman captive, for *this* we faced jail, so Roger could carry a paper sack, like a badge of martyrdom, around with him and inform anyone who asked how he *knew* from *much past experience* that jail food was uneatable? Better to be prepared at all times, he advised. Carry peanut butter sandwiches in paper bags. Be ready when the fascist bust comes.

"Want a sandwich?" Roger offered, holding a dripping, gooey glob of peanut butter and grape jelly oozing between the bread. My stomach turned. "No, Roger."

"Are you sure? I've got plenty, enough to last a couple days."

"Quite sure, Roger." Sadist.

I closed my eyes again. I woke to the sound of WKCR, the campus station, blaring out over the room. It was around ten o'clock. Roger had left, leaving only curled orange skins in the ashtray to mark his passing.

Students were relaxing in the room, some reading the *New York Times* and laughing, some playing chess, a few gathered around a card table painting posters: GYM CROW MUST GO! Over WKCR a pompous professor was bitching about the fact that the majority of the Columbia students opposed the liberation (perhaps) and that the "overwhelming number" of students in the buildings were being "duped" by SDS. So what? It mattered for nothing, since this was the first event in most of our lives where we felt effective, where what we were doing belonged to us. I had been involved in the peace movement since the Student Peace Union of the early sixties, where the main concern was to oppose an SDS takeover. I had worked through countless protests, picking up friends at each: Mel and Craig at the Pentagon, Roger at Princeton, Frank and Brian at the UN, Tish at Whitehall Street—where we stood outraged, held back by the police, and watched our friends beaten up in Battery Park by ignorant, half-assed longshoremen.

I sat there and wondered where Lionel Trilling was, hoping that somehow he, who wanted to understand so badly what was happening to us, would come over to our side. I remember telling him that in relation to his generation we felt disregarded, unconsulted, powerless—powerless to affect the quality of our lives in his America. Our lives, without roots in history, seemed diminished to gesture without power, to desperation without probable hope, to fantasy. With that fantasy our politics and art were being created, a fantasy of revolution and ritual murder and the giving way to a clean violence and a final peace. Even sitting in Math was a bit fantastic, unreal, hopeless, for I knew that they could bust us anytime they wanted. There will be no revolution, and good, rich, respected men will die, as always, in their beds. Because we knew this—the futility of our arrogance—we increasingly lost a true relationship with actuality and with history, and our responses to life became melodramatic and false and dangerous.

But it did not matter. None of it. Not the bust to come, nor the degrees and careers in jeopardy, nor the liberal faculty insulted and lost. All that counted was the two hundred of us in solidarity for the first time, together in our place in our time against the cops outside and the jocks outside and the fucking American nation hoping for our blood. HIT THOSE RED PUNK FAGGOTS AND HIT 'EM HARD! It did not matter, for if you truly believe—and we were true believers—that your hope of change is all you have, even in as narrow a situation as Columbia, and if you suspect that it is false, that you can finally do nothing effective to act on its behalf, then you have to choose between throwing it over or keeping it and acting against your suspicion. We acted against our suspicion. Our outrage grew and, in time, fermented into hatred. In five days inside the commune at Columbia I learned again to hate with a passion, to hate things I had once loved.

But I could not see any alternative to being in the building with my friends, to acting in every situation in rebellion against the System. What other choices were there? Trilling's generation had covered all the options. We were left with our resistance, and in this culture, that meant acting in danger to ourselves. It always cost *us*. At the anti-Rusk demonstration I saw young men rush at mounted police in the hope of being clubbed. At the Pentagon we waited late into the night—Lowell and MacDonald had parties to attend—in the growing tension and the cold, waited around fires built on the steps before that massive, ugly building, waiting, hoping in the dark that the troopers' fingers would tighten and bullets would fly and it would be over for us. We wanted to force them to act irrevocably. We wanted a response *to us*. Any kind. And now at Columbia I waited, knowing they could not act affirmatively in regard to us, they could give nothing without endangering the whole fucking System. "We have to consider," President Kirk had said, "what effect our actions will have on other American universities." I wanted them to act as they must, to act against us, to reveal themselves for what they are—a stinking, rotten group of venal men. I and the others had reached the point where we could no longer tolerate being disregarded. I and the others had to own our lives.

Frank came into the dining lounge and asked, "When do we eat?" I told him around noon as usual. He sat down beside me, took a notebook out of his pocket, and started writing. He looked up once to ask me if I knew a word that rhymed with Trotsky. I didn't.

Frank's father is a landlord, a conservative. Frank had walked out a year ago and gone to Haight-Ashbury and become active in the Oakland anti-draft riots. When he came back he said, a bit dramatically, "I saw the face of America out there. And it is made of violence." Frank is very bright and very gifted and yet he does not want to go back to school, he does not want to go to graduate school, and he will not go into business or government. He does not want money or power. He does not want to live off someone else's labor. He does not want to sell out. He said to me that he felt like someone lying on his back in a cellar with a low ceiling. And he can hear music and laughter filter down to him. And he presses his hands against the ceiling trying to find out where it is weak, where it will break and let him into life. Yet it will not break for him.

On Friday morning when we entered the liberated building, I asked him if he knew he was liable for arrest. He nodded that he knew. "It is part of the game," he said. He wants a revolution in America. He does not know how to make one. So he hangs loose. "I am looking for the inside of a jail." He thinks it is pure there because he sees the outside as being corrupt and deadly. "A jail is in all our futures," he said. And he wrote, "I see my manhood in the streets." That was in Oakland in the riots.

Frank wrote. I read the *Times*. I was astonished at the inaccuracy of the reporting of the Columbia rebellion. Remembering that Sulzberger was on the Columbia Board of Trustees made it seem sinister. The radio was still blaring out reports of activities on campus; jocks had surrounded Low Library and they were mumbling about Taking The Situation Into Their Own Hands. Acting Dean Coleman, seeing a real, permanent, high-paying, high-status deanship in his future—the lure of it all shimmering just beyond those trustee asses, bow and kiss—was going around trying to keep the boys cool, telling them that "Harlem surrounds us. They'll burn the place down if we're not careful, fellows. Let's have the police handle the situation. You can trust President Kirk, etc." The boys were getting impatient. It is no fun to be called dummy jocks by long-haired, dirty—but oh so bitterly bright—radicals and not want to beat them up. Especially when they whispered that there was something peculiar about your masculinity in your posturing love of violence.

The jocks were grouped on the lawns before the buildings. The police sat muzzled in the basement of Low and other buildings, waiting to be unleashed. And outside, along the walls of Math, more cops stood in the sun, looking up now to see the students throw Sunday flowers down on them from the lounge. Faggots with their flowers. Sick!

We had tuna fish and tomatoes for lunch. After eating, I went on to the ledge overlooking Broadway and sat down by Dave. He had his shirt off— well-built, handsome—and I took mine off, and we sat together in the sunshine passing Coke bottles and cigarettes from mouth to mouth. Beautiful. Down below, people walked by, some of them stopping to put money or food in our bucket, others calling out obscenities, most, however, simply raising their fingers in a Churchillian V, our symbol of victory. As usual, there were a dozen or so cops leaning against the wall, most of them quite young, some even well disposed to us. Privately.

A contingent of Harlem demonstrators marched by with signs protesting the construction of the gym—HANDS OFF HARLEM—and shouting, "Strike! Strike!" They were the poor. In the street the middle-class Uncle Tom niggers swept by in their shiny new cars trying to look as disdainful as possible, Thoroughly East Side Token Nigger, more white than us, giving us sliding glances of contempt as they roared by; some, playing White Tourist, slowed their cars and rolled down the windows and pointed up at us sneeringly, gracing us with queenly "we-are-amused" type smiles just like the Man does when he goes slumming in Harlem on Sunday afternoons. It was sad, their self-hatred.

A blue Ford pulled up and double-parked in front of the building. A middle-aged man, stout, gray-haired, looking like a Prussian shopkeeper or a Southern preacher, got out of the car, a Bible carried in his right hand. He strutted over and stood a few feet from the Math building, his hands on his hips, and looked up at us, trying to shrink us with his prissy contempt. He yelled up at us: "If My people which are called by My Name shall humble themselves and pray and seek My Face I will heal their land. . . ." Dave, seeing his Bible, hearing God shouted in the street, interrupted him, "Thou shalt not steal, Columbia!" The man began again, louder: "If My people which are called by My Name. . . ." "Thou shalt not kill, America!" The man stopped. He gave Dave the finger. "Fuck you commie bastards," he shouted, "God fuck you bastards!" And then seeing the girls lining the ledge with us, twenty feet above him, out of reach, casually dressed, flower children, lovely in the sun, seeing them smile down on him, he started to shout hysterically: "Bitches! Whores of Babylon! Where would you be if some big, black buck was raping you in an alley? Red sluts! Who'd you call, you commie cunts! Who'd you call for help? The *police*, that's who you'd call, you communist. . . ." While he was spewing forth into the street, a rookie cop calmly walked over to his double-parked Ford and gave him a parking ticket. We applauded. The cop grinned and bowed in reply.

Dave slapped my thigh and laughed, "Beautiful, Baby. The world's beautiful! You, the cops, life . . . life's so goddamn beautiful!" I smiled back at him. He put his hand to my head and playfully mussed my hair.

Sitting on the ledge that Sunday afternoon, caught by his friendship, I felt a great sense of oneness with the people in the commune. We were together until it was ended for us. Our building—our *home*, for Christ's sake!—where we slept and ate and talked and bathed and worked together. And our sensitivity to the goodness of the commune experience was born out of a consciousness of its contingency—that in point of fact it was bounded by time and place, fatally weak, impossible of survival. We had to make it last as long as we could. We had to make it good. Our tolerance of each other was immense. In the week, I heard not one word said in anger against anyone in the commune. And sitting with Dave on the ledge, full of love for him, I thought of Camus's celebration of human solidarity in *The Plague* and of Alyosha in *The Brothers Karamazov* with the children at the funeral, telling them to remember their sometime oneness with each other. It was a tender sentiment, new to me, and it was decidedly unusual in my America. It was, at the risk of sounding hopelessly sentimental, a precious thing.

Around five the general meeting of the commune began in the main lounge. There was one held each night. Participatory democracy. Hayden chaired them. Frank and Dave and I sat on a rug in the back of the room, not paying much attention until an announcement was made by the Steering Committee that it had broken off negotiations with the Ad Hoc Faculty Group. This frightened me since I assumed that the administration would not chance mass resignations by calling a police bust while the faculty was negotiating with the students to end the occupation of the buildings. That, of course, was precisely what happened, there being no honor among liberals or thieves. Not with so much at stake, so much *loot* to peddle one's liberal ass for—research grants, government appointments, secret funds, POWER. Not even the faculty is worth losing Percy Uris's millions. Not to mention the Rockefellers'. *Gawd!*

There was a brief debate over the accuracy of the announcement; two students disagreed about what exactly had happened at the Steering Committee meeting they had both attended. I was getting nervous so, true to left-lib form, I took the floor and made a brief and, as I remember it, magnificent speech in defense of Trilling and Westin and Anderson, the professors who had just come under attack. I remember calling them "eminent men, fair-minded," and saying that the students could act in "complete good faith" with them. The radical leaders particularly disliked the "eminent men" line, thinking, probably correctly, that it sprang from a nasty little case of intellectual elitism—most undemocratic—that I was coughing up into the room. To protect the commune from my counterrevolutionary remarks, they proceeded to attack the faculty all over again, this time

Up Against the Wall!

making it most personal. Undeterred by the evidence, I made another neat speech and offered a motion directing the Steering Committee to do what it was most unwilling to do—reopen negotiations with the faculty. I was not the only closet elitist in the room, for my motion passed overwhelmingly.

It *is* hard to see your professors overnight as enemies tainted by bloody CIA funds. It is hard but, more often than not, it is true (as I would learn as the contents of Kirk's private files began to seep out). The university was corrupt. And much of the faculty was complicit in its corruption.

Flushed with the victory of my motion, I stood, not really knowing what to say, to propose other motions. *Many* of them. I did not want to let my moment of power pass. I had the Majority! I was a Leader! Not like the others, who had only one gripe to bitch, I discovered as I stood to the floor, Hayden looking impatiently in my direction, that I had hundreds of silly motions whirling in my head, motions about the use of the bathrooms, the lousy food, the Defense Committee, and, *most important*, the ban on drinking. I could have stood the entire day offering motions to be rubber stamped by *my* majority. But Hayden interrupted me. Juan, a Puerto Rican who was an SDS marshal, came rushing in and handed the chairman a note.

"Please sit down." Is he speaking to *me*? My power went, untasted.

"This is an important announcement. We have definite word that there will be a bust before nightfall." I instinctively glanced at the window. Still light. "Anybody who has to leave may leave now. No one will think any less of you if you have to go. It's OK." No one left.

I looked at Frank and shook my head. "I guess this is it," I said. I was frightened for him and for Dave and Brian and the others, especially for the girls. I had seen the police whip into young demonstrators before, seen the delight with which they attack. The brutality of their assault almost always corresponded to the youth and weakness of the victim. And the people in the commune were young, most in their late teens and early twenties, and not strong. They would be torn apart, and there was nothing I could do to help them when it came, nothing to prevent it, to make it less costly. I could do what I had to do—stand with them, share their hatred and their defeat, witness and work to make those who allowed it to happen pay. This desire for vengeance was my primary response to life in the commune. I had had enough of war and injustice. I was ashamed of my country and of its leaders. The rich had grown too rich, the poor too wretched, and it was time to demand an accounting. And if it meant destroying universities, disrupting a nation, if it meant jail and beatings, so be it. I had a deep terror of the police, but my anger was deeper and harder, and when my fear passed—

and it usually passed as soon as the cops began to move—only the clean anger remained.

A member of the Legal Committee handed each of us an arraignment form, which we filled out. He gave us a telephone number to call if we were isolated from the group and needed a lawyer. I wrote the number on my arm. The head of the Defense Committee stood and showed us the best position to assume if the cops attacked: fall into a fetal position on the ground, arms over your head and neck, legs drawn tightly to the stomach to protect your genitals and internal organs. Then our gas expert—an anarchist from the East Village—gave us a vivid description of the effects of tear gas and Mace, warning us that Mace only needs a small area of the skin to contact to be assimilated by the blood. Thus we were to seal our cuffs with string, put cigarette filters in our nostrils, plastic bags—airholes in the back—over our heads, and Vaseline to close the pores of skin exposed to the air.

The meeting broke up. The passage window onto campus was sealed. Students started collecting bags and filters and gobs of Vaseline. We were instructed to disperse ourselves throughout the building to make it as difficult as possible for the cops to pull us out. I agreed to meet Frank, Brian, and Roger—lunch bag in hand—in the attic when the cops appeared.

I went into the dining room and made a cup of coffee and sat down on the couch and waited.

About two hours later the news came that the bust was off. It was a false alarm. I was elated by the news of the reprieve. I saw Tish, blond, lovely, tough, and kissed her and said, "Isn't it great! Jesus, I'm glad!" She smiled, "So am I. It'll give us time to make more clubs." Tish, the Irish peasant wife singing her men off to war.

The whole commune was relieved that the bastards had given us more time. And at the same moment, we were proud of ourselves because no one had walked out, no one had panicked. We had stayed solid. The barricade was taken off the passage window. The singing and dancing started. Someone got a guitar and sat down on the second floor landing and sang Bob Dylan's "It's All Right, Ma." Students sat on the steps before him like a tiered choir and sang along: *though the masters make the rules for the wisemen and the fools, I got nothing, Ma, to live up to.*

About an hour later, a bagpiper came into the building, and we joined hands in a long chain and danced behind him, snaking through the building, up and down the stairs, playing, shouting happily, singing about how we weren't going to study war no more. And later still, I stood with Frank on the balcony beside the red flag in the coolness of that lovely night and tore sheets of paper and threw them down in lieu of rice on the couple who had been married that night in one of the liberated buildings and were walking toward us, now under the balcony, now on the lawn, lighted candles in their hands, a wedding party of tired professors, flower children, and red-banded communards dancing behind them singing. We raised our arms and shouted out into the night: "We've won! We've won!"

Sunday, feeling happy, I went to sleep upstairs on the couch listening to Frank and Brian talk about how the bust might not come at all, how they were going to hold out until the administration gave in on every demand, and if they tried to bust them, they would make them regret it.

Monday I left campus shortly after noon, going over to the West End Bar—deserted—for lunch and a few drinks. I tried to fortify myself to the task of meeting my parents, returning from their goy First Class Biblical Tour of the Great State of Israel, lunches included. I took a cab out to Kennedy. I felt better about the Columbia liberation, sure now the bastards would not bust us for at least a few days. I knew the tension was growing. The radicals—Roger among them—had made a pathetic charge against the hundreds of beer-happy jocks lined below Low [Library]. Fistfights had broken out. There was a chance that we would not wait until the administration acted. It is difficult to live in a tense situation, threatened, swept by rumor, the balance held by your enemies; it is tough when you are young and when you believe deeply that what you are doing is right and necessary. In spite of the growing tension and the threat of a bust—you could taste it in the air—I felt we had won.

I was mistaken.

I went back to the West End bar, relieved my parents had left New York. It had gone easily, the past avoided, the truth skirted. Our conversation had been limited to Israel and the eighteen led through the artillery-pocked hills into Gethsemane for the service and the sunrise. My duty again would be limited to letters home. No need to justify the lust for violence to them (the politics of cultural despair, Trilling had called it, lifting Fritz Stern's term, a politics where ends had been diminished to the acts themselves), the hatred exhilarating and new, years of guilt and accumulated failure, powerlessness, the ingrown despair released daily like jism in the communes where we reassured ourselves daily of our pacific intent while we panted for the bust. Anything, however violent, to end the growing tension. I did not have to tell them that I was filled with hatred for men and institutions and, yes, for the country I had loved days before. In me and in the others I had discovered a hunger for violence, almost carnal, that admitted no reason. Put the motherfuckers up against the goddamn wall. Them. The cops. The asshole Trustees. The bumbling, duplicitous President. The Middle Class. The Company Students. The Liberal Faculty. Up Against The Wall. Motherfuckers.

"But why?" Mother asked, Israeli-tanned and lovely, "Why get yourself hurt over a bunch of Communists?" She had not read a paper in weeks and already she saw *conspiracy* brooding over the city. She should have been an editor of the *Times*. My son the Commie dupe. "For *this* we educate and raise you, for this stealing of buildings and deans?" In her mind the St. Paul papers: LOCAL BOY ARRESTED AS RED AGENT AT COLUMBIA. Revolutions were to be read about, not made, in America. "You part of such a thing? At your age? For this we left Europe?"

I had a double Scotch at the West End. I wanted to get high before I crawled back into the liberated zone. Math was dry as an Iowa county, by democratic vote. Who needs it?

It was nearly midnight. The West End was empty of students, except for a few misplaced jocks who usually hung out at the Gold Rail or, failing that, at the Gay Way. Holding the drink in my hand I looked across the bar to the booth where four of them sat dressed like street hustlers in tight shirts and whites and sneakers. Drinking beer. They were out of place here, where Ginsberg and Kerouac drank before pot and acid and age and tiredness and fear pressed in on them, drawing them from the world (Ginsberg drunk and bugging Trilling on the phone in the back of the bar . . . *we're both Jews, man, let's admit it*). Time had taken them.

And the Liberation had taken a new generation of Columbia students, leaving in its wake their posturing indifference, their hustling, their cool, their reality, thinning in the smoke that sometimes covered an unadmitted hollowness. And the hippies inside Math, before the liberation, had fanatically denied the actuality of the future in order to avoid judgment, had rejected political action as a sellout. These same people, after a few days inside the commune, had become obsessed by a Future and its power. Now they crouched inside Math and Avery and Fayerweather and Low waiting to meet the violence once opposed in the name of Love. Children of the Present, proud of it, hung up on it, now were captives of a Future. Buckley had said, archly, dryly, that they wanted to "imminentize the Eschaton." True. The Revolution-To-Come justified everything. All had become judgmental.

The West End was strangely quiet. Smokeless. It made me uncomfortable.

The air there is usually unbreathable, but Monday night, emptied of heads and drunks spilling urine on the bathroom floors, and old lady wings, and students crowded over beers, the air was clean. I could not get high. And I wanted to in order to confront Hayden in the name of Moderation and Reason. That was my bag. But I was so politically untrained that I had to have a few drinks to convince myself I was winning him when, if ice sober, I would see I was losing miserably. All was politics. Even the West End, like the university and the community, drooped with thick rhetoric, smelled of politics. Joyless. "All within the Revolution," Hayden had declared, half-facetiously, the age not weighing yet the resurrected terms, the retread revolutions of the East. It was still 1825 in twentieth-century America by Hayden's calendar. And he worked to press the year with decades.

The bartender asked me if I had seen Juan. I told him he was in Math. "He owes me money," he said, "the filthy spic."

Even Juan had changed. Somehow he found a grim sort of manhood, contingent though it was, situationalist, separate but equal, in darting between the communes playing Professional Puerto Rican to the whites. We listened. The blacks did not. No whites or spics welcome in Malcolm X (Hamilton) Hall.

Juan's rhetoric was limited to a hoarse but well-meant "I am for *my* America, Whitey, after we burn *your* America to the fucking ground!" Effective, especially when he delivered his speech with his greatcoat thrown over his shoulders and his red armband glistening below his clenched fist. It was pretense, though it was delivered with such ease in telling that it made his past dissolve one week, and fiction grew inside his mind, stretching his revolutionary past back beyond last Friday to Lenin—this Puerto Rican pimp—back to Herzin and Belinsky—this pusher, pornographer, pimp—back to where his memory was lost to names and race and all violence took the name of Freedom. As I drank in the West End he was over in Math, his greatcoat discarded on the fifth floor, playing revolutionary general to the whites. Outwardly cool. His stomach tight. Feeling less white as the cops moved onto campus. "How does a black cop feel clubbing us?" Dave had asked Juan. "It makes him feel white," he had replied on Sunday.

The liberation had taken Juan with the rest. I remembered the joints bought, the speed. I remembered the night in his pad at 124th, his old lady in the kitchen with her Gallo, a lighted candle before a saint on the wall stand, San Juan beaches nearing in the wine. Juan pinned a sheet to the wall and, at five bucks a head, I and Frank and Brian watched three blue movies, Cuban export. Dogs fucking women. Men eating each other. Old men eating little girls. During each flick his old lady wandered into the room, looked a minute and mumbled in Spanish that she had seen it, cursed, and wandered out. And now Juan was donning grease, a shield, his face too dark, and waiting for the bust. A prison record. Would the bastards give him bail?

It was twelve-thirty. I ordered another drink. When the bartender slid it across the bar to me he said, low, "They get those red punks tonight."

"Who does?"

"You haven't seen it? Christ, they're piling out of buses on Amsterdam. Looks like a goddamn army camp over there."

Tonight. Impossible. We are negotiating. They promised. Negotiate and no bust. "Are you sure?"

"Dead certain. It's for real this time. The fucking punks!"

For real. I left quickly. Outside and cool, a light breeze coming over the Hudson from the west. Fear tasted in my mouth, so soon, so soon, as I ran across Broadway toward the 116th Street gates. I had to get back inside Math. I belonged there. All I could think of as I ran was the fear that I would arrive too late, that before I could reach the entrance window into Math, the blood already would have won. My friends. Frank . . . a poet's mind . . . Brian . . . who laughs at violence and believes . . . David . . . Crazy Mel . . . Tish . . . Tish who made the clubs and got the gasoline . . . they'll be cut apart, the fucking walls washed with them, bled over the floors, along the steps, broken.

At the gates. "I've got to get onto campus!" I showed my ID card.

"Campus is closed. Move or face arrest."

"This is important! I'm part of the Math commune. My friends are there. I *belong* there!" Goddamn asslicking cops.

"Move!"

I moved. Up Broadway, trying to circle the campus at 120th and over to the Amsterdam gates. The shouting of the crowds inside the campus was starting, my fear pushing like a hard knot in my chest. Running, I pictured my head being clubbed by eight-foot-tall cops, swaddled in shiny leather, bulging, and my brain damaged . . . years later my limping dramatically through leftist assemblies, people awed and drunk with sweet pity—the Martyr!—as I, a one-man Abraham Lincoln Brigade, stumbled half-wittedly through the crowd, a Crippled Veteran of the Columbia Rebellion.

Two horse vans were lined along 120th Street, across from Teachers College and Union Theological Seminary. Horses filled the street. Twenty or so uniformed cops, smug in leather, tall, tough, strutting like leather queens on Christopher Street, their hands itching to swing, to prove manhood again and again. Jogging by them, I instinctively put my hand in my pocket and covered my cock protectively. The smell of manure and piss, the smell that would cling to Broadway and the walks for days after, was there in the street. Blood has no smell.

I reached Amsterdam. There, along the walls of Columbia, hundreds of cops stood in line facing the street, waiting. Five, ten city buses marked SPECIAL, filled with sadistic plainclothesmen looking like bouncers from dockside bars, or pimps . . . cops in other buses . . . cops inside the gates, hundreds . . . cops belching and itching to kill, leaning butch under the ledges above which Trilling and Quentin and Steve Marcus wrote . . . police vans, paddy wagons, two ambulances, police cars, red lights playing on the university buildings, reflecting on the windows of Philosophy Hall where the Ad Hoc Faculty Group had argued and lost, where the wounded would be taken that night. Crowds of whites packed across the street from the gates, along the walls under the Law Bridge, jeering the cops . . . fascist motherfuckers . . . and where was Harlem? Two old colored ladies—one screaming hysterically at the cops, "You's evil! You's evil!"; the other knocking over a litter basket and kicking it toward the cops. Futile anger. Harlem was asleep.

No entrance. Closed. A cop at the gates jabbed a billy club hard into my stomach. Move! Breathless. I ran to 114th and over to Broadway again, west of the fenced gym site over which the press and administration and students fought to avoid the meaning of the fight. On Broadway, three ABC cameramen were laughing as they talked. The noise from the campus grew louder. The shouting would build and fade and build again. "Kill 'em!" came from the jocks gathered at Low. The bust was still to come.

Near the Broadway gates I saw a professor I knew. I went up to him and told him I had to get on campus. He understood.

Professor Dodson was an hour away, told the bust was called off, two drinks later, driving toward Sparkill . . . Trilling was home exhausted . . . Quentin was in front of Hamilton renewing the thirties and his credentials as a man . . . Dean Platt was home . . . the president and vice president were held in the basement of Low listening to Captain Denesco reassure them of the cops' professionalism . . . Coach Balquist, who had planned the attack with the cops, sat in the corridor in Low, his hands sweating, waiting for the commie bastards to get fucked but good . . . in Fayerweather the barricades were being checked once more and the commune reminded of its pledge to nonviolence . . . the cops were moving onto Low silently . . . the captain raising his bullhorn, "In the name of the Trustees of Columbia University I order. . . ." The blacks had given in in Hamilton, led like sheep by the cops through tunnels into paddy wagons, like Jews moved into the showers . . . Avery was pulling on plastic bags . . . in Mathematics the students were in the middle of their anti gas preparations, and one boy, seventeen, was sobbing out his fear in the second-floor bathroom. It was an hour to the bust.

The professor and I walked to the gates. The cop barricades were in place. A junior faculty member was in charge. He stopped us.

"No one admitted. The gates are closed." He sounded very official, smug, enjoying his power as gatekeeper.

"Do you know who I am?"

"Yes, Professor, but no one is to be admitted."

"I'm going through and he is coming with me."

The gatekeeper glanced nervously at the police a few feet away. Television lights lit the gates. "I can't, sir."

"Do you want tenure at this university?"

He let us through.

On College Walk, just before I darted up the steps toward Math, the professor grabbed my arm and stopped me. "Why, Dotson, why all this coming violence, this playing at revolution?"

I looked at him carefully. He had spoken with great sadness, almost out of defeat, and I was moved by the concern expressed in his voice. His face, the pain of it, reminded me of Lowell. "I guess because we are trying to make the world safe for our friends. At least I am. And I don't know any other way."

I ran up the steps. He called out behind me, "Protect yourself."

The crowds of angry students were being shoved by cops away from Low Library to the steps of Earl Hall. They were militant and loud, shouting at the cops. The plainclothesmen had begun their deadly infiltration of the crowds, some of them dressed like students, carrying books. On College Walk cops were trooping onto campus, vans and paddy wagons lined from Kent to Dodge halls. Over Alma Mater's head someone had fixed a sign that read: RAPED BY THE COPS. I heard screaming in the distance and shouts that echoed through the quads across the lawns. The communes had begun to take up the defiant slogan, hurling it at the cops from the window and roofs: UP AGAINST THE WALL MOTHERFUCKERS.

I stood on the grass in front of Math, begging admission. The building was sealed. I shouted up to the windows, cupping my hands over my mouth, "I'm with you, Baby, all the way!" They shouted back encouragement.

I got in front of the Mathematics Building and leaned against the glass doors behind which tables and chairs and pathetic board barricades were built for defense. Only the barricades and the bodies of us before the door stood between the cops and the commune.

I stood before the doors, linking arms with four other young men, all of us frightened, all beginning to sweat. In front of us another line. And in front of that three professors, one with white hair, a tiny man. That was all the army of faculty—liberal, boasting that they would never allow the cops on their campus, we will stand by you, before you, behind you—that was all the army of faculty that bothered to appear before Math. We held each other's arms and waited. Hank, at the end of my line, started screaming hysterically at the cops as they came by the hundreds through the Earl Hall gates around the side of Math, and another contingent came to us across from Low. As they assembled in long, tight lines before us, hundreds of them facing nine young men and three old men barring their entrance, as they grouped and waited, it seemed for hours, unmoving, the tension mounting, Hank yelled, "Motherfucking, cocksucking bastard cops! Fascists! Fascists!" over and over again. I glanced over at him and shrugged. His face was red, his hair wet with sweat. He had not shaved in five days and he looked tired and drawn. He was eighteen. And he looked utterly terrified and defiant and beautiful to me as he screamed his outrage against the fucking liberal world. The white-haired professor, after Hank had gone on for a while, broke ranks and went up to him. "Son," he said quietly, his hand on his shoulder, "You're showing your fear. Calm yourself. We're all together. Those fascist animals will have to get through us to get to you. And I'll wear the bastards out." Hank quieted down.

I took out my contact lenses and put them in their case and shoved it in my pocket. I took off my tie to prevent strangulation. Then I waited with my friends while behind me, beguilingly, magnificently, my friends, those brave and sad young men, shouted into the night: UP AGAINST THE WALL MOTHERFUCKERS. The cry was taken up by other buildings and by the crowds and carried into the darkness.

A man in a tan trench coat stood about fifteen feet before us, and said into a bullhorn: "In the name of the Trustees of Columbia University I order you to leave. . . ."

They came at us fast and hard. The three professors were moved out quickly. Then the line of students in front of us folded quickly, some of them knocked to the ground. They were dragged away. Then the motherfuckers reached us. The boys at each end of the line braced themselves against the building. We held our arms tightly, legs spread, heads down. They kicked our legs and stomachs trying to make us break. We held for several minutes until the bastards took each of us by the hair and yanked us apart. I was thrown to the ground, kicked in the stomach, and then lifted by two plainclothesmen and thrown ten feet over the hedges onto the lawns. When I tried to get up they kicked me down. Two cops, each grabbing a leg, dragged me down the Earl Hall steps and ordered me to wait. Then Hank was dragged out. After a while we stood and ran down Broadway, the cops chasing us about a block. The motherfuckers.

While I was being pulled off campus, the cops were making their way into the building, pulling the furniture out of the doorway and throwing it on the lawns. It took them fifteen minutes to clear the building; rope and hoses held the barricade in place. They were met by six boys sitting, arms locked, on the soaped stairs. They were arrested. Then Hayden and a few others were pulled out.

After the first floor was cleared, the cops went from room to room methodically axing down every door, smashing furniture and walls, beating kids, pulling them along the stone stairways face down, their heads leaving blood smeared like thin paint along the steps.

At 114th Street I climbed over the Ferris Booth gate and jumped back on to campus. Paddy wagons filled with students were being driven out of College Walk, crowds of students on the lawns shouting their solidarity at the fucking cops: UP AGAINST THE WALL MOTHERFUCKERS!

The plainclothesmen started to clear South Field of thousands of students milling in rage, viciously driving them like frightened deer, trapping them between buildings and police, moving them in terror one way and then another, playing with them, dropping like animals on top of them when they fell—three, four plainclothes cops to each fallen student.

I was driven out of campus with the main contingent of students, several thousand of us running from the police to Broadway, there to be met by mounted police. The horsemen drove into us as we flooded into the street, crushing some of us against the gates and the sides of buildings.

I broke ranks and ran past a score of cops down Broadway to Furnald Hall. The French windows were open. I shouted, "I'm coming in!" and climbed the grating to the ledge and fell into the dormitory lounge, my ass being clubbed by a cop as I went inside. I saw Doug, a friend of mine, and we collected liquor from the rooms for the infirmaries in Philosophy and Ferris Booth halls.

Then Doug and I climbed four flights and stood on the upper ledge of Furnald, the windows filled with angry students shouting at the fucking cops, and looked down Broadway, my chest constricted with anger and impotence, hating the cops and the goddamn administration and half-assed president and the cocksucking university itself, and hating—gloriously, patriotically, beautifully, cleanly—America. Hating her fucking cops and troopers and her ways and manners and indifference, her lack of human sentiment and kindness, her arrogance, her pious *Christian* people who justified violence and spread death over the earth. Doug, his young, strong face contorted in anger, his body tense with outrage, started yelling obscenities at the cops. And I, hatred breaking me, joined his rage: UP AGAINST THE WALL MOTHERFUCKERS. ASSLICKING FASCIST FAGGOT COPS. PIMPS. GODDAMN CUNTEATING CORRUPT BASTARDS. My imagination dead, I clung to the epithet, "bastard," and hurled it monotonously, repetitively at the cops. We threw empty beer cans and lighted cigarettes down on them as they herded the terrified students up and down Broadway, allowing them no exit, whipping them with clubs, driving them into walls, making them fall again and again to be kicked and pummeled and arrested. I spit at them, shouted, hating them—and if I could I would have edged my ass over the avenue and dropped my hatred and my disgust on my America with her child-beating fascist cops and bloody, senseless wars, with her hypocritical, deadly leaders, her lack of compassion, her endless racism and inbred hatred, her balling, imperialist violence; America the violent, the disreputable, the outrageous, the incestuous land, devouring her children, feeding us bile and hunger for death; my unhappy America, my pathetic, bloody, stupid country, self-righteous and vicious, my evil land, beating her sons and daughters, killing her young men in useless wars, exploiting her weak, making victims of the young and poor and powerless; my country, led by fools and asslicking Company Men who terrorize the earth. America, how I hated you that night, and how clean and good and redemptive that hatred was.

Around six-thirty Tuesday morning, I walked back inside Mathematics. Empty. The floors and walls wet. I climbed the stairs. Blood smears on the walls. Broken glasses. Single shoes. Pieces of torn clothing. Bloody clumps of hair.

The place had been vandalized by the police. Ink thrown against the walls. Papers strewn everywhere. Furniture and doors and walls destroyed by axes and crowbars.

I went into the attic. "Who's there?" someone said. I stopped, standing under the light. "It's Dotson. I'm part of the Math commune."

Roger came out from behind a partition, his lunch bag in his hand. "God, you should have seen it. It was unbelievable. Oh, the fucking bastards, the bastards!"

"How did you escape?"

"I climbed out the window in the roof and hung over the side by my hands until they left. The fucking bastards. Somebody's got to pay for what they've done. Somebody's got to pay."

From *Dead Meat*

VEAL SLAUGHTERHOUSE, MONTREAL

THE BOSS WOULDN'T LET ME draw or take photos in the slaughterhouse, so I wrote this a day later. Veal calves are slaughtered in lots, each lot containing ten to twenty veals. The calf is three to four months old at slaughter and weighs between 250 and 300 pounds. Veals are kept off feed for eighteen hours before slaughter and handled with care to avoid bruising. Veals have to be dragged to the slaughterhouse, as they are too weak to stand and walk.

The animals are forced into the restraining pen, two at a time. The veals can see their comrades having their throats cut. The calves' eyes become practically white. Foam is pouring out of their mouths.

The man with the stun gun waits until there is enough space in the conveyor belt to receive the newly stunned veals. A large metal bolt strikes through the animal's skull. People who think this is a "humane," painless process are deluding themselves.

According to the meat industry's handbook, *The Meat We Eat*, twelfth edition, veal calves struggle for a longer period after sticking than other classes of livestock, so it is good to hoist them. The veal is hung upside down by a chain, and the throat is slit. The animal bleeds to death, which takes up to five minutes, as it moves along the conveyor belt.

The head is taken off. The body is slit open and steam comes out with all the entrails. Hooves come off. The carcass is cut into parts.

The conveyor belt starts up and all the bodies move down one. I see one calf with its throat slit, #6 on the conveyor belt, move one front leg in a last movement. This must have taken a massive effort as its body was drained of blood—a denial of death. The inspector wore a face mask.

The owner of the veals gives twelve dollars to the owner of the slaughterhouse for killing them. I keep bumping into the inspector, he pops up all over the place. The inspectors all look like surgeons, and they are clean of any blood. They are government employees.

The "jobber" is the person who chooses the best pieces of freshly slaughtered meat and transports them to the sales people. A jobber and I look into a giant vat full of brains, maybe 300 brains. Larger than human brains, they are white with blood clots. We look into another vat and the jobber tells me, "that's all livers." They are very large and yellow. He says yellow liquid oozes

Compression Stunner

From *Dead Meat*

out of them, which means they have been pumped up with hormones. There is a long line of workers as far as the eye can see. They cut meat off bones and ribs. They work so fast I can't see their hands moving. The forty full-time union workers get fifteen Canadian dollars an hour and kill 1,000 to 3,000 head a week.

ABATTOIR, MONTREAL

This slaughterhouse is thirty-five minutes from the center of Montreal. We drive along the highway in a freezer truck, go through a housing estate, then onto a deserted road, along which are several meatpacking buildings. These buildings look typically innocuous. They are one-story link and corrugated structures, with no clue as to what goes on inside, except for the stream of trucks backing in and out. We go into the front office, and I wear a hard hat and white coat. I've heard stories about this place. The boss, according to all accounts, is a multimillionaire, who closed the plant down for three years sooner than have a union. This is the largest slaughterhouse in Montreal. In the end, the union and the boss came to an agreement. Workers in blood-stained coats come in and out of the office. They all have cellular phones. They are taking orders from jobbers. Cattle and veals are to be slaughtered in ten minutes, so advanced orders are being taken. The men have white hair nets on under their hard hats. One of the jobbers tells me to get rid of my hair and tuck it up under my hat. The boss's daughter glides by, looks at me and then says to my guide Ian, "What's *she* doing here?" Ian says that I am his new assistant, and he wants to show me the kill floor. All the white workers here are Greek, in fact Greeks control most of the meat production in Montreal. The majority of Greeks speak fluent English and are second generation. This differentiates them from French Canadians, who generally don't speak English. There are also many African Canadians.

New trucks drive up to the back, and Martin, my fellow assistant, says jokingly, "It's their last journey." Martin has a lot of physical work to do, carrying carcasses and "sweetmeats." We go into the main room, which has a vast conveyor belt. It has two levels, on the top are the cut-up pieces of meat, on the bottom, rib cages and big bones. Along one side are workers, mostly Black, wearing hair nets and white clothes. They are cutting, chopping, slicing, and throwing the neat bits on the top belt. When I watch this, I can't believe humans are capable of this type of labor. It's just so hard. The conveyor goes so fast. I know they are making about 1,500 cuts an hour. I understand why these workers get carpal tunnel syndrome, because these are the same forceful movements over and over. I wonder what it's

From *Dead Meat*

Veal Slaughterhouse

From *Dead Meat*

like in the winter here. This meat is cold, having come from the cooler. This reminds me of when I worked in a factory, the mind-numbing boredom, the hypnotic effect of counting the minutes until the break. It's like splitting yourself up into parts.

I see no older workers. How would it be possible to do this labor, over the age of forty? They have to stand all day in ice water and blood. When they get home, all they can do is eat, maybe watch TV, and sleep, before it starts all over again. A loud buzzer sounds and the workers disappear, everything stops. It must be the break. The meat inspectors are wearing protective eyewear, hard hats, and earphones. They patrol everywhere, looking and listening.

We go into a huge room through a very heavy door, like the door of a safe. I look down, and I'm standing on a grid drainage floor. There is a conveyor belt with the corpses of cows and a large steel table, where one worker is scooping out brains and throwing them in a steel cart. There is a lot of crashing metal and shouting, and all the men are wearing ear protection. The corpses swing along with speed, the weight giving the impetus to move. I suppose the tracks on the ceiling must be at an angle to allow for momentum. The intestines, brains, livers, and kidneys are being taken out and put in steel carts with wheels. I'm told these parts are valuable, and there are thousands of dollars worth in each cart. The organs are yellow with blood spots. Maybe there are 500 brains in one cart and 500 livers in another and so on. Many tongues also. I keep thinking of the phrase, "They cut out their tongues, to stop them talking."

The room is quite dark. I always thought my memory of past slaughterhouses was colored by my emotion, but I can see now that the hanging, moving corpses obscure the overhead lighting. I wish I could take photos, but that would compromise Martin and Ian who have to work here, and they are taking a risk as it is. The workers drag and cut out innards, standing on a raised platform. And the liquid and guts drip and fall through the grid to the floor below. There is steam, as the hot intestines come out. I think there are about five workers doing this with an inspector watching. There is nowhere for us to stand, since we don't have a specific job to do. I am walking carefully on the grating, as it is slippery. Ian opens another door, a really heavy steel one, and we are on the kill floor, also called the "hot floor" because the animals' blood is hot, and the rest of the packing plant is kept cool.

In fact, the animal goes from being alive and hot, through different cooling procedures, until it's frozen in the butcher shop or supermarket. Meat that doesn't go through these stages is called "hot meat" by the

From *Dead Meat*

industry. Although not illegal, this meat hasn't cooled sufficiently to cut it cleanly and hasn't obtained a red, crisp appearance. The meat is dangerous to the workers, because it is hard to cut. Hot meat happens when the demand exceeds the supply, and the carcass is rushed through.

There is no place for observers to stand on the kill floor, so we have to keep moving and ducking under the swinging corpses, which move along very fast. The workers slow down to allow us to stand somewhere. I realize the meat inspector has to constantly do a balancing act along the raised platform where the workers stand.

A huge steel door opens, and two calves are forced through with an electric prod. They are pushed into a restraining crate, a metal box. It is very hard for them to squeeze in, and they don't want to, as they can see everything and it scares them. It takes a long time to force them. Veals can barely stand anyway, because they have lived their short lives in a crate and been given only milk to drink, no roughage to build bones. So their bones can't support them. The veals' fur is usually caked with diarrhea. The person on the other side of the restraining crate is getting frustrated, because the veals won't move all the way inside. They are two-thirds of the way in. The door keeps dropping down on them. It's a steel door, and it keeps rising up and dropping. It crashes down on their backs again and again. So the veals are getting electrocuted with the prod from behind and smashed from above. They finally go into the crate. They are squished together and can't move. I see their ears are stapled with their lot numbers. They look around wildly, making no sound, their heads are trembling, as if they have palsy.

White foam is dripping from their mouths. One calf looks at me with what appears to be trust. They wait. The worker with the either the bolt pistol or the electrolethalizer (I am not sure which, as I was absorbed in watching the animals) runs one hand from the head of the calf, right down to the flank. I am mesmerized by this action, so much so, that I didn't see him shoot the calves. Now we are in the second stage of the killing—the "sticking." I look down and realize I am standing on the drain for the blood. The drain is made out of wire mesh, and although I can't see it, I know the blood is going into containers under the floor. There is no heavy odor of blood, which exists when the blood is drained directly into water.

One stunned veal swings towards us, hanging upside down, chained by the legs. I have seen a lot of animals not properly stunned before throat cutting, but this one is stunned. It's a misconception that animals are dead

From *Dead Meat*

at this stage. It's important that the heart pumps the blood out of the animal, once its throat has been cut. Every time I go to a slaughterhouse, I try to see aspects I have missed before. In this case, I pay particular attention to the sticking. The tongue hangs out of the mouth. The man cuts the carotid artery. Because of the weight, this hole becomes elongated, looking like the throat has been cut, but it has not. The blood comes out like a red glass rod, a moving, solid rod. The next stunned veal is waiting to come down the line. I am thankful not to be splattered with blood, but notice my shoes are covered, and I am standing by slivers of flesh. The veal then swings along the line, with a slight push, and the blood continues to drip. The veals wait in line to be decapitated and to have their hooves cut off by power tools. As I watch, I see one veal that is about to be decapitated—alive. Although almost completely drained of blood, this veal has come out of the stun, which means there was not enough electricity or the captive bolt did not hit the right point.

Before decapitation is "rodding the weasand" (esophagus), which means separating the esophagus from the stomach to prevent the contents of the stomach from spilling. (The contents will make a mess and taint the meat.) The abdomen comes out, separated from the trachea. The esophagus is tied off. As I'm watching the "continuous, mechanical-powered rail system," the veal moves down from rodding to decapitation. In this case, I'm watching "dressed veal," a veal that hasn't been skinned. I hope by this time the veal is dead. I can see the front legs move, like an animal dreaming, when the limbs look like they are running in slow motion. This poor, pathetic veal can have no memory of actually running, because it was restrained in a crate for its entire life. As I leave the kill floor, I touch a veal. The fur is so soft and long, silky almost. I thought it would be coarse. I touch the ears and realize the last heat is leaving the face. What was alive a few moments ago in helpless misery is now dead, an eight-inch bolt fired into its brain. A power clipper takes off the head in two snips, another clipper takes off hooves—four snips for four hooves. They clatter to the steel mesh. These are hooves that never ran or walked on grass. This creature was kept in darkness its entire life, to keep that flesh tender and white on this day. Someone calls out, "That's the end of the veals. Cattle next." A buzzer sounds and the line stops.

I ask Martin about politics. He says he doesn't ever think about them. He says that he gets unemployment and works off the books at a cash job. Martin also works as a DJ on weekends—his favorite bands are Led Zeppelin and

From *Dead Meat*

Carcass – Skinner has lost three fingers

From *Dead Meat*

Public Enemy. He wants a car and tells me he had a cellular phone like all his friends, but his first bill was $350, so he got rid of it. His brother is getting married at age twenty-eight. The whole family will go to Greece for the wedding. Martin wonders when he will get a girlfriend, then he says he doesn't care if he ever gets one. He's twenty-one years old. Martin shares his cigs and his soda with me. He doesn't want to do this job. It's too much heavy lifting and doesn't pay enough. When we go to look at the killing floor, he jokes about it, but then he gets upset. "It's wrong." I am amazed that although he handles the dead corpses all day, he hadn't seen the actual killing.

In a back alley, Martin unloads veals, a hundred veals, hung and unskinned. They go into a white-tiled room behind the butcher shop. There is a deep white sink, and many sharp knives neatly arrayed on the draining board. An elderly man, the skinner, waits as Martin hoists the veals on to a rail of meat hooks. The veals slide down, and the skinner expertly separates the hide from the flesh. The furry hides fall to the floor like cast-off dresses. I look at the skinner's hands; there is something wrong. I look more closely and see each finger has been severed at the joint—he has only stumps and thumbs.

Last Bit of Daylight

From *Dead Meat*

SLAUGHTERHOUSE, NEW YORK STATE

This slaughterhouse is within the prison system. The meat is produced for the prison. The slaughterhouse workers are training the prisoners to be slaughterers. I spend a long time with Bill, the head slaughterer, and some of the workers. It is nonunion, and the workers have come from other meat-packing plants which have been forced to close down. One of the workers has seen me in the company of an animal rights activist and also has seen something about me in the *Village Voice*. They are, not surprisingly, hostile and suspicious of me, as some have already lost jobs and have large families to support. Also, the local animal rights group is very actively trying to close this place down. Bill swings from very hostile behavior to pleading with me to understand his circumstances. I am in a quandary. I support the views of the local animal rights activists, but not necessarily their tactics. In general, they are from a higher income level than these workers, so the activists are less understanding about the consequences of closing the plant. The workers are very hostile towards them. In a cushy office, the boss gets none of this aggravation. He gets $80,000 per annum for doing *zilch*. Very cunningly, he has used the workers as a buffer from the activists.

The workers and I have a raging debate right on the kill floor. I sit on the steel cutting table, and the workers smoke cigs. We talk about *The Jungle* and the industry, and the fact that they can't lose these jobs. I get the impression that these workers are wanderers, wandering the United States looking for meatpacking jobs. On the one hand, they desperately need a union, but on the other, they feel the union betrayed them in past struggles. I find myself thinking that if I get too much information, too many agendas, I will never make another picture. Animals are mute. But humans can communicate verbally, and as the workers carry on talking—even though I'm still sitting on the kill floor—the animals fade away. The men's reality becomes paramount. I identify with them very quickly. They feel under siege.

The day before, I went with Bill in the elevator, a steel platform which rises over the larger animals, and he asked me if I wanted to "participate in the slaughter." I declined, although it makes very little difference to the animal, since I'm standing right there. Bill pointed the bolt pistol at me and said half-jokingly, "This is to kill artists, women, and animals." I looked down the barrel of the gun and made a kind of little girl giggle, as though it was a joke to me too. I saw all the faces of the men looking up and laughing. Bill then told me that he always kisses the animals before he shoots them through the brain. Luckily at this point, the government

inspector came in. I questioned him, and he knew nothing about farm animals, workers injuries, or anything. To every question I had, he replied, "it doesn't happen here." I seriously suspect he is on someone's payroll.

The next day, Bill has mellowed toward me somewhat. He now sees me as "a babe," and he gives me his cherished animal slaughtering books. *How to Slaughter Sheep*, for example. Milton Friedman would be pleased. Bill believes in the free market, social Darwinism, and that we "need meat to eat . . . it's natural." He believes he is teaching the prisoners a good trade and that the meat-cutting business is good rehabilitation. He calls the prisoners "his boys." It's a bizarre sight to enter a slaughterhouse where the head slaughterer is holding a gun, the prisoners have knives, and the guards of the prisoners have guns. I feel unarmed, along with the animals.

Bill takes me to the "chilling room." This place is the most scary for me, as I always imagine I'll get locked up with all the hanging corpses in the dark. The door is very heavy, and without a coat, it would be hypothermia for sure. The hogs hanging here have been freshly killed, despite what Bill

From *Dead Meat*

told me earlier. I wanted to see the hogs slaughtered, but Bill said they hadn't killed any recently. He's covering up the slaughter because he doesn't want the activists to know when the killing starts—he's afraid of demonstrations.

As for politics, these men don't want to be aggravated. Their lives are so hard, the American dream so relentless that they balance in midair with no place to land. To them, politicians are corrupt scum, and it's as though the government exists on a separate planet (which it does). Yet on a dime, they turn with the flag, joining the racism against Blacks and Jews. But they have big hearts, and I'm not generalizing about all "working people," I am talking about these four men. They are very loyal to the prisoners. Bill has adopted homeless children. But to the bosses, the lives of these workers have the same value as the lives of the animals on the killing floor.

MOTEL, COLORADO

I arrive late at night and check into a small motel. The curtains are drawn on the bay windows. I watch TV all night. At 6 A.M., I am tuned in to the Home Shopping Network, mesmerized by glinting cubic zirconium on a twirling red-nailed finger. The room begins to shake, and then stops, and then starts shaking again. I go over to the window and look through the curtain. Outside the window a few feet away, a train has come to a standstill. It is a cattle train. The sun is rising. A thousand eyes are reflecting in the light, staring into the motel room. I can see the cattle between the wooden slats. They are silent and motionless. The temperature is below zero, and the cattles' breath makes a white mist.

The train starts up again, very slowly. This is the longest train I have ever seen. It takes a full thirty minutes to pass by. There are hundreds of cars, packed with thousands and thousands of cattle on their way to slaughter. Six billion animals are killed each year in the United States for human consumption. The suffering of these animals is mute. For the defenseless, the gentle, the wounded, the ones who cannot speak, life consists of indescribable suffering.

From *Dead Meat*

PAUL KRASSNER

The Parts Left Out of the Kennedy Book

*An executive in the publishing industry, who obviously must
remain anonymous, has made available to* The Realist *a pho-
tostatic copy of the original manuscript of William Man-
chester's book,* The Death of a President.
   *Those passages printed here were marked for deletion
months before Harper & Row sold the serialization rights to*
Look *magazine; hence they do not appear even in the "complete" version published by the German magazine* Stern.

IN THE SUMMER OF 1960 the Democratic National Convention in Los
Angeles was the scene of a political visitation of the alleged sins of the
father upon the son. Lyndon Johnson found himself battling a young,
handsome, charming, and witty adversary, John F. Kennedy, for the presidential nomination.

The Texan, understandably anxious, allowed his strategy to descend to a
strange campaign tactic. He attacked his opponent on the grounds that his
father, Joseph P. Kennedy, was a Nazi sympathizer during the time he was
United States ambassador to Great Britain, from 1938 to 1940. The senior
Kennedy had predicted that Germany would win the war and therefore had
urged President Franklin D. Roosevelt to withhold aid to England. Now
Johnson found himself fighting pragmatism with pragmatism. It did not
work; he lost the nomination.

Ironically, the vicissitudes of regional bloc voting forced Kennedy into
selecting Johnson as his running mate. Jack rationalized the feasibility of
the situation, but Jackie was unable to forgive Johnson. Her attitude toward
him expressed itself as a recurrent paroxysm of barely controlled scorn.

It was common knowledge in Washington social circles that the chief executive was something of a ladies' man. His staff included a Secret Service
agent, referred to by the code name Dentist, whose duties consisted mainly
of escorting to and from a rendezvous site, either in the District of
Columbia or while traveling, the models, actresses, and other strikingly
attractive females chosen by the president for his not-at-all-infrequent trysts.

"Get me that," he had said of a certain former Dallas beauty contest winner when plans for his campaign tour were first being discussed. That particular aspect of the itinerary was adjusted, of course, when Mrs. Kennedy decided to accompany her husband.

She was aware of his philandering, but would cover up her dismay by joking, "It runs in the family." The story had gotten back to her about the late Marilyn Monroe using the telephone in the bathroom of her Hollywood home to make a long-distance call to *New York Post* gossip columnist Sidney Skolsky.

"Sid, you won't believe this," she had whispered, "but the attorney general of our country is waiting for me in my bed this very minute—I just had to tell you."

It is difficult to ascertain where on the continuum of Lyndon Johnson's personality innocent boorishness ends and deliberate sadism begins. To have summoned then-Secretary of the Treasury Douglas Dillon for a conference wherein he, the new president, sat defecating as he spoke, might charitably be an example of the former; but to challenge under the same circumstances Senator J. William Fulbright for his opposition to administration policy in Vietnam is considered by insiders to be a frightening instance of the latter. The more Jacqueline Kennedy has tried to erase the crudeness of her husband's successor from her mind, the more it has impinged upon her memories and reinforced her resentment of him.

"It's beyond style," she would confide to friends. "Jack had style, but this is beyond style."

When Arthur Schlesinger Jr. related to her an incident he had witnessed firsthand—Lyndon Johnson had actually placed his penis over the edge of the yacht, bragging to onlookers, "Watch it touch bottom!"—Mrs. Kennedy could not help but shiver with disgust. Capitol Hill reporters have long known of Mr. Johnson's boasts about his six-o'clock-in-the-morning forays with Lady Bird and of his bursts of phallic exhibitionism, whether on a boat, at the swimming pool, or in the lavatory.

Apropos of this tendency, Drew Pearson's assistant, Jack Anderson, has remarked: "When Lyndon announces there's going to be a joint session of Congress, everybody cringes."

It is true that Mrs. Kennedy withstood the pressures of scandal, ranging from the woman who picketed the White House carrying a blown-up photograph supposedly of Jack Kennedy sneaking away from the home of Jackie's press secretary, Pamela Turnure, to the *Blauvelt*

Family Genealogy that claimed on page 884, under "Eleventh Genera-tion," that one Durie Malcolm had "married, third, John F. Kennedy, son of Joseph P. Kennedy, one-time ambassador to England." But the infideli-ties themselves gnawed away at her—as indeed they would gnaw away at any wife in this culture—until finally Jackie left in exasperation. Her father-in-law offered her $1 million to reconcile. She came back, not for the money but because she sincerely believed that the nation needed Jack Kennedy and she didn't want to bear the burden of possibly causing him to lose enough public favor to forestall his winning the presidency.

Consequently, she was destined to bear a quite different burden, with great ambivalence—the paradox of fame. She enjoyed playing her role to the hilt but complained, "Can't they get it into their heads that there's a differ-ence between being the First Lady and being Elizabeth Taylor?" Even after she became First Widow, the movie magazines would not—or could not—leave her alone. Probably the most bizarre invasion of her privacy occurred in *Photoplay*, which asked the question, "Too Soon for Love?" then pro-ceeded to print a coupon that readers were requested to answer and send in. They had a multiple choice: "Should Jackie (1) Devote her life exclusively to her children and the memory of her husband? (2) Begin to date, privately or publicly, and eventually remarry? (3) Marry right away?"

Mrs. Kennedy fumed. "Why don't they give them some *more* decisions to make for me? Some *real* ones. Should I live in occasional sin? Should I use a diaphragm or take the pill? Should I keep it in the medicine cabinet or the bureau drawer?" But she would never lose her dignity in public; her faith in her own image ran too deep.

American leaders tend to have schizophrenic approaches toward one another. They want to expose each other's human frailties at the same time that they do *not* want to remove their fellow emperors' clothes. Bobby Kennedy privately abhors Lyndon Johnson, but publicly calls him "great, and I mean that in every sense of the word." Johnson has referred to Bobby as "that little shit" in private, but continues to laud him for the media.

Gore Vidal has no such restraint. On a television program in London, he explained why Jacqueline Kennedy will never relate to Lyndon Johnson. During that tense flight from Dallas to Washington after the assassination, she inadvertently walked in on Johnson as he was standing over the casket of his predecessor and chuckling. This disclosure was the talk of London, but did not reach these shores.

The Parts Left Out of the Kennedy Book

Of course, President Johnson is often given to inappropriate responses—witness the puzzled timing of his smile when he speaks of grave matters—but we must also assume that Mrs. Kennedy had been traumatized that day and her perception was likely to have been colored by the tragedy. This state of shock must have underlain an incident on Air Force One that this writer conceives to be delirium, but which Mrs. Kennedy insists she actually saw.

"I'm telling you this for the historical record," she said, "so that people a hundred years from now will know what I had to go through."

She corroborated Gore Vidal's story about Lyndon Johnson, continuing: "That man was crouching over the corpse, no longer chuckling but breathing hard and moving his body rhythmically. At first I thought he must be performing some mysterious symbolic rite he'd learned from Mexicans or Indians as a boy. And then I realized—there is only one way to say this—he was literally fucking my husband in the throat. In the bullet wound in the front of his throat. He reached a climax and dismounted. I froze. The next thing I remember, he was being sworn in as the new president."

[Handwritten marginal notes: 1. Check with Rankin—did secret autopsy show semen in throat wound? 2. Is this simply necrophilia or was LBJ trying to change entry wound from grassy knoll into exit wound from Book Depository by enlarging it?]

The glaze lifted from Jacqueline Kennedy's eyes.

"I don't believe that Lyndon Johnson had anything to do with a conspiracy, but I do know this—my husband taught me about the nuances of power—if Jack were miraculously to come back to life and suddenly appear in front of Johnson, the first thing Johnson would do now is kill him." She smiled sardonically, adding, "Unless Bobby beat him to it."

WILLIAM S. BURROUGHS

Mind War

EARLIER I HAVE SUGGESTED THAT the CIA, the Russians, and the Chinese have all set up top-secret centers to study and apply psychic techniques to political ends. Those of you who have read *Psychic Discoveries Behind the Iron Curtain* will infer that the Russians are ahead of us.

Now, anyone who has lived for any time in countries like Morocco, where magic is widely practiced, has probably seen a curse work. I have. However, curses tend to be hit-or-miss, depending on the skill and power of the operator and the susceptibility of the victim. And that isn't good enough for the CIA or any similar organization: "Bring us the ones that work, not sometimes but *every* time." So what is the logical forward step? To devise machines that can concentrate and direct psychic force with predictable effects. I suggest that what the CIA is, or was, working on at its top-secret Nevada installation may be described as *computerized* black magic. If Curse A doesn't make it, Curse Program B automatically goes into operation—and so on.

I recommend to your attention a book called *The Mind Masters* by John Rossmann. This is ostensibly a fantastic science fiction novel, interesting more for its content than its style, that may well contain some real inside information. The story concerns a researcher who has been disillusioned by his work on Project Pandora, an American psychic training center run by a Colonel Pickett, who is strongly reminiscent of the mad General Ripper in *Dr. Strangelove*, right down to the cigar. Only he is unloosing *psychic* warfare rather than nuclear bombs, having convinced himself that this form of warfare is more effective and more easily controlled by elitist objectives. The disillusioned researcher, one Britt St. Vincent, is contacted by Mero, a private institution dedicated to opposing these black magic centers. (It should be obvious that only *black* magic has "military applications.")

After he has been taken to Mero's secret headquarters, Britt is briefed by Dr. Webster on the purposes of Mero. Dr. Webster cites an early report by columnist Jack Anderson that the reason the Johnson-Kosygin summit conference in 1967 at Glassboro, New Jersey, was held in such a remote spot was that this was the world's first summit conference on *psychic warfare*. He recalls for Britt how the CIA, while making an electronic sweep of the U.S. embassy in Moscow for listening devices, discovered some very unusual electromagnetic emanations pulsing through the building. (Later it came out that the Soviets had stepped up the power to a point where embassy officials and their families were in danger from the high-voltage microwave radiation, which can cause confusion, migraines, and even death.) Not long after, the CIA confirmed that this was in fact part of a much larger psychic attack on the embassy. When the Defense Department launched its top-secret psychic counterattack, according to columnist Anderson, it was code-named Project Pandora.

Dr. Webster goes on to tell Britt: "Glassboro wasn't the end of it, Britt . . . obviously. By easily diverting funds within their mammoth defense budgets, small groups of supermilitarists here and in Russia covertly continued psychic programs. . . ."

The violent student rioting of the late sixties was largely instigated by electronic mood-control devices that were derived from the psychic discoveries of Project Pandora. The riots, it is now evident, were the first phase of a massive plot. The students were used by U.S. military extremists for two purposes. First, the riots tended to discredit the student causes. Secondly, the civil disturbances conveniently provided the plotters with the necessary reasons to reinstate some of their psychic weapons programs under the guise of "crowd control" research. Britt learns that similar secret psychic research is still advancing rapidly in China, France, Israel, Egypt, South Africa, and Chile, in addition to the United States and Russia:

> Although these scattered groups are currently working to beat *each other* to the secret of powers that will give them world control, there is a good possibility that they could even now join forces and make a *combined* psychic bid for world control—and at this moment they appear to stand an almost even chance of succeeding if they joined forces.

And what would the future look like if such groups actually exist and if they do combine and take over? An elitist World State very much along the lines laid down by the Nazis. At the top would be a theocracy trained in psychic control techniques implemented by computerized electronic devices that would render opposition psychologically impossible. Entry to this privileged class would be permitted only to those whose dedication to the World State was absolute and unquestioning. In short, you don't get in by merit or ability but by being an all-around one-hundred-percent shit. Under this ruling elite of power addicts would be an anonymous service collective of functionaries, managers, and bureaucrats. And below them, the slave workers.

There would be no place for dissent or independent research. The troublesome artist would be eliminated or absorbed. The elite lives happily ever after at the top of a control state that makes *1984* seem cozy and nostalgic.

The Courage To Kill: Meeting the Panthers

I FELL IN LOVE WITH the Black Panther Party immediately upon my first encounter with it; it was literally love at first sight. It happened one night at a meeting in a dingy little storefront on Scott Street in the Fillmore district, the heart of San Francisco's black ghetto. It was February 1967. The meeting was the latest in a series of weekly meetings held by a loose coalition functioning under the name of the Bay Area Grassroots Organizations Planning Committee. The purpose of the coalition was to coordinate three days of activities with the worthy ambition of involving the total black community in mass action commemorating the fourth anniversary of the assassination of Malcolm X. The highlight and culmination of the memorial was to be the appearance of Sister Betty Shabazz, Malcolm X's widow, who was to deliver the keynote speech at a mass meeting at the Bayview Community Center in Hunter's Point.

Among the topics on the agenda for this fortuitous meeting was the question of providing security for Sister Betty during the twenty-four hours she was to be our guest in the Bay Area. There was a paranoia around — which I did not share — that assassins by the dozens were lurking everywhere for the chance to shoot Sister Betty down. This fear, real or imagined, kept everybody uptight.

I had arrived at the meeting late, changing at the last minute a previous decision not to attend at all. I was pissed off at everyone in the room. Taking a seat with my back to the door, I sat there with, I'm sure, a scornful frown of disdain upon my face. Roy Ballard (if the normal brain had three cylinders, his would have one) sat opposite me, across the circle formed by the placement of the chairs. He, above all, understood the expression on my face, for he had done the most to put it there; this accounted, I thought, for the idiot grin on his own.

On Roy's left sat Ken Freeman, chairman of the now defunct Black Panther Party of Northern California, who always looked to me like Dagwood, with his huge round bifocals and the bald spot in the front of his natural. On Roy's right sat a frightened-looking little mulatto who seemed to live by the adage, "It's better to remain silent and be thought a fool than to open one's mouth and remove all doubt." He probably adopted that rule from observing his big, fat, yellow wife, who was seated on his right and who had said when I walked in, just loud enough for me to hear, "Shit! I thought we agreed after last week's meeting that *he* wouldn't be allowed to attend any more meetings!"

Next to her sat Jack Trueblood, a handsome, earnest youth in a black Russian cap who represented San Francisco State College's Black Students Union and who always accepted whatever tasks were piled upon him, insuring that he would leave each weekly meeting with a heavy load. On his right sat a girl named Lucky. I could never tell why they called her that—not, I'm sure, because she happened to be Roy Ballard's old lady; maybe because she had such a beautiful smile.

Between Lucky and myself sat Marvin Jackmon, who was known as a poet because after Watts went up in flames he had composed a catchy ditty entitled "Burn, Baby, Burn!" and a play entitled *Flowers for the Trashman*. (It is hard for me to write objectively about Marvin. My association with him, dating from the third week of December 1966, ended in mutual bitterness with the closing of the Black House. After getting out of prison that month, he was the first person I hooked up with. Along with Ed Bullins, a young playwright who now has a few things going for himself off-Broadway, and Willie Dale, who had been in San Quentin with me and was trying to make it as a singer, we had founded the Black House in January 1967. Within the next two months the Black House, located in San Francisco, became the center of non-Establishment black culture throughout the Bay Area.)

On my right sat Bill Sherman, an ex-member of the Communist Party and at that time a member of the central committee of the Black Panther Party of Northern California. Next to Bill was Victoria Durant, who dressed with what the black bourgeoisie would call "style" or, better yet, "class." She seemed so out of place at those meetings. We were supposed to be representing the common people—grassroots—and here was Victoria ready to write out a $50 check at the drop of a hat. She represented, as everyone knew, the local clique of black Democrats who wanted inside info on everything even hinting of "organizing" in their stomping grounds—even if the price of such info was a steady flow of $50 checks.

Then there was Marianne Waddy, who kept everybody guessing because no one was ever sure of where or what she really was. One day she'd be dressed in flowing African gowns with her hair wrapped up in a pretty *skashok*, the perfect picture of the young Afro-American lady who had established a certain identity and relationship to traditional African culture. The next day she would be dressed like a man and acting like a man who would cut the first throat that got in his way.

Next to Marianne sat a sneaky-looking fellow called Nasser Shabazz. Sitting between Nasser and Ken Freeman, completing the circle, was Vincent Lynch, as smooth and black as the ebony statues he had brought back from his trip to Nigeria and the only member of the Black Panther Party of Northern California I ever liked or thought was sincere. Somewhere in the room, too, was Ann Lynch, Vincent's wife, with their bright-eyed little son, Patrice Lumumba Lynch. Ann was the head of Black Care, the women's auxiliary to this Panther Party. These sisters spent all of their time talking about the impending violent stage of the black revolution, which was inevitable, and how they, the women, must be prepared to care for the men who would be wounded in battle.

I had come out of prison with plans to revive the Organization of Afro-American Unity, the vehicle finally settled upon by Malcolm X to spearhead the black revolution. The OAAU had never really got off the ground, for it was stopped by the assassin's bullets that felled Malcolm on the stage of the Audubon Ballroom in New York City. I was amazed that no one else had moved to continue Malcolm's work in the name of the organization he had chosen, which seemed perfect to me and also logically necessary in terms of historical continuity. The three-day memorial, which was but part of the overall plan to revive the OAAU, was to be used as a forum for launching the revival. In January, I had put the plan on paper and circulated it throughout the Bay Area, then issued a general call for a meeting to establish a temporary steering committee that would see after things until the start of the memorial. At this time we would have a convention, found the Bay Area branch of the Organization of Afro-American Unity, and elect officers whom Sister Betty Shabazz would install, giving the whole effort her blessings in a keynote address on the final day of the memorial.

By February the plan had been torn to shreds. If the plan was a pearl, then I had certainly cast it before swine, and the biggest swine of all, Roy Ballard, had hijacked the plan and turned it into a circus. It soon became clear that if the OAAU was to be reborn, it would not be with the help of this crew, because all they could see was the pageantry of the memorial. Beyond that, their eyes blotted out all vision. Far from wanting to see an organization develop that would put an end to the archipelago of one-man showcase groups that plagued the black community with division, they had each made it their sacred cause to insure the survival of their own splinter group.

The Courage to Kill: Meeting the Panthers

From the beginning, when the plan was first put before them, they took up each separate aspect and chewed it until they were sure it was either maimed for life or dead. Often, after an idea had gone around the circle, if it still showed signs of life they would pounce upon it and rend it some more. When they had finished, all that was left of the original plan was a pilgrimage to the site where a sixteen-year-old black youth, Matthew Johnson, had been murdered by a white cop; putting some pictures of Malcolm X on the walls of the Bayview Community Center; a hysterical speech by Ken Freeman; and twenty-four hours of Sister Betty Shabazz's time.

In all fairness, however, I must confess that the whole plan was impossible to achieve, mostly because it did not take into account certain negative aspects of the black man's psychological heritage from four hundred years of oppression here in Babylon. Then, too, I was an outsider. Having gone to prison from Los Angeles, I had been paroled to San Francisco. I was an interloper unfolding a program to organize *their* community. Fatal. It didn't matter to them that we were dealing with the concept of the Black Nation, of colonized Afro-America, and that all the boundaries separating our people were the stupid impositions of the white oppressors and had to be obliterated. Well, no matter; I had failed. Proof of my failure was Roy Ballard, sitting there before me like a gaunt buzzard, presiding over the carcass of a dream.

Suddenly the room fell silent. The crackling undercurrent that for weeks had made it impossible to get one's point across when one had the floor was gone; there was only the sound of the lock clicking as the front door opened, and then the soft shuffle of feet moving quietly toward the circle. Shadows danced on the walls. From the tension showing on the faces of the people before me, I thought the cops were invading the meeting, but there was a deep female gleam leaping out of one of the women's eyes that no cop who ever lived could elicit. I recognized that gleam out of the recesses of my soul, even though I had never seen it before in my life: the total admiration of a black woman for a black man. I spun round in my seat and saw the most beautiful sight I had ever seen: four black men wearing black berets, powder-blue shirts, black leather jackets, black trousers, shiny black shoes—and each with a gun! In front was Huey P. Newton with a riot pump shotgun in his right hand, barrel pointed down to the floor. Beside him was Bobby Seale, the handle of a .45-caliber automatic showing from its holster on his right hip, just below the hem of his jacket. A few steps behind Seale was Bobby Hutton, the barrel of his shotgun at his feet. Next to him was Sherwin Forte, an M-1 carbine with a banana clip cradled in his arms.

Roy Ballard jumped to his feet. Licking his lips, he said, "For those of you who've never met the brothers, these are the Oakland Panthers."

"You're wrong," said Huey P. Newton. "We're not the Oakland Panthers. We happen to live in Oakland. Our name is the Black Panther Party."

With that the Panthers seated themselves in chairs along the wall, outside the circle. Every eye in the room was riveted upon them. What amazed me was that Roy Ballard did not utter one word in contradiction, nor was there any other yakkity-yak around the room. There was absolute silence. Even little Patrice Lumumba Lynch seemed to sit up and take notice.

Where was my mind at? Blown! Racing through time, racing through the fog of a perspective that had just been shattered into a thousand fragments. Who are these cats? I wondered at them, checking them out carefully. They were so cool and, it seemed to me, not unconscious of the electrifying effect they were having on everybody in the room. Then I recalled a chance remark that Marvin Jackmon had once made. We were discussing the need for security at the Black House because the crowds were getting larger and larger and we had had to bodily throw out a cat who was high and acting like he owned the place. I said that Marvin, Ed, Dale, and I had better each get ourself a gun. As I elaborated on the necessity as I saw it, Marvin said: "You need to forget about the Black House and go across the bay and get with Bobby Seale." And then he laughed.

"Who is Bobby Seale?" I asked him.

At first he gave no answer; he seemed to be carefully considering what to say. Finally he said, "He's arming some brothers across the bay." Though I pressed him, he refused to go into it any further, and at the time it didn't seem important to me, so I forgot about it. Now, sitting there looking at those Panthers, I recalled the incident with Marvin. I looked at him. He seemed to have retreated inside himself, sitting there looking like a skinny black Buddha with something distasteful and menacing on his mind.

"Do you brothers want to make a speech at the memorial?" Roy Ballard asked the Panthers.

"Yes," Bobby Seale said.

"OK," said Ballard. "We have the program broken down into subjects: Politics, Economics, Self-Defense, and Black Culture. Now which section do you brothers want to speak under?" This was the sort of question which in my experience had always signaled the beginning of a two-hour debate with this group.

"It doesn't matter what section we speak under," Huey said. "Our message is one and the same. We're going to talk about black people arming themselves in a political fashion to exert organized force in the political arena to see to it that their desires and needs are met. Otherwise there will be a political consequence. And the only culture worth talking about is a revolutionary culture. So it doesn't matter what heading you put on it, we're going to talk about political power growing out of the barrel of a gun."

"OK," Roy Ballard said. He paused, then added, "Let's put it under Politics." Then he went on to start the specific discussion of security for Sister Betty, who would pick her up at the airport, and so on. Bobby Seale was jotting down notes in a little black book. The other Panthers sat quietly, watchfully.

Three days before the start of the memorial, I received a phone call from Los Angeles. The man on the other end identified himself as Hakim Jamal, Malcolm X's cousin by marriage. He would be arriving with Sister Betty, he said, and both of them wanted to talk with me. They had liked, it turned out, an article on Malcolm that I had written and that was published in *Ramparts*. We agreed that when they got in from the airport I would meet them at the *Ramparts* office in San Francisco.

On the day that Sister Betty and Hakim Jamal were to arrive in San Francisco, I was sitting in my office tinkering with some notes for an article. One of the secretaries burst through the door. Her face was white with fear, and she was shouting, "We're being invaded! We're being invaded!"

I couldn't tell just who her invaders were. Were the Chinese coming? Had the CIA finally decided to do *Ramparts* in? Then she said, "There are about twenty men outside with guns!"

I knew that Hakim Jamal and Sister Betty had arrived with their escort of armed Black Panthers.

"Don't worry," I said, "they're friends."

"*Friends?*" she gasped. I left her there with her eyes bugging out of her head and rushed to the front of the building.

I waded through *Ramparts* staff jammed into the narrow hallway, fending off the frightened inquiries by repeating, "It's all right, it's all right." The lobby resembled certain photographs coming out of Cuba the day Castro took Havana. There were guns everywhere, pointed toward the ceiling like metallic blades of grass growing up out of the sea of black faces beneath the black berets of the Panthers. I found Hakim Jamal and Sister Betty surrounded by a knot of Panthers, who looked calm and self-possessed in sharp contrast to the chaotic reactions their appearance had set off. Outside, where Broadway ran in four lanes to feed the freeway on-ramp and to receive the heavy traffic from the off-ramp, a massive traffic jam was developing, and sirens could be heard screaming in the distance as cops sped our way.

I took Jamal and Sister Betty to an office down the hall. We talked for about fifteen minutes about Malcolm. Sister Betty, her eyes concealed behind dark glasses, said nothing after we were introduced. She looked cool enough on the surface, but it was clear that she felt hard-pressed. Huey P. Newton was standing at the window, shotgun in hand, looking down into the upturned faces of a horde of police. I left the room to get Sister Betty a glass of water, squeezing past Bobby Seale and what seemed like a battalion of Panthers in the hall guarding the door. Seale's face was a chiseled mask of determination.

A few yards down the hall, Warren Hinckle III, editor of *Ramparts*, was talking to a police lieutenant.

"What's the trouble?" the lieutenant asked, pointing at the Black Panthers with their guns.

"No trouble," Hinckle said. "Everything is under control."

The policeman seemed infuriated by this answer. He stared at Bobby Seale for a moment and then stalked outside. While I was in the lobby, a TV cameraman, camera on his shoulder, forced his way through the front door and started taking pictures. Two white boys who worked at *Ramparts* stopped the TV man and informed him that he was trespassing on private property. When he refused to leave, they picked him up and threw him out the door, camera and all.

When it was agreed that it was time to leave, Huey Newton took control. Mincing no words, he sent five of his men out first to clear a path through the throng of spectators clustered outside the door, most of whom were cops. He dispatched a phalanx of the Panthers fast on their heels, with Hakim Jamal and Sister Betty concealed in their midst. Newton himself, along with Bobby Seale and three other Panthers, brought up the rear.

I went outside and stood on the steps of *Ramparts* to observe the departure. When Huey left the building, the TV cameraman who had been tossed out was grinding away with his camera. Huey took an envelope from his pocket and held it up in front of the camera, blocking the lens.

"Get out of the way!" the TV man shouted. When Huey continued to hold the envelope in front of the lens, the TV man started cursing, and reached out and knocked Huey's hand away with his fist. Huey coolly turned to one of the score of cops watching and said, "Officer, I want you to arrest this man for assault."

An incredulous look came into the cop's face, then he blurted out, "If I arrest anybody, it'll be you!"

Huey turned on the cameraman, again placing the envelope in front of the lens. Again the cameraman reached out and knocked Huey's hand away. Huey reached out, snatched the cameraman by the collar, and slammed him up against the wall, sending him spinning and staggering down the sidewalk, trying to catch his breath and balance the camera on his shoulder at the same time.

Bobby Seale tugged at Huey's shirt sleeve. "C'mon, Huey, let's get out of here."

Huey and Bobby started up the sidewalk toward their car. The cops stood there on the point, poised as though ready to start shooting at a given signal.

"Don't turn your backs on these back-shooting dogs!" Huey called out to Bobby and the other three Panthers. By this time the other Panthers with Sister Betty and Jamal had gotten into cars and melted into the traffic jam. Only these five were still at the scene.

At that moment a big, beefy cop stepped forward. He undid the little strap holding his pistol in his holster and started shouting at Huey, "Don't point that gun at me! Stop pointing that gun at me!" He kept making gestures as though he was going for his gun.

This was the most tense of moments. Huey stopped in his tracks and stared at the cop.

"Let's split, Huey! Let's split!" Bobby Seale was saying.

Ignoring him, Huey walked to within a few feet of the cop and said, "What's the matter, you got an itchy finger?"

The cop made no reply.

"You want to draw your gun?" Huey asked him.

The other cops were calling out for this cop to cool it, to take it easy, but he didn't seem to be able to hear them. He was staring into Huey's eyes, measuring him.

"OK," Huey said. "You big fat racist pig, draw your gun!"

The cop made no move.

"Draw it, you cowardly dog!" Huey pumped a round into the chamber of the shotgun. "I'm waiting," he said, and stood there waiting for the cop to draw.

All the other cops moved back out of the line of fire. I moved back, too, onto the top step of *Ramparts*. I was thinking, staring at Huey surrounded by all those cops and daring one of them to draw, "Goddam, that nigger is c-r-a-z-y!"

The Courage to Kill: Meeting the Panthers

Then the cop facing Huey gave it up. He heaved a heavy sigh and low-ered his head. Huey literally laughed in his face and then went off up the street at a jaunty pace, disappearing in a blaze of dazzling sunlight.

"Work out, soul brother!" I was shouting to myself. "You're the bad-dest motherfucker I've ever seen!" I went back into *Ramparts* and we all stood around chattering excitedly, discussing what we had witnessed with disbelief.

"*Who was that?*" asked Vampira, Warren Hinckle's little sister.

"That was Huey P. Newton," I said, "Minister of defense of the Black Panther Party."

"Boy, is he gutsy!" she said dreamily.

"Yeah," I agreed. "He's out of sight!"

The quality in Huey P. Newton's character that I had seen that morning in front of *Ramparts* and that I was to see demonstrated over and over again after I joined the Black Panther Party was *courage*. I had called it "crazy," as people often do to explain away things they do not understand. I don't mean the courage "to stand up and be counted," or even the courage it takes to face certain death. I speak of that revolutionary courage it takes to pick up a gun with which to oppose the oppressor of one's people. That's a different kind of courage.

Oppressed people, Fanon points out, kill each other all the time. A glance through any black newspaper will prove that black people in America kill each other with regularity. This is the internalized violence of oppressed people. Angered by the misery of their lives but cowed by the overt superior might of the oppressor, the oppressed people shrink from striking out at the true objects of their hostility and strike instead at their more defenseless brothers and sisters near at hand. Somehow this seems safer, less fraught with dire consequences, as though one is less dead when shot down by one's brother than when shot down by the oppressor. It is merely criminal to take up arms against one's brother, but to step outside the vicious circle of the internalized violence of the oppressed and take up arms against the oppressor is to step outside of life itself, to step outside of the structure of this world, to enter, almost alone, the no-man's-land of revolution.

Huey P. Newton took that step. For the motto of the Black Panther Party he chose a quotation from Mao Tse-tung's *Little Red Book*: "We are advo-cates of the abolition of war; we do not want war; but war can only be abol-ished through war; and in order to get rid of the gun it is necessary to pick up the gun."

The Courage to Kill: Meeting the Panthers

When I decided to join the Black Panther Party, the only hang-up I had was with its name. I was still clinging to my conviction that we owed it to Malcolm to pick up where he left off. To me, this meant building the organization that he had started. Picking up where Malcolm left off, however, had different meanings for different people. For cats like Marvin Jackmon, for instance, it meant returning to the ranks of Elijah Muhammad's Nation of Islam, denouncing Malcolm as a heretic and pledging loyalty to Elijah, all in Malcolm's name. For Huey, it meant implementing the program that Malcolm advocated. When that became clear to me, I knew what Huey P. Newton was all about.

For the revolutionary black youth of today, time starts moving with the coming of Malcolm X. Before Malcolm, time stands still, going down in frozen steps into the depths of the stagnation of slavery. Malcolm talked shit, and talking shit is the iron in a young nigger's blood. Malcolm mastered language and used it as a sword to slash his way through the veil of lies that for four hundred years gave the white man the power of the word. Through the breach in the veil, Malcolm saw all the way to national liberation, and he showed us the rainbow and the golden pot at its end. Inside the golden pot, Malcolm told us, was the tool of liberation. Huey P. Newton, one of the millions of black people who listened to Malcolm, lifted the golden lid off the pot and blindly, trusting Malcolm, stuck his hand inside and grasped the tool. When he withdrew his hand and looked to see what he held, he saw the gun, cold in its metal and implacable in its message: Death-Life, Liberty or Death, mastered by a black hand at last! Huey P. Newton is the ideological descendant, heir, and successor of Malcolm X. Malcolm prophesied the coming of the gun to the black liberation struggle. Huey P. Newton picked up the gun and pulled the trigger, freeing the genie of black revolutionary violence in Babylon.

The genie of black revolutionary violence is here, and it says that the oppressor has no rights that the oppressed are bound to respect. The genie also has a question for white Americans: Which side do you choose? Do you side with the oppressor or with the oppressed? The time for decision is upon you. The cities of America have tested the first flames of revolution. But a hotter fire rages in the hearts of black people today: total liberty for black people or total destruction for America.

The prospects, I confess, do not look promising. Besides being a dumb nation, America is mad with white racism. Whom the gods would destroy, they first make mad. Perhaps America has been mad far too long to make any talk of sanity relevant now. But there is a choice and it will be made, by

The Courage to Kill: Meeting the Panthers

decision or indecision, by action or inaction, by commission or omission. Black people have made their choice; a revolutionary generation that has the temerity to say to America that Huey P. Newton must be set free, also invested with the courage to kill, pins its hopes on the revolutionary's faith and says, with Che: "Wherever death may surprise us, it will be welcome, provided that this, our battle cry, reach some receptive ear, that another hand reach out to pick up weapons, and that other fighting men come forward to intone our funeral dirge with the staccato of machine guns and new cries of battle and victory."

Kick Out the Jams, Motherfucker!

The *"Total Assault on the Culture!"* issue of the Warren-Forest Sun *was one of our last formal actions in Detroit—a few weeks later we packed up everything and moved en masse to Ann Arbor after the Board of Zoning Appeals and the Detroit Police Department combined to run us out of town. We couldn't get any printers in the state to touch our paper, but the* Sun *continued as a mimeographed free street paper, and our total assault program intensified with the crazed rock and roll guerrilla warfare we were waging with the MC5 and the Up. In Ann Arbor we copped two big houses next door to each other and had everybody in one place for once—both the bands were right there with us, our operation tightened up, and we had the added advantage of a greatly increased base in the mushrooming freek community as well as a much smaller and much less dangerous police presence to deal with. We suffered a serious setback in June with the arrest and incarceration (under a $20,000 bond!) of brother Pun Plamondon by narcotics officers from Traverse City, who snatched up Pun on a charge of giving away one roach three months earlier and held him until the middle of September. They came with a warrant for Gary Grimshaw too, but Grim beat it out of town before they could get to him and remained underground until the summer of 1970, when we finally got him back.*

During the summer of 1968, we started running into more and more hassles with the police and other mother-country authorities as we refined our total assault campaign and struck deep into the heart of honkie-land with the MC5 night after night. We followed the principle of relying on the people and using the police assaults on our activities to expose the repressive nature of the mother-country system while building up our base of support among the people and constantly increasing the scope of our operation. Every two weeks I would write up what had happened for the Fifth Estate *and try to interpret it so our people could understand what was going down. What follows is a series of "Rock & Roll Dope" columns,* Sun *stories, and press releases from that period, which culminated in the band's ill-fated recording contract with Elektra Records and the founding of the White Panther Party after Pun was finally released from jail in September. We didn't understand exactly what was happening when all this shit was going down, because there'd never been anything like it before, but the increasing harassment and repression we were encountering in Michigan, coupled with the massive police stomp scene we experienced in Chicago at the "Festival of Life" in August (where the 5 was the only band to show up for the opening of the celebration), pushed us out of our hippie dropout peace-love consciousness and into an explicitly political-radical stance which grew directly out of our experience that summer.*

More than anything else, we learned that our culture itself represented a political *threat to the established order, and that* any action that has a political consequence is finally a political action. *The result was that we became* consciously *political, and the White Panther Party became the formal expression of our new consciousness. But the documents tell the story better than I can do it now. . . .*

1. ROCK & ROLL DOPE #2

A strange polarization (or maybe it's a natural one) seems to be happening with rock and roll fans right now, with white teenage audiences turning toward either total freek scenes or greasy reactionary hostility when confronted with the revolutionary guerrilla tactics of the MC5. Three incidents in the last three weeks illustrate the current scene.

Friday, May 31, the MC5 was booked into the Grosse Pointe Hideout, an eastside teen dance joint. We produced our own handbill for the gig, a Grimshaw design featuring a picture of the band naked against a backwards American flag and the legend, "Break through American stasis with the MC5!" Four hundred kids jammed into the tiny hall to dig the 5—the Hideout's biggest crowd in months—and were first treated to two fine sets by a new Detroit trio, the 3rd Power. MC5 drummer Dennis Thompson and I stepped outside during the second set for a smoke and met some young brothers in the parking lot next to the building. The young rock and roll addicts produced some grass, and while the sacrament was being ingested, two rent-a-cops strolled onto the scene, surprising one brother with a joint in his hand.

The two associate pigs called their big brothers, the Harper Woods Police, who appeared on the scene some thirty minutes later to see ten freeks lounging against some cars under the watchful eye of the hired guards. Questioning followed, and the ten were told that we'd be taken into the station and booked on marijuana charges. I asked that the rest of the band be informed of this revolting development, which was done, and band members Wayne Kramer, Fred Smith, Rob Tyner, and Michael Davis, along with equipment manager Ron Levine, immediately burst upon the scene woofing at the cops and demanding an explanation, causing enough confusion that those in the assembled company who were holding the sacrament could get rid of it. Then the real shit went down.

Levine hassled the pigs until he was sure that subtle persuasion wouldn't work (resulting in one cop pushing Fred Smith in the chest and threatening him with a whupping) and then returned to the club, turned on the PA, and informed the eager MC5 fans that me and Dennis were getting popped in the parking lot and that the only way they'd get to hear the band would be to surround the cops outside and *make* them give us up. While Levine was rapping, the club's manager had a cop drag him off the stage and then closed the doors, trapping the kids inside. He was sufficiently shook up, however, to persuade the police to release the suspects, except the one who was caught with the weed and the two under-seventeen "juveniles" who were taken in and released later to the custody of their parents. By this time Kramer was on the phone contacting LEMAR attorney Bill Segesta, and Dennis and I were threatening the clumsy suburban police with false-arrest suits and extralegal retaliation.

When the band, intact once again, returned inside to play their first set, the crowd went into a spontaneous scream scene to welcome them back to reality. And when Tyner kicked off the first tune with "KICK OUT THE JAMS, MOTHERFUCKER!" it was madness all the way, with wild applause and jubilation before and after every jam.

The Hideout's manager was furious by this time, but he was caught in a simple capitalist contradiction: he couldn't move to censure the band because the paying customers were behind us all the way, and they were a lot more than "paying customers" by that time too—they were *ready!* When the chomp shut off the electricity during the closing energy-orgy "Black to Comm" to get the band off the stage, the crowd joined Fred Smith in chanting *"Power! Power! Power!"* until the juice came back on and the music soared to its natural climax.

The next Friday the MC5 joined the Cream for the Grande[*] Ballroom show. Excited by the success of the previous week's guerrilla theater event, the band planned to burn an American flag on stage during "Comm" to make their feelings about this shit clear once and for all. Ballroom owner Russ Gibb got wind of the scheme through the underground grapevine and left word for us that if any burning went on, he would have the police sent in to capture the ragged symbol and take appropriate action against the traitors, so we came up with a last-minute alternative plan and went ahead as scheduled.

[*]Prounounced "Gran-dee"

Kick Out the Jams, Motherfucker!

When the 5 danced on stage for the second set of the evening, the temperature in the Grande was over 100 degrees on Detroit's first boiling weekend, and there were close to two thousand sweating rock and roll fiends packed onto the floor, lured into action by the promise of the Cream *and* the dangerous hometown favorites the Motor City 5. Again a huge cheer erupted from the crowd when Tyner announced his purpose, and the people carried on like that all through the explosive hour-and-fifteen-minute set in the sweltering heat.

As "Black to Comm" built to a screaming frenzy, equipment manager Steve "the Hawk" Harnadek introduced a tattered plastic-nylon American flag onto the stage, and he and Tyner ripped it to shreds while the audience freeked and cheered. The symbol of imperialism and oppression demolished, Tyner then struggled back to his feet and raised his freek flag high: a 4' x 5' red banner inscribed with a rampant marijuana leaf, green in a yellow circle, in the upper-left-hand corner, and the word FREEK scrawled across the body of the banner. Again the freeks in the crowd—most everybody—screamed and cheered in a burst of patriotic frenzy. Simultaneously, the specter of madman Jerry Younkins (of the Magic Veil Light Company) materialized on stage with the band, fully naked, and the cheers turned to gasps of disbelief as Younkins settled cross-legged on the lip of the stage and began chanting "OM" into a microphone, merging his spectral voice with the distant humming "OM" of the amplifiers. The music faded into history and the band stumbled off stage, leaving the people stretched out on the floor in exhausted awe.

Repercussions followed immediately: Ballroom manager Larry Feldmann was called on the carpet by building owner Gabe Glantz and was summarily discharged from his duties. Glantz also started ranting at Tyner and me about "committing crimes" and "obscenity" and "is that what you think of your country?", threatening us with eternal expulsion from the Grande, which was pretty comical, all in all. The next day Feldmann reported scores of phone calls from irate parents, we were lectured by our booking agent, and everyone involved in this heinous caper was met with frosty silence from "Uncle Russ" Gibb, who carried on as usual about freedom, dope, police brutality, and rock and roll music on his radio show. Only the Cream, it seemed, were unaffected by the whole scene, as they didn't bother to show up at the Ballroom until the beginning of their set, which began half an hour after the 5 had left the stage and continued until they collapsed from the heat an hour later.

The following Wednesday, June 12, we traveled to Lansing for a gig at the (yes!) Lansing Hullabaloo. Our audience seemed at first to be 90% grease and maybe 10% freeks, and there was a lot of hostility generated throughout the three sets by young, short-haired anti freek forces in front of the stage. Warned by our booking agent against any un-American and/or obscene acts, the 5 merely kicked out the jams throughout the evening and into the last set, holding their rap down to their usual blasphemous cant and raunchy music. Kramer periodically swept the front row of the audience with his guitar held like a gatling gun to cool the greasers out a little bit, the band worked its magic on the rest of the kids to warm them up, and by "Comm" time the polarization was down to maybe 50-50. As "Comm" climbed to its howling climax, the freeks in the crowd began howling with the music and waving their arms in the air, flashing a two-handed "V" and jumping up and down with glee.

The converted shorthairs joined them, while the most hostile elements raised their middle fingers in the traditional gesture of rejection and disgust. The Tommy James fans made menacing gestures toward the stage, and one of their number responded to direct musical attacks by Wayne and me (I was playing saxophone) by climbing up on the stage and shaking his fist in our faces. He was pulled back down by his friends in the audience before anything physical could jump off, and it seemed that a lot more V's went up, starting with those on the bandstand, as the music decrescendoed into the everlasting cosmic drone of the assembled Sunns. Rumors of toughs waiting outside filled the dressing room as the freeks rushed to join the band backstage, but the purity and accuracy of the music as usual equalized the bad vibes, and we rolled home unscathed.

As everyone wonders what will happen next, the MC5 is girding its loins and readying some new tactics. Our itinerary for the rest of June includes dates at the Sarnia (Ontario) Arena, the Birmingham-Bloomfield Teen Center, the Michigan State Fairgrounds, the Benton Harbor Scene, the Grande again, with Blue Cheer and the Psychedelic Stooges, a return to the Grosse Pointe Hideout, the Jackson Hullabaloo, and the Greenlawn Grove in Romulus. The MC5 will also headline the first Saugatuck Pop Festival on the Fourth of July, with the Amboy Dukes, the Rationals, the Up and the Flock. See you on the street!

2. ROCK & ROLL DOPE #3

I promised you when I started this column that I'd take you behind the scenes in the rock and roll industry so you can see what your bands have to go through just to be able to do their thing on stage, and ever since I said that, so many weird things have been going on that I hardly know where to start. But the Grande Ballroom scene last Sunday was probably the weirdest of all, and if you just paid your money and sat and waited for the MC5 that night, you deserve to know that it wasn't the band that kept you waiting in all that heat—it was the creeps who took your money. Be advised.

The MC5's freek scene at the Grande June 7 (as reported in the last issue of the *Fifth Estate)* has touched off a string of creep scenes with club owners around Michigan, starting at—you guessed it—the Grande itself. So far only two major incidents have gone down, but if they're any indication, you can look for a lot more shit to hit before the fan is shut off.

There was a long line of rock and roll fiends waiting outside the Grande last Sunday night (June 23) when the 5 arrived at 6:45 to play the evening concert with Blue Cheer and the Psychedelic Stooges. The band was ready to kick 'em out like never before, but we were accosted by greedhead Glantz before we could even get to the dressing room and warned not to use any "dirty words," no nakedness on stage, and no incidents with the American flag, "real or simulated," during the band's performance.

We told him that we just wanted to do our show and make the people happy, but he didn't seem to be too convinced and ended up threatening to turn off the power onstage (I guess he meant the electricity) at the first sign of any obscene language or any other tomfoolery. At this point I overheard the conversation and told Glantz to go away and count his money and leave us alone, whereupon he ordered us not to play the evening's performance and stomped off to the ticket office.

I had been talking with reinstated Ballroom manager Larry Feldmann about the order of performance when the business with Glantz went down, and Feldmann immediately got on the phone to Russ Gibb, who made it down to the Ballroom with his attorney to see what was going on.

Meanwhile the Stooges were forced into starting the first set—by this time it was maybe 8 o'clock and getting hotter all the time, and the Grande was still filling up with easily recognized MC5 addicts who began to wonder what the fuck was going on when the Stooges finished and the record player went back on.

No MC5. The band was in the downstairs office with Gibb and his attorney, talking it out. Management contended that for the band to go on stage and kick out the jams would result in an immediate bust—if not of the band then of the Ballroom itself. The band maintained that Glantz had created the whole affair (there were supposed to be three detectives there ready to snatch the Grande's license if any more un-American shit went down) because he wanted to get rid of us, and that if we couldn't do our show at the Grande without being submitted to prior censorship then the place might as well be closed, because we didn't even want to play there anyway if we couldn't play what the people wanted to hear.

This argument went back and forth for more than an hour, with us trying to get Gibb to understand the significance of what he was trying to do—to see that the Grande had been created by the people as a place where they could get down and do what they wanted to do, and that he was actually destroying the beautiful thing that has been built up in that place over a period of two whole years—but nothing was happening toward a resolution until a brother named Gut, one of Blue Cheer's managers and a righteous freek himself, came into the office and told Russ that his band couldn't go on unless the MC5 went on, "because the audience wants to hear the MC5 and won't settle for anything less."

Upstairs the people were chanting "MC5! MC5!" and getting madder and madder by the minute. By this time it was way after 9 o'clock, and Russ was still wondering what to do. He had to be reminded that the MC5 had opened the Ballroom with him, had worked there for free to get it off the ground, was still working for peanuts ($125 a night!), our light show (Trans-Love Lights) was getting $25 a night for six people working five hours, Grimshaw still gets $25 a poster, the Ballroom is packed every weekend now, and it's bad enough that the people who were supposed to share in the profits don't share in them. But now if people can't talk like they want and do what they want there, then the whole thing just ain't worth it. He had to be reminded that we hadn't started the bullshit about the "dirty words"—we *always* used them—but Glantz had, and that all we wanted to do was play our music or else go home—forever. And take the light show, the Trans-Love store, and everything else we'd brought—including the Ballroom's *mojo*—with us.

The act of workers' solidarity by Blue Cheer seemed to've been the decisive factor in the whole thing—after all, they were the "big band from out of town" and we were just the local chumps—and at 9:30 Russ decided that the MC5 had better go on, even though his attorney advised him that the police could easily lift his license if they wanted to. (We had tried to tell him that they could lift his license anytime *anyway*, if they really wanted to, but that only scared him even more.) Actually, the final decision was made when Glantz appeared in the office and told Russ that the alleged defectives were no longer upstairs. That was all he needed to get out of this mess.

Kick Out the Jams, Motherfucker!

When the MC5 charged on stage, the crowd exploded. The audience, estimated at some fifteen hundred on a Sunday evening (the biggest Sunday-night crowd in the Grande's history), knew something funny was going on, but they'd waited for the 5 through a whole hour of silence as the heat level in the place mounted, and when Wayne Kramer kicked off the show with Ted Taylor's old smoker "Ramblin' Rose," they were really ready for it. And when Tyner leaped out and hollered "KICK OUT THE JAMS, *MOTHERFUCKER!*" everything broke loose. Hands shot up in the air and never came down as the band truly kicked out the motherfucking *jams*.

Our original plan had called for an hour-and-a-half set of new and established material which the band had been working on all week so the people would get as much music as they deserved for being so far out, but four songs into the set, Gibb sent word to the stage that his attorney (who had been "monitoring" the show) had to leave, and that the band would have only one more piece to play.

I relayed the message to Tyner in between tunes, and Tyner *blew up*. He ran the whole thing down to the people, telling them it was "another bullshit Grande Ballroom scene" and that they were being cheated out of what they were supposed to get because of the creeps who ran the place. The freeks in the audience started hollering for Gibb's ass. "Kick out Uncle Russ, motherfucker!" someone shouted from the middle of the room. Tyner was furious, looking around the place for Gibb, and finally spotting him, screamed into the microphone: "One of these days / and it won't be long / you'll look for *me* mister / and down the road I'll go . . . cuz I *believe*, to my *soul*," and everybody knew exactly what was being said. Tyner directed all his energy at that one spot and made Gibb leave the room, only to send his flunkies back to shut off the electricity to the stage before the music could be fully realized. But things won't be the same there for quite some time now, and the people are getting hip to what the real deal is.

On Tuesday (June 25) our booking agent called to report that the job at the Jackson Hullabaloo for that night had been cancelled when the local police read about the flag scene in the *Fifth Estate* and took the Hullabaloo manager to the city council, which threatened to rip up his license if he allowed the MC5 to play his club. The club owner was pissed off because he knew he would've made some money, but he was so thoroughly convinced that the police would pull a stomp scene that he broke his contract with the band and canceled.

Other club owners around the state are beginning to realize that it would be in their best interest to hire the MC5, no matter what they think of our show. The people who have to have the music are the ones who control the scene anyway, once you let these club owners know what they have to do to keep you coming back. Let them know, and we'll see you then. Kick out the jams!

3. Rock & Roll Dope #4

In the past two weeks since the last issue of this paper, a bunch of new developments have taken place. Almost every job for the MC5 brings a new and different creep scene into being.

At a Wednesday-night job in Tecumseh, Michigan, at the local teen center, Wayne Kramer ripped a pair of pants early in the second set and went off to change them. Later in the same set, he ripped the second pair, this time accidentally exposing his genitals to the tender crowd. Everybody just laughed, Wayne changed pants again, and the music went on to its natural conclusion with no untoward incidents.

We didn't think anything about it until the musicians' union and our booking agent both sounded us out about it, claiming that some insane Tecumseh woman had written them a letter describing the accidents in lurid detail, among other claims asserting that Kramer had purposefully "exposed his personal self" to the shame and dismay of the teenage audience. The union made vague threats about "expelling" the band, and so on, but so far nothing has been done about the matter. Honk on!

The Fourth of July brought the Saugatuck Pop Festival on the west coast of Michigan, and it showed how beautiful things can be if you keep the police off the grounds and out of the people's way. There wasn't any creep scene at all, but there *was* a huge freek scene that warmed the hearts of everyone there.

The festival was presented by a Detroit promoter as an attempt at a local version of last summer's incredible Monterey Pop Festival, and it featured, among other things, a totally pigless performance area. With no police on hand and a cooled-out promoter, the band's natural chemistry was free to work its magic on the crowd without interruption, and we were surprised to see a whole raft of MC5 addicts from around Detroit out there in the sun waiting to get down with us. They called for the MC5 all throughout the afternoon, and their chant spread through the whole crowd—over three thousand people, a mixture of stoned-out freeks and drunken frats—until the 5 took over the stage from the mighty Up around 9 o'clock.

It was the Fourth of July, and everybody was ready to get down. The people cheered their asses off all the way through the show, and when Rob

Tyner called out "Kick Out the Jams, Motherfucker!" so many arms shot into the air that it looked like the end of World War II. By the time "I Believe to My Soul" surged into "Black to Comm" the whole crowd was on its feet, screaming and waving their arms in the free night air for the 5 to bring it all back home NOW!

The band was ready for them. Kramer had had his Stratocaster decorated for the Independence Day festivities: red-and-white striped body, blue pick-guard with white stars, and tiny flags hanging from the tuning pegs: truly an all-American guitar and fit to be freed. The energy built up and up and up until people couldn't stand it any longer, and finally Kramer stepped back, unstrapped his star-spangled Fender, and began smashing the motherfucker against the top of the stage, on his speaker cabinets, on the floor and every solid object in sight, smashing it to smithereens. Dennis kicked his drums over and they sprawled across the stage. Fred Smith lunged for his speakers and leaped on them, kicking over everything in his path. The people hollered and screamed and surged at the stage as the band staggered off, and the energy level in that field got so high, it was almost unbelievable. That's rock and roll, people, the way it's supposed to be!

On Monday night we returned to the Grosse Pointe Hideout, where the weird shit had started the first of June, and it just got weirder. The fire marshal was there, the Harper Woods pigs were there, the same rent-a-cops were there, the owner was running around in circles from all the hassles he was getting, our booking agent was there trying to cool him out, and the kids were there too—in full force. The fire marshal made the Hideout management turn people away and keep all the lights on during the band's two shows. The police lined up outside the doors complete with riot helmets and grim pig faces, the heat mounted, and the manager kept breaking in with announcements all during the show: "Please stop smoking grass in the girls' toilet," "You'll all have to fold your chairs up and sit on the floor," "No dancing," "No obscenity or they'll take our license away," "You've got to turn down, it's too loud for the fire marshal," and so on. Warnings and threats cluttered up the air, but the kids were right there and they didn't wanna hear no shit—they wanted the 5 and nobody was gonna stop them from getting it.

Kramer kicked off the second set with "Ramblin' Rose," and when it came time for the magic moment, Tyner strolled onstage and told the kids he needed some help. Everybody knows what comes next, he said, and we need your help in calling off the tune because we've been hearing all kinds of weird stuff about it. Everybody knows it's all right, don't you now

(YEAH!!), so I'll just count three and then we can get this old tune started. But everybody's gotta do it together, or else it won't be any good.

Tyner counted to three—the whole band counted—and then the place exploded: "KICK OUT THE JAMS, MOTHERFUCKER!!" four hundred deranged teenage freeks screamed in unison, and the band *got down*. The pigs were infuriated, but they would've had to've arrested everybody in the place on the phony rap to get *anyone*. And after that it was freedom all the way.

Tuesday night we rested. Wednesday night we drove down the street to the new Ann Arbor Hullabaloo for a scheduled gig, our first in Ann Arbor. Everything was cool while the first band, the Sugar Cube from Dearborn, did their thing, although we noticed that there were a lot more rent-a-cops than you would expect in such a small place. The shit hit the fan when the MC5 started playing: by the time "Borderline" was over, at the start of the first set, the squad cars had started to turn into the parking lot, and before five tunes had been played, there were seven squad cars, at least two cars full of detectives, Lt. Staudemire of the Narcotics Bureau, and other assorted officials hassling the club owners about the "noise." When the band refused to alter their amplifier settings and protested what we saw as an attempt at artistic censorship (something to be expected since Staudemire's seizure of the flick *Flaming Creatures* the year before), the police moved inside and shut off the power to the stage.

The enraged audience started yelling with the band: "Power! Power!! Power!!!" But the electricity stayed shut off. Tyner started running it to the people, without benefit of a microphone, about the pigs and how they're trying to cut off our power on all levels, and how we have to go ahead for ourselves and do it however we can, *together*. The saxophones and gongs and bells and drums came out as Tyner was rapping, and then everyone merged in a nonelectric orgy of music and feeling, chanting and dancing around and jumping up and down with glee in the face of the outraged police bandits. A police official in a white shirt with gold trim—obviously a lieutenant or an inspector or something—came up to the stand where I was playing my saxophone and handed me . . . a ticket! A ticket! For having "a noisy band"! I took one look at it and then tore it up in his face and went on playing like everybody else. We kept on until everybody was tired out, for another hour at least, and then packed up and went home, grinning.

We matched our magic against the pigs' brute tactics, and it worked— any respect any of the people there might have had for "law and order" as represented by the Ann Arbor police just disappeared, and their futile tricks

Kick Out the Jams, Motherfucker!

were exposed to the light. All this bullshit was totally unnecessary—we just wanted to do our thing and let the people do their thing with us, but the police just won't let that happen without trying to stomp us out one way or the other. The old people seem to want to pretend that the world is just the way it is on television and that other peoples' lives have no validity. They don't want people to know—or if they know they don't want it acknowledged—that men have cocks in their pants, that women have tits and cunts under their clothes, that people can say and do whatever they want as long as it doesn't *hurt* anyone else, that their guns and orders and phony laws and honkie power are all bullshit, that there's no way any common words can "shock" and "corrupt" kids who are really hip to the whole deal and who are instead shocked and hurt by the insane disregard for human freedom that the police and other authorities practice as a matter of course.

People are getting hip to all of the old people's lies and perversions, and they aren't gonna stand for it much longer. We sure aren't!

4. ROCK & ROLL DOPE #5
Poet/MC5 manager John Sinclair and MC5 guitarist Fred Smith were brutally assaulted, beaten, Maced, and arrested by members of the National Security Police, the Oakland County Sheriff's Department, and the Michigan State Police while performing at a teen club in Oakland County last Tuesday, July 23. The two victims of police terrorism were charged with "assault and battery on a police officer" and are presently free on $2,500 bond pending their pretrial examination September 12. The charge is a high misdemeanor and carries a maximum two-year sentence.

The scene took place at the Loft, a converted barn in Leonard, Michigan, where the MC5 had been contracted to play a dance job. What follows is Sinclair's account of the incident.

We had worked at the Loft twice before in the past month or so and never had any trouble out there, just great crowds of high-energy kids, you know? But the club owner had bounced two checks on us for a total of almost $400, and we were going to take him to court and also try to get his place closed down by the musicians' union because he had beat a bunch of other bands around here too. This dude, Harold Boumer, his name is, called our booking agent and told him that he wanted to settle everything with the bands he had ripped off, and he set up this date for us to go out there the 23rd and play again in exchange for all the money he owed us plus 40 percent of the gate for that night. We didn't want to hang him up anyway—we just wanted to get our money—and we dug playing out there because the kids are so far out. So we agreed to the deal and drove out there the night of the 23rd.

When we arrived, and before we could even get out of the van, we were confronted by this rent-a-pig named Capt. Kenneth Osborne and told that he didn't want us to play "that song with motherfucker in it." I told him that he didn't have anything to do with our show and that if he wanted to say anything to us he could say it through the manager, because we worked for him and not for some rent-a-cop, right? This pig had given me some shit the last time we were there anyway, about moving the equipment out faster or something, and I didn't wanna talk to him at all.

When we went inside, Boumer ran up to me and apologized for Osborne's actions. I told him that we would just as soon turn around and go back home if there was gonna be any funny shit, because we were giving this dude a break in the first place and we didn't haveta stand for any of his pig's madness. Boumer said never mind Osborne, just play the gig, and I'll pay you your money afterwards. Well, we were supposed to get it all in front, but he only had $100 and he said he'd give us all the money that came in that night, because he had a full house and he knew he'd have all the money by the end of the night.

So I took the $100 and the band went on stage to kick 'em out. The 5 smoked through the first three tunes and were really flyin', but this chomp Osborne had the house announcer stop the show "because of obscenity." We asked the people if we should stop, explaining that we had come to play for them and we'd let *them* decide what we should do. They told us to keep on playing, but we decided to play one more thing and then go right into "Comm" so we could get out of there in case this pig started any shit. We didn't wanna stop right there because we didn't wanna leave the people with nothing, you know, but on the other hand we knew this fool was crazy and we wanted to get outa there as soon as we could.

Meanwhile the rent-a-pigs apparently called the Oakland County Sheriff's Department and told them there was a "riot" going on because we wouldn't stop playing and were "inciting the kids to violence." That was a bunch of bullshit, because what we actually told them was that there were a bunch of crooks running this place and they should never come back because the owners were cheating the bands and pulling funny shit all the time, right? Anyway, Osborne and his flunkies blockaded all the exits to the place so nobody could get out—evidently they figured they'd better *have* a riot situation when the real pigs got there or else they wouldn't look so good, you know?

Kick Out the Jams, Motherfucker!

I had the equipment dudes pack up all the shit and take it out to the van, and got the band changed and all the guitars and shit packed up and sent them downstairs to wait for me. I didn't know that the doors were shut off or anything. I was up there checking the stage area to make sure all the equipment was taken care of and checking the dressing room and all the stuff you have to do before you leave, so you won't leave anything behind, you dig? I'm standing by the stage when this dude Boumer comes up to talk to me. We sit down on the edge of the stage, and he apologizes again for the police and asks me to bring the equipment back up so we can play another set and he won't have to give the kids their money back! *What?* I couldn't believe what I was hearing! I told Boumer he was stone crazy if he thought we'd stick around that madhouse for another minute—we wanted our money and if he didn't want to pay it right there, we'd see his ass in court. I also told him that we were going to put the word out on him to all the bands in the area, and that I was going to get the musicians' union to shut him down for good—not just because he beat us out of the money but because he couldn't control his police and he was cheating all the people who went there.

Boumer kept talking, mumbling on about a second set and dodging the money issue, when all of a sudden the rent-a-pigs and a bunch of uniformed police in riot gear appeared at the top of the stairs and started marching over to where we were sitting. Osborne was in the lead, and he came up to me and started oinking in my face.

"Sinclair, get out of here!" Osborne grunted. I asked him what the fuck he was talking about, looking at Boumer expecting him to explain what was happening. Osborne oinked again: "I told you to get out of here—*now!*" I told him I couldn't possibly leave until I got the money. Osborne and his partner snatched me by the arms and yanked me up, but I broke free for a minute and smashed him in the face. Then the whole force jumped on me and beat me down to the ground. Osborne squatted on top of me and kept hitting me in the face while the other porkers were smashing me with nightsticks, blackjacks, fists, and booted feet while I tried to cover up my head and genitals. During the melee, an Oakland County pig, Donald Gilbert, badge number 81, squirted me in the face with Mace, and another pig handcuffed me.

There were still about a hundred to a hundred and fifty kids on the dance floor, standing around in horror as this bloody scene flashed into action in front of their eyes. They were just as dumbfounded as I was, and it all happened so fast that it must've been hard to believe that it was really happening. Girls were screaming and crying, everybody was trying to figure out what was happening, and by this time the pigs were beating on Fred Smith, who had run up from downstairs to help me when he heard all the noise. Fred leaped into the pile of pigs who were beating on me, but two of them pulled him off and beat his ass with clubs. They subdued both of us, got us handcuffed, and dragged us over into the corner before they started clearing the room. A bunch of sisters, righteous MC5 addicts who came to all our gigs, came over and started wiping the blood off of us, but the pigs grabbed them and pushed them down the stairs. One sister had a camera and I told her to get pictures of this shit, but the pigs spotted her and grabbed her camera and broke it before they pushed her down the stairs too. They beat up quite a few kids and shoved everybody else out of the place, finally letting the doors be opened so people could leave.

They took me and Fred and put us in the car and started for the county jail in Pontiac, with about fifteen cars full of kids following them all the way. One kid tried to set the place on fire, he was so mad! When we got to the jail, they booked us on charges of assault and battery on a police officer, but when Osborne tried to sign the arrest warrant, the desk sergeant told him that he wasn't a police officer and couldn't legally arrest us. So one of the Oakland County pigs stepped up and said he'd sign it—that was Gilbert, the one who Maced me, right? All these kids were milling around outside, but the deputies all went outside and started threatening them, so they yelled up to us one more time and then pulled up. When we got in court to be arraigned the next morning, some other pig's name was on one of the warrants too. We pleaded not guilty and our people posted $2,500 bond for each of us, which was the highest bond the judge could set, you dig? We're gonna fight this as hard as we can, and then we're gonna sue all these creeps. These fascist dogs are trying to stomp *all* of us out—DON'T LET THEM DO IT!

5. Flash! MC5 Arrested in Ann Arbor for Playing Free Music in the Parks—Charged with Disturbing the Peace!

Rob Tyner, Wayne Kramer, Fred Smith, Michael Davis, and Dennis Thompson—the MC5—were arrested by Ann Arbor police Friday, July 26, and charged with "disturbing the peace" and "disorderly person" as a result of a free concert they played in West Park last Sunday (July 21). The band posted $125 apiece in bond money and will face the charges in Ann Arbor Municipal Court next Monday.

The warrants stem from complaints by neighbors of the park about the alleged "noise" created by the band last Sunday. The principal complainant,

Johannah Lemble, whose name appears on the warrant, charges the brothers individually with "creating an unreasonable and disturbing noise" and with "disturbing the peace" by being "loud and boisterous" in violation of city ordinances. Mrs. Lemble and her husband are active in the local chapter of the John Birch Society.

What went down is this: last summer, free rock and roll concerts were held in West Park every Sunday through the middle of September. Ron Miller, bassist for the now-defunct Seventh Seal (who is presently in Europe with his new band, the Pigfuckers), would pay the city the $10 permit fee every week, and the Seal as well as bands like the Prime Movers, Charles Moore's avant jazz group, Billy C and the Sunshine, the Up, the Roscoe Mitchell Unit from Chicago, and the Grateful Dead when they were in town took the stand every Sunday afternoon to play for the people in the sun.

Ron Levine and I applied for a permit to use the West Park bandshell some weeks ago and received a flat refusal. Apparently a new ordinance was passed during the winter months outlawing amplified music in the parks, so there couldn't be any more concerts, but we knew the people had to have the music. So after giving the matter some serious consideration, including consultations with attorneys and local heads, we decided to just go down to the park and set up and kick out the jams, since the parks belong to the people anyway. Two Sundays ago (July 14, Bastille Day), the MC5 set up in the picnic shelter in the park and played for about an hour for a great audience of freeks and black people from the neighborhood. The police showed up to douse it out, but the mayor was on the set and held them off until he could talk to us and see what the deal was. I told him that these were important community functions and that we were donating our time and energy to the people so they could have some of the free music they need to survive, and he said he could dig it. He promised to get in touch with us during the week, but two weeks went by with no word from the city, so we decided to make it on down to the park again and rent our own generator so we could play in the bandshell this time. Word of mouth spread the news, and a large, grooving audience was there on Sunday ready for it.

The Up played the first set and smoked all the way through, with a short interruption when two uniformed patrolmen mounted the stage in an attempted suppression scene. Lt. Staudemire emerged from out of the audience, where he had been digging the proceedings, and cooled out the lowly patrolmen. He explained to us that the neighbors around the park were complaining about the noise and could we turn down a little to see if that would work out? Sure. The Up did the rest of their set, and the 5 followed them for an hour with the dangerous jams the people love to hear. When it came time for the magic moment Tyner got the whole crowd to scream "KICK OUT THE JAMS, MOTHERFUCKER!" with him, *three times*, and you could hear it all over town. This brought down the self-righteous wrath of the Birchers in the neighborhood, however, and led to the arrests of Friday.

There was no music in the park this weekend, but one interesting development has taken place: city officials have expressed a further desire to meet with the Trans-Love freeks this next week to see what can be worked out in terms of free outdoor concerts somewhere else around town. Meanwhile petitions are being circulated among Ann Arbor's hip citizenry to demonstrate the need and support for such concerts.

More News as it happens.

FLASH! More news happened. On Sunday, July 28, as this *Sun* was going to press, the MC5 was traveling to Oakland University to play in a benefit for ALSAC (Aid to Leukemia-Stricken American Children) when we were met by our equipment crew, who had gone on ahead of us. They reported that they'd been at the gig and were greeted by more than ten Oakland County Sheriff's cars. Apparently the legendary Oakland pigs had warrants for Rob Tyner, Mike Davis, and Wayne Kramer dating back to 1966 and were determined to cash them in at Oakland U when we showed for the benefit. We just turned around and beat it back home.

Stay tuned to the paper radio for more news as it happens.

6. Flash! Free Music in Gallup Park Every Sunday! Rock and Roll Emerges Triumphant!

Following the tremendous success of the first Gallup Park free concert last Sunday, local heads and rock and roll maniacs will carry on on the banks of the Huron River every Sunday afternoon until further notice. Last Sunday's concert, which featured the Black & Black Boo Funny Music Band, Billy C and his Killer Blues Band, and the dangerous MC5, went off with no trouble whatsoever, just groovy vibes all around. No cops appeared all afternoon during the three-hour fest, but Lt. Staudemire could be seen with his lady, digging the music quietly from the riverbank on an unofficial off-duty visit. Staudemire, who has emerged as the city's liaison man with the hip community, was instrumental in freeing the Gallup Park location for the free concerts, working in conjunction with Asst. City Administrator Don Borut and Trans-Love heads to find a home for the music the people need.

The Gallup Park location, on the south bank of the Huron River near the corner of Geddes Road and Fuller Road, is so isolated from complaining neighbors that the city called us up Monday morning to see if there had been a concert the day before! When they realized that everything is cool, they granted permission to use the park whenever necessary, which is pretty incredible.

This Sunday's concert will start at 3 P.M. and will feature the Wilson Mower Pursuit and the MC5, with other community bands due to fall by for a set. Bands who want to do their thing for the people are urged to bring out their equipment and kick out the jams with us Sunday afternoon. The concerts are presented by the people for the people—free for all!

7. Flash! MC5 Set to Kick Off Festival of Life! Yippie!

The long-awaited Youth International Party Festival of Life will surge into being Sunday, August 25, in Chicago's Lincoln Park, with a kickoff concert by Ann Arbor's own MC5!

The *Sun* talked with YIP music coordinator Ed Sanders in New York yesterday and got the latest dope on the already legendary Festival of Life (YIPPIE! CHICAGO! AUGUST 25–30!), which will be held in the Windy City at the same time as the Democratic Party National Death Convention. The YIPPIE Festival will be built around the music of the international youth culture—rock and roll!—and will also focus on two other favorite activities of *Sun* readers—dope and fucking in the streets. In addition to other YIPPIE! activities, Sanders has scheduled rock and roll concerts for each afternoon and evening of the festival, which should create enough energy to keep everyone going through the less musical aspects of the program. Other Ann Arbor bands scheduled to play during the Festival of Life are the mighty Up, the Psychedelic Stooges, and probably some others.

In his telephone interview with the *Sun*, Sanders (who is otherwise known as editor-publisher of *Fuck You: A Magazine of the Arts* and founder of the fuck-rock group the Fugs) revealed that the festival will indeed be held and that the city of Chicago is expected to grant the Lincoln Park permit with the added stipulation that the festival area is to be left alone by Chicago police, who will be busy enough carrying out their assignments at the Democratic Death Convention and trying to keep the candidates from getting murdered on stage in the Amphitheatre.

Sanders and other festival organizers will be flying to Chicago from New York today to confer with city officials and straighten out this permit business as well as other necessary arrangements. Sanders is confident that the city *will* grant the permit, although they may hold off until the last minute to spread further confusion among the millions of young people who are planning to make it to the YIP gathering. The festival will go on no matter what the city says, according to Sanders, and the officials are well aware of that fact by now.

With all the other shit going down in Chicago during the week, it should be kept in mind that the Festival of Life is *not* a "protest" of any kind but is a presentation of an alternative way of life which will provide a sharp contrast to the way of death epitomized by the Democratic Death Convention. Drunken delegates in restrictive ugly suits and ties and wingtip shoes courting plastic prostitutes will be exposed as the pigs they are by hordes of long-haired freeks in brilliant colors and free bodies dancing to rock and roll, smoking dope, and fucking in the streets and parks of Chicago. For many Americans this will be their first contact with the dynamic Life Culture, as legions of maniacs explode into the streets and onto the sacrosanct TV screens of America, bringing some free life to the nightly death news reports. And unlike the Democrat scene, no one will be barred from the YIP Convention, and we damn sure don't need "15,000 police, troops, and FBI personnel" to keep us from murdering each other while we do *our* thing! Kick out the Jams! YIPPIE!

8. Flash! Elektra Buys 5!
In a lightning move, Elektra Records signed the MC5 and the Stooges to long-term recording contracts in New York September 26.

The move was engineered by Elektra's publicity director, the young Danny Fields, who flew out to hear the bands last weekend at the Grande Ballroom in Detroit during the 5's triumphant return to their old stomping ground for the first time since they were barred after the Blue Cheer hassle June 26, and at the Union Ballroom in Ann Arbor, where the 5 and the Stooges were playing a benefit for the Children's Community School.

The 5's first album will be recorded live at the Grande Ballroom late this month, probably on Wednesday and Thursday the 30th and 31st— Zenta New Year! The two dances will be free for all the people in the community so all the freeks who have supported the band all these years can get on the record too.

A single release is tentatively scheduled for early December, with the album itself due for release around Christmas or early January. A 16-mm color film of the 5 will be produced by Trans-Love Energies for release with the single, which will undoubtedly be "Kick Out the Jams" and probably "Motor City Is Burning."

Kick Out the Jams, Motherfucker!

After the recording is completed, the 5 will travel to the East Coast, where they will be introduced to the people of New York with a free concert at the Fillmore East right around Christmas. Motor City maniacs who can make it are invited to come out with us and show our brothers and sisters out there what we're doing here. Rock and Roll!

POSTSCRIPT

Everybody knows what happened in Chicago that August, but it had a tremendous effect on us because the suppression of the Festival of Life confirmed our suspicions that it was our culture which was really dangerous as a political force in this place. We had been following all the developments in the radical movement throughout the summer, looking for some way to tie what we were doing with rock and roll maniacs into the political scene, but of all the individuals and groups which were active at the time, only the Yippies and the Black Panther Party seemed to understand the revolutionary potential of the people we were working with. We were knocked out by the total assault tactics of the Yippies, and we were even more impressed with the propaganda and the actions of the Black Panther Party, particularly the way Eldridge Cleaver related to our culture and Bobby Seale and Huey P. Newton called for "mother-country radicals" to organize their own people into a conscious political force. Pun got out of jail in September ready for action, and we started talking about how we might be able to hook up with these people so we could give the kids who related to the band a clearer political focus for their wild, inarticulate, antiauthoritarian thrust. When we got the recording contract with Elektra, we knew that we would be able to reach a whole lot more kids all over the country with our total assault propaganda, and the time seemed absolutely perfect for putting our ideas into action. Immediately after we recorded the album at the Grande Ballroom, we announced the formation of the White Panther Party, which we conceived as "an arm of the Youth International Party," and from that point on, the MC5 was identified as "the White Panther band." We had thousands of White Panther buttons printed up, which we would pass out at all our gigs, and we started rapping about "revolution" before every show in an attempt to put the music and the "cultural revolution" into an explicitly political context. I stopped writing so much about our exploits with the police and started trying to sum up our experience and make some sense out of it so the kids who followed the band could see that they were part of a revolutionary movement and not just "rock and roll fans." The "White Panther State/meant" is the first of those documents.

Portrait of a Young Man Trying to Eat the Sun (the life, legend, & mysterious death of d. a. levy)

I THOUGHT THEY WERE WIND *chimes / in the streets at night / with my young eyes / i looked to the east / and the distant ringing of ghost ponies / rose from the ground / Ponies Ponies Ponies . . . / (the young horse becomes / a funny sounding word) / i looked to the east / seeking buddhas to justify those bells / weeping in the darkness / The underground horses are rising / Cherokee, Delaware Huron / we will return your land to you / to purify the land with their tears / The underground horses are rising / to tell their fathers / in the streets at night / the bells of Cherokee ponies are weeping.*

—d. a. levy, "The Bells of the Cherokee Ponies"

There never has been enough to go around. The right questions aren't asked. Meaningful answers never appear. Even words get lost. Lost words, wild words without a home wander endlessly for years, sometimes lifetimes, before they resurface and make an impression on a public of a different time. This is the story of d. a. levy, a controversial master of those wild words, who like an American Rimbaud, remains a major poetic influence long after he stopped writing. Just over 25 years ago, at the height of his powers, he was arrested and put on trial in his hometown basically for the crime of being a poet, and then after almost two years of extreme harassment by authorities and adulation by local hippies, either committed suicide or, as a number of his friends still believe, was murdered just as he was starting to be recognized as one of the major voices of his generation.

levy's story is a modern *Roshamon*, filled with contradictions illuminating the dichotomies that appear on the path of the warrior-artist. His story, with a hint of some deep dark secret hiding in the shadows of counterculture history, is either about the corruption of a society destroying an artist, a kamikaze in search of immortality, a young mystic seeking spiritual transcendence, a tragic leader of a failed revolution, or a major undiscovered post-beat literary movement. Unquestionably it is the story of not only a genuine counterculture hero, but a major unrecognized artistic influence of the times, certainly a martyr on a collision course with his environment. Color it gray, set it in a very volatile-repressive time, and you have Cleveland, Ohio, in the heart of the '60s.

Somehow in all of the hoopla of the times d. a. levy got lost. levy, little l, big force, had an extraordinarily large and powerful body of work that was published in underground presses and literary magazines all over America by the time he died at 26 years old. Working literally without the benefit of money, but with a driven energy and focus, he almost single-handedly created a scene in Cleveland, producing hundreds of chapbooks, pamphlets, magazines, and newspapers on a small hand letterpress his brother found for him. From 1963 to 1968 his *Seven Flowers Press, The Marrahwanna Quarterly*, and *The Buddhist Third Class Junkmail Oracle* published scores of poets, writers, and artists, as well as many then relatively unknowns from all over the underground press circuit, such as Charles Bukowski, R. Crumb, and Ed Sanders, to name but a few who went on to achieve acclaim.

Maybe if he had gotten out of Cleveland he wouldn't have been swallowed by the times, his reputation and work would have already transcended the boundaries of a regional underground cult figure. Or perhaps 26 years after this ancient young buddha-head supposedly opened his third eye by cradling a .22 rifle between his legs and (as the story has been constructed and embellished) totally relaxing all the muscles in his body before triggering the blast with his own bare toes, he, like most poets who refused the sanctuary of academia, might still have trouble getting paid for his work in the world. But without question, two and a half decades after his still controversial death in a poorly furnished one-bedroom apartment in East Cleveland, his voice rings as strong and true as it did after he was charged with obscenity by a grand jury in November 1966, and arrested and put on trial in March of the following year for contributing to the delinquency of minors (for reading poetry in a church-sponsored coffeehouse in front of two high school kids).

A scrawny, shy, half-Jewish kid (on his father's side) who embraced Buddhism, levy grew up in a working-class neighborhood around 65th and Lorain, innocuously went through Rhodes High, collected stamps, and Bs, and was remembered simply enough in his senior yearbook as, "Hey you." He was advised to go to college, but joined the Navy instead. Seven months later, however, he was back, discharged for "manic depressive tendencies." Much later, after he was arrested, he wrote, "Unable to find competent leaders or teachers, unable to discover intelligent persons in places of authority, unable to find anything other than pseudo-christian bigotry and ignorance—i decided to commit suicide at 17. Changed my mind at the last minute and started to read everything and wrote poems." Hundreds and hundreds of poems. Poems about Cleveland, poems about growing up in America, poems about transcending his own consciousness, in the midst of the overwhelming chaos of the times.

Dropping his name to the lower case, Darryl Allen Levy first became known to other Cleveland poets as d. a. levy while he was living in a grungy garret overlooking the Cuyahoga River and the Cleveland Flats, with poet Russell Salomon. There, looking out on the sprawling industrial waste, he started composing hundreds of long, rambling odes filled with references to the arcane Eastern religious texts he devoured, mixed with the language of the streets he walked.

"We were going to make Cleveland famous," Salomon recalled. "I was in college—we met at a poetry reading. He was still living with his folks in Avon, 30 miles west of the city, on Lake Erie. He'd already been around—hitched to Mexico twice and San Francisco once. He was very impressed with the way they treated poets in Mexico. Not like here. He moved in with me—I had this five room place on the bluffs overlooking the Flats—it had a great picturesque view of downtown and the polluted river running through it. The woman underneath us had something like forty cats, so it always smelled. levy used the living room. I told him as long he produced he could stay (rent free). He was writing *Cleveland Undercovers* at the time. And I was writing another long poem called *Descent into Cleveland*. I remember he always used to say, 'When I finish writing this poem I'm gonna kill myself.' But he was so busy he always got hooked into something else. He was about to throw away *Cleveland Undercovers*—he couldn't make it work, so I said 'lemme take a look at it.' I reversed stanzas two and three, really nothing else, and he said, 'that's it.' And it was, except for a few minor things."

He reminded Salomon a lot "of that character Japhy Ryder (based on Gary Snyder) in Kerouac's *Dharma Bums*. He was really into Eastern mysticism, totally against drugs. He advocated using 'em because he advocated the freedom to do so.

"That stuff about him being a manic depressive was absolute bullshit. He joined the Navy, he made a mistake. It took him about a month to decide he wanted out—so he faked being crazy. The highs and lows he went through, naturally come with what he was doing. But make no mistake, he did it! He was planning to do it, and he did it! It was an explanation point. He was hooked into Rimbaud, the idea that he just walked away

Portrait of a Young Man Trying to Eat the Sun

from poetry. He was going to stick around Cleveland and make a point.
Like the Indians, he tied himself to a spear. He was a spiritual being—
believed in the continuance of the soul—he was ready to leave his body
behind . . . I got drafted in '65, so I missed that real heavy time there. I
came home in '69, and asked, 'where's levy?' I wasn't surprised by what he
did, but fuck . . . fuck . . ."

The heavy time, the years '66, '67 & '68 were also the days of "*the Mimeo
Revolution*," according to what that infamous dirty old man, Charles
Bukowski, told me in 1988. Like levy in Cleveland, Bukowski was cranking
out literary mags in Los Angeles, like *Laugh Literary* and *Humping Guns*.
"We were the Meat poets, baby. We got down to the bone. levy, Doug
Blazek in Chicago, *Ole*, some pretty good writing came out of that period.
Not like today. Too many out there with too little to say."

Bukowski, whose fame in America (because of *Barfly*) was just starting to
catch up with what the Europeans had known since the mid '70s, took a long
pause when thinking back, and in his inimitable Fieldsian twang reflected,
"levy published a little book of mine, *The Genius of The Crowd*, but I never
really knew him except through his letters and the mags. I guess I played the
Ezra Pound role of the group, and had some luck. levy didn't have the luck,
it's a terrible shame, he was just starting to develop. What killed him? I don't
know, baby. Cleveland, the cops, lack of money, I don't know . . . He should
have held on."

From the start his mimeoed poetry and underground newspaper stuck in
the craw of the sleepy city fathers. He used language that Cleveland had
never seen in print before. Like *The Chicago Seed, The Berkeley Barb, RAT,
The Great Speckled Bird, The San Francisco Oracle*, and dozens and dozens
of others across America, Cleveland was under attack from the counterculture and levy assaulted his city saying *fuck you* with both political & artistic
purpose. He went directly after the real estate interests, after the police and
the narcs, and became the most visible figure in Cleveland's burgeoning
youth culture. He and his friends (D. R Wagner, rjs, T. L. Kryss, Kent Taylor,
John Scott, Geoffrey Cook, Steve Ferguson, Franklin Oskinski . . .) became
known as *The Underground Thought Patrol*. Like a matador taunting a bull,
they took the battle straight to the enemy, and probably were initially surprised, like most kids who joined "The Revolution," by the ferocity and dirty
tactics of the establishment's response to their public undressing.

On December 1, 1966, James Lowell's Asphodel Bookshop was raided
downtown, on the excuse of a search for non-existent drugs. The Asphodel,
the sole outlet for levy's publications at the time, was a nationally known

literary mecca, filled with crates of levy's material, to be used as evidence for the obscenity indictments of levy and Lowell, and were never returned, even after the charges were dropped. Nor was the mimeo machine, levy's printing press, the voice of the underground that the police took from his apartment. To this day, Lowell can barely speak about it, or about levy. "What would be the point?" he asks. "It's too late now." An attitude a number of people who were part of the scene embrace, with a full house of emotions, ranging the obvious blocking of an open wound to the blood flowing out in anger.

Allen Ginsberg, who came to Cleveland with The Fugs for a benefit for levy at Case Western Reserve University, recalled, "[levy] seemed to be very much affected by the put down and the jailing or arrest and trial. It was obviously a trumped up charge. Cleveland was a very heavy police state in a very literal way. The Cleveland police were notorious for their outrageousness and for their storm trooper tactics." Now in California, but then a Chicago poet and one of levy's closest allies, Doug Blazek concurred: "The Cleveland police made the Chicago police look like Boy Scouts."

"It was a grim scene," according to cartoonist R. Crumb, who came to Cleveland from Philadelphia when he was nineteen, because he had a friend who dropped out of Kent State and invited him to share an apartment. "What did I know? Cleveland was a place where a lot of sensitive middle class kids—outcasts—committed suicide, and this was before LSD! The scene was filled with depression, a beatnik kind of sensibility. I remember getting giggly on grass once, and they all turned on me." Crumb met levy in '66, and thought he "took everything to heart—took it all so personal. And there was no relief. They lived like the ultimate cool thing to do was blow yourself away. He was very depressed and didn't seem to have a sense of humor. I remember the last time I saw the guy his face was just contorted in pain."

"He was one of the funniest men I ever met," D. R. Wagner disagreed. Now a visual artist who makes miniature tapestries, Wagner was one of levy's closest friends, and with his magazine *Runcible Spoon*, one of the major forces, along with levy, in the concrete poetry movement. "(levy) published a very early book of Ed Sanders called *King Lord Queen Freak* when Sanders was doing *Fuck You: A Magazine of the Arts*. It was one of the first things that Sanders ever published. levy was inspired, I think, by Tuli Kupferberg, the poet and composer and co-founder of The Fugs. Tuli's *Birth Press* published many things (probably the best known was *1001 Ways to Beat the Draft)* . . . all silliness . . . using a lot of linocuts. I think levy liked the style of those things." levy was supposedly getting out of Cleveland, coming to California to stay with Wagner, when his body was found.

Tony Walsh, a Cleveland lawyer and friend who lived around the corner from levy when he died, and made the funeral arrangements, always saw a bit of Woody Allen in levy. "He was very funny despite what was happening to him." Walsh laughed. "I have his ashes, actually half his ashes. His family has half—I have half. Sometimes I wonder which half. He laughed again.

"The Noel Coward of Bohemia," Tuli Kupferberg, couldn't find anything particularly funny about dying in Cleveland. "Cleveland has always been known as one of the assholes of America—levy could've been one of a dozen different guys living in the Village, but for some reason he had to live in Cleveland."

Poet Kent Taylor, who like many Cleveland poets now lives in California, was married to levy's cousin, so besides being in the inner circle, was family. "He didn't really function well outside of Cleveland. We went to the west coast together, but he couldn't wait to get back. He always went back to Cleveland like it was a magnet, even though it was an evil magnet for him."

When he did get out on occasion, and came to New York, he stayed with poets Carol Berge or the late Allen Katzman. In Berge's opinion, "levy *was* suicidal—he saw the world as it really *is* at a too early age," she recalled years later, from her studio in Santa Fe. "He was truly looking for a way to accept the way things were." Later, after she thought about it, she exploded. "Why bring him up? Let him rest! There's no immortality! levy quit: I'll never forgive him for that!"

Woodstock Renaissance man and lead Fug Ed Sanders, who had a close correspondence with levy during those years, still feels the loss after all this time. "For me personally, it was the first time that a death created a wound. d. a. was intense—he didn't want to be driven out of Cleveland like Hart Crane. The whole thing, cleaning up the poets, the reason they wanted to get rid of them was a real estate scam as I understand it. They were going to re-develop the area: Its origin was greed."

"That whole corner (115th & Euclid) mysteriously burnt down a couple of years later," according to Franklin Osinski, another Cleveland poet who lives in Northern California. "levy wrote about the scheme to take over University Circle in the early issues of *The Buddhist Third Class Junkmail Oracle*. He named names, and laid out their plan, which was to get many of these homes that were dilapidated, properties that were run down and getting them real cheap. Whether arson was involved, who knows? But in that winter of '66–'67 was when the kids got wind of it. That summer, what the media called *The Summer of Love*, all the teenagers moved into the scene. At that point the city fathers and authorities saw it as rather dangerous. They didn't want their daughters being involved. They evidently saw levy as dangerous. As a dangerous type of youth leader."

Steve Ferguson, who along with R.J. Sigmund (rjs) found the body, and took over publishing *The Oracle* after the poet's death, said that levy was not unaware of his effect on people. "He knew he was the great Poo-Bah, and he wore the crown."

John Scott, a man with a definite sense of black humor, held the unofficial title of levy's bodyguard. "My job," he laughed from Northern California, "was to protect him from himself. You've got to understand, I wasn't a poet, I was a hard-core greaser. levy was my best friend, for a lot of different reasons. He was a good person, a genuinely good person. But he was not happy in the world. He'd always been suicidal—he knew his perceptions were different from other people. One time I asked him, 'What if there isn't anything else, what if this is it?' He got quiet then retreated. If there was somewhere else to go, he was going."

Scott was in the workhouse when levy died, doing thirty to life. Set up, he claimed, by an informer inside the group. "The scene was totally littered with informers." Scott did two years. When they arrested him he said they told him, "It isn't you we want, it's d.a. If you *make* d. a. you're home free." Scott said, "In my opinion he did not want to die. From what I heard he borrowed suitcases from Cuz (levy's real cousin). You don't pack your bags for that kind of journey. The only ones who might really know are Ferguson and rjs." Scott laughed again. "I guess I'm the only one with an airtight alibi."

Besides Scott, a number of others including levy, and then rjs, did time for contributing to the delinquency of minors. Many years later, George Moscarino, the former assistant county prosecutor who handled the case, told *Cleveland Magazine*, "Most of our information came from young people who were arrested, they gave us information about their friends."

While most American kids grew up playing *Cowboys & Indians*, in the late '60s that game had evolved to *Feds & Heads*. In Cleveland it was known as *Cowboys & Poets*. Though there's little doubt that poets would become ignored in any other time frame, this was not any other time frame. It was the heartbeat of the counterculture, the beginning of the psychedelic revolution, and the kids poured out of Cleveland Heights and Shaker Heights to be a part of it. Mostly they congregated on Euclid Avenue, just east of 115th Street, on the edge of University Circle. They poured into Adele's Bar, Stanley

Heilburn's head shop, the Coffee House, and Sam Dogan's Bookspot, where levy helped stock the shelves with poetry, and where he met Mara (Dagmar) Ferek.

Fresh out of Cleveland Heights High, with the looks of a working-class Madonna, she immediately got caught up in the scene on Euclid. She was across the street at Adele's, then went into the bookstore. "I had no idea he was a poet," she told filmmaker Kon Petrochuck, while he was researching his award-winning levy documentary (*If I Scratch, If I Write*). "He acted like he was doing me a favor by going out with me," she recalled. "I wasn't attracted to him as a poet, he could've been a garbage man. I was attracted to him as a person. It was kinda funny, he really pushed the idea he was a poet all the time. I didn't really care, but he sure did! He was a scrawny little dude [5 foot 7, 117 lbs.]. He looked like he needed a mother. Poet in search of a mother," she laughs. "I don't know, he was used to people running after him. I didn't understand it. I mean, I was at an age where I was trying to find something better than the other people, ya know, my parents, etc., had gotten. And I was smoking and hanging around with interesting people, like musicians and stuff. I guess he just kinda fit in that whole thing."

Steve Ferguson, a writer and graphic artist who still lives in Cleveland, recalled, "levy was very concerned with style to the point of being silly. When too many people started growing their hair long he thought it didn't mean anything anymore. Truthfully, he wanted the kids to all go back home and let us create our own alternate universe." The *us*, which became known as *The Underground Thought Patrol*, was not really a gang. "It wasn't that tight-knit, it was really an island of lost souls," Ferguson explained. "As for drugs, levy was a wimp. Couldn't drink more than a beer, beer and a half—couldn't do more than a couple of tokes. At his worst he was paranoid. He was crippled by the police attention. He had become the scapegoat for every Cleveland daughter that ran away during that period."

According to Jonathan Dworkin, levy's first lawyer, "Drugs to levy was an experience, not a way of life—they were an attempt to find a real error through trial and error."

Dagmar recalled, "People wanted to think he was into drugs because a lot of people were into drugs, and they felt they should get him on something—so the police tried that, but he was almost anti-drugs. The only thing he was into was hallucinogenics—and he used those very sparingly. He believed people should consciously put themselves in a place and then come back consciously, rather than take a drug, get somewhere, and then not know how you got there or how you got back. Because some people didn't come back! That was one of the things about his whole interest in Buddhism; it taught consciousness expansion that was a gradual process. It was kinda like a school—you get so far and you learn where you're at, and then you come back, and then you go back out again."

"It all started over the existence of God," according to Ferguson. "That single fact has more to do with levy's suicide than anything else. It's my speculation that because he was a heavy student of Buddhism, which believes there's no God, he had no support system to fall back on. I think he was trying to work his way through a puzzle and just ran short of hope."

"He was like Jeremiah," Ed Sanders whispered. "He had the potential to be a great religious writer—a prophet. No doubt, he could have developed . . . The weight of all his different hats crushed him before he even reached Shelley's age."

Going through his archives, while being interviewed by a young reporter and photographer from *Interview* (about the regrouping of The Fugs' *Star Peace*, the full-scale American opera he wrote and recorded with them, and of course those not so peaceful days of *Auld Lang Hippie*) Sanders pulls a letter from levy (Jan 12, 1965) out of his files.

    dear ed,

    i have no words . . . when on paper i think perhaps i am losing everything or leaving everything via negation behind . . . with drugs . . . but i don't take drugs anymore or haven't for a long time . . . someone told me (a Philly chick) "last year the world turned over . . . its doing it again this year." what the fuck is happening? all i know is its a mind thing from one end of this country to the other . . . perhaps the whole world but i am not in contact with any place other than the US. A voice in mexico city, also trembling from canada. How much do you know? Have you read "The Sacred Mushroom—Key to the Door of Eternity." It is a bridy murphy thing in egypt. How aware are you of yr Egyptianish poems? I am not finished with the book but turn on like a light bulb cosmic high when reading it.

    last night (No time anymore) went to adele's bar with friends . . . i drank a little ginger ale and got euphorically drunk . . . maintained high degree of control knew where

people were in their heads (or felt consciously where they
were at—could not definitely pin it down)

I still get paranoid . . . the cia fbi are going to get me for
something (burn this letter) many people here becoming very
sensitive perceptive.

Geoffrey Cook, who considered himself best friends with levy in 1966,
recalled the pressure of the times. "He was a big fish in Cleveland. He was
a writer of place like [Robinson] Jeffers. He was living his life at a brutal
speed. He wasn't getting enough food, his teeth were falling out—he virtually broke down when he went through the legal trouble. He closed himself
off—his friends stopped being his intellectual and artistic peers—rjs was
one of those friends. He got paranoid about myself and Kent Taylor. I don't
know why. There was a lot of stress on all of us. A lot of us moved out to the
West Coast. The rumor was that he was dying—no doubt, the Assistant D.A.
murdered levy by hounding him to the point of suicide."

But the lead prosecutor in the levy trial, George Moscarino, had a hard
time remembering the facts in the case, and questioned why the story was
at all "newsworthy." In a telephone interview from his law office in Cleveland he continually suggested that it would be more appropriate to talk to
the levy defense attorney, Gerald Gold. Speaking in rapid-fire staccato
burst, Moscarino said, "I don't know where the story is, though I do
remember he was a poet. And I do remember it was a cult time and it was
a time of a lot of drugs. Whether he was involved in other things or not I
don't know, although the court records don't show that. So the man's dead,
may he rest in peace. I believe he's dead, isn't he? I remember that there
were people who liked his poetry, and I did not judge his poetry. I'm a lit-
erate person and—talk to Gerry [Gold], he'll tell you a little about my reputation. But I just don't have a reputation for keeping files or remembering
what happened that far back."

He certainly couldn't remember who James Lowell was, or that his
books and levy's press were confiscated and not returned. "He probably
never asked for it," Moscarino insisted. "There are ways to get property
back. I don't think there's a story there. If he didn't ask for his property back,
he didn't get it, right. That's not newsworthy. If he had had me as his lawyer,
if his bookstore was raided, if it was illegal or even done legally, I'd have
gotten his books back for him.

"I'll tell you one thing," Moscarino said, "I didn't have anything to do
with that, I'm sure of that!"

Portrait of a Young Man Trying to Eat the Sun

Gerald Gold put it somewhat differently: "George Moscarino now defends criminal cases, big ones, for one of the biggest law firms in the country. He was the prosecutor then, and he was out to get d. a."

In November 1966, a grand Jury indicted levy on charges of obscenity. He found out about the charges in the morning newspaper delivered to his door, but before police arrived that morning he had moved into John Scott's apartment in Collinwood and went into hiding. Shortly afterward, on December 1, Lt. Burt Miller, the head of the Cleveland Narcotics Bureau, raided Lowell's bookstore, and along with levy's material confiscated the dangerous works of Robert Duncan. On January 16, 1967, levy wrote in *The Oracle*, "to prevent the police from further harassment, I have decided to turn myself in."

In court the next day, the prosecutor told the Judge, "this man is not eligible for personal bond. He has evaded police since his indictment, which has been publicized for two weeks. He has no job and no address."

"You write poetry . . . do you sell it?" Municipal Court Judge Frank Celebrezze asked.

"I sell poetry for eighty-nine cents a day," levy replied, though it wasn't quite that much, and he lived on Dagmar's waitress earnings.

"Bail of twenty-five hundred dollars is not excessive for a great poet. Maybe you should charge more than eighty-nine cents," proclaimed the Judge.

A New York art dealer posted levy's bond, and he was set free after spending about a week in the county jail. By this time his conflicts with the police were rapidly turning him into a public figure, by far the major spokesman in the city for the counterculture. Both newspapers, the *Plain Dealer* and the *Cleveland Press*, called for an end to what they saw as harassment, and they devoted generous space to each new development in the drama, thus helping to build the legend and enhance his reputation.

In response to his arrest, he wrote in *The Oracle*, "Not having money, the only escape mechanism i have had is very much an American tradition. i started swearing at each new piece of bigoted flotsam as it drifted past my mind's eye—the city administration often appeared. So now my freedom of expression is being stomped on by the local psychotics, who in their stupidity, think i am a leader, and in their own personal blind hallucinations have visualized me as having a following.

"With their cooperation i have been turned into a symbol, and i sincerely hope that in their incompetence they do not attempt to turn me into a martyr. This is absurd and i certainly don't want to be reborn into a world

Portrait of a Young Man Trying to Eat the Sun

in which everyone is attempting to imitate a foul-mouthed saint. The city is working overtime to turn me into a myth, i haven't been able to reach them yet, perhaps you can—Think nice thoughts about them, perhaps they will grow into civilized human beings."

Just about two months later, on March 28, 1967, levy was arrested at his apartment and charged with five counts of contributing to the delinquency of minors—specifically for reading so-called obscene poetry at *The Gate*, in the presence of a seventeen-year-old boy who levy had published (a political poem praising the Hough riots of the previous summer), and a fifteen-year-old girl. The boy's parents had found a copy of the *Marrahwanna Quarterly* in their son's room and complained to the police. The girl, once levy's friend, had agreed to carry a tape recorder into the reading and turn over the tape to the police.

Gerald Gold, who took over as levy's lawyer, recalled, "Of course d. a. was trying to get publicity. You have remember, things were far more puritanical then—in fact—one of the exhibits we had for the trial, which never took place by the way, was a painting from the May Show at the Cleveland Art Museum which had FUCK written in it. If it's the contemporary standard in the Art Museum, why isn't it the contemporary standard in the coffee houses?

"What had happened—you know d. a. never had any money, people were raising money to defend him—he was a scared, little worried guy, and we really had a deal where he didn't have to go to the can. He was scared to death of going to jail. And you know, dealing in a Catholic-in-more-than-a-religious-sense community, we were kind of concerned that he was going to go to jail. So we finally made a deal, which in retrospect I'm sorry we made. Because I think as long as he had this fight he probably would have stayed alive. I think he just kinda got tired. He had nothing to live for, not love or hate, so he did himself in apparently.

"We always told him we thought we could win the case, but it was a case we could have lost too. You know, in Juvenile Court, it was and still is a pretty vague thing what is contributing the delinquency of a minor. So that was the end of it—I don't think I ever saw him again." On February 20,1968, levy pled "no contest" to the charges of contributing, in return for probation and the dropping of the obscenity counts. He paid a $200 fine and walked out, but according to his friends, he was never the same again.

levy and his friends had always been considered justifiably paranoid— according to Dagmar, levy was followed, their apartment was secretly searched, and an informer had infiltrated their inner group—identity unknown. And levy's friends, who to start hadn't always been close to each other, drew even farther apart in their growing paranoia over who the informer was.

According to Franklin Osinski, "Cleveland had a 'Subversive Squad,' going back to the McCarthy era. What they were doing mainly was breaking and entering and going through everybody's files. Today we can almost laugh about it, but back then it was like being under the thumb of the Nazis."

A law student then, Tony Walsh lived around the corner from levy. "East Cleveland," he explained, "was very diversified—mostly blacks down by Euclid, whites up in the hills in Forest Hills, which is divided by Forest Hills Park, a John D. Rockefeller estate. So when the Hough riots broke out levy was in the middle of it, trying to bring it together."

Suburban Monastery Death Poem described levy's reaction to the riots:

> Only 10 blocks away / buildings burned—perhaps burning now / the August night broken by sniper fire, / Police men bleeding in the streets / A sniper surrenders (perhaps out of ammunition) / Gun jammed? / some sed he was framed in a doorway / like a picture—his hands in the air / when they shot him—/ Only 10 blocks away / from my quiet apartment / with its green ceramic Buddhas / & science fiction books, / unread skin magazines to be / cut up / for collages / only 10 blocks away / from my total helplessness / from my boredom enforced by the state / they are looting stores / trying to get televisions / so they can watch the riots / on the 11 pm news.

Kent Taylor recalled that levy told him he used to walk around the city "with a lethal dose of Seconal" on him at all times. When he managed to duck out of the chaos he had partly created, levy would disappear and crash at Jonathan Dworkin's house. "He'd come over for a night or two—for something to eat or some money for paper—he always left something in return—a picture, a poem, and then he went back to it."

"One day he told me 'There's no security in the universe,' " Steve Ferguson recalled. "When I replied, 'Oh?' levy said, 'Well don't tell anybody I said it—if the wrong people hear it I'm in trouble.' "

Dagmar recalled, "sometimes he'd go off on a tangent for consciousness' sake. He was a real manic-depressive—one minute he'd be up, the next he was down. He rarely ever lived in the middle. He seemed to like being up or down. He seemed to like being down as much as he liked being up. Ya know, he just liked having to say, 'I feel this and I feel this.' He wasn't able to appreciate any kind of a middle place where things are just OK. To him that wasn't good enough, things had to be very intense one way or the other. It had to be very good or bad, right or wrong. He didn't appreciate the subtle values in-between that I think life is all about. He felt uncomfortable unless he could label and place it. And basically he only had these two places he could put 'em."

"She lived with him, but she didn't really know him," says John Scott about the four-year relationship that like almost everything else in levy's life was starting to fall apart. Ed Sanders, among others, tried to get levy to come to Chicago for the 1968 Democratic Convention, but levy, though he supplied Sanders with a poem to be read, turned down the invitation. In a long, soul-wrenching letter to D. R. Wagner, at the end of that summer, he explained:

> i said "no" i wanted to go but inside i said "no" and Mara [Dagmar] said "please no" but she would let me do whatever i had to do—she is a "good person" & she loves me & she is growing & we are sometimes very close—but'. . . me & mara . . . Will we grow into each other? i still want someone else—will she become someone else? perhaps i need two women? or three? or none—i couldn't go to CHICAGO!
>
> so im stuck here til at least Dec-Jan most likely spring—& then? do i come to calif to die? to live? to grow? to rest? some good things could come together for me here & i don t want to make a wrong decision—i don't want to jump the gun—& despite what you may think—i am not hung up on cleveland & haven't been for a while—it is just that i am here & i can get things done here.

According to Osinski, besides everything else, politics was starting to take its toll on levy's poetry too, and on top of that he felt his angels—the voices that guided him—had deserted him. This was not a metaphor.

"levy, Scott and I were driving to Toronto one time in the middle of a blizzard," Wagner recalled. "I think Cuz was there too. And levy turns and says to me [about the telepathy], 'You don't really believe this shit, do you?' And I said, 'No, I don't.' He said, 'That's too bad, because you're the best transmitter of us all. Listen.' Then he and Scott proceeded to have a conversation, back and forth between themselves, without opening their mouths or saying a word, and I heard every word they were saying in my head."

That fall levy was invited to Madison, Wisconsin, by Dave (not D. R.) Wagner and Morris Edelson, to be Poet in Residence at the new Free University. As Edelson described it, in the introduction to *The Madison Poets,* this "little, black-haired, pasty-faced, nervous intense fellow showed up in black pants, white socks, black shoes and one of those long-sleeved Hawaiian patterned shirts that recall the Greyhound Bus depot rather than the beach at Waikiki. He was coping with his Lenny Brucehood, having been busted for purveying porn to adolescents via his poems and newspaper and being generally harassed in Cleveland to the point of extreme nervous exhaustion. . . . He visited my class, we set some poetry readings up for him, and we set up his Free University meeting room and place. I think the title of the class we said he would teach was Tantric Yoga—no it was Telepathic Communication. His class was a tremendous success, though not because of his lecturing on telepathy. The first night he was supposed to teach it, we walked with him to the student union building. The room was on the first floor and was packed with people sitting quietly, intently, as though waiting for Jim Jones to pass the Kool-Aid. Either it was that or something else, something false, levy picked up on, and he simply walked on by the door and out the side. I thought for moment of going in and telling them it was another no-show, but what the hell. We all walked over to the 602 Club and then thought no more about it, until Ann Krooth told me that levy's class was one of the most successful in all the Free University. People there assumed he was trying to reach them telepathically, and many of them heard him, as they sat there, meditating in the classroom. That class went on for several months after levy had returned to Cleveland—months after levy was no longer alive."

Many years later, trying to make sense of what happened, Dagmar remembered, "When he came back [from Madison] he got an invitation to be a poet in residence over there, and he also got an invitation to be a poet in residence at Athens too. And I don't understand whether it bummed him out or not. It seems he had gotten to where he had wanted to be, but then within twenty-four hours he was dead. I wasn't there, I don't know what happened, but it was certainly bizarre—he spent a lot of energy saying no one appreciated him, and then people are saying come to our place, and he decides to do himself in.

"I had gotten to the point where I was really not happy with our relationship, and when he came back I wasn't living at our place anymore.

Portrait of a Young Man Trying to Eat the Sun

People say that he said goodbye to them. I don't know what happened. If he committed suicide I certainly blame his friends as much as himself, because they thought it was so cool that he wanted to commit suicide—he talked about it all the time and they thought it was funny. I don't find anything funny about it. I couldn't understand why they thought that was so neat. I still don't understand what happened to this day." As to whether she actually believed he committed suicide, her voice broke, "So it would seem! The police didn't investigate it that much. I don't know if it was a very obvious case or they didn't want to bother."

Though he has no evidence that would hold up in a court of law, Osinski told filmmaker Petrochuck, "My personal feeling based upon what I know is that levy was murdered. Another possibility," he said, was that "[levy] may have allowed himself to be murdered, realizing that he was not going to be permitted to leave [Cleveland]. There were quite a few people really who did not want to see him leave. Like if you're a young child, and your father leaves, you'd be very upset. You want him to stay. And in a sense, when he talked of leaving Cleveland it was the same thing. Many of us did not want him to leave. It was kind of like having a loved one take off and leave and not come back for a long time, or not come back at all."

For years the rumor has circulated that levy was getting out of Cleveland, that he had made up his mind to go to California, get a job at the post office, move in with D. R. Wagner, and that he had sent Wagner a postcard letting him know he was on the way. He supposedly spent the last three or four weeks of his life methodically preparing to leave, although it wasn't clear where he was going. He gave a reading at Antioch College, came back, deliberately picked a fight with Dagmar to drive her out, then after she was gone, went and got her, brought her back to the apartment, asked her to stay with him, and told her he realized his "poetry wasn't where it was at—it's just another game," and threw all his unpublished manuscripts in the incinerator. Dagmar, not knowing what to make of his behavior, supposedly told him she'd be back, but didn't return. levy then went to Jeanne Sonville's house, told her he was going out of town, offered her one of his two Siamese cats, and gave her some uncashed checks from *Oracle* advertising to publish a friend's book of prints. Then, as the story goes, he called his brother Jim and asked to borrow a suitcase. Then he called his parents. He wanted to speak to his father, but he wasn't in. According to his mother, levy, who although he had a license didn't drive, wanted his father to come pick him up. "I believe Darryl was thinking of coming home," Carolyn Levy (now deceased) told a reporter.

"My wife was the last person to see him alive," said Osinski, who six months before the death, moved into levy's building, catty-corner on the floor beneath him. Convinced more adamantly than ever that levy was murdered, he explained to me, "There was a peculiar thing about levy's apartment, you would have had to have lived here to have known this. It was an older type of building, and it had the locks, the little buttons you had to push on the side of the door. He always had it pushed so it was unlocked. He always kept his door unlocked . . . The thing is, I don't know if you've heard, in psychology, the person who's always talking about suicide is not the one that does it! It's the person who doesn't talk about it. levy was into what we call psychic violence—I remember I had an argument with him that was witnessed by rjs, and I warned levy that psychic violence was dangerous, and if he continued it, in about six months or so he'd probably be dead. It was about nine months after that he was dead.

"The thing is he always left his door unlocked. Especially the last week or so he was alive, because I used to go up to his apartment. Of course, after he came back from Madison he wasn't seeing anybody—his old lady, Dagmar, split from him, but he still had the door unlocked . . . and that day he was taking care of things—in fact, he and my wife met at the A&P, 'cause he had gone to get some cat litter for his cats. And he helped my wife bring the groceries in—I was sound asleep because at the time I worked the night shift—I woke up kind of groggy, and there's my wife and there's levy bringing in the groceries, and he was happy! He looked happy. There was no way you would have suspected anything was going to happen. I was too groggy to talk to him, but I remember he talked about going to Africa."

The postcard to Wagner about coming to California was dated Nov. 18, 1968. It had a picture of Meher Baba on the front, with the quotation, "I am the divine beloved who loves you more than you can ever love yourself." On the other side levy wrote: *d.r., cuting through the illusions i find i need the illusions to live & grow, or its that another illusion? HELP- reply necessary—short.*

Sometimes levy thought of escaping to college, but every time he got a scholarship form he ended up writing "FUCK" all over it. He said that once he was asked by a kid why he didn't go to college, and he told him, "They didn't have the courses I wanted. I told him I wanted to study angels." Or as he wrote in *Tombstone as a Lonely Charm (Part 3)*:

> if you want a revolution / return to your childhood / and kick
> out the bottom / don't mistake changing / headlines for changes
> / if you want freedom / don't mistake circles / for revolutions. /
> think in terms of living / and know / you are dying / & wonder
> why. / if you want a revolution / learn to grow in spirals / always
> being able to return / to your childhood / and kick out the
> bottom. / This is what i've been / trying to say—if you attack /
> the structure—/ the system—the establishment / you attack
> yourself / KNOW THIS! / & attack if you must / challenge your-
> self externally / but if you want a revolution / return to your
> childhood / & kick out the bottom. / be able to change / your
> own internal chemistry / walk down the street / & flash lights in
> yr head / at children

With his angels apparently still not speaking to him, and the newfound acceptance of his poetry leaving him both confident he was pulling it off and depressed that it was all just a game, he decided to make his move. Whether that move was to actually leave Cleveland or someone stopped him from leaving is still a mystery almost thirty years later.

Ferguson and Sigmund, who was generally thought to be the last person to see levy alive at the time, found the body Sunday night, November 25. levy supposedly turned over the flats for the next issue of *The Oracle* to rjs, and he and Ferguson put it out.

"He was peaceful and beautiful," Sigmund said to the reporter at the wake. "He had more knowledge than anyone I ever knew. He said he thought of himself as three or four hundred years old and lived that way. Everybody does the same thing. It's all a game. Some people are remembered, some people are forgotten, at least he'll go out as a legend, like Hemingway."

After *The Oracle* came out rjs, who had a very exclusive and intense rela-tionship with levy, generally made himself unavailable for comment, and began severing all his contacts with d. a.'s other friends, building an aura of sus-picion around himself that to this day still exists in the minds of many of the others. Ed Sanders didn't know what it was, but he felt there was something wrong. He and the Fugs were on tour, on the way to Notre Dame, when the gig got canceled. When he got to Cleveland he had the strange feeling that some-thing was being covered up. Something he still can't put his finger on today.

Steve Ferguson, who thinks of himself in biblical terms as "a simple shepherd," pauses, then says, "People have said to me that it's guys like you who drove levy crazy. But you can't be held responsible for what you don't know! I used to say 'sure' to almost everything," he recalled, so when rj called and said he was worried about levy and wanted me to go over with him, I said 'sure.' I think he wanted somebody else along, perhaps he had a premonition that something was seriously wrong and he didn't want to take the trip alone. . . . I don't know where I was living in those days—levy and rj were within a block of each other. So we went over and tried to push in, but the door was locked—it was necessary to get the lady who did the cleaning to open the door. Which she did—swung it open, and he was there in the first room.

"I reconstructed the lotus theory myself—one foot was back under the bend behind the other knee, the other one had dropped down to the floor. The knees were both forward, it was a full lotus that had broken as the body fell backwards. The rifle was still propped up in between the legs. The police were not content with their investigation and they kept fiddling with theories. One of the unusual things they noted was there was no tension in the muscles. In a suicide case there is always tension in the muscles anticipating the impact of the bullet. The other thing was the angle of the entry of the bullet, which came from above. These are things I heard—I never had my hands on any of the documents.

"They were trying to speculate how he with his short arms could haul a .22 rifle up into that position. It seemed perfectly obvious to me that he sat on the edge of the mattress, leaned over the rifle and pulled the trigger. There was a splatter of blood on the wall behind him where the body had pitched backwards and flipped that splatter back there. Because it was a .22—there wasn't much else. A small clean hole right in the third eye, which is black poetry, thank you very much. The police of course have their own methods of dealing with things—one cop said, 'Aw, this is nothing, we had a guy who blew his head off with a shotgun last week.' "

For the next several years, he's not sure how long, Ferguson kept *The Oracle* running sporadically. "I wasn't literally equipped at the time. I just felt I had to do something. Later, I figured out there's a kind of complicit feeling when somebody commits suicide. You feel responsible, like it was your fault 'cause you didn't know, or you weren't there. Later on I experienced a lot of the things I'm sure that levy was experiencing, and developed a better understanding of it. I had my own series of religious visions, I went through my own very long period of carefully chemically, psychologically balancing myself. And that, really in the last few years, was a lot of what levy was doing—he had this paranoid internal balance that he was keeping—which is man's relationship with God kinda thing. The suicide story sits with me because fundamentally we're talking about a pretty unforgiving personality—he had written a lot of stuff he wasn't that pleased with anymore, but he was so committed to making himself a poet he was unable in himself to go back and tear it up and throw it away. He was committed to taking every word as gospel, and that could catch up with him, especially if he was starting to get the recognition. I've never gone this far with it before," Ferguson suddenly realized. "I may regret I ever said this, but look, he was a pretty vain guy. Perhaps it was his feeling that ultimately the most dramatic thing he could do would be to split right now, while the mythology was at its peak—before he got sold off and the chicken salad dinners started rolling in. He was a master of impact, I have to grant that. There was a lot of confusion, ya know, there was confusion about what exact role Dagmar had and what exactly he owed her—common-law wife, companion, partner, girlfriend, whatever . . . He actually wrote the list down a few times—he didn't know exactly what to think of her or what his relationship should or would be with her, and it tore his heart out that he couldn't provide better for her, but part of that was a dominance game too—if he had had money he wouldn't have had to take a lot of shit from her either.

"She was not the easiest woman to be around, she was inclined toward depression and moping around the house and not much talking to anybody—I think she was just another person trying to work her stuff out, and levy was there, and between supporting him and not supporting him she couldn't find much of a value one way or another, so she supported him. She wasn't happy where she was . . . A week and a half before he killed himself she moved off to live with this real screwball—the guy that did the eyeball paintings. The paintings were awful—eyeballs perched on these walls in space—twenty or thirty eyeballs per painting—he had a wife that he called Mouse, and a series of sado-masochistic steps to enlightenment that he ran her through. Dewey Fagenberg and I went over and tried to spring [Dagmar] from the joint, but she allowed that that was where she wanted to be. Of course levy had just come back from Madison—it had a big effect on him being up there because enough people were finally treating him seriously as a poet to gratify some of those tremendous drives, which were perhaps the most profound part of his personality. He was dead serious about it. He wanted to be a poet and goddamit he was going to be a poet—he willed himself to be a poet He didn't do anything mechanical—wouldn't take a job around machines. Avoided most jobs anyway because they conflicted with what it was he wanted to be doing.

"There have been dark rumors about his relationship with rj—speculations about the egocentric game playing, back and forth, that they did. I never witnessed them but I heard some pretty graphic stories—holding knives to one another's throats, stuff life that. It was all about love, death and poetry . . . I grant you that rj's behavior in calling me [to go to levy's] is a bit suspicious—I've been asked about that before, and . . . I don't put . . . He was a pretty crazy guy himself—another of these people who carried with himself a conviction of his own genius and his destiny. He was driven to the point where he couldn't stand correction—couldn't stand criticism—he couldn't entertain another point of view: *Be reasonable, see it my way!* You know the line from Ecclesiastes, 'Vanity, vanity, all is vanity'? Almost everybody forgets the last line of that passage: 'All is vanity and vexation of spirit,' so says the preacher. If you wanted to cast these two in a morality play, levy could play vanity, and rj could play vexation of spirit. As for the darker theories with rj—I think that was just the way it looked emotionally to a lot of people. rj's relationship with levy was certainly trying for them both. They ran into each other and they were certainly equal opposites of some sort or another. I think that was clear to everybody around them. It's the kind of thing where you say, 'Oh no, this isn't going to work.'

"I think it's possible nothing physical happened between them. I think it's equally possible that the suicide happened in rjs's presence—that he locked up the room and came back two or three days later with a witness. And I think it is unlikely that in our lifetime anybody's going to know for sure unless rj tells us. And I sincerely doubt rj is going to say anything.

Robert J. Sigmund, better known as rjs, first met d. a. levy in the fall of '65 at Cleveland State, where he was running a coffeehouse and a newspaper, and in his own words, "Was kinda being the local radical there." In the last several years of levy's life he was closer to the poet than anyone else, and collected and edited the most complete work on levy, *ukanhavyrfuckinciti back*, which was published by t. l. kryss's *Ghost Press* in a limited edition of 1000 copies. Concluding a monumental five page introduction to that book, rj wrote, "maybe this book is here to fuck with levy the same way the early christians fucked with christ. create a mythology around d.a. & kill him with his own words so he can't be human anymore. that's kinda mean, u mite believe me. why else would've i used that analogy? why else would such a book appear?"

Two months before his death, levy questioned the relationship in a letter to D. R. Wagner:

rjs thinks i am telling him to commit suicide when i tell him
to go after the light! am i? i don't think so—the ego dies
slowly—a little on each level of consciousness—poet or
prophet. artist or saint. all the same—but i wanted to be a saint
& a magician & be invisible & do good things turn people
on—& this country is not the place to be a prophet! too much
death & wanting death subconsciously—too much misdirected energy while the city sleeps & pretends . . .

Surprisingly, rjs, who lives in the countryside outside Cleveland and
spends most of his time working an acre-and-a-half garden, was willing,
though somewhat hesitant in the beginning, to talk about his relationship
with levy. "Whatta ya wanna know? How close were we? We were like partners in a business—I lived two hundred feet away from his building—we
had breakfast together every morning, that's roughly how close we were . . .
To me he seemed to be telegraphing what he was going to do all along, but
we were missing it. It as an amazing stunt, that's what I felt. and it rang like
a bell afterwards, that's all I can say . . . Why'd he do it? Was he incapable
of getting out of Cleveland? He left Cleveland! That was the whole point,
he left Cleveland. That was the whole point, leaving Cleveland. He left. He
went to Israel. Get it?" After a long pause he says, "I was engaged in a lot of
mundane activities and I wasn't paying attention to what he was saying. He
was saying those things and I did not connect—he would talk in terms of 'if
we both pulled our energy out of Cleveland the whole thing would collapse'—that is the whole thing in the sense of whatever network was in
Cleveland at the time. The community. There was a community in East
Cleveland which was somewhat more subdued—a greaser-beatnik background, more intellectual. There was the hippie community in Cleveland
Heights, which we weren't really into. We had something different happening. What we had going was more like covens in East Cleveland.

"Of course, I'm long since burned out . . . And like Tom Kryss said—he
didn't say it in these words—I'm trying to paraphrase, 'all the bullshit in the
world isn't gonna raise his eyebrows again.' Read the introduction to *Suburban Monastery Death Poem*: the existential games we play to make ourselves do something real. Whereas what does it all mean after the maggots
have eaten our corpse, or what does it mean after you have taken that last
stop, once you've left Cleveland, once you've gone to Israel, what do all these
games we're playing on this level mean? It's an existential enlightenment . . .
I have always been, from the age of seventeen, into existentialism—I'd cut

my teeth on Sartre, Camus and that gang. It never crystallized itself until the way it was then, and probably continues to do so now in a different way. Of course, over a period of twenty years you lose a lot of what you had then too. My outlook did become more . . . I stopped fooling myself almost completely for a while there.

"Ya know, there's a biological imperative that forces you to continue building games to fool yourself, because if you continue, if you continue to live, your biology overcomes your intellectual understanding of reality. If you are alive, the biological imperative that keeps you alive is going to create games that will gradually pull your eyes shut OK. Does that make sense?

"I can't really place [the last conversation with d. a.] in time. It was either two nights before or three nights before we discovered his body. There was kind of an instinct after he hadn't been around for a while and his cousin and Kent Taylor dropped off a suitcase at my apartment because levy hadn't answered his door and he's leaving Cleveland and wants the suitcase. And all those things come together for me at that point in time. I got hold of Steve Ferguson—without saying it in words there was some kind of concurrence between Steve Ferguson and myself that levy was dead. And we went over to his apartment and asked his landlady for the keys—we believed we were going to find his body. We knew at that point, at last that's my recollection of it—I didn't want to go myself—there was something to me that was frightening about going myself and finding his body—and his landlady screamed! The strangest thing that happened to me was that I happened to be carrying a pocketknife or something—the police come and I think they're gonna search me for weapons—I don't know, there's this paranoia that sets in when the police are around . . . The last conversation . . . I don't know . . . He kept dragging me through the same kind of existential philosophical conversation that we had had several times over nothing meaning anything at all and all of that I didn't have an answer for it—It's all meaningless so where do you go from here—and I would sit there dumbfounded like a dummy. Whatta ya mean where do we go from here? He was trying to communicate to me, OK, *this is all bullshit, it's all meaningless and it's a pain in the butt. I mean, it's no fun being here, that kind of thing. We're miserable being alive. And it doesn't have any meaning—anything you accomplish is just a game you're playing to fool yourself. So where do we go from here?* That was our last conversation, the best I can describe it.

"It ran maybe six hours, it ran very long into the night, into the next morning. He kept coming to me and I couldn't answer him. It wasn't clear to me. I was doing stupid things like painting my apartment, those kind of things, ya know. The day I was over there I was borrowing painting equipment, a scraper, stupid things like that. Ya know, here I was operating on that level at the time—I had fallen off the high ground and I was down operating on the planet, and he was planning on leaving. Like I said, I hadn't realized how far away he was because I was too dense to see it. If you're dense, someone can be way ahead of you and you never realize they're way ahead of you. I mean, when somebody's way ahead of you you only see as far ahead of you as you are capable of seeing. You can't see how much farther they may well be in front of you because you're not there.

"levy was kinda my mentor, and I would usually sit behind in the background and not say much of anything. levy would introduce me and I would just kind of keep to myself and listen and then afterwards levy would go over what he thought had happened, and I would contribute—I was kind of the shadow that was out of the picture that would supply additional information to d. a. as to what I thought was going down, if that makes any sense. All I can say is it's been twenty years, and I sure as hell have been through a lot of things that haven't any relationship to the level I reached in those times—I mean, I've done everything from fighting the utilities company to playing the demagogue for the local citizens of the area, The most recent thing I wrote was on the effects of the drought in China on the U.S. and world food supply.

"There ya go again," he laughs. "You go through all kinds of things and I know what that means. I'm playing the same games that are keeping me away from the enlightened . . . The lights are all out, OK. And you can't turn the lights on without approaching that same decision [levy made]— you have to get near that edge, you have to go on that cutting edge to begin to have any kind of light, you have to be on the point of the sword ready to fall before the real lights come on, and if you're not there, then you don't see it. You know, you see past it. It's the Analogy of the Cave, the Aristotle [*sic*] thing, where you're looking at the shadows on the wall, and you're one of the people sitting there seeing the shadows on the wall. And how can somebody who understands you're looking at shadows on the wall communicate to the people who only see the shadows on the wall that it is the fire behind them and they are here in the room, and the shadows are just a reflection?"

Twenty years after his death, in the fall of 1988, a three-day festival celebrating d. a. levy's life and work was held in Cleveland at Case Western Reserve University. Almost thirty years ago, this letter from Jim Sorcic of Gunrunner Press circulated all over underground America, the day after levy's body was found:

Portrait of a Young Man Trying to Eat the Sun

LETTER TO THOSE WHO HAVEN'T HEARD: D. A. LEVY IS DEAD 11.26.68 morgan came over about 12:30 last nite & told clarissa to wake me up. when i came downstairs he told me rjs had just called from cleveland. i have bad news/ d. a.'s committed suicide/ levy's dead/ blew his brains out with a shotgun/ d. a.'s dead/ died blew himself apart/ dead/ he's dead i don't understand what it all means. i go back to d. a.'s letters & try to find him/ bring him back somehow . . . he wrote me the day before he died—it was a 3 page thing—the longest he's ever written to me: if you don't hear from me for a while its ok since time is non existent (that's what my angels tell me when i get impatient) —til dec 1 —only—maybe —i keep trying to find out what it all means/ what i'm supposed to do. & like maybe it wasn't the police chief briers & richard nixon that killed d. a. maybe it was you & i who pushed him in to dying. maybe if we had all just left him alone/ stopped pushing him & writing him/ telling him its all worth it/ all the shit is really worth it in the end/ maybe if we had just gotten off his fucking back for once & given him room to live HE DIED BECAUSE HE WAS TIRED. because i don't understand all this. because this morning i received books from d. a. that had been mailed the nite before he died. because i can't cry anymore over a package from a dead man. because i loved him even before he died. because he's dead & i don't understand what it means . . . there have been only 2 people i've cried for in my life: my grandfather & levy. i don't think i'll ever cry again. stay well, motherfucker, law & order is back in Cleveland. & d. a. levy is dead.

POSTSCRIPT

When I first started writing about levy in 1988 there was an incredibly diverse response from everyone I interviewed. Some, like Frank Osinski, kept insisting levy was murdered by one particular member of the inner circle. Others kept insisting it had definitely been the Subversive Squad. Others claimed he did it because Dagmar was sexually involved with one or more of his closest friends. And even others claimed levy had been tripping for close to two weeks before the fatal day he made his decision.

At one point, while Ed Sanders and I were both in Cleveland for the twentieth anniversary festival celebrating levy's life and work at Case Western University, Osinski called from Northern California, demanding

Portrait of a Young Man Trying to Eat the Sun

that a kangaroo court be held to settle things once and for all. Charges and countercharges were hurled back and forth, but that was as far as it went.

When the article came out, the reaction was fairly positive from most of the people who knew levy, though neither rjs or Steve Ferguson was very happy with the way they came off. Neither, however, complained that they had been misquoted.

In 1990 I met a musician from Cleveland named Tim Wright, who once upon a time had a band called *Pere Ubu*. Wright had read the article on levy but had made no effort to contact me until we were introduced by a mutual friend. Like a postmodern Stan Laurel imitating W. C. Fields, his first words to me were, "Are you ready for some brand new lies?" Wright told me that not long after levy's death Ferguson and Dagmar got married. Ferguson never mentioned that bit of critical information. But the news of the marriage wasn't the end of Wright's surprises. "There are a lot of salacious rumors about what happened," he said, "but about six months after they got married Ferguson supposedly went to San Francisco and did a lot of acid with the [Jefferson] Airplane. When he came back he was fried, and when his head didn't clear Dagmar had him committed and they gave him electroshock." Wright drove Ferguson to the hospital, and "tried to talk him out of doing it, to Dagmar's dismay." He even went back to the hospital by himself and brought Ferguson some R. D. Laing books and tried to talk him out of it again, but failed.

What's the truth? There are too many different sides to the story, too many different people pointing their fingers at each other. At this point, even if someone claims they were in the room with levy when he died, the only truth we can be sure of is the poetry that levy left behind, because basically, as Ferguson said, "It was all about love, death and poetry."

Liner Notes for the Jefferson Airplane's 2400 Fulton Street

"We were very much a creature of our times." That's one way Paul Kantner explains the Jefferson Airplane, the group that he and Marty Balin forged together two long, strange decades ago. Well, yes, they were. And all of us who were alive—really alive—back then were creatures in arms.

But somehow, the Airplane were more monsters than creatures. They scared authorities and made things happen. They pushed boundaries and helped define the times.

The times, of course, were the most cataclysmic decade in the history of this country, a decade that got going around 1965 and ended anywhere from 1969 (Altamont) to 1974 (Watergate).

The sixties was a decade of which it can truly be said: You had to be there. As Robin Williams put it, "If you can remember the sixties, you weren't really there."

Try and conjure up that decade, and all you come up with is a laundry list of clichés having to do with tie-dyes, Gods' eyes, Day-Glo, posters and light shows, patchouli and incense, with the language of those days, those incredible, far-out, psychedelic, flower-powered days. The times saw the escalation of civil rights activists' war on segregation and of the United States' war on North Vietnam. In music, folk singers, Bob Dylan chief among them, led musical protests. On the flip side, there were the carefree Beatles, who, in the fall of 1965, were about to get high for the first time, courtesy of some marijuana provided by one Bob Dylan.

Around the time of that momentous pot party in New York, a band was making its public debut in San Francisco: Jefferson Airplane, named after a mythical blues artist ("Blind Thomas Jefferson Airplane") and influenced by the Beatles, Bob Dylan, and marijuana.

As such, the Airplane were no different from many of the people around them, especially a growing community of students, dropouts, artists, pacifists, post-Beat bohemians and other adventurists who lived or hung out in a low-rent, Victorian-housed neighborhood called the Haight-Ashbury.

But the Airplane, by dint of their music, by their approach to the business of music, and by the relationships they nurtured within the community, became the musical symbol of the Haight-Ashbury movement, its ambassadors to the outside world. They were by no means the weirdest, the funkiest, or, who knows, the hippest. But they had two crucial things going: a willingness, if not eagerness, to balance art with business, and the stuff it took to cross over toward, if not into, the mainstream.

And so it was that the Airplane not only scored the first hit records out of San Francisco but helped change the way musicians related to the industry. Which is to say they refused to be slaves or puppets. In 1966, they scored a contract with an unprecedented advance of $25,000. (Other bands thought they were doing well getting $5,000 for signing with a label.) With success, they demanded artistic freedom and stretched musical boundaries, tapping into root music: folk, jazz, blues, and beyond. At the top, despite all their human weaknesses, they refused to set up barriers between themselves and their audiences. Yes, they bought a seventeen-room mansion on a border of Golden Gate Park—the address: 2400 Fulton Street—for what they thought was an outrageously high price: $70,000. There they lived, rehearsed, and partied.

But they were constantly in the streets, playing free concerts and street parties.

"It was a very *encouraging* scene," says Paul, emphasizing that word. "The bands encouraged one another; at radio stations we'd take tapes of the [Grateful] Dead, Quicksilver [Messenger Service], or whoever we'd meet. There was a sense of 'We're all in this together.' "

No one who knew the Airplane, then, was surprised when the band showed up at the Gathering of the Tribes, better remembered as the San Francisco Human Be-In in Golden Gate Park on January 14, 1967. Or when they sang "Let's Get Together."

And love one another right now. Right now. Right now. Right now!

The Haight became history quickly; pushed by commercialism, media attention, and drugs, it was swamped by the rush of young seekers who came for the "Summer of Love" in 1967, and it died a fast, painful death.

The Airplane went through much of what the Haight endured. The band had a tough time handling the weight of success; it, too, succumbed to the temptations of drugs and free love, and their attendant zigs and zags; it, too, became a fragmented, volatile, many-headed monster, some passionate, some passive. For many surrealistic moments, it was beautiful, a time to behold and hold on to. But it was also destined to fall apart.

After nearly two decades of changes, the Airplane became the Starship, with Grace Slick the sole surviving link. Paul Kantner, Marty Balin, and

Liner Notes for the Jefferson Airplane's 2400 Fulton Street

Jack Casady have a new band, KBC. Jorma Kaukonen is back where he began—a solo act, happily gigging at small blues clubs. And Spencer Dryden, drummer through the prime times, is a member of a band with a typically self-deprecating (and accurate) name: The Dinosaurs.

To talk with Marty, Paul, and Grace is to confront the many-headed monster once more. Memories are vague or conflicting. Grace doesn't care to wax nostalgic, anyway. "It's hanging on to something that doesn't exist. It's looking at ghosts." Paul looks back with affection at the things the Airplane accomplished musically, reflecting each band member as well as the times. Marty looks back with sourness at how short a time the Airplane really flew. Listening to them talk takes me back to the Fillmore, where between songs the band noodled endlessly, trying to get in tune for the next number. It took a while, but when they got into sync, they soared like few others and took us to places we'd never been and would never see again.

BEGINNINGS

Before Grace, it was Marty Balin's band. In fact, it was the Airplane, performing at Marty's nightclub, The Matrix, that inspired Grace to sing rock and roll. "It's No Secret" was the Airplane's signature song and, in 1966, it was their first single, but Balin didn't write it for his own band. "I wrote it for Otis Redding," he says. "We worked on the same bill a couple of times at the Fillmore." Grace: "Marty's a lover/loner kind of guy. At one point he wanted to be Otis Redding."

"Come Up the Years," another showcase for Balin's soaring tenor, was co-written by Marty and Paul. Paul: "It was an idealization of that whole element of beautiful young (and underage) girls who were very bright, who left their families and were on their own." Marty: "It was based on this one girl who looked like thirty-five but was twelve or something. I met her mother and father and had dinner with them once 'cause she was so infatuated with me; I wrote the song about her."

"My Best Friend," the first single from *Surrealistic Pillow*, is by Skip Spence, a guitarist who, legend has it, Balin found at an audition for the band that would become Quicksilver Messenger Service. Marty recruited him to be the Airplane's drummer because, he told Skip, "You look like you should be a drummer." Skip didn't argue, but when he joined Moby Grape after leaving the Airplane in fall of 1966, he was a guitarist again.

By the time the Airplane were ready to record *Surrealistic Pillow*, they had a new singer. Signe Toly Anderson, who worked primarily as a harmony

Liner Notes for the Jefferson Airplane's 2400 *Fulton Street*

backup to Marty, left to have a baby. In stepped Grace Slick, who was a lead singer for Great Society. Besides giving the Airplane a galvanizing new force, she brought a couple of songs. "Somebody to Love," the biggest of the Airplane's two hit singles (it reached number five), was written by Darby Slick, her brother-in-law and a fellow member of Great Society. Darby: "I'd broken up with a girl around then. And one night I took some LSD. . . ." Grace wrote "White Rabbit" around the same time, he says. "And we knew, instantly, that these songs were hits."

"Comin' Back to Me," a thoughtful soliloquy by Marty, was one of his fastest efforts, written in his Los Angeles motel room one evening during the two-week sessions for *Surrealistic Pillow*. "I'd smoked this really strong joint, and I wrote it. Then I went back to the studio—'cause we used to stay up all night—and the engineer, Grace, Jack [bassist Jack Casady], and Garcia [Jerry Garcia, all-around handyman on the album], were still there, so I said, 'I'd like to record this, please.' " Manager Bill Thompson: "They rehearsed it a couple of times: Jerry played guitar; Grace played recorder. They did one take, and Marty said 'I like it. It's a love song and it's rough. That's the way I want to convey it.' "

"Embryonic Journey" is an instrumental solo by Jorma Kaukonen, a piece he performed when he worked folk clubs in Palo Alto and San Jose. "I was a Bay Area folk figure," says Jorma, who sometimes played with Janis Joplin and other times with Steve Talbot, a blues singer who originally came up with "Blind Thomas Jefferson Airplane" as a joke on blues names.

"She Has Funny Cars" is credited to Jorma and Marty. Grace recalls adding a line or two. The song, she says, is a good example of the early Airplane's method of writing. "We didn't sit down together to write. If you were around, and somebody made a comment, you'd write it down and have it for a year, and then you say it fits in with something you're writing. It was us honestly stealing from each other." Paul: "We'd come in with pieces and run at each other and see what meshed."

On *Surrealistic Pillow*, deeply felt love songs meshed with acid dreams, offbeat tunes with multiple layers of meanings, and the first instrumental adventures by Jorma and Jack. *Pillow* was a landmark, the Airplane's *Rubber Soul*. The songs Grace brought in were hits and helped keep the album on the charts for more than a year, peaking at number three. But almost more than the music, it was the very idea of the Airplane that struck a million nerves. In their rush to help create the Summer of Love, writers for magazines like *Time* and *Look* suddenly became Keseys and Wolfes, and they could not get enough of Grace—or "Gracie . . . a turned-on girl," as

Look called her in a trippy essay. The more cautious *Life* magazine came calling a year later—in 1968—with a cover story about the Airplane and the "vibrating world" of "The New Rock."

PSYCHEDELIA

The Airplane, as the *Rolling Stone Illustrated History of Rock and Roll* has stated, "were of, by, and for the acid community." As such, it might be said that all of their music was informed by their adventures in chemically charged wonderlands. Almost any song they did, then, could have fit under that most elastic category, "Psychedelia."

And it's poetically just that the first song, "Plastic Fantastic Lover," really doesn't. Marty: "It's just about a TV set. I was sitting one night watching television; I had no girlfriend or anything, and I wrote this song to this TV set. True story!" Yeah; but what a bringdown. . . .

Which can't be said for "Wild Tyme" by Paul. Pointing out the line, "I'm doing things that haven't got a name yet," he explains, "That referred to all the new designer drugs that were coming out, as well as the whole renaissance of experiences that was going on, exploding out of the restrictions of the fifties. There was the breaking away from parents; the sexual revolution; drugs became OK. Everything became OK, worldwide."

After Bathing at Baxter's was a chaotic time for the band; they were set up in a Hollywood house previously rented to the Beatles; stars because of the success of *Surrealistic Pillow,* they found themselves flying out for concerts and TV dates, all on top of their recording schedule. That schedule became a shambles. Where *Pillow* took thirteen days to record, *Baxter's* would take seven months. On the road and at the house, Marty found himself unable to work—all the band members had their own entourages, he recalls, and he couldn't get through to them. Bill Thompson: "It was absolutely crazy. Nude swimming going on all the time; Jorma firing his gun in the pool; kids sneaking through the doors looking for the Beatles. . . ." "Pure LSD, among thirteen other things," Paul says about that album. But whatever those things were, Paul managed to write most of the songs, including "The Ballad of You & Me & Pooneil," a combined paean to childhood (Winnie the Pooh) and an ode to a folk-music hero, Fred Neil.

"A Small Package of Value" must have been another of those things. "It was improvisational," says Bill Thompson, and that says it all.

One of the two songs that paid for the Airplane's license was "White Rabbit," which followed "Somebody to Love" by two months into the Top Ten in 1967. It started simply enough. Long before Bo Derek, Grace heard

Ravel's *Bolero* two ways: musically and sexually. "I've always liked the way it works, as an exercise for an orchestra. And people turn it on for sex because that's the way things ought to work. You don't come slamming in at somebody. You start and build up to the crescendo." As for the infamous words, so often interpreted as a commercial for drugs:

> The lyrics come from having read what they call the great children's books. All of them talk about how your life will be spectacular given some kind of chemical. Peter Pan—you sprinkle dust on your head, you can fly. Oz: You fall into a field of poppies and all of a sudden there's Oz. Alice had five or six kinds of drugs that took her places.
>
> Adults were ragging at us for taking drugs. What I wrote the song for was to say, "Why did you read me this stuff? Look at what this stuff says!"

But how did she think to combine the Alice imagery with Ravel? "What I did was take acid and listen to Miles Davis's *Sketches of Spain* for about twenty-four hours straight." And a hit was born.

While the Summer of Love was going on, the Airplane were shuttling between the road and their Hollywood house, supposedly getting *Baxter's* together. Needing a song, Paul thought back to the Human Be-In and came up with what he calls "just a celebration of the Renaissance, as it were." It was the almost journalistic "Won't You Try Saturday Afternoon." In fact, says Paul, some of the words came from an article about the Be-In by the late Ralph J. Gleason, who championed the scene through his jazz and pop column in the *San Francisco Chronicle*.

For a time in the late sixties—nobody remembers exactly when—the entire band took up residence at the Airplane House at 2400 Fulton Street. The only couple among them was Grace and Spencer Dryden, a jazzer who'd stepped in as drummer in time for *Surrealistic Pillow*. For the band's fourth album, *Crown of Creation*, Grace wrote "Lather" to make fun of Spencer. "Lather was thirty years old today; they took away all his toys. At the time," Grace explains, "it was the old 'You can't trust anybody over thirty.' Everybody's dead at thirty, and Spencer was turning thirty. The situation amused me."

REVOLUTION

By the *Crown of Creation* album, says Paul, the music was "starting to swing into darker directions." It almost had to. The year began with the Beatles, as usual, on top of the charts, singing "Hello Goodbye" from *Magical Mystery Tour*. But 1968 was nothing less than a hard year's night. It was a year of battle lines being drawn.

Perhaps a quick dirty-laundry list will do: The Viet Cong's Tet offensive; student draft deferments abolished; by spring, ten thousand U.S. dead in Vietnam; "Hell, no, we wont go"; Columbia students' strike; Martin Luther King murdered; George Wallace for President; Bobby Kennedy for President; RFK assassinated; Nixon for President; Humphrey for President; Yippies; bloodshed in Chicago. Nixon wins.

The Airplane continued to extol love and psychedelics, but the sound began to toughen. As Grace Slick commanded an increasingly greater share of both media attention and the spotlight on stage, her duets with Marty became high-pitched battles.

"We Can Be Together" was their first anthem for the social revolution. Now the Airplane—and all of us who flew with them—were "outlaws in the eyes of America." It was, says Paul, "a love song for a movement of people towards brightness."

Revolution or no revolution, Paul was writing a song, and he remembers being musically stuck. "I was looking for something to resolve the chorus, and Crosby [his old pal from the folkie days, David Crosby] came up with this banjo lick. It was an old fiddle lick, and none of us knew where it came from. But it resolved "We Can Be Together," and we wrote the whole other song with that lick alone." The other song was "Volunteers," which is credited to Marty and about which the composer has a story of his own:

> We were all living in the mansion at the time. One morning, somebody was banging the garbage cans outside my window. I looked out, and it said on the truck, VOLUNTEERS OF AMERICA. I leaned over and wrote, "Hey, what's happening on the street, da-da-da. . . ." I gave it to Paul, he put some music to it (apparently adding the phrase, "Gotta revolution," along the way), and it became kind of an anthemic thing for us. I say it's about a truck picking up some garbage, and people don't believe me. I had no idea about writing about any revolution or anything.

But Paul did. "Crown of Creation," for example, was written to the hated

Liner Notes for the Jefferson Airplane's 2400 Fulton Street

Establishment. "They were saying that they were the crown of creation, and we were pointing out that 'You're not necessarily the crown of creation.'"

By then, Paul had begun mixing his lifelong fascination with science fiction into his music. He got a chance to use some long-dormant lyrics in "Wooden Ships." "Crosby had written this beautiful music and didn't know what to do with it. I took it and we played with it; Casady would put lines in it, and it went on for a year and a half." One day, after going sailing with David, "Wooden ships on the water" came to Paul. "Just an ideal escape movie. The survivors go off to a wonderful life forever, Amen." So why is Stephen Stills included in the credits? "He added the one dour verse, 'We'll watch you die. . . .' We stuck it in there. And David wrote the intro about the purple berries."

To which Grace can only smile a grown-up, clearly-over-thirty smile. That song, she says, is a fair representation of one facet of the Airplane. "The idea is so naïve: we'll have some berries and share them. It's cute. It represents a bunch of kids looking to be characters in a children's book," just as Paul did with Pooneil, and as she did with Alice in Wonderland. "We were all out there, wanting to be children."

"Nothing wrong with that," says Paul. "I still believe in that. Much of my writing is still born of looking for some quality that's childlike, utopian. That's what characterizes mankind in its best moments."

"Rejoyce" is nothing but grown-up, an exercise in literature and jazz, with Grace paraphrasing lines from James Joyce's 1922 novel *Ulysses*. "Writers just knock me out," she says. "What you try to do when you read is to see the similarities in your own life, in the culture. Since I was always older than everybody, I take the teacher's role, to take these things and make them interesting."

In contrast, Grace wrote "Mexico" after reading newspaper accounts in early 1970 of the Nixon administration's Operation Intercept, a campaign to stem the flow of marijuana from south of the border. Grace considers more recent governmental battles against drugs. "It's still the same," she says. "We don't have funding for the one-third of the people who are illiterate in the country, but we have funding for nuclear stuff. They spend too much time on things that are really stupid and unimportant."

The drug scare of 1970 came in the aftermath of the summer of rock festivals, a summer that included the three days in Bethel, New York, that gave us the Woodstock Nation. There the Airplane performed Marty's garbage-truck song, among others, but few of the band remember what they did. "We were on at 7 A.M.," says Paul. "Our slot was supposed to be 9 P.M. the night before, but it was typical hippie organization. Time wasn't of consequence." On stage, Paul didn't have a clue about how the Airplane sounded. "Half the crew was asleep or naked in the pond, and I remember the film cameras were pointed in the sky half the time." Paul himself was up there half the time; he'd been dosed with LSD shortly after arriving in the sixties version of the *Twilight Zone*.

Airplane Parts

In 1970, Spencer left, to be replaced by Joey Covington. By then, Grace was living with Paul, and when she became pregnant, the band stopped touring. A long-disenchanted Marty Balin left in 1971. By then, Jorma and Jack had formed a side band, Hot Tuna (which they'd tried naming Hot Shit). The end was near.

The first post-Marty album, *Bark*, included "Pretty As You Feel," a jam that originally lasted almost half an hour and involved Jorma, Jack, Joey, and visitor Carlos Santana. After it was edited, Joey added lyrics. The result: the Airplane's fourth-highest-ranked single.

"Martha" takes us back to *Baxter's* and to memories of one of those free and beautiful young girls Paul used to know. With an obvious sweet relish for the chance to recall some of the abandon of youth, he describes the inspiration for the song: "She was the daughter of the mayor of a nearby town, and she was hidden in the rock and roll community from the FBI because she was underage and the daughter of a mayor. Martha moved quite freely amongst the society as a very young girl. She was bright; almost painfully bright for her own good." He allows himself a moment of nostalgia. "Martha," he says, "stimulated several songs."

"Today," which has Marty at his most achingly romantic, was originally two songs, says Paul. "The first part was from a song Marty wrote. Then I finished up with a song I'd written. Then Marty wrote the lyrics." Marty: "When I recorded it, I was thinking, in the back of my mind, of Tony Bennett at age twelve as a choirboy singing this song. That's how I sang it." He adds: "Heavy drugs in those days made you think of a lot of things."

"Triad," by David Crosby, is the infamous ode to a ménage à trois that got him in trouble with the Byrds. "It happened I was part of a triangle, and there was one that worked out long and really righteously," he once told me. But his band, he said, "was very uptight about that song." Paul, who found the song "quite moving," gave it to Grace. Without blinking, she recorded it for the *Crown of Creation* album.

"Third Week in the Chelsea," by Jorma, signaled the end of his line with the Airplane. "We were at the Chelsea Hotel," Bill Thompson remembers. "It was a bad time, nobody was working together; nobody was playing together. It was kind of the end, even if it didn't really die."

The last Airplane studio album was *Long John Silver* in 1972. Marty, the founder, the original visionary and voice, had been gone for two albums. In his mind, the band was over long before—say, around the time their records began to turn to gold. He had been the leader. "Once it clicked, everyone was free and they were their own leaders and did whatever they wanted to do, and that democracy immediately destroyed it." In the beginning, he was the fiery young man with all the plans. "Then—around *Baxter's* time—I realized everybody was off their ass and didn't give a shit about anybody or anything else. So I lost interest."

Jorma and Jack left for good in the fall of 1972. Paul and Grace, with assorted musician friends, carried on with solo and joint projects and in 1974 introduced the Jefferson Starship, which, soon enough, included a familiar, soaring tenor: Marty Balin. Marty went, came, and went again. Grace left in 1978 and returned three years later. Paul left in 1984.

And these days, says Darby Slick, he's getting bigger checks than ever before for "Somebody to Love."

In September 1985, the Airplane House was sold (for $650,000). A few days before the Starship staff moved out, I dropped by 2400 Fulton Street one more time. With the pool table and the funky furniture gone, I could see more clearly than ever the mix of classic, turn-of-the-century Victoriana that was the house and the crazed collage of colors and clippings that was the sixties. Upstairs, where most of the band used to live, was the bathroom with the chartreuse walls; there was Paul's octagonal room; in another room, the walls were still papered with photos of nude women, of Dylan and the Beatles, of protests. It was the laundry list as art.

Downstairs, before opening the front door, I turned once more and spotted one more poster left behind. It was a blow-up of the cover story I'd done in 1980 in *Rolling Stone.* There was Grace standing tall, surrounded by six men, including Paul and Marty. The headline read, "STARSHIP WARS: The Band Plays On."

So what happened here? What did the Airplane accomplish? They'd set out, like so many of us, to change the world.

Grace considers that overly optimistic, once a great notion. "When you get older," she says, "you see that, unfortunately, it doesn't change that much. Maybe you make a small dent, but making a small dent in a giant doesn't really do anything.

Liner Notes for the Jefferson Airplane's 2400 Fulton Street

"We thought"—she corrects herself—"I thought that with an incredible amount of media blitzing and books and knowledge, you could change people. But you can't. The only person I can change is me. That's it."

Well . . . maybe. I think Grace, as a person, and part of a band, and part of the times, had an impact on those times, and those times still reverberate today. At the very least, the Airplane helped push out the boundaries of music. Just as they "honestly stole" from each other and from musicians before them, so did they teach listeners, then and now, that rock and roll can be music without rules, and that in rock and roll, for better or for worse, and for richer or for poorer, it is the artist who ultimately wears the crown of creation.

Liner Notes for the Jefferson Airplane's 2400 Fulton Street

From *America: A Prophecy*

REPORT FROM AMERICA

PARDON ME, BUT I'VE left New York. I've been touring the United States, and believe me, it's different. People actually wear those clothes that look so amusing in Times Square—yellow shirts and golf pants—they wear them *all the time*. Cash registers in supermarkets speak in a female voice, and no one says, "I saw Dave." They say, "I saw Dave's car."

Everyone curses more than in Manhattan and takes more drugs. An informal survey made while hitchhiking indicates that 75 percent of the men in America have spent at least $100,000 on cocaine.

Americans work less than New Yorkers, or maybe it just seems like less. After work they come home and sit on a sofa, listening to the crickets. They don't go out every night to Bartók string quartets and transvestite beauty pageants like we do. By and large, they have no desire to be famous.

On Passover, no American supermarket had ever heard of matzoh. When I defined it as a "Jewish cracker" the manager looked startled and conducted me to their vast selection of Ritz.

Americans prefer foods whose colors match their handbags. Their idea of eating out rarely involves leaving the car. Yet they all have lush gardens out back (Americans have an "out back") where they pull up glowing carrots even more beautiful than the Korean ones on Dyckman Street.

America is a land of contrasts.

The most tragic side of the USA is its visual impoverishment. There's almost nothing to look at in the whole country. One block of St. Nicholas Avenue is more interesting than the entire drive from Florida to Texas.

America is very relaxing. It's quiet and it's easy to fall asleep. Those characterless Top Forty songs out of L.A.—bland remakes of *California Girls*—that sound so foolish on Amsterdam Avenue sound good here. They fit this slow world of freeways and trees.

Shopping centers are like little fake cities, where families wander aimlessly around, buying ice cream and staring at each other. There's a B. Dalton bookstore, tennis clothes, and teenage girls with curly hair.

No one is America is political—all their extra energy goes into running triathlons, bicycling, and canoeing. The more adventuresome fly little planes.

One meets grown men who have lived their entire lives in trailers.

Americans love plastic because it's brighter than everything else, and every main street is like a Kandinsky-that-went-wrong. Just as New York seems a city of adults and one feels like a child looking up the steps of the Metropolitan Museum, so in America one feels an adult among children—passing towns where the best movie is *13 Going On 30*.

In the souvenir shops there are no more "Tune On, Tune In, Drop Out" stickers, but there are lots of license plates that say, "I'm Spending My Children's Inheritance," and one commonly passes motor homes piloted by elderly couples with mischievous grins. My guess is the new hippies are over sixty-five.

The best thing about America is there are real cowboys here, who *know* cows, and pause about ten minutes between sentences, and seem aware of some mystery that never makes it into New York, except maybe by subway.

And there are clean restrooms everywhere, and no one minds if you use them.

MY SEX WITH A HORSE

In Kansas, I met a horse. I saw it the moment I left the plane. The horse supported a member of the Kansas Guard. Its eyes looked directly into mine—black, trusting eyes. A horse had never looked at me so tenderly before.

As I walked by the horse into the Cyrus Wheeler International Airport, I scanned its underbelly for a penis. There was none.

Wichita is a small city, and I encountered the horse two days later, on Weaver Street. The same Kansas Guardsman sat on her outside the Trentworth Cemetery. "Good girl, Shirley," he said, patting her flank.

I have always loved the name Shirley.

"Where do the Kansas Guardsmen keep their horses at night?" I asked my friend Barry, whom I was visiting—the same way Holden Caulfield asked where the ducks in Central Park go in the winter.

"By the railroad tracks on Sandford Avenue," Barry said, looking up from the *Wichita Times-Leader*.

That night, by a gibbous moon, I climbed in an open window of the Lt. Moorman Memorial Stables. In the huge room, I saw breath rising in mist from the many stables. How would I find her? I wondered. I dare not turn on the light.

Then I heard a sort of purr to my right. It articulated into a whine, resembling speech: "Doooo meeeee." I had a chilling memory of Mr. Ed.

From *America: A Prophecy*

Looking over a wooden wall, I saw those dark, trusting eyes, now gleaming with a kind of mischief. I jumped up on the wooden partition.

For a long moment neither of us spoke. Then slowly, offhandedly, Shirley raised her mouth and tugged at the cuff of my pants.

I jumped down, loosened my belt, and she pulled my pants off—then my underwear.

Her tongue licked the tip of my penis. How did she know *that!* Had she and the Kansas Guardsman . . . been intimate? I feared he would sneak up behind me, the Jealous Lover.

Then Shirley lay down gently, turned her belly to me, and opened her legs. Her vagina tasted like buttered oats.

A sudden anxiety gripped me. Shirley was accustomed to horses. Compared to a stallion, I was not large.

Then she trained on me her sweet, beguiling eyes. "Doooooo meeeee," she said. I lost my fear.

Don't most animals have sex for thirty seconds? I thought, but we went two hours. I woke at dawn, warm against the beast's belly.

Will I ever return to women, so small and hairless? I wondered.

We kissed deeply, and I climbed out the half-opened window.

INTERVIEW WITH A SUPREME COURT JUSTICE WHO VOTED AGAINST FLAG-BURNING

> *We interviewed one of the Supreme Court Justices who voted flag-burning should be a crime. For reasons of confidentiality, we refer to him only as Madame X.*

Ruse: What are you, some kind of fucking idiot? You think a flag is *holy*, like God or something?

Madame X: Excuse me, sir, you must apologize for your language. I will not converse with you unless you apologize.

Ruse: Fuck *you*, apologize! Bull*shit*, apologize! I'll be a flame-thrower for the South Korean Army before I apologize!

Madame X: Lawrence, remove this man. *[Lawrence, a balding butler, appears. He wears a black armband.]*

Ruse: *[Struggling, as Lawrence holds us by the arms.]* You haven't removed me forever! You will see me again, in sunglasses! I'll follow your children to school!

[Lawrence ejects us. Silence, in the carpeted foyer. Doorbell rings.]

From *America: A Prophecy*

Lawrence: Who is it?

Ruse: I apologize.

Madame X: Show him in, Lawrence. *[We seat ourselves, uncap a Papermate pen.]* You may continue.

Ruse: So what got into you? Are you a colossal jerk in knickers? You think the flag is worth more than a half ounce of paste?

Madame X: That's a little better. You are closer now to the English language.

Ruse: Aah, you big fuddy-duddy.

Madame X: My mother was an alcoholic and swore a great deal. I came to hate profanity, as well as birdcalls.

Ruse: Birdcalls?

Madame X: Sometimes she would lock me out of the house all night, and I would sleep on the porch. I'd wake to the sound of birds. Then I could not return to sleep.

Ruse: I'm very sorry to hear. And the flag? How is it sacrosanct and uninflammable?

Madame X: The flag is highly flammable, and of course inflammable. Unfortunately the English language finds itself in the unenviable position of 'inflammable' meaning both 'able to catch on fire' and 'unable to catch fire.' If only every word meant its opposite! Then our life would be easier—particularly the life of judges. We could declare a man guilty and he could go free. Or flag-burning could be a crime and also no crime.

Ruse: But each word *doesn't* mean its opposite meaning.

Madame X: No, except for a word like "elope" which exists inside "cantelope" and "antelope" as a sort of *hex*.

Ruse: Anyway, the flag . . .

Madame X: Ah, God bless the flag. That is exactly what we're discussing. What is speech? Who speaks? The government protects our right to speak, but is burning something speech? Hitler burned books. Was that speech? Do we have a right to burn? I suggest that burning is not speech.

Ruse: Suppose we burned a speech of Hitler's?

Madame X: A burning speech cannot speak.

Ruse: Suppose we came to the end of a speech, a speech we

From *America: A Prophecy*

poured into all our glory and singing voice, and then said: 'Now, to show you what I mean, I will burn the words "America the Beautiful"—because how can America be so beautiful when it trains men in Honduras to kill nurse's aides over the border?'

Madame X: Must you burn something to speak?

Ruse: I must burn the flag or be burned myself.

Madame X: Now I, too, speak no more.

AUTUMN NOW

Written a month after September 11, 2001.

I was born in the autumn—born into a regretful season. The days before and after my birthday are ones of lonesome walking, over susurrant leaves, days in which one recalls the cadences of Ecclesiastes:

> *All things are wearisome;*
> *more than one can express;*
> *the eye is not satisfied with seeing,*
> *or the ear filled with hearing.*

Viewing thousands of abandoning leaves, one senses the futility of a worldly career. One publishes an article in a newspaper, for example—perhaps to full acclaim. Two days later the same newspaper billows down an avenue, pushed by the October wind.

So strong is the October wind, it blows all accomplishments—all diplomas, money, press releases—before it. And in this wind is the first taste of winter's grueling breath.

But this fall is different, for me. Walking in Phoenicia Park, toward the rising Tremper Mountain, now beginning to show its varied color, I am not melancholy. The recent horrors in Manhattan and at the Pentagon change the tone of this autumn to reassurance. Stepping over deep-red maple leaves, I observe: *This is not blood.* Here are a thousand deaths I need not mourn. The leaves did not leap from a burning tower; they simply fell as gravity tugged. The earth is designed with four seasons—at least in the higher latitudes—one of birth, one efflorescence, one of harvest, one of contemplation. Despite war, and acts of ruthlessness, Nature preserves her subtle intent.

There are years one resents Nature's inevitable plan, and there are years

From *America: A Prophecy*

one is thankful for this same inevitability. I would rather be helpless before autumn than before soldiers and grim battle.

THE EAST VILLAGE MILITIA

> *In 1996, The East Village Militia was founded to protect the East Village of Manhattan from natural disasters and capitalism. Sparrow held the rank of Specific Commander. In one of their daring escapades, the militia gave away books in front of Nobody Beats The Wiz, an electronics store on Broadway, to prevent people from buying televisions. The militia handed out this flier:*

The Second Commandment says "Thou shalt make no graven image of anything that 'creepeth' on the earth or 'swimmeth' in the seas or 'flieth' in the air." By emphasizing these verbs, God is forbidding us to show motion. Static art—paintings, drawings, engravings, etc.—are perfectly acceptable to God. It is television that God despises. TV is the idol of our age—and its heroes are commonly known as "television idols."

Repent ye!, before ye lose your souls. We offer free books to you, that your souls may be preserved. Read, look at paintings, listen to poetry, study modern dance! Do meditation! Pray! But buy no new TVs, and bury your present TV in the earth!

Love,
The East Village Militia

From *America: A Prophecy*

From *Unrepentant Whore*

I Want to Change the Laws That Punish Prostitutes

We don't protect ourselves because we are prohibited and inhibited. We can't share information about dangerous tricks. We are discouraged from any kind of organizing or self-protection by laws that prohibit "communicating for the purposes" or collective organizing (charged as pimping). It's hard to protect yourself from the rapists while you're busy protecting yourself from the police.

Laws Against Prostitution = Violence Against Women

I am appalled that the state assumes jurisdiction over my sexuality. To me, cops seem like rapists with badges. I read the newspapers: "Ex-Cop Linked to Hooker Slayings" and "Rapist Lures Prostitutes with Phony Police ID." The serial killers are the police—or at least, there's no way to tell the difference. It isn't fair.

Prostitution busts are a form of rape. When an emissary of the government (a cop) coerces me to engage in fondling and petting through fraud (pretending to be a client), then pulls his weapon and arrests me for my sexual behavior, I call that institutionalized rape.

That's why I'm always angry. That's why I'm angry at everyone who isn't angry.

I hate the idea that a group of men who are the arms of the state are entrusted to enforce my behavior in the boudoir, whether it is for money or not.

I hate it that there are young women all over the country who are being told to ignore this violation of our rights and, instead, to spend their time suppressing sexual expression. I'm not one to deny the relationships between imagery and action, but sluts and whores and erotic entertainers are not the enemy of the matriarchy.

I am trying to understand everything. Sometimes I don't fuck for love, pleasure, or money. I just fuck in defiance.

"The stigmatization of prostitution underlies the social control of all women," says friend and activist Gail Pheterson.

Sexual control is part of social control and part of all societies, I imagine, though I'm not exactly an *anthro-apologist*.

"DON'T FUCK 'TIL AFTER THE REVOLUTION"

I suppose it isn't fair to blame women for making prostitution illegal. Of course, I can't blame contemporary feminists. But historically women did play an important role in the process. To put it nicely.

The criminalization of prostitution was a cruel mistake promoted by feminist moralists near the turn of the nineteenth century. Poor women on our city streets pay for the classist follies of our predecessors. Are protectionist strategies just naturally a part of women's political contribution? I wish it weren't so, but my library is full of books about misguided campaigns to end women's sexual exploitation and to preserve women's purity. The punitive legislation that has emerged targets poor women and women of color, creating a climate that supports the cop rapists and leaves prostitutes with no recourse. My whore friends are very upset because they are the ones being sacrificed to preserve the "good" woman's illusion of safety.

I'M TRYING . . .

I've been an ardent feminist for twenty years. I love feminism like I love my mom. I'm trying to be open-minded. Maybe slut-positive women can seem like the enemy. Maybe we *should* be treated like outcasts, excluded from the family of feminists, labeled liars.

> In general, those who most adamantly promote this view, organizing various 'whores' conferences' and positioning themselves as prostitutes' spokespersons with the male-dominated media, do not choose prostitution for themselves; some have abandoned it; some never worked as prostitutes; some work as 'madams,' selling other women's bodies but not routinely marketing their own; a few actually work as prostitutes.
>
> —"Prostitution as 'Choice,' "
> *Ms.* magazine, January/
> February 1992

Anyway, I'm going to try and relax. I can't let this get to me. I can't expect too much of women or of humanity in general. Society has its own cycles. As politicos we play our parts, fulfill our responsibility by participating. Everyone has a right to her or his analysis. Variety is the spice . . . I can't blame women for thinking I'm an evil-sellout-dupe-of-

From *Unrepentant Whore*

the-patriarchy. It's the lot of a modern libertine. We all feel like we're losing. The slut radicals abhor the pornophobes.* I don't want to fight my sisters, and pornophobia is not quite a recognized social ill at this point, so I just better relax.

I've got to be open-minded. Just because my life offers vast evidence of the value of including whores in the family of womynkind doesn't mean it is the only truth, right? For some women, my philosophy could be dangerous. The freedom that I demand for myself is, for some women, the rope to hang herself with. I have to relax. It's just a difference in philosophy. I won't take anything personally. I'm not even mad at Phyllis Schlafly. It takes all sorts to make up the world. Some people think abortion is murder. Some people like war and nukes. I'll give everyone a break. After all, this is the patriarchy, and being a prostitute teaches me patience.

*From the Greek root *porne* referring to prostitutes and *phobia* meaning fear. Pornophobia means the fear of prostitutes. Pornophobia can also refer to the fear of sexual expression and sexual representation—that is, fear of pornography. Whore activist claim the term that was used as a weapon against them, pornography, as their own.

From *Unrepentant Whore*

Obscenity

Riah Fagan Cox was a gallant and pretty little woman from Columbia City, Indiana, which is in the northeast corner of the state, about halfway between Fort Wayne and Winona Lake. She was born into a so-called "good family," but her father was an alcoholic. He could not hold a job.

So, although little more than a child, Riah set out to rescue herself and her brother and eventually their descendents from want and obscurity. She sent herself to the University of Wisconsin and took a master's degree in the classics. Her thesis was a high school textbook on the Latin and Greek roots of common words in English. It was adopted by many school systems all over the country and earned enough money to enable Riah to put her brother through medical school. He set up practice in Hollywood and became the beloved obstetrician of many famous movie stars.

She married a lawyer in Indianapolis who did not make much money. She took jobs teaching Latin and Greek and English and became the Indianapolis representative for touring lecturers and musicians. She also sold silly, witty short stories to magazines from time to time. Thus was she able to send her son and daughter to the best private schools, even during the Great Depression. Her daughter became a Phi Beta Kappa at Swarthmore.

She died three years ago and is buried in Crown Hill Cemetery in Indianapolis, somewhere between John Dillinger, the bank robber, and James Whitcomb Riley, the "Hoosier Poet." I liked her a lot. She was a good friend of mine. She was my first mother-in-law.

I mention her in this chapter on obscenity because she imagined that I used certain impolite words in my books in order to cause a sensation, in order to make the books more popular. She told me as a friend that the words were having the opposite effect in her circle of friends, at least. Her friends could not bear to read me anymore.

Indianapolis Magazine said much the same thing in its article about me. . . . It praised the themes of my early books, *Player Piano, The Sirens of Titan,* and *Mother Night*: "anger at war and killing, at the void that technology is creating in contemporary life." But it went on to say: "From then on, though the themes remained constant, his style began to change. Small obscenities crept in, and four-letter words became frequent in

Breakfast of Champions in a riot of indecorous line drawings and misbegotten words that were suggestive of a small boy sticking out his tongue at the teacher."

This small boy sticking out his tongue was fifty years old at the time. It has been many decades since I have wished to shock a teacher or anyone. I did want to make the Americans in my books talk as Americans really do talk. I wanted to make jokes about our bodies. Why not? Why not, I ask again, especially since Riah Fagan Cox, God rest her soul, assured me that she herself was not wobbled by dirty words.

If I had gone to Riah's friends, they would have told me, too, that they had heard all the dirty words I used many times before, that the words did not astonish them. They would have insisted that the words should not be published anyway. It was bad manners to use such words. Bad manners should be punished.

But even when I was in grammar school, I suspected that warnings about words that nice people never used were in fact lessons in how to keep our mouths shut not just about our bodies but about many, many things—perhaps too many things.

When I was in the fourth grade or so, I had this hunch confirmed. My father hit me for my bad manners in front of guests. It was the only time either one of my parents ever hit me. I hadn't said "shit" or "piss" or "fart" or "fuck" or anything like that in front of the guests. I had asked them a question in the field of economics. But my father was so offended by my question that I might as well have called the guests "silly shitheads." They really were silly shitheads, by the way.

The Great Depression was going on. The year would have been 1932. I had been taken out of private school a couple of years before, so that my classmates were no longer the children of the rich and the powerful. They were the children of mechanics and clerks and mailmen and so on. I thought it was wonderful that their mothers could cook. That was more than my own mother could do. Also, their fathers could fart around with motors and so on. Peer pressure, which is the most powerful force in the universe, had actually made me a scorner of my parents' class.

But I was polite enough when these two silly upper-class shitheads came over to our house one night. They were husband and wife. I remember their names well enough, but I will call them "Bud and Mary Swan." This was at a time when securities had become nearly worthless, when many banks had closed forever. Factories and stores were dead. But the Swans had arrived in a new Marmon, and Mrs. Swan had a new fur coat and a new star sapphire ring.

We all had to look out through the front door at the car, and then at the coat and the ring. So Mother and Father, with their nice manners, said they were glad that things were going so well for the Swans. The whole thing looked fishy to me. Everybody else was broke. Where would the Swans get all that money? It was as though this one couple had been allowed to defy the law of gravity.

Mother and Father told me to take another look at the sapphire, so I could see the beautiful star in there. So I did. But then, to get a better understanding of what was going on, I asked Mr. Swan how much the ring had cost him. That was when Father hit me. He hit me with an underhand blow to the seat of my pants. It lofted me in the direction of the staircase, and I just kept on going upstairs to my bedroom. I was mad.

Now then: as my parents would eventually discover, to their grief, the Swans were cat's-paws for confidence men. They had been bankrolled by crooks to put on a show for friends of theirs who might still have a little money squirreled away somewhere. My parents would want to know where the Swans got all their easy money. My parents needed some easy money, too. If they didn't find it somewhere, they would be bounced forever from the upper class. As I say, I myself had already sunk into the lower orders.

The Swans said that they had invested what little they had left after the crash of the securities market in a wonderful company that wanted to keep itself a secret. It was quietly putting together a coal monopoly which would be as rich and powerful as Standard Oil. It was buying mines and barge lines and controlling interest in coal-hauling railroads, was getting them for a minor fraction of their true value since it was paying cash. Almost nobody else had cash. The cash was coming from individuals like the Swans and my parents, who could keep a secret, and who could scrape up a little something from the bottoms of their barrels, if they really tried.

The value of the company would increase at least a hundred times, the instant prosperity returned to the world. Meanwhile, the company was already paying dividends because it was so efficient. It was the dividends that had bought the Marmon and the coat and the star sapphire ring.

My parents of course invested. They found buyers somewhere, I suppose, for some of their oil paintings or oriental rugs, or for some of Father's fine guns. During the boom years, Father had been a collector of guns.

My parents had been taught such nice manners in childhood that it was actually impossible for them to suspect that these old friends of theirs were in league with crooks. They had no simple and practical vocabularies for the parts and functions of their excretory and reproductive systems, and no such vocabularies for treachery and hypocrisy, either. Good manners had made them defenseless against predatory members of their own class.

There we have our old friend peer pressure again, of course.

And there was no coal monopoly, of course. Whoever got my parents' money spent most of it on racehorses and chorus girls, probably, except for maybe a quarter of it, which they sent to the Swans as dividends.

I had a telephone conversation recently with a young Indianapolis cousin, a married woman, during which I said that I dreaded coming out there, since I did not consider it possible that my older relatives could love me but hate my books so. She replied that I had to understand that they were all Victorians and too old to change. They could not help themselves when it came to loathing dirty books.

So I thought about Victoria, queen of the United Kingdom of Great Britain and Ireland and the empress of India, who lived from 1819, long before my first ancestor arrived in this country, until 1901, when my father was a junior in Shortridge High School. And I asked myself why any mention of bodily functions should have pained this queen so.

I cannot believe that Victoria herself would have suffered a moment's genuine dismay if I had shown her the picture of my asshole which I drew for my book *Breakfast of Champions*. My asshole looks like this:

I also feature my asshole in my signature, which looks like this:

What would Queen Victoria really feel in the presence of what she had declared to be obscenities? That her power to intimidate was being attacked ever so slightly, far, far from its center, was being attacked where it could not matter much as yet—was being attacked way out on the edge? She created arbitrary rules for that outermost edge to warn her of the approach of anyone so crude, so rash as to bring to her attention the suffering of the Irish, or the cruelties of the factory system, or the privileges of the nobility, or the approach of a world war, and on and on. If she would not even acknowledge that human beings sometimes farted, how could she be expected to hear without swooning of these other things?

What a subtle scheme Queen Victoria evolved to make people hesitant about discussing their entitlement to more control over their lives. She persuaded them that they would deserve to be self-governing only after they had stopped thinking about all the things that human beings can't help thinking about all the time.

Genteel mothers of the era could do no less than to similarly discipline their children and their servants—and their husbands, if they could get away with it, and on and on.

What was the dirtiest story I ever wrote? Surely "The Big Space Fuck," the first story in the history of literature to have "fuck" in its title. It was probably the last short story I will ever write. I did it for my friend Harlan Ellison, who printed it in his anthology *Again, Dangerous Visions*. It was copyrighted by him in 1972, and appears here with his kind permission. It goes like this.

The Big Space Fuck

In 1987 it became possible in the United States of America for a young person to sue his parents for the way he had been raised. He could take them to court and make them pay money and even serve jail terms for serious mistakes they made when he was just a helpless little kid. This was not only an effort to achieve justice but to discourage reproduction, since there wasn't anything much to eat any more. Abortions were free. In fact, any woman who volunteered for one got her choice of a bathroom scale or a table lamp.

In 1989, America staged the Big Space Fuck, which was a serious effort to make sure that human life would continue to exist somewhere in the Universe, since it certainly couldn't continue much longer on Earth. Everything had turned to shit and beer cans and old automobiles and Clorox bottles. An interesting thing happened in the Hawaiian Islands, where they had been throwing trash down extinct volcanoes for years: a couple of the volcanoes all of a sudden spit it all back up. And so on.

This was a period of great permissiveness in matters of language, so even the president was saying *shit* and *fuck* and so on, without anybody's feeling threatened or taking offense. It was perfectly OK. He called the Space Fuck a Space Fuck, and so did everybody else. It was a rocket ship with eight hundred pounds of freeze-dried jism in its nose. It was going to be fired at the Andromeda Galaxy, two million light-years away. The ship was named the *Arthur C. Clarke*, in honor of a famous space pioneer.

It was to be fired at midnight on the Fourth of July. At ten o'clock that night, Dwayne Hoobler and his wife Grace were watching the countdown on television in the living room of their modest home in Elk Harbor, Ohio, on the shore of what used to be Lake Erie. Lake Erie was almost solid sewage now. There were man-eating lampreys in there thirty-eight feet long. Dwayne was a guard in the Ohio Adult Correctional Institution, which was two miles away. His hobby was making birdhouses out of Clorox bottles. He went on making them and hanging them around his yard even though there weren't any birds anymore.

Dwayne and Grace marveled at a film demonstration of how jism had been freeze-dried for the trip. A small beaker of the stuff, which had been contributed by the head of the Mathematics Department at the University of Chicago, was flash-frozen. Then it was placed under a bell jar, and the air was exhausted from the jar. The air evanesced, leaving a fine white powder. The powder certainly didn't look like much, and Dwayne Hoobler said so—but there were several hundred million sperm cells in there, in suspended animation. The original contribution, an average contribution, had been two cubic centimeters. There was enough powder, Dwayne estimated out loud, to clog the eye of a needle. And eight hundred pounds of the stuff would soon be on its way to Andromeda.

"Fuck you, Andromeda," said Dwayne, and he wasn't being coarse. He was echoing billboards and stickers all over town. Other signs said, "Andromeda, We Love You," and "Earth Has the Hots for Andromeda," and so on.

There was a knock on the door, and an old friend of the family, the county sheriff, simultaneously let himself in. "How are you, you old motherfucker?" said Dwayne.

"Can't complain, shitface," said the sheriff, and they joshed back and forth like that for a while. Grace chuckled, enjoying their wit. She wouldn't have chuckled so richly, however, if she had been a little more observant. She might have noticed that the sheriff's jocularity was very much on the surface. Underneath, he had something troubling on his mind. She might have noticed, too, that he had legal papers in his hand.

"Sit down, you silly old fart," said Dwayne, "and watch Andromeda get the surprise of her life."

"The way I understand it," the sheriff replied, "I'd have to sit there for more than two million years. My old lady might wonder what's become of me." He was a lot smarter than Dwayne. He had jism on the *Arthur C. Clarke*, and Dwayne didn't. You had to have an IQ of over 115 to have your jism accepted. There were certain exceptions to this: if you were a good athlete or could play a musical instrument or paint pictures, but Dwayne didn't qualify in any of those departments, either. He had hoped that birdhouse-makers might be entitled to special consideration, but this turned out not to be the case. The director of the New York Philharmonic, on the other hand, was entitled to contribute a whole quart, if he wanted to. He was sixty-eight years old. Dwayne was forty-two.

There was an old astronaut on the television now. He was saying that he sure wished he could go where his jism was going. But he would sit at home instead, with his memories and a glass of Tang. Tang used to be the official drink of the astronauts. It was a freeze-dried orangeade.

"Maybe you haven't got two million years," said Dwayne, "but you've got at least five minutes. Sit thee doon."

"What I'm here for—" said the sheriff, and he let his unhappiness show, "is something I customarily do standing up."

Dwayne and Grace were sincerely puzzled. They didn't have the least idea what was coming next. Here is what it was: the sheriff handed each one of them a subpoena, and he said, "It's my sad duty to inform you that your daughter, Wanda June, has accused you of ruining her when she was a child."

Dwayne and Grace were thunderstruck. They knew that Wanda June was twenty-one now, and entitled to sue, but they certainly hadn't expected her to do so. She was in New York City, and when they congratulated her about her birthday on the telephone, in fact, one of the things Grace said was, "Well, you can sue us now, honeybunch, if you want to." Grace was so sure she and Dwayne had been good parents that she could laugh when she went on, "If you want to, you can send your rotten old parents off to jail."

Wanda June was an only child, incidentally. She had come close to having some siblings, but Grace had aborted them. Grace had taken three table lamps and a bathroom scale instead.

"What does she say we did wrong?" Grace asked the sheriff.

Obscenity

"There's a separate list of charges inside each of your subpoenas," he said. And he couldn't look his wretched old friends in the eye, so he looked at the television instead. A scientist there was explaining why Andromeda had been selected as a target. There were at least eighty-seven chronosynclastic infundibulae—time warps—between Earth and the Andromeda Galaxy. If the *Arthur C. Clarke* passed through any one of them, the ship and its load would be multiplied a trillion times, and would appear everywhere throughout space and time.

"If there's any fecundity anywhere in the universe," the scientist promised, "our seed will find it and bloom."

One of the most depressing things about the space program so far, of course, was that it had demonstrated that fecundity was one hell of a long way off, if anywhere. Dumb people like Dwayne and Grace, and even fairly smart people like the sheriff, had been encouraged to believe that there was hospitality out there and that Earth was just a piece of shit to use as a launching platform.

Now Earth really was a piece of shit, and it was beginning to dawn on even dumb people that it might be the only inhabitable planet human beings would ever find.

Grace was in tears over being sued by her daughter, and the list of charges she was reading was broken into multiple images by the tears. "Oh God, oh God, oh God—" she said, "she's talking about things I forgot all about, but she never forgot a thing. She's talking about something that happened when she was only four years old."

Dwayne was reading charges against himself, so he didn't ask Grace what awful thing she was supposed to have done when Wanda June was only four, but here it was: poor little Wanda June drew pretty pictures with a crayon all over the new living-room wallpaper to make her mother happy. Her mother blew up and spanked her instead. Since that day, Wanda June claimed, she had not been able to look at any sort of art materials without trembling like a leaf and breaking out into cold sweats. "Thus was I deprived," Wanda June's lawyer had her say, "of a brilliant and lucrative career in the arts."

Dwayne meanwhile was learning that he had ruined his daughter's opportunities for what her lawyer called an "advantageous marriage and the comfort and love therefrom." Dwayne had done this, supposedly, by being half in the bag whenever a suitor came to call. Also, he was often stripped to the waist when he answered the door, but still had on his cartridge belt and his revolver. She was even able to name a lover her father had lost for her: John L. Newcomb, who had finally married somebody else. He had a very good job now. He was in command of the security force at an arsenal out in South Dakota, where they stockpiled cholera and bubonic plague.

The sheriff had still more bad news to deliver, and he knew he would have an opportunity to deliver it soon enough. Poor Dwayne and Grace were bound to ask him, "What made her *do* this to us?" The answer to that question would be more bad news, which was that Wanda June was in jail, charged with being the head of a shoplifting ring. The only way she could avoid prison was to prove that everything she was and did was her parents' fault.

Meanwhile, Senator Flem Snopes of Mississippi, chairman of the Senate Space Committee, had appeared on the television screen. He was very happy about the Big Space Fuck, and he said it had been what the American space program had been aiming toward all along. He was proud, he said, that the United States had seen fit to locate the biggest jism-freezing plant in his "L'il ol' hometown," which was Mayhew.

The word "jism" had an interesting history, by the way. It was as old as "fuck" and "shit" and so on, but it continued to be excluded from dictionaries long after the others were let in. This was because so many people wanted it to remain a truly magic word—the only one left.

And when the United States announced that it was going to do a truly magical thing, was going to fire sperm at the Andromeda Galaxy, the populace corrected its government. Their collective unconscious announced that it was time for the last magic word to come into the open. They insisted that *sperm* was nothing to fire at another galaxy. Only *jism* would do. So the government began using that word, and it did something that had never been done before, either: it standardized the way the word was spelled.

The man who was interviewing Senator Snopes asked him to stand up so everybody could get a good look at his codpiece, which the senator did. Codpieces were very much in fashion, and many men were wearing codpieces in the shape of rocket ships, in honor of the Big Space Fuck. These customarily had the letters "U.S.A." embroidered on the shaft. Senator Snopes' shaft, however, bore the Stars and Bars of the Confederacy.

This led the conversation into the area of heraldry in general, and the interviewer reminded the senator of his campaign to eliminate the bald eagle as the national bird. The senator explained that he didn't like to have his country represented by a creature that obviously hadn't been able to cut the mustard in modern times.

Obscenity

Asked to name a creature that *had* been able to cut the mustard, the senator did better than that: he named two—the lamprey and the bloodworm. And, unbeknownst to him or to anybody, lampreys were finding the Great Lakes too vile and noxious even for *them*. While all the human beings were in their houses watching the Big Space Fuck, lampreys were squirming out of the ooze and onto land. Some of them were nearly as long and thick as the *Arthur C. Clarke*.

And Grace Hoobler tore her wet eyes from what she had been reading, and she asked the sheriff the question he had been dreading to hear: "What made her *do* this to us?"

The sheriff told her, and then he cried out against cruel Fate, too. "This is the most horrible duty I ever had to carry out—" he said brokenly, "to deliver news this heartbreaking to friends as close as you two are—on a night that's supposed to be the most joyful night in the history of mankind."

He left sobbing, and stumbled right into the mouth of a lamprey. The lamprey ate him immediately, but not before he screamed. Dwayne and Grace Hoobler rushed outside to see what the screaming was about, and the lamprey ate them, too.

It was ironical that their television set continued to report the countdown, even though they weren't around any more to see or hear or care.

"Nine!" said a voice. And then, "Eight!" And then, "Seven!" And so on.

That is a made-up story. Here is another true story:

When I was little, there was a female friend of my parents who was particularly admired for her vivacity and good taste and impeccable manners and so on. She married a German businessman.

When she came back to Indianapolis after the Second World War, she was as attractive as ever. She said vivaciously that Hitler had been right about most things, and that Germany should be admired for fighting so many powerful enemies all at once. "We almost won," she reminded us.

I had just come back from Germany, too. I had been a prisoner of war there. So I took my father aside, and I said to him, "Father, I can't help having mixed feelings about this old family friend."

He told me that I should pay no attention to her when she spoke of political matters, that she understood nothing about them, that she was just a charming, silly, innocent little girl.

He was right. It was impossible for her to think coherently about assholes or Auschwitz or anything else that might be upsetting to a little girl.

That's class.

Obscenity

Hellfire Club

In 1979, after just one week back in the Big Apple, I discovered the one and only Hellfire Club—an illegal, after-hours club in a dark, underground, run-down, damp space where anything sexual and/or kinky could—and did—happen. In the previous century, the space had been a stop on the Underground Railroad, which helped slaves escape from the South. Now it was home to an entirely different kind of slave. It was a meeting place for people of every sexual persuasion: gays, bis, straights, drag queens, sadists, masochists, exhibitionists, voyeurs, fist-fuckers, foot fetishists, masturbators—you name it—they came together (literally) in all kinds of ways.

It was the heyday of the gay leathermen, who taught us what kinky sex was all about. You could piss, shit, or ejaculate anywhere you wanted. In the back was a maze of walls with glory holes (the management added two cutouts especially for my breasts). There was a leather sling for fisting and lots of S/M equipment, which was always in use. Leather-trimmed bodies hung from the ceilings, crawled under the tables, and lay on the bathroom floors. Lubricant was supplied at the bar, big cans of Crisco that everyone dipped their greasy hands into. When the movie *Cruisin'* with Al Pacino was filmed there, the production team left a few decorations, like an electric flag, a play jail cell, and some silver chains. Otherwise, there was only a crude wood bar, black-painted brick walls, and water dripping from the ceiling. It reeked of that S/M charm. (Madonna later rented the place to shoot some of the photos for her wonderful book *Sex*.)

For about two years, every Friday and Saturday night from midnight to 8 A.M. I could be found there, undressed in the sexiest of costumes, doing what most women wouldn't even dare fantasize about, having one wild sexual encounter after another. It was a place where I could experiment freely and even be appreciated for my sleazy, slutty, nasty ways.

One night I wrestled in oatmeal, and when it was over, two dozen men pissed on me to get the oatmeal off my body (there was no regular shower). Another time I orchestrated a circle-jerk, with about twenty-five guys jerking off around me. Often, gay men who had never had sex with women would choose me to be their first, which I always enjoyed. There was David, the

Jewish guy who got off on wearing a Nazi uniform, and there were dozens of guys who begged me to hit their behinds with a whip, crop, or cane until they were bloody. There was the Hasidic masochist who wanted to suck on my bloody tampon, and Timmy, who looked like an alien from outer space. He had been in a fire that burned off his lips, fingers, eyelids, ears, and nipples. His body was covered with the most fantastic textures, which turned me on to no end. There were dozens of foot-worshipping slaves, many a slutty transvestite, and some tantalizing transsexuals. There were unforgettable piercing scenes, a Great Dane who licked pussy and liked to get blow jobs, and an eight-foot boa constrictor who slithered on nude bodies. There were men who liked to be danced on by women in high heels. There was Billy Kerr, who could take a whole rack of billiard balls up his butt. He loved me to fist-fuck him up to my elbow, curve my arm around, and gently massage his heart from the inside.

Some nights when I had a lot of sex, I would actually hallucinate, without any drugs. I had several incredibly powerful experiences in which I went into a trance and into some underworld where there was no ego and no sense of time or of normal reality. (As my friend Lily Burana says, drugs are just the lazy person's sex.)

When I wasn't playing at the Hellfire Club, I was working at the Hell Hole Hospital, an S/M house on Twenty-seventh Street and Third Avenue, as a professional dominatrix and occasional submissive. Straight prostitution had become boring. S/M work was more creative, challenging, and interesting, and it allowed me to take out some of my pent-up anger on willing, well-paying men.

It was at the Hellfire Club that I did my best performance pieces, which I don't think I will ever be able to top. It was a totally outrageous time. Eventually, of course, things changed. By 1982, the new management replaced the hypnotic drum music with disco and encouraged dancing. "Tourists" came just to stare at us, bad-mannered, heterosexual, "dirty old men" lurked in greater and greater numbers, professional dominants came only to look for clients and vice versa, the gay guys gradually stopped coming, there were fights, undercover police, and then a deadly plague hit. As far as I was concerned, the Hellfire had climaxed. It was over.

For the Love of Women

I'VE ALWAYS BEEN WILD WHEN it comes to females, and I can see how my long line of love affairs finally busted up my marriage. I'll tell you more about that later, but now I want to set out the preamble to my constitution regarding women.

In spite of my old-fashioned attitudes, I believe that women have been the victims of society's oppression as much as anyone. They've been taught that they can't stand alone, they've been beaten down and treated like servants, they've been waiting on us men like slaves. I realize that, and I see the pity and the shame of it all.

On the other hand, I came up at a time when those attitudes were not argued—by men or by women. No one was challenging them, and I took them all for granted. In my middle age, I see the cracks in the old foundation—our thinking has certainly been fucked up—but I'm also a product of my time.

Women's lib is good to me, so I don't fight it. I want chicks to be more independent. I'm happy if they don't ask me for stuff. How can any right-minded man argue against that? But sometimes I wonder whether families can take too much competition between men and women.

A man has to feel like he's protecting something or somebody. If he doesn't, he's apt not to consider himself a man. That may be dumb, that may be ignorant, that may not be modern, but I bet you that 90 percent of the cats you meet on the street really feel that way.

It's been my experience that even strong gals finally lose respect for a man if he can be pushed around. They might go after you a little bit and test your ass, but when it gets down to the getting down, most of 'em still want you on top.

I'm one of those cats who looks at a cow pen and sees one bull; I look at a chicken house and see one rooster; I look at the lion's den and see one lion. But this bull has many cows, this rooster has many hens, this male lion has many females.

As far back as I can read, I see that man has been slipping around. The Bible talks about it time and again. And I do believe that deep down we've got a natural drive for more than one woman.

I recognize all the sexual differences—that there are men who lust for other men, women who dig other women, and people who go every which way. I respect those differences; I believe those desires are legitimate and wholesome, and what people do in their bedrooms is strictly their own business.

But there's a certain male drive—even though all males don't have it—which keeps us wanting more and more women: different kinds, different shapes, different sizes, with various voices, with sweet and salty smells and touches and feels which have us guessing and wondering and searching and switching.

I can see why, in the old days, a cat would pick out fifty or sixty women and put his seal on them. He was doing the same thing as a rooster or a bull, saying to the other cats, "Look, this is my territory, these are my women; hands off or I'll murder your ass."

Now I've never done that. But I have known more women than I can literally remember. I don't mean that as a brag, only as a fact. I don't ascribe it to anything unusual in me. In fact, I think that many, many other cats would do exactly what I do if they had the chance. But I don't have to do much; often I just turn around and there she is.

There are lots of cats who do the same thing. They conceal it, though, with their money and power. You'll have to wait till they die before you're hipped to what's actually coming down. Actors, kings, prime ministers, chiefs, presidents—these are gentlemen with similar situations as mine. They're names. And they're exposed to many women who are willing, ready, and able to satisfy them at any given moment.

That's a lovely fate—at least it can be—and Lord knows I've taken full advantage of it. I wasn't cut out to discipline myself sexually; few human beings are, and when they are, watch out: They usually take out the frustrations on something or somebody else.

Having female singers around me also opens up many possibilities for me right at home. Don't get me wrong. If I was forced to look hard, I'd certainly look. I don't like to conclude a day without female companionship.

I'm probably a fatalist. I don't know if I have two more years to live, forty years, or another two hours. I've always felt that way. I don't want to be unhappy. Not if I can control it. Fate will lay enough unhappiness on me; I don't need to look for any of my own. So as long as I can generate my own good times, I'll be doing just that.

I meet a gal. She digs me. I dig her. The chemistry's right. She's clean, she talks nice, she's attractive, she's enticing, her voice is pleasing, and she's anxious to get down—well, that's enough for me.

My relationships with women have been loose. I've slipped in and out of many different situations, but I've tried to follow some rules.

I have no interest in trying to keep tabs on every move a woman of mine makes. If she tells me she's going to the store, fine. I ain't gonna follow her to see whether she's gonna meet some dude at the Holiday Inn. I don't want to aggravate myself.

Naturally, like everyone else, I'm jealous. I ain't made of stone. But if a chick says she's through with me, I don't argue and I don't try to talk her out of it.

I assume she's serious. It takes courage to say that, since some men will stick a knife in a woman for such statements. They'd rather have their ladies dead than fucking someone else.

In my young and foolish days, I might have popped a gal upside the head on a rare occasion. But that's when I was stupid. That don't solve nothing, and besides, if you're blind, you're really dumb to start that kind of shit. You don't know what's coming back at you, and there ain't no way you gonna duck in time. A gal can kill your ass.

I think everyone's jealous. Even God. The Bible says somewhere that God is love, but it also says that God is a jealous God. So even He's got those same feelings. Those two—love and jealousy—will be mixed together forever. The trick is learning to walk away from the bad feelings and say, "Hey, Mama, you got it. Shine it on. Do what you feel you have to do. But I don't think we need to destroy each other."

I'm the kind of cat, for example, who doesn't ask a lot of questions. If I'm gone for six months, I won't ask the little lady if she gave it to anyone. If she say no, I might not believe her. If she say yes, I don't want to hear it.

Or if I walk in on a lady friend balling some cat in my apartment, I ain't gonna kill the guy. I'm just gonna tell him to get his ass out. Ain't gonna kill her either, but I'll blame her more than him. She ought to have the sense to say, "Look, I'm gonna give you this pussy, but you going to have to take me somewhere. You sure ain't going to get it here." Certain amount of decency is due everyone—even a dog.

Oh, my nose has been open very wide. I can suffer at the hands of a woman. Cut me and I bleed as much as any man. If I dig a chick, I don't want it to end. There's something about the finale which is tragic—like death—and the pain will burn inside me for a long time.

That's why I believe in options. If a woman tells me she's through, I'll want to know two or three others who'll take me in. I got to be that way, since I'm not willing to tell any female, "That's OK, honey, let me tuck you under my wing and keep you there forever."

I can't characterize my love affairs as lighthearted or silly. They're often serious. Even when I was a kid I hung around older women. Maybe that's 'cause I was thrust into the world of adults so young. Or maybe it's just because I didn't like silly girls who giggled and acted the fool. I like to have fun, but I prefer women who are women—mature and worldly. Let me tell you about a few of such friends.

Margie Hendrix was a great lead singer, a great Raelett. She fitted very well with my own style. I thought she was a big talent. She was also a lovely and sweet lady.

There's one thing, though, that Margie had a hard time with: learning her harmony part. I'd have to take her aside and go over it with her for hours on end. She must have been trying *too* hard. But once she learned her part, she'd have it forever.

Anyway, because of those extra hours spent alone with Margie, she and I got closer and closer, and one thing led to another. Soon we became lovers. We didn't live together—we always had separate hotel rooms on the road—but we saw each other often and grew especially tight.

Long 'bout 1959, she became pregnant. She told me about it and asked me what I thought she should do.

"What do *you* want to do?" I said.

"I think I want to have the baby."

"Well, that's what I want too."

And that was that. I'm not for or against abortions. That's the woman's business. So I would never—*ever*—even hint to a lady who I got pregnant that she should or shouldn't have an abortion. It's her decision. I'd never put any pressure on her one way or the other. I feel obliged to lend the kind of support that she wants.

Why should I do otherwise? I've never liked rubbers and therefore don't use 'em. So I certainly don't help prevent pregnancies. I feel obligated to live with the consequences.

Margie had a baby boy—Charles Wayne she called him—and I've supported him. I haven't seen him as much as my kids in California, but that doesn't mean I love him any less. I don't think one brother loses his love for another just because he lives far away. And that's how I feel about all my children. They are me.

Margie died a few years back, and it hurt me very deeply. We were together for a long while—up until she left the band in 1964—and there was something special about what we had. When you hear us sing together, you can tell how close-knit we were.

Today Charles lives with Margie's sister in New York, and I see him whenever it's possible.

I had a child with Louise, I had a child with Margie, I had three with my wife B, and there are four other times when I fathered kids.

Two of those times didn't result in any trouble. In the early fifties, a gal I was going with in Atlanta turned up pregnant. She had a little girl, and everything was cool. Same thing happened out here in California in the sixties. Another pregnancy, another baby girl.

I always made it plain that I'd support the children. I never denied being the father. How could I? My friends told me the babies looked like I'd spit 'em out. And besides, what man—married or single—really knows?

On the other hand, I didn't believe in supporting the child and also setting up mama in some luxurious crib with a Mercedes and two or three mink coats. No, sir. That ain't me. She wouldn't starve, and neither would the baby; but I didn't figure she was entitled to a lifetime of jewels and caviar.

That's how I got myself entangled in two nasty paternity suits. The first happened with a woman I knew in New York, and that's a story which is begging to be told.

. . . I met the mother of one of the younger Raeletts when I had to get her permission to have the girl join the band. This was when I was in New York so often that I even had an apartment at the Beaux Arts Hotel over on Third Avenue. From '59 through '63, all my business was in New York—my publishing firm, my lawyers, my booking agent, my accountant, most of the studios where I recorded, and ABC itself.

Well, this woman and I hit it off right away. I dug her so hard that I rented us an apartment on Ninety-seventh Street and Central Park West. For me, that was a big commitment. Shows you how much I was into her.

Our relationship went on for some time. I couldn't live in New York— I've never wanted to live there—but I was there for long spells.

New York always seemed like an experiment some scientist dreamed up. Instead of rats, you crowd as many people together as you can, let them crawl over each other and live with their asses sticking in each other's face. You do that for a while and watch the results—wholesale craziness.

Anyway, my lady friend became pregnant in New York, and once again

For the Love of Women

I didn't protest or encourage her to do anything but have the child. She did; she had a girl, and I was prepared to do what I had always done: support the baby. But my lady friend was listening to other folk. Friends started whispering in her ear:

"What, with all his bread! Well, listen here, if I was you—" That kind of chatter. She also talked to a lawyer, something which caused even more discord. Finally, she demanded more bread. *Demanded.* Well, I resent demands, especially when I think they're unreasonable. So I refused. She filed suit, it was later transferred to Los Angeles, and I lost. Again, I wasn't denying that I was the father. I was just denying that I was the Bank of America.

Exactly the same thing happened with a lady I had met in Ohio, who later came out to L.A. to work. She and I were very close for a while, she wound up pregnant, she had a little girl who looked just like me, and she demanded far more bread than I was willing to pay. Another paternity suit, another trial, another loss for me. By this time, you can see I wasn't exactly knocking 'em dead in the courts.

But that's not the point. I believe in doing what's fair and right. And it's very hard to threaten me. Even all the publicity and the embarrassment to my wife didn't make me budge. I considered those kinds of threats—"You gonna be exposed, Ray Charles"—blackmail, and I can't be blackmailed.

I've had fights with the musicians' union over the same kind of issue. A cat once missed his flight with me and I was supposed to pay him back wages of $600. Screw it, I said, it's *his* fault. The union screamed bloody murder, put me on their blacklist, harassed my friends. Even my lawyer said it wasn't worth fighting, that the legal fees would be double the $600. Didn't matter, I said. It was the principle.

In the case of both paternity suits, I think the ladies now regret what they did. They see I've forgiven them, but I haven't forgotten. I pay exactly what the court ordered and not a dime more. If any of my children need help, I'm there. But except for emergencies, I do no more or no less than what the judge ruled.

If they had only cooled it and let the thing ride out naturally, they would have wound up with more bread. But they misunderstood, got a little greedy, started pushing, and found out I wasn't budging.

Now, I don't believe in comparing women, and I don't believe in comparing my children. Every relationship is different. Naturally, I grew closer to the sons I had with B, because I was there more and got to watch their little joys and sorrows. I was also close with Evelyn, and that's because Louise and I were so tight. And besides, Evelyn was my first. She came out of some very strong love between two people. Louise and I had the kind of thing that you don't outlive.

I couldn't very well integrate all these children into my life. They live in faraway places, leading lives of their own. They exist on the outside of my day-to-day grind. But then again, even the boys I had with B—the kids who see me the most—have grown up with an absentee father.

Naturally many of my children are now under the jurisdiction of other men. And there's nothing I can do about that. I'm not about to break down doors and pry into other families' lives just 'cause my kids are there. And I don't really want to get involved with their mothers any more than absolutely necessary.

But the women and the kids know how I feel.

How can any of my children *not* be legitimate? "Illegitimate" sounds like the kid is damn near nonexistent. That's some cold shit. The law makes the man and woman feel like they committed some mortal sin. It's like the rape laws where a gal is asked all these jive questions to make it sound like she halfway coaxed the cat into attacking her.

It's what we were talking about before: marriage only got started when men wanted a way to fence off their property. So we set up these rules and started marrying gals. The gals felt like they were being protected. To them, it was their sole method of survival.

Many times women weren't allowed to learn to read or write. And they were held back the way blacks had been stifled by whites. That's how men have controlled women for so long. And that's how our attitudes got so crazy and one-sided.

I'm not a reformer and I'm not a crusader. I carry the sins and the silliness of my generation. But when it comes to children, I'm not like the rest of society. There are certain raunchy, hypocritical distinctions I just don't make.

Rape Scenes

I REMEMBER THE FIRST TIME someone stuck his hand down my pants when I didn't want him to. My roommate and I were mugged and molested in San Francisco while walking home from a movie. What I remember most was that my assailant was a full head shorter than me. He looked to be about fourteen and he had the tip of his knife pushed against my breastbone. I was scared stiff, unable to move, pleading. Our two mugger boys were so inexperienced themselves that one of them handed my roommate's key ring back to her so he could use both hands to unfasten her pants. She blew the silver whistle that hung off her keys, and as if she had fired a warning shot, the armed and dangerous brats scattered like rabbits. It was over. I felt like shit and I continued to feel like shit for months. I moved out of that neighborhood.

I remember the first time I had a rape fantasy. I was quite young and had gotten my hands on a very naughty book. This naughty book was actually a serious volume on true tales of juvenile delinquency which I found in the library. One story described a teenage girl pinned to a cross, just like Jesus, on a grassy hill outside her suburb; all the boys in her school had their way with her. Another story was about a little girl who didn't obey her parents' warnings not to talk to strangers. She was kidnapped by a couple who sequestered her in their apartment and introduced her, day by day, to various sex acts which she first resisted and then (of course) became addicted to. I was attending Catholic school at the time, and my head was already filled with stories of romantic martyrdom and the wages of sin. The juvenile delinquents' dramas played over and over again in my head at night as I rubbed myself through layers of sheets, pajamas, and underwear, always coming very hard. I never left *that* neighborhood.

I did not acknowledge having masochistic or submissive turn-ons until I was in my twenties. In a feminist college course, our teacher asked us if we had experienced arousing rape fantasies. One girl tearfully raised her hand and said this was true for her. My heart started beating so fast, it was all I could do to stay put. I was just as ashamed as she of these fantasies, but I would never have admitted them. Our professor was actually quite kind to her, if misinformed. She comforted the girl by saying that, as women, we had been brainwashed by the patriarchy to eroticize our subordination to men. She said these fantasies were very common, which is true, and that we could "overcome" them by exposing our fantasies to feminist analysis and by our increasing self-esteem.

She was dead wrong. In fact, I knew she was wrong later that same night. Despite my assertive self-confidence, rock-hard feminist analysis, and weekly shift at the rape crisis hotline, I could still crawl into bed and successfully masturbate to those same disturbing fantasies that had aroused me since I was a child. Feminism and self-esteem had no more effect on my erotic hot spots than the Communion wafers I used to take every Sunday, hoping they would wash away the devil's seed inside of me. Clearly, religion and linear politics were useless in explaining the unconscious and subversive quality of eroticism.

Two years later, I started reading about sexuality for the first time: the stuff that comes after the birds and the bees. At an airport newsstand, just before boarding, I picked up the mass-market edition of Nancy Friday's *My Secret Garden* in idle curiosity. The back cover quoted some eminent psychiatrist who said the book revealed "the hidden content of our own sexuality." I wondered what it would reveal about me, other than that I was a hopeless pervert.

It was a long trip from L.A. to Detroit. In fact, I would say it was the most excruciating five hours I have ever spent in the air. My face was scarlet; my floatable seat cushion was wringing wet. Friday quoted her "first name only" correspondents—Marie, Debbie, Jessica—describing fantasy after fantasy on subjects I had never spoken out loud: incest, anal sex, erotic kidnappings, dog lickings, gang bangs, screwing on altars, and panting in total darkness with nothing on but a blindfold. As flabbergasted as I was that these women came from every background and corner of the map, I recognized that I had been arousing myself with similar themes for as long as I could remember. I never consciously said to myself, "Oh, I think I'll fantasize about my sex-slave circus tonight." But each time I climaxed, at the moment of truth, those tigers and cowering slave girls flashed through my mind. The whip cracked.

I was one of Nancy's kids. According to the book's cover copy, I was one of a million women who read this book and, I assume, had a similar reaction. Either we were a million perverts clutching our grimy handbooks in shame, or these sexual fantasies were as normal as apple pie.

I had never really thought about what created an erotic fantasy. I thought a sex fantasy was some *Tiger Beat* scenario where you scored a dream date with this month's current tanned celebrity. I had masturbated since I was eight, but when I squeezed my eyes shut and bore down so hard on my arm that my fingers went numb, I never saw Paul Newman drift across my orgasmic screen. Or Mick Jagger. Or Bianca Jagger, for that matter.

Nancy Friday broke down the closet door of female sex fantasy by presenting the unfiltered erotic confessions of hundreds of women. Unfortunately, she also insisted on providing, in the same pages, her misguided analysis of female sexuality. Her lengthy introductions to each section of fantasies were designed to legitimize the book's intent, but sad to say, her stab at explaining why women are aroused by this taboo material was an intellectual disaster area. On the one hand, she was a feminist who believed her respondents were thriving, healthy women who had a lot of guts to speak out like this. On the other hand, she hinted that the whole lot of them had seriously ruptured relationships with their mothers. Or fathers. Or maybe society at large. It was pop psychology at its most awful.

Instead of providing the delicate framework needed to understand how erotic fantasies come from all manner of triggers, both deeply personal *and* cultural, Friday tried to read fantasies like they were Tarot decks. Oh, you have a lesbian fantasy? That must be the "longing to be close to mother" card. Every time I read one of her explanations, I felt like someone was trying to stuff my foot into a shoe that didn't have a prayer of fitting. Later, when I recommended the book to friends, I issued strict instructions: Read the fantasies *only* and draw your own conclusions.

Friday has continued to collect fantasies since My *Secret Garden* and its sequel, *Forbidden Flowers*, came out in the mid-seventies. She has finally compiled an anthology of fantasies for the nineties: *Women on Top*. As you can guess from her title, she not only has new stories to share but also claims that women's lives and wet dreams have changed extraordinarily since she did her first interviews twenty years ago.

On one score she's right. Most of the women in her new book are young—the end of the baby boomers. Their attitude toward masturbation is utterly matter-of-fact. One of the rare fifty-year-old contributors ends her fantasy with the exclamation of a post-feminist convert: "Masturbation is GREAT." The younger women consider sexual satisfaction a completely reasonable expectation in their lives.

Nancy is full of evidence to document the End of the Good Girl Era. Sex toys are commonplace in her respondents' bedrooms, and in their fantasies these sometimes take on Terminator-style proportions, as in one story

Rape Scenes

about a woman who imagines herself being penetrated and stroked along a relentless conveyer belt.

The fantasies are just as wild when they come from virgins as when they're from women with plenty of experience. "Connie," who has never had sex with anyone besides the boyfriend she met in fifth grade, tells a hot story about her turn-on for cops in uniform. She imagines being pulled over in her car and given a thorough pat-down. "[He] titillates my clit like a marble in oil."

Friday's research is an erotic marathon. The Gorilla Science Lab Experiment, where the woman scientist seduces her subject, alone is enough to send you to bed for a week. It becomes clear, reading story after story, that no territory is so fantastic that it cannot arouse you or remind you of your own provocative daydreams. Each woman prefaces her fantasy with a little information about her real life, making it obvious how normal, how common it is to fantasize about the bizarre, the taboo, the things that in real-life circumstances would trouble us, frighten us, or maybe just make us laugh. Erotic fantasies take the unbearable and unbelievable issues in life and turn them into orgasmic gunpowder.

Switching genders was a new issue in *Women on Top*, although I know women who were fantasizing this sort of thing long before Friday published it. One woman explains that when she massages her clitoris she imagines it growing "larger and larger until it is the size of a penis. I imagine I can feel the sensation of a man during intercourse. I also imagine that the man is having sex with me . . . hence I can feel the sensation of both partners at the same time."

As excited as Friday is to show off new fantasies where women experiment with men's traditional roles, her political agenda is still at odds with her story material. What she wants to prove is that today's groovy heads of households have dumped those nasty old oppressive rape fantasies in favor of turning the tables on their oppressors—dominating men and loving it. "Women in *My Secret Garden* who may have had very controlling natures in reality invented elaborate fantasies of rape," Friday recalls. "It was all they dared themselves. Then once *My Secret Garden* was published, overnight the rape fantasy was rejected by the women in this book who wanted total power over and domination over men."

Oh, horse feathers. Women are not newcomers to fantasies where they wield the sexual power, nor have we abandoned fantasies of being ravished just because this is the macha nineties. A woman's place in her job or home is no forecaster of what her fantasies may be. How can Friday not know this yet? A woman or man CEO can have the most hair-raising rape fantasy on the block, and it will have nothing to do with lack of courage. A willing submission is every bit as powerful as a domination fantasy. And in our fantasies, no matter how much we struggle to deny it, we control every frame. Whether we are standing tall in thigh-high boots or are breathless on our knees is simply a matter of our well-lubricated position. As Friday knows from her survey of men's fantasies in *Men in Love*, men have submissive fantasies in even greater numbers than women. So spare us the pseudofeminist Bible stories.

Friday devotes a full chapter to "Women Controlling Men," and while it is certainly a delightful treasure trove (Lou Ellen and her fifteen well-endowed male housekeepers are particularly fabulous), it is downright irritating that Friday buries the numerous submissive and masochistic fantasies in chapters whose titles don't hint at their contents.

Lesbian fantasies get the worst treatment. Friday insists that "all fantasies with other women begin and end with tenderness." Then, in the very next fantasy, a girl named Brett says her favorite fantasy is to be dominated by a group of ruthless bulldykes. Not one particle of tenderness is mentioned. In many of the other lesbian fantasies, the feminine attraction is bitchy or masculine rather than narcissistic or maternal.

Friday's prejudiced image of lesbianism as the last word in sisterly, dewy-eyed breast worship is dead wrong. She misses the variety of gay life, and the fantasies she has collected don't accurately represent the spectrum of lesbian desire.

Friday took all the fantasies that didn't fit her new "dominant-woman theory" and scattered them throughout the book in the most unlikely places. I had to search and search to find the very best innocent babysitter fantasy ("I am babysitting two boys. They decide to play Indians and tie me up. Here their father comes in. . . ."), which was stuck in a chapter called "Women with Bigger Appetites than Their Men." If this was *my* anthology, I would have had chapter titles like "Sweet Innocent Babysitters," "Secret Spy Agents," and "True Tales from the Catholic Church."

In her claim that women are now "on top" in their sexual fantasies, Friday cultivates a dangerous party line. She imagines that women's economic independence is somehow tied to the content of our sexual fantasies. We don't need to make a case for feminism by claiming that women are now entertaining new, improved, ringmaster or revenge fantasies. This kind of thinking unwittingly censors the diversity and complexity of real women's fantasies. It is the same as my Women's Studies teacher claiming that only unliberated women have rape fantasies and that as soon they get their consciousnesses raised, those ugly stains will wash right out.

What really happens when you get your consciousness raised is that you can't be afraid of your fantasies any longer. You see the difference between your real-life anxieties and limitations versus your potential to go to any extreme in fantasy. Now, *that* is empowering. Erotic dreams certainly communicate powerful and very personal messages. But to read them as if they were tea leaves amounts to some pretty tacky fortune telling.

We can't assume that certain labels lead to certain behavior and vice versa. After I was mugged and fingered by the fourteen-year-old prick, I had several fantasies. In one, my revenge fantasy, I walked in on him at home during Sunday dinner and shamed him in front of his family. His mother told him to get out, that he could never come back again. In another fantasy, I imagined my "if only" scenario, where I raised my long arm, disregarding his blade cutting into my chest, and decked him. I spit on him lying in the street, and the blood from where he nicked me dripped into his eyes.

But in the third fantasy, he kept fucking me with his hands, and I was frozen, naked on the sidewalk. He talked to me nasty, he was arrogant, and he teased the knife against my nipples. Neighborhood people gathered; he invited them to take his place.

I had this last fantasy twice, both times culminating in orgasm. Then it became impossible to conjure up. My old rape fantasies from childhood came back in its place.

A year later, I moved back into the old neighborhood, the "scene of the crime," but I was smarter and, in a first for me, I was territorial. Welcome to my neighborhood—all of it.

Rape Scenes

Transmissions from Camp Trans

UNLESS YOU'VE SPENT SOME TIME as a lesbian or perhaps are a hippie sort of woman, you've probably never heard of the Michigan Womyn's Music Festival (MWMF). It's been happening for the past twenty-eight years, taking place each August on a lush chunk of woodland in northern Michigan, planned to coincide with summer's final full moon. While womyn's music is the festival's alleged purpose—the guitar stylings of folksters like Holly Near and Cris Williamson as well as post-riot-grrrl acts like Bitch and Animal, the Butchies and Le Tigre, to draw in the younger generation—the real purpose is to hunker down in a forest with a few thousand other females, bond, have sex in a fern grove, and go to countless workshops on everything from sexual esoterica to learning to parade around on stilts, processing various oppressions, and sharing how much you miss your cat. Women strut around half or fully naked because it's hot and they can. The festival aims to be a utopia, and in most ways it hits its mark. Performers are paid well, and all performers are paid the same amount, regardless if they're famous, like the Indigo Girls, or some virtually unknown girl band. You can come for free as a worker, taking on jobs like child care, kitchen work, or driving shuttles on and off the land, and even women who pay the hundreds of dollars to come in are required to pull their weight by picking up a couple of work shifts. The only dudes allowed in the space are the ones who rumble in, late night, on giant trucks to vacuum the sludge from the hundreds of porto-potties, called porto-janes. They are preceded by a woman who hollers, "Man on the land! Man on the land!" a warning to skittish nymphs to hop into a tent or a bush. I've been to the festival four or five times and can attest to the deeply stunning feeling of safety and peace there. The absence of guys does make for an absence of threat; everyone's guard is down, finally, and a relaxation level is hit that is probably impossible to access in the real world. It is an emotional experience to realize how tense you are all the time, the low level of fear and defensiveness that radiates off your body. Pretty much everyone who attends bursts into tears at some point, saddened at all the psychic garbage females are forced to lug around, grateful for this week of respite. It's no wonder that the women who come to the festival are zealots about it, live for August, get totally obsessed with and protective of the culture that springs up within its security-patrolled boundaries.

In 1991 a transsexual woman named Nancy Jean Burkholder was evicted from MWMF. Transsexual women, for those not up-to-date with the growing transgender revolution, are women who were born in male bodies and have been fighting against that ever since. They may or may not be on hormones, which can be costly or unavailable. Same goes for sex reassignment surgery, which is often prohibitively expensive and not covered by insurance. Nancy Jean's eviction is famous in Michigan lore, for it sparked a fierce debate about the inclusion of transsexual women that has been raging over a decade. A lot of women inside the festival want to keep trans women out. Some staunchly insist that the individuals are not women, they are men in dresses trying to ruin the feminist event. Others concede that trans women are women but because they were born boys and may still have penises, the festival is not the place for them. Trans women and their growing number of allies say that these feminist justifications are straight-up discrimination, no different from the rest of the world, which routinely denies that trans women are "real" women and bars their access to everything from jobs to housing, domestic violence counseling to health care. Off and on for the past decade, a small group of trans people and their supporters have set up a protest camp, Camp Trans, across the road, in hope of changing the policy that left Nancy Jean stranded in the Midwest twelve years ago.

NANCY JEAN BURKHOLDER

I appreciate women's space, and after checking with festival literature, I couldn't see that I wasn't welcome. I had talked to people, and their opinion was: If you think of yourself as a woman, you're welcome. I'd gone with a friend of mine, Laura. We drove out together and we were number thirty-three in line. We got there early, we were really excited about going. We set up camp up in Bread & Roses. It's kind of the quiet area. Then we each did a work shift—shuttle duty. Hauling people from the front all the way back. That evening Laura was having a friend come in on the shuttle bus from Grand Rapids, so we walked down to the gate about 9 P.M. to meet the bus. Turned out the bus was late and didn't get there 'til about eleven. We were hanging out at the fire pit, just kind of joined the group of people that were hanging out and talking. When the bus came in at eleven, Laura went up to the gate to meet her friend, and I waited by the fire pit. At that point a couple of women approached me and asked if I knew that this was a festival for women. It kind of surprised me. I said, "Yeah, uh-huh." About that time Laura was coming back, so I asked her to come over, something didn't seem right about what these women were asking. I think one of them asked me if I was transsexual. I said, "My history is none of your business." I asked, "Why are you asking?" and she said that transsexuals weren't welcome. I think I remember saying, "Are you sure? How do you know?" And so she went at that point and talked to the festival producers. She came back in about an hour, it took a while, and said that transsexuals were not welcome at the festival, and was I transsexual? At one point I offered to show them my driver's license, which said female, and also to drop my drawers, and she said, "I wouldn't be comfortable with that." Which I thought was kind of off, given the amount of nudity at the festival. She asked again, "Are you transsexual?" and I said, "It's none of your business." At that point she said, "Well, I'm empowered to expel any woman, at any time, for any reason. You have to leave." I knew there was no arguing with them.

They wouldn't let me leave the area around the main gate. Instead, Laura went with a couple of festival security guards back out to my campsite, scooped up all my equipment and brought it back to the main gate. It must have been about one o'clock in the morning by then. They arranged for us to stay at a motel in Hart. I think we got there around two o'clock. And it was a dump. It was cold, there was mildew in the carpet, wet, trucks running by on Route 10. I couldn't believe it. I was devastated. The next day Laura took me down to Grand Rapids, and I paid for a plane ticket and flew home to New England. I flew to Worcester, Massachusetts, and Laura's partner arranged for a taxi to take me back to their house, where my car was. Laura went back to the festival, for two reasons. She was doing a workshop, and also she went back to tell my friends what happened to me. Otherwise I would have disappeared without a trace. One of the friends she told was Janis Walworth. Janis and Laura spent the rest of the festival talking to people and telling them what happened. I was back in New

Hampshire, and I called *Gay Community News*, a newspaper in Boston, to tell them what happened. I think they were a little taken aback and weren't quite sure what to do with this. They did say, "If you want to write an editorial, we'll publish it." So Laura wrote a letter to the editor, and they published it with my editorial, and we took up a whole page in the newspaper. That kind of started the whole controversy.

The important piece that doesn't always get reported is that Janis organized a bunch of people to go back in 1992. She brought her sister, a male-to-female postoperative transsexual, and also an intersex person and a butch female. They distributed buttons and leaflets and did a survey. The survey indicated that 72 percent approved of transsexuals being at the festival; 23 percent did not, for a variety of reasons. Out of that, Janis categorized the reasons why people didn't want transsexuals, and she compiled Gender Myths, twenty-four of them.

Twenty-four Gender Myths
1. Although male-to-female transsexuals have surgery to change their anatomy and take female hormones, they still act like men.
2. Male-to-female transsexuals are not women-born women (or womyn-born womyn).
3. Male-to-female transsexuals have been socialized as men, and this socialization cannot be changed.
4. Male-to-female transsexuals are trying to "pass" as women. They try to make themselves as much like nontranssexual women as possible.
5. Transsexuals take jobs away from women because they had access to better training when they were men.
6. To lessen the power of patriarchy in our lives, we must purge our community of everything male, including women who once had male anatomy.
7. Most women can easily prove they are not male-to-female transsexuals, if they are challenged to do so.
8. Male-to-female transsexuals have been raised as boys, have never been oppressed as women, and cannot understand women's oppression.
9. Women's space is not "safe" space if male-to-female transsexuals are allowed.
10. Transsexuals have surgery so they can have sex the way they want to.

11. Male-to-female transsexuals are trying to take over the lesbian community.
12. The sex assigned to a person at birth is that person's "real" sex.
13. The lesbian and women's communities have nothing to gain by including transsexuals.
14. Nontranssexual women have the right to decide whether transsexuals should be included in the women's community.
15. Transsexuals are guilty of deception when they don't reveal right away that they are transsexuals.
16. Male-to-female transsexuals are considered men until they have sex-change surgery.
17. People can be categorized as transsexual or nontranssexual—there's no in-between.
18. Women who want to become men have bought into societal hatred of women or are hoping to take advantage of male privilege.
19. A person's "true" sex can be determined by chromosome testing.
20. Transsexualism is unnatural—it is a new problem brought about by sophisticated technology.
21. "Real" women, certainly those who belong to the lesbian community, rejoice in their womanhood and have no desire to be men.
22. Now that festival policy has been made clear, there are no transsexuals at Michigan.
23. Transsexuals have caused trouble at Michigan, resulting in their expulsion.
24. Nontranssexual women at Michigan don't want male-to-female transsexuals here.

AIRPLANE OVER SOUTHWEST, AUGUST 15, 2003

And I'm reading *Jane* magazine because my plane could of course crash, this could be my last moment alive, and I will not deny myself the small delight. *Jane* is the most innocent of the guilty pleasure that is women's magazines, as it at least aspires toward a sensibility that affirms women shouldn't look starved for cheeseburgers and gay people are cool. Running beneath a small column in which the actor who plays the exchange student on *That '70s Show* gives advice to lovelorn teenage girls is this bit of information: "Wesleyan University now offers the nation's first 'gender-blind' dorm for students who don't label themselves as male or female."

I am zooming through the air toward a patch of National Forest presently populated by a horde of people who don't label themselves as

male or female, as well as bunches of folks whose identities settle somewhere beneath the banner *transgender*. Now, before we land in Grand
Rapids, an emergency glossary.

Emergency Glossary of Gender Identity Terminology
   [partially plagiarized from the Antny's Place Web site]
   Genderqueer: Individuals who may identify as both male and female, or
       sometimes male and sometimes female, or decline to identify with any
       gender whatsoever. Not necessarily on hormones or pursuing surgeries.
   Transsexual: 1) A person who feels a consistent and overwhelming desire
       to transition and fulfill their lives as members of the opposite gender.
       Generally taking hormones and pursuing surgery. 2) One who believes
       that his or her actual biological or "born" gender is opposite the one it
       should have been.
   Trans man: A female-to-male transsexual (FTM). Also trannyboys, if
       younger.
   Trans woman: A male-to-female transsexual (MTF).
   Pre-op: Has not had sex reassignment surgery.
   Post-op: Has had sex reassignment surgery.
   Non-op: Has no intention of having sex reassignment surgery.

I am headed to Camp Trans, now in the tenth year of its on again/off again
standoff with the Michigan Womyn's Music Festival across the road.
Started by Nancy Jean and friends in the years after her eviction, the protest
camp faded away in the mid-nineties. A new generation of young transgendered activists picked up the torch in 1999 and resumed the con-
frontational face-off. In the scant four years since, there has been an
unprecedented boom in people identifying as trans, mostly female-assigned
people transitioning to men or staking out a third-sex genderqueer territory.
Flocking to Camp Trans for both the political struggle and the party, they
have changed the outpost in significant ways. The focus of the trans
struggle in recent years has drifted away from its original intention of getting trans women into women-only and lesbian spaces. Trans men have
generally been welcomed—if not totally fetishized—by contemporary dyke
communities, particularly young, urban enclaves. The same is not true for
trans women, even lesbian trans women. This influx of trannyboys and
their lesbian admirers has not only alienated many of the trans women at
Camp Trans, it's also blown up attendance so high that they can no longer
set up right across the street from the festival gates. The encampment is

now located up the road a bit, in a forest-lined field between the music festival and a nudist camp.

I've never been to Camp Trans, though I stopped attending MWMF a
few years back, too conflicted about this exclusion of trans women. Today
I'm picked up at the airport by a girl named Ana Jae who volunteered to get
me so that she could get the hell out of the woods. Ana hates camping; she
says the bugs are attacking like mad, and it's really bad when you drop your
shorts to piss in the woods and they start fluttering around your bare ass. Ana
can't use the porto-potties because she is traumatized by the 1980s B-horror
flick *Sleepaway Camp II*, where terrible things happen within one plastic,
fetid chamber, so she is forced to piddle among the bugs. I'm antsy to hear
of the mood at Camp Trans, and Ana confirms that the trans men by far out-
number the trans women, complains about a general devaluing of femininity in the young, post-dyke, queer scene, and tells me about a sex party
that somehow went awry the night before and is this morning's main drama.
Our immediate drama is that we get outrageously, wildly lost on the way
back to the woods, careening through quaint Michigan townships for hours,
hopelessly passing farm stands selling fresh vegetables, rows of exploding
sunflowers and cornstalks, trees and trees and more trees, gigantic willows
with long whipping branches that drape and swag, and large, one-family
homes with porches and pools and tractors in the front yard. We know that
we've descrambled our cryptic directions when we pass a gas station that has
a flapping sign reading WELCOME WOMYN in its parking lot and loads
of sporty females loading cases of beer into their cars. We follow a camper
with a bumper sticker that reads SEE YOU NEXT AUGUST down a road
so heavily traveled that the foliage that lines it is coated in a thick dust of
brown dirt, like an apocalyptic snowfall. We pass the front gates of the festival, see its huge parking lot crammed with vehicles, women in neon-
orange vests directing the flow of females through the gates, and we keep
going. It's a disappointment not to see Camp Trans boldly arranged there at
the mouth of the festival, and I wonder how their political point can be
clearly made if they are tucked out of site around the curving road. The
former vigil has turned into a sort of alternative to the festival, one that's free
of charge, one that a lot of MWMF attendees mistake as a happy, friendly,
separate-but-equal campsite. A place for dykes who think trannyboys are hot
to spend a night cruising, partying, then returning to their gated community
up the road. For the trans women relying on Camp Trans as a site of protest,
this new incarnation as a sort of Spring Break for trannnyboys and the dykes
who date them has been infuriatingly sucky. Which is why Sadie Crabtree,

a trans woman and an activist from D.C., has emerged as the sort of head leader this year. It is her intention, backed up by the other organizers, to bring the focus of Camp Trans back around to the trans women it was originally meant to serve.

CAMP TRANS WELCOME STATION

Everyone who comes to Camp Trans, either to camp or on a day pass from the festival, has to pause at the welcome tent and check in, and MWMF attendees who arrive tonight for entertainment will be charged $3. Behind a table made from boards and sawhorses sits a couple of Camp Trans welcomers, women doing their work shifts acclimating visitors to their new environment. Like the festival across the way, everyone here is expected to lend a hand. The camp isn't nearly as large as the music festival—their parking lot is bigger than Camp Trans's entire area—but it still takes a lot of work to make it run. I spy a kitchen tent with a mess of pots and pans and water jugs strewn before it. Another tent is garlanded with Christmas lights that are beginning to shine as the hot summer sun starts to sink. This is the performance area, bulked with DJ and other sound equipment. There's a medic tent and a roped-off area for "advocates," armbanded individuals whose job is to answer touchy questions, listen to complaints, and diffuse conflicts.

At the welcome tent I sign in, and the form I sign in on doubles as a petition that calls for the dropping of the festival's womyn-born-womyn policy. I'm handed a slip of paper welcoming me to Camp Trans.

From "Welcome to Camp Trans 2003"
> Camp Trans is an annual protest against the Michigan Womyn's Music Festival's policy that bars transsexual women from attending. MWMF's so-called "womyn-born-womyn" policy sets a transphobic standard for women-only spaces across the country, and contributes to an environment in women's and lesbian communities where discrimination against trans women is considered acceptable. For trans women who are consistently refused help from domestic violence shelters and rape crisis centers, this is a matter of life and death.

Posterboards stuck with Post-It notes outline each day's workshops and meetings, another posterboard is cluttered with bright notes soliciting *amour* in the woods. One bemoans a throat atrophied with lack of use, another is looking for couples to participate in a Floridian retiree role-play. Interested parties can respond by slipping scrawled replies into corresponding envelopes. There are 'zines for sale, silk-screened patches that say "Camp Trans Supporter" in heavy metal letters, buttons that squeak "I (heart) Camp Trans," and T-shirts reading "Not gay as in happy but queer as in fuck you." There is also a notebook labeled "Letters to Lisa Vogel."

Lisa Vogel is the sole captain of the SS Michigan Womyn's Music Festival. There is no one but her behind the wheel; she wrote the policy and she is the only one who can lift it. Of the many rumors I hear this weekend, most involve her. One is that she offered Camp Trans a sum of money somewhere between $7,500 and $75,000 to start their own damn festival. This is totally unlikely, as her own festival is suffering financially. Another is that transsexual women will be allowed into her festival over her dead body, an extreme pledge that makes me think of Lauryn Hill's "I'd rather my babies starve than white kids buy my records" quote. Who knows what's true. Lisa Vogel is famously tight-lipped about the whole controversy and has never made an attempt to negotiate with Camp Trans. In the face of past protests she has simply reiterated the policy, which, I also hear, has suddenly been removed from all MWMF Web pages. There is much speculation on what this means, but no one is naïve enough to believe that it means the policy has been dropped and trans women welcomed. More likely the immense controversy, which now involves a boycott not just of the festival but of the individual artists who perform at it, is wearing on festival producers, and targets for attack are being shuffled out of the line of fire.

Excerpts from "Letters to Lisa Vogel"

> I love the festival and it has to become a safe space for everyone. It can happen, everyone would benefit. As feminists we can not become our oppressors.

> A transpositive environment will only improve the festival experience for all. There are plenty of information sources on how to do this.

> I've been to many trans-inclusive events in my hometown, including a woman's bathhouse. I feel totally safe around trans women, and I know lots of other women my age who feel the same way.

Behind the tree line is where people are camping, and the arc of green has been segmented into three campsites: *loud substance*, which means campers are getting bombed and fucking right outside your tent; *loud no substance*, meaning sober people lashed to trees and moaning loudly; and *quiet no substance*, which means everyone sleeps. This is where I camp. I actually unknowingly plop my tent right in the center of a sand patch being used for AA meetings. Next to me is a camper van all tricked out with a sink and a fridge, the outside painted [like a] checkerboard. It looks straight out of *Fast Times at Ridgemont High* and it is occupied by, lo and behold, my friend Chris, who is out on his makeshift patio, smoking a lot of pot and triggering the substance-free campers. He's sharing his pipe with a lesbian named Mountain, who lives on a women-only commune in Oregon that has successfully integrated trans women into their home. It is, essentially, no big whoop. Life goes on, wimmin are still wimmin, they tend their organic gardens and print their lunar calendars and life is good. Mountain is one of those women who live for Michigan, and it's a real big deal that she's not there this year. She's here at Camp Trans in solidarity.

The sun is dipping and people are scurrying around full of purpose. Tonight is the big dance and performance, and the number of people on this land will rise with an influx of girls from the festival. Camp Trans's population, which hovers at around seventy-five, will shoot up above a hundred with the visitors. Which is nothing compared to the eight thousand or so women hunkered down in the vast woods across the way. Sadie is dashing around, all stressed out. She's got a sweet, kind face with sparkly eyes and short hair; her all-black outfits seem like military gear, especially with the big black women-symbol-raised-fist tattoo on her shoulder. She's still dealing with fallout from last night's sex party, and now she just found a note from a Camp Transer looking to host a Camp Trans workshop inside the festival, where trans women can't go. There is a feeling that the action is spinning out of the organizer's hands, and she's upset that a so-called Camp Trans event would happen in a place where trans women aren't allowed. Sadie, needing a drink, bustles off with tears in her eyes.

Sadie Crabtree

> My number-one goal was to make Camp Trans a safe and empowering space for trans women. I told myself that even if only twenty people showed up, even if we didn't do any actions or outreach with the festival, that as long as trans women went home feeling better about the space, about ourselves, and about

organizing to improve the conditions of our lives, I'd count that as success.

One problem was that some festival attendees were unclear on the mission of Camp Trans and didn't see it as a protest but rather as a part of their Michigan experience. Kind of a suburb of MWMF where fest attendees could go to hang out with hot trannyboys. That's another problem—the fascination with and fetishization of FTMs in some dyke communities makes trans women even more invisible. At least one fest attendee last year had spoken openly about how she totally supported Camp Trans and loved trans guys but just didn't like trans women. We tried to solve some of those problems this year by having a very clear mission statement on all the materials, providing suggested talking points for all campers, and having discussions about the experiences of trans women at Camp Trans. We had volunteer advocates whose job it was to listen to people's concerns—especially those of trans women—and help organizers plan solutions. Another thing we did was designate certain workshops and decompression areas "wristband-free zones" where fest attendees were asked not to go. Having a space to retreat from interactions with fest attendees was a need that had been expressed by trans women last year, but it also sent a message. It wasn't to stigmatize festival attendees but to help people think a little more critically about what it means to give hundreds of dollars to a transphobic organization for permission to do activism inside, what it means to speak in a space where others' voices are forbidden, what it's like to have a space that specifically excludes you. When people asked about the wristband-free spaces, we offered them scissors. You have that choice. Some people don't.

Another goal I had for this year was to move the strategic focus from just education and outreach with attendees toward a real direct-action organizing strategy. Because there's really one decision maker in the campaign to change the policy, and she's said clearly that trans women will never be allowed at MWMF. You don't convince someone like that. That's why you have to organize—to get someone who has more power than you to give you something they don't want to give. You have to understand your own power in order to do that. So we did list building this year. We started building a base of constituents who attend the festival. After our work this year, we know who several hundred of our supporters are. We know what they're willing to do to change the policy, and we know how to get in touch with them before next year. We know that we can send a stack of letters that will cost Lisa Vogel tens of thousands of dollars. One of the questions on the constituent sign-up form is "Would you support a coordinated action to end the policy if it meant skipping the festival one year?" That's power we can measure, and that's what we need to change the policy. Vogel can do the math just like we can. Maybe the numbers aren't big enough this year, but next year they might be. Eventually, they will be.

I want more trans women to attend. I want more trans women to feel safe and empowered and to be involved in the yearlong planning of Camp Trans 2004. The approaches we used with festival attendees this year worked, and the lists we built are crucial. We just need to stick with it, because we're going to win.

LEMMY AND OTHER PROBLEMS

Another MWMF policy is no male voices on the land, meaning no one is allowed to slip a Michael Jackson tape into their boom box and start moonwalking. Perhaps it also means the porto-potty men take a vow of silence when they roar through the gate. Who knows? This rule has been broken, or bent, with the rise of drag kings—female performers who costume themselves as men, both lampooning and celebrating masculinity in a sort of burlesque, often via lip-synchs. When, some years back, the Florida drag king troupe House of Ma took an MWMF side stage during a talent show, the audience was given warning that a male voice would shortly boom from the sound system. Offended women hightailed it out of the vicinity, one step ahead of Neil Diamond. This, of course, is not an issue at Camp Trans, so the music is a little varied—better—on this side of the road. The dance party under way on the patch of sandy brown earth which has been designated both "stage" and "dance floor" is shaking to Dr. Dre and The Gossip, Motorhead and Peeches, Billy Idol, Northern States, Ludacris, and Fannypack. I'm standing beside Benjamin, a genderqueer boy. Meaning he was born a boy and remains a boy but he's gorgeous like a girl and does hella fierce drag. His hair is an architecture of multiple hairpieces that look like feather dusters, protruding from his scalp in feathery pom-poms. "Everyone is so beautiful," he muses at the crowd, and he is right. Mostly young, late teens and twenties, they are kicking up Pig Pen–sized clouds of dust as they dance in their silver plastic pants and marabou-trimmed spandex, their starchy crinolines and pink ruffled tuxedo shirts, their neon-orange nighties, push-up bras, and outfits constructed from shredded trash bags and duct tape. Everyone is gleeful, happy to be smashing the gender binary, to be partying down for a cause, to be part of a revolution of good-looking gender-ambiguous people. In the process of deconstructing gender identity, I muse, sexual preference may become obsolete. If you're an old-fashioned lesbian purged of transphobia, you'll be hot for the trans women. Bunches of dykes are already hooking up with trans men, and if you're dating trans men, it's probably a good time to reckon with your bisexuality and attraction to the equally male, if perhaps less socially evolved, non-trans men of the world. And that's pretty much everyone. Yeah. Maybe I'm just trampy, but I'm attracted to pretty much everyone here.

Showtime starts with an introduction by an organizer named Jess who instructs the crowd—part Camp Transers, part festie-goers—on proper behavior while in such an unusual space, a space where trans people out-number the non-trans. Because last year's visitors didn't understand how to act, pissing off a lot of trans women, this year we get a tiny schooling. Do not assume anyone's pronoun. There's really no way of guessing at who is a "he" and who is a "she," and besides all that, there are gangs of genderqueers pro-moting the use of a third pronoun, "ze," which I am not going to conjugate for you. Others say to hell with pronouns all together and dare us to be more creative in the way we were refer to them. Also, Jess instructs, do not ask anyone rude questions about their bodies. If you're bursting with curiosity or just freaking out, please see an armbanded advocate. Last year at Camp Trans, the weight loss guru Susan Powter paid a visit and was greeted by an advocate named J.J. Bitch. "J.J. Bitch!" she shrieked, waving her arms around like a nut. "J.J. Bitch! I love that name! I want that name! I'm J.J. Bitch!" J.J. Bitch was stunned and delighted by the somewhat manic celebrity guest. Advocate work can be quite emotionally draining. It had to have been a lift.

First there's skits, one of which demonstrates the simply cruelty of turning trans women away from the festival gates. Another enacts the trau-matizing experience of having perfect strangers trot up and inquire about the state of your genitals because you are transgendered and expected to answer this. Last-minute creations, the skits are shaky but effective. The audience ripples out from the spotlit performance area, sitting in the dirt, getting hopped on by grasshoppers and crickets and weird brown beetles with little wings folded beneath their shells. A moth as big as a sparrow keeps charging into one of the lightdishes glowing up from the ground. A gang of women come out all dressed in trash bags and duct tape. They are The Fat-tastics and they deliver a smart performance about fat power and fat oppression, ending in an empowering cheer replete with pom-poms fashioned from more shredded garbage bags. A lanky punk-rock trans women named Geyl Forcewind, who has a red anarchy sign sewed into her ratty T-shirt, sets up a puppet theater with some chairs, a blanket, her hands, and the hands of some friends. A good radiance sort of shines off Geyl; her combat boots are patched with gummy straps of duct tape, and she spits a lot. Here are some of her jokes.

Geyl Forcewind's Jokes, Which She May Not Have Made Up Herself
What's white and can't climb trees?
Yogurt.
What's red and bad for your teeth?
A brick.
What's red and invisible?
No tomatoes.
Where do hippies have sex and what's it like?
In tents, man, intense.

A duo of trans boys or genderqueers dressed like Gainsborough's Blue Boy enact a randy ballet. Nomy Lamm, an artist who has arranged a petition for artists who oppose MWMF's policy, howls heartbreaking songs into the warm night, accompanied by a honking accordion. The camp feels like some medieval village on a pagan holiday, bodies close in the darkness, being serenaded by a girl in striped tights and crinoline, harlequin eye makeup shooting stars down her cheeks. Benjamin is a total trooper when the CD he's lip-synching to keeps skipping, and skipping, and skipping. Eventually Julia Serano reads. Julia is a trans woman spoken-word poet. She's got a girl-next-door thing going on, with strawberry-blond hair and a sprinkling of freckles. She performs a piece about her relationship with her girlfriend. It's got sweet and honest humor; it charms the crowd. Then she recites another, "Cocky":

> and if i seem a bit cocky
> well that's because i refuse

to make apologies for my body anymore
i am through being the human sacrifice
offered up to appease other people's gender issues
some women have a penis
some men don't
and the rest of the world
is just going to have to get the fuck over it

Julia gets a standing ovation, everyone hopping up and brushing the dirt off their asses, brushing crickets from their chests, hooting and hollering at the poet as she leaves the "stage" and falls into a hug with her girlfriend and Sadie.

JULIA SERANO

As part of Camp Trans, so much of our work is dedicated to convincing the women who attend MWMF that trans women won't flaunt their penises on the land or that we won't commit acts of violence against other women. I have yet to meet a trans woman who has acted violently towards another woman and/or flaunted their penis in public, but I know I need to take the MWMF attendees' concerns seriously in order to gain their trust. At the same time (to borrow an analogy), it's like someone of Middle Eastern descent having to convince every person on a flight that s/he won't hijack the plane in order to be allowed on board.

Having talked to several festival-goers, I was distressed at how often people centered the debate around "the penis." Everyone talked about the significance of penises being on the land without much acknowledgment that these so-called penises are attached to women's bodies.

Like most trans women, I have a lot of issues surrounding both my penis and the fact that I was born a boy. I have worked through too much self-loathing about these aspects of my person to allow other people to throw salt on my open wounds. It has taken me a long time to reach the point where I can accept my penis as simply being a part of my flesh and tissue rather than the ultimate symbol of maleness. I find it confusing that so many self-described feminists spend so much effort propagating the male myth that men's power and domination arises from the phallus.

Transmissions from Camp Trans

It was surreal to have MWMF festival-goers talk to me about their fear that transsexual women would bring masculine energy onto the land one minute, then the next tell me that they never would have guessed that I was born a man.

I also found it distressing that so many women would want to exclude me (a woman) from women's space under the pretense that my body contains potential triggers for abuse survivors. That line of reasoning trivializes the abuse that trans women face day in and day out. I have been verbally and physically assaulted by men for being who I am. Like other women, I have had men force themselves upon me. In addition, I can't think of a more humiliating way to be raped by male culture than to be forced to grow up as a boy against one's will. Every trans woman is a survivor, and we have triggers too. The phrase "womyn-born-womyn" is one of my triggers.

I'm wiped out, exhausted, can't make it through the rest of the show. With my little flashlight I traipse through the scratchy, weedy terrain, locusts dashing away from my sneakers, toward my tent. My tent may be toxic. Earlier I dumbly spritzed a wealth of bug spray onto my body, fearful of West Nile virus. I did this inside my tent, then had to quickly unzip myself out, a step ahead of asphyxiation. It's aired out a bit but still retains its chemical tang. I eat a bunch of valerian, herbal Valium, and crawl into my sleeping bag. The dance party has revved back up, I hear the shrieks of dancers over the thump of Outkast, and then I fall asleep.

Day Two

One thing I made damn sure to do before leaving civilization was brew a two-liter container of coffee, and it is this I grab at when I wake up. My tent is already starting to bake. I scramble into some jeans, grab my toothbrush, and stumble out into the searing sunlight. I am the only camper—the only camper!—who did not camp in the shade behind the tree line. I camped in front of the trees, the scary trees that I imagined were dripping ticks, ticks poisoned with Lyme disease; the disgusting trees where many spiders live, with a carpet of old leaves slowly rotting away, where mice no doubt burrow, and any number of things that bite can be found. No, I arranged my borrowed tent right in direct sun. Not so smart.

The smart campers are emerging from their shaded glens, getting right into their cars, and driving the fuck to the lake. There's a lake nearby, and a creek, too, and everyone I speak to confirms that going to the lake is definitely part of this "Camp Trans Experience" I am hoping to document; they urge me to hop in for a swim. A fat caucus had taken place at the lake yesterday, as did an attention deficit disorder caucus, though no one managed to stay very focused for that one. I am beyond tempted to ride along, to float in the lake in my underwear under the guise of journalism, but I am too scared of missing out on some crucial bit of drama. The vibe at Camp Trans is intense—it's flammable like the parched ground beneath our various feet. Something was bound to happen, and I couldn't be splashing around like a fool when it did.

I was standing at the welcome tent when the festival workers showed up. Two of them, a femme girl with curly red hair, a cowboy hat, and glamorous sunglasses, and a butch girl in thick horn-rims and a baseball hat. They carried a box of 'zines they had made, a compilation of the various opinions held by the women who work the festival across the road. The femme girl handed it off to the Camp Trans welcome worker. "It's our effort at having some dialogue," she said, something like that. She seemed a little shy, scared probably, and I had a few thoughts, watching the welcome worker accept the gift, a caul of skepticism on her face. I thought the festie was brave to come over with a box of MWMF opinions, I thought the opinions were probably already well-known to Camp Trans campers, I thought shit was going to hit the fan and these workers and their good intentions were going to get creamed. The two festival workers walked off to the side, leaned against a parked car, lit cigarettes, and hung out. I stuck my 'zine in my back pocket and headed over to a tent for the morning meeting.

I guess the morning meetings happen every morning, just a rundown of what's happening that day, a space for people to make announcements. A sort of exhilaration was blowing through the crowd as word of the 'zine, or the 'zine itself, hit them. People were hunched over, their faces stuck in the xeroxed pages, gasping. It didn't look good. Simon Strikeback, a camp organizer, one of the activists who resuscitated Camp Trans after Nancy and company let it go, is facilitating the gathering. Like everyone, he is very cute. He's got blond curls spiraling out from his baseball hat and is grimy in a fun way, like he's been playing in the dirt. He says yes, there can be a circle to process the 'zine. He announces some other events—a Feminism and the Gender Binary workshop I plan to check out, despite its terrifying title. A dreadlocked white girl with facial piercings announces that she has anarchist T-shirts for sale and is looking for partners to hitchhike to Mexico for an anti globalization rally. Someone else holds up a silkscreen emblazoned with a Camp Trans image designed by the cartoonist Ariel Schrag and asks for help screening T-shirts. I announce that I'm attending the festival as press. It's a good-faith thing I did at Sadie's request, so that everyone knows what's up and people who think it's terrible and exploitative that I am writing about their camp can glare at me from afar and not wind up, against their consent, in my story. I'm even wearing a dorky sticker that says "PRESS" in red Sharpie. At one point a boy walks up and presses it. "I thought something happened when I pressed it," he explained, perhaps disappointed. I try to remedy suspicious looks by volunteering to help clean up breakfast over at the kitchen tent.

OVER AT THE KITCHEN TENT

There's not much to do until the water gets here. There are various pans with muck being swiftly baked on to them by this relentless sun of ours. There is a giant bucket of beets that people are wondering what to do with. I move it into the shade, sure it'll keep a bit longer. In another bucket a whole bunch of beans soak, plumping up for that night's chili dinner. Culling the rotten vegetables from the vegetable boxes is what I'm told to do, so I join the others inside the tent. There is an abundance of vegetables, mostly donated from a co-op states away. Cardboard boxes of squash, zucchini, bulbs of garlic. I deal with a plastic bag filled with liquifying basil, pulling the top leaves, still green, from the blackening herb below. The stuff that's no good, the dried-up rosemary and yellowed cilantro, the split tomatoes and the peppers sprouting cottony tufts of mold, all gets tossed in the compost. A woman is picking beets as large as a child's head and slicing their wilting greens off with a knife. When she discovers the mouse inside the beet box, she shrieks. "Oh, that's no good," says the person culling squash beside me. "You can get really sick. I ate food contaminated with mouse shit once and I got really, really sick." We try to scare the mouse away, but it just burrows deeper into the beets. I leave the tent, walk behind it and pull the beet box out backwards, into the grass. The mouse leaps out and scrambles into the forest. We look for visible mouse turd, but everything is sort of brown and crumbly from the dirty beets. I decide not to eat a bite of the Camp Trans food while I'm there. I'm too worried about getting a tick in my armpit to take on the additional neurosis of hantavirus. I've got six energy bars stuffed in my suitcase, two packs of tuna, and a few cans of chili. That's what I'll be eating. Deciding that I saved the day by ridding the beets of the mouse, I retire from my cleanup duties. It's too hot—I need some tuna or I'll get heatstroke. I stop by Chris's stoner van to glob a bit of cool, refrigerated mustard into my tuna and listen to his instructions that I gulp down at least fifteen gulps of water each time I hit my bottle. That's the number, fifteen. "Till your stomach's all bloated," he advises. I do as he says. He does seem like an experienced camper, and the heat is killing people all over the globe, knocking them down by the thousands in France. His little dog, Poi, who looks just like Benji, has burrowed a cool hole beneath the van and lies there, panting.

BULLSHIT

I am very glad I didn't go to the lake. Now we sit in a ring in a small, shaded clearing not far from where I've camped. It's bunch of Camp Trans campers and the two festival workers who delivered the box of 'zines. The 'zine is called *Manual Transmission* and people hate it. It's an anthology, essentially, of festival workers' opinions on the trans-inclusion issue. There is talk about throwing the box of them onto that evening's campfire, a good old-fashioned book burning. Ana Jae is set to facilitate the discussion, and Benjamin is by her side, "taking stack," which I think means keeping a list of everyone who raises their hand to speak, so that everyone gets to.

EXCERPTS FROM MANUAL TRANSMISSION

Let's be clear about what womyn born womyn means. It's not about defining a goddamn thing. It is about saying this is what I'm gathering around for this particular moment. It is saying that this festival, this period in time, is for women whose entire life experience has been as a girl and who still live loudly as a woman. Period. How is that defining you? Why do you think we are so ignorant as to not "get" that, to not figure out that we also have privilege for not struggling with a brain/body disconnect? But can you be so obstinate, can you be so determined to not understand that we have an experience that is outside yours? And that that experience, even though we have greater numbers, still entitles us to take separate space? Do you not see it as full-on patronizing that you act as though these "thousands" of women's shelters can't make up their own minds and policies? Doesn't it make you sick to have the same objectives as the religious right? Why is it okay to totally ignore the need of women who do *not* want to see a penis? How and what world do we live in that you can completely divorce these things? Like being white and telling everyone your skin color doesn't matter because you are not a racist? Stop assuming our ignorance.

Dicks are not useless signifiers. Even unwanted ones. You who I love and call my community of political bandits, you who grew up being seen as, treated as, regarded as boys (and perhaps miserably failing that performance), you did not grow as I. You did not experience being held out as girl and cropped into that particular box. You gotta understand, you are my sister, but you don't have that experience. And taking my experience and saying it is yours don't make it yours, makes it stolen.

"This is bullshit. In my opinion," Ana Jae states. The overall feel about the 'zine and its arrival is, first: We know this already; and second: How dare you bring it into this space that we are trying to keep free from such hurtful sentiments. People take turns expressing themselves.

The Hitchhiking Anarchist Girl: takes issue with a passage defending MWMF's $350 entrance fee, calling it classist.

Simon: frustrated; only open to discussing changing the policy; sick to death of back-and-forth arguing about penises and girlhoods.

Guy to My Left: generously concedes that the festie workers had good intentions but delivered a flawed product.

Festie Workers: admit they were rushed, that though they specified no submissions degrading or attacking trans people would be published, they did not get to read all the writings. They feel bad for the discord their 'zine has caused, but maintain that these are the opinions of workers inside the festival, like it or not; they didn't feel it was proper to censor anyone's thoughts—who can dictate what is right and what is wrong?

Sadie: maintains that as an activist, it's her job to declare her views the good and right and true views; is only interested in talking to people who agree and want to help further the cause.

Festie Workers: weakly remind of their good intentions.

Girl to My Right, in Wheelchair: offers that she is hurt every day by people with good intentions.

Femme Festie Worker: cries; doesn't know how to help this situation.

Girl I Can't See: says that it's everyone's responsibility to educate themselves on trans issues.

Girl with Camouflage Bandanna: sympathizes with how painful the education process can be; urges please don't let that stop you from learning.

There's a lot of fear here—everyone afraid of each other, afraid of their own ability to do the wrong thing from simple ignorance, their own ability to bungle a peace offering, offend the person you sought to help. It starts to rain. Light at first, and then heavy. The weather out here can turn violent in a finger snap, the dust suddenly flooded into muddy ponds, the sky cracking thunderbolts and sending threads of lightening scurrying across the cloud cover, occasionally touching down and setting a tree on fire. I run back to my tent and fling the rain cover over it, and by the time I get back to the circle, it's over—the process, the rain, all of it. I talk briefly with a girl I know from my Augusts at the festival, she's usually a worker. Last year she caught a lot of shit for taking a festival van over to Camp Trans for a date, so this year she's camping here, back in the trees where everyone seems to have gone. I go back to my tent to grab a notebook. Inside it is hot and smells strongly of sulfur, like hell itself. I take my notebook back to the now-empty clearing, sit in someone's abandoned camp chair, and write some notes.

HERE'S GEYL, THEN PAM
Geyl collapses into the chair next to me and asks how my "project" is going. She's teasing me, I think, but it's perfect that she's appeared, because I wanted to talk to someone about the proliferation of trans men and tranny-boys and the small numbers of trans women or genderqueers who enjoy the trappings of femininity. I love girls, I love girlness, and though I love trans men—my boyfriend is trans—I wish there were more females around these genderqueer parts. The face of the transrevolution is, presently, a bearded one. "Riot grrrl made being a dyke accessible," Geyl reflects, "And now those people are seeing that they can be genderqueer and it's not so scary. There's none of that for MTFs." Pam, a trans woman who had been quietly strumming her acoustic guitar in the woods behind us, strolls up and joins our conversation.

Pam: Trans women get abused a lot more in our society.

She's right, of course. Because it's often harder for them to pass as women in the world, and because they're likely to get way more shit for it, lots of would-be trans women just don't come out.

Geyl: Being a girl is not as cool. I actively try to recruit.
Pam: Yeah, there must be something wrong with you if you want to be a woman.
Geyl: I tried to be really butch when I first came out.
Michelle: I tried to be really butch when I first came out, too. It seemed cooler and tougher—and safer—to be masculine.

Pam looks like just the sort of woman the music festival across the way embraces—smudgy eyeliner, long brown hair, rolled bandanna tied around her forehead, and that acoustic guitar in tow. She's even a construction worker, and isn't that one of the most feminist jobs a woman can work? After Pam came out as a trans woman, her co-worker threatened to toss her from the very high building they were working on. Her foreman said, "You should expect that sort of thing" when she complained about it. She was soon fired from the job for "being late."

Pam: If I watch Jerry Springer, I don't want to come out.
Geyl: All the trans women on that show aren't really trans. They're a joke.
Pam: I think Jerry is a trannychaser. And I think he's resentful of it and wants to take it out on the community.

Soon we're informed that we're sitting smack in the middle of the space reserved for the Feminism and the Gender Binary workshop.

Geyl: I'll feminize your gender binary. If anyone quotes Judith Butler, I'll punch them.

FEMINISM AND THE GENDER BINARY

This workshop was very exciting for the four or so aspiring gender theorists and of varying levels of excruciating for the rest. While terms like *"biological determinism," "social determinism,"* and *"social constructivism"* are bandied about, I dwell heavily on how, in a space where everyone's "isms" are sniffed out and deconstructed, this workshop drenched in academia is, well, classist. Presumptive. Dull as a doorknob. But I don't get mad, I space out. I love the hot-pink color of the gender-theorist girl's hair. The trannyboy-genderqueer in the bright-orange shirt is so cute, and the trans guy in the plaid shirt becomes my hero for asking if, please, more accessible language can be used. Who else is cute? The genderqueer girl named, perhaps, Kooky, whose outfit is candy-pink and decorated with skulls and metal studs; her hair is the faintest blue in pigtails, and her glasses are vintage cat's-eyes. "What's cultural relativism?" Geyl whispers over to me at one point. When Emily the facilitator observes that the vibe in our brainy glen has gone "slimy" and Geyl suggests we fix that by having everyone select a single word to describe how they're feeling, Kooky says, "Dissociated." Others words include "alienated," "frustrated," "murky," "muddy," and "my butt hurts." Later Kooky critiques the whole theory business, saying, "It tends to turn people into abstractions, and I don't like being an abstraction." Amen, sister. I go back to my tent to crack open a can of chili, and hear the venting cries of frustrated workshop survivors. "So much academic bull-shit!" I go out and sit with them. They also eat from cans of beans. "Hi, I'm Rock Star," says a thin girl in what appears to be a nurse's uniform. We talk about the night's big event—a group of festival women are supposed to meet up at their dinner, parade through the festival grounds, and march up to Camp Trans for a rally. Rock Star wants to sneak into the festival, and so do I. As we're mulling over how to make it happen, a faint roar comes into the air, widens until it fills it, a booming chant that ricochets off the trees, that rolls down the dirt road like the first wave of a flash flood. "Oh my God, they're already here!" I gasp, and dash away from Rock Star and Co. I'm really excited. I run across our scabby land toward the welcome center, getting a chill from the rising holler of voices that yell, call-and-response-style, "What do we want? TRANS INCLUSION! When do we want it? NOW!" Chants at marches are usually so tedious, but holy shit, the yells sound fierce and righteous, not the monotone intonations of burnt-out organizers but the heartfelt cries of what sounds like a nation of women. I bounce in my sneakers. The chant comes closer, gets louder, changes— "Michigan will be so great / when they let trans women through the gate!" The first of the parade trickles in, followed by another trickle, a bit more trickle, and then—done. That's it. About twenty-four women. They sounded so gigantic out there on the road, an army, the trees cupping their chant and lifting it into the air. It was all a big echo. This parade has been being planned all week long. Twenty-four out of approximately eight thousand in attendance. It's really disappointing. It's also ahead of schedule. Sadie is frantically rounding up individuals to speak at the rally, but it's going to take a while. Someone pulls out a volleyball net to entertain the twenty-four women, prevent them from leaving. The Gainsborough Blue Boys from the night before emerge from the woods in a new costume of luxurious wigs, oversized sunglasses, billowing scarves flounced round their necks, and tight white clothing. Who are they? They begin to play badminton. One takes two of the, um, shuttlecocks, stuffs them into his shirts like breasts, and runs away.

I'd seen the postcards advertising the inner-festival action parked on the welcome table, a takeoff on the *Free to Be . . . You and Me* album cover stamped with the plea "This is NOT the feminism my mother taught me about! Help end the exclusion of trans women from the Michigan Womyn's Music Fest!" The back features quotes from old-school feminist icons Adrienne Rich on invisibility and Gloria Anzaldúa on rigid thinking, as well as a zinger from third-wave transfeminist Emi Koyama which ends, "If the festival insists on removing certain groups of women because their genital structure or other physical characteristics are reminiscent of male violence and domination, it should also tell white women to peel off their skin."

THE RALLY

There's that girl Mountain again, on the mic this time, letting everyone know that if her feminist-separatist farming commune can let the trans women in, anyone can. "I always have said that if I didn't go to the festival each year I'd die," she tells the crowd. "Well I didn't go, and I didn't die, and I'm not going until they change the policy!" Everyone cheers. Sadie's on the mic, revving everyone up by insisting that we're going to change the policy. I guess it's impossible to engage in any sort of activism with a fatalistic view, and who knows, maybe MWMF will surprise us all and roll out the trans carpet, but I just don't see it happening. I remember glimpsing Lisa Vogel in the festival worker area years ago, after Camp Trans had brought a protest onto the land. They'd been kicked off, of course, and a reiteration of the womyn-born-womyn policy was swiftly typed up, xeroxed, and distributed throughout the festival. Lisa was smoking; she looked pissed. Someone told me that she saw it all as a class issue and an age issue. Camp Trans were a bunch of teenagers freshly released from liberal New England colleges with a head full of gender theory and blood bubbling with hormones and rebellion. Lisa Vogel is loved the way that saints are loved by the women who attend her festival, and why shouldn't she be. She's provided them with the only truly safe space they've ever known. She's a working-class lesbian who built it all up from scratch with her hands and the hands of old-school dykes and feminists, women who claim, perhaps rightly, that no one knows what it was like, what they went through, how hard they fought. It has taken a lot of work to create the MWMF that's rocking across the way, sending its disembodied female voices floating into our campsite. It's taken single-mindedness and determination. Lisa Vogel, I fear, is one severely stubborn woman.

Transmissions from Camp Trans

Emily is speaking and she's saying things that could turn around some of the more stubborn festival women. Unfortunately, I don't think anyone has come over from the fest who wouldn't love to see the policy junked. Emily is preaching, as they say, to the choir. She's talking about her girl-hood, how the girls all knew she was a girl like they were, and how powerful and lifesaving it was to be recognized like that—your insides finally showing through. A young friend wishing Emily would get a sex-change operation so she could come to her slumber party. It's a great response to the festival's insistence that trans women didn't have girlhoods. Anna speaks next. Not Ana Jae—this is a brand new Anna, you haven't met her yet. She's got big dark eyebrows and wide lips painted red, she's holding the mic, and she's come to lecture the lesbians for dating trans men but justifying this shades-of-hetero behavior by saying, "He's not really a guy." Sacrificing trans men's maleness so that their lesbian identities can stay intact. Sheepishly explaining, "He's trans," again invalidating the real masculinity so as not to be confused with a straight girl. For fetishizing, as a community, this sexy new explosion of trans men but remaining unwelcoming to trans women. It's all so true, my frickin' eyes well up. I'd spent the first year and a half of my boyfriend's transition explaining to everyone—women on the bus, strangers in line at Safeway, people I sit next to on planes—that my boyfriend, he's transgender. So don't go thinking I'm some stupid straight girl, the confession implies. I'm QUEER. Okay? It tended to be more information than anyone wanted. Everyone's uncomfortable, but at least no one thinks I'm heterosexual, and that's what counts. Oy vey, as my Jewish friends say. And I know lots of lesbians who date trannyboys but freak out if a trans women struts into their space. It's all so fucked up and heartbreaking and overwhelming. Or maybe I'm just really sleep-deprived from a night on bumpy ground, sleeping atop sticks and hard mounds of dirt. Before me are the Gainsborough Blue Boys, lying side by side on separate chaises longues, still in their wiggy tennis outfits. They clutch paper bags of what I assume is beer, and make out. Seriously—who are they? I love them. I wipe my soggy eyes, grab Anna as she shuffles past with her boyfriend, and thank her for her speech. I confess my past as a shameful tranny-dating lesbian, I heap upon her how sad and scared I get when my dyke friends start talking shit about trans women. I want Anna, beautiful strong Anna with the microphone, to absolve me and also solve all my social problems. She seems so capable. I think I overwhelm her. She gives me her information, phone, e-mail— "She loves being interviewed; it's her favorite thing," her boyfriend encourages. Of course she does—she's a genius. She walks away into the darkness, her beaded, sequined shoulder bag glinting in the night.

The rally is over, and everyone's dancing again. On the sidelines I find Carolyn, a writer and a trans woman from Brooklyn. Carolyn must have found some way to construct a shower from rainwater and tree branches. Every time I see her she looks really, really clean. Every night, before I sleep, I wipe a thick coat of grime from my body with some sort of chemical gauze pad called a Swash Cloth. It's all I've managed to do, hygiene-wise, and I look mangled. Carolyn admits that others have commented on this. "I don't know—I haven't showered for four days! I'm just lucky," she says modestly. Here's what else she says.

CAROLYN

I came to Camp Trans because I realized that the organizers were really focused on organizing around the policy and making Camp Trans an empowering experience for the women there. The background of this is, in the dyke community in general and Camp Trans specifically, transgendered women are the minority. There are ways that even trans spaces can be not so empowering to trans women.

I've only gained from being a part of women's spaces and a part of feminists spaces. When I came out as a trans woman, one of the first things that I did was get involved with the New York Clinic Task Force because Operation Rescue was coming to block clinics during the Democratic Convention. For me the issue of women's right to choose and the phrase "biology is not destiny" has a particular sort of resonance. I've always felt really welcomed in lesbian spaces, but there's a profound lack of information about trans women's lives. I think it's really important because I'm sick of having the same conversations—yes, I have a G-spot, I have a clit, I have orgasms. There's such a basic lack of information. Or, it's not okay to ask me about my surgical stature unless you want to have sex with me! Only if you're asking 'cause you want to have sex, not because you want to find out all the lurid details of what's in my pants.

I have to make decisions all the time, when I meet women and go on dates, how I will respond to what really are hurtful questions from a person who don't think they're doing anything

wrong. Really inappropriate questions about my gender identity and my life.

The main thing for me is that I'm coming back next year.
It was worth it. And I'm coming back because of the community that was at Camp Trans, and how that community is a
model of what Michigan should be. We are part of the same
community. There are ways that even trans spaces can be not
so empowering to trans women, and it was really empowering
to me to see so many non-trans dykes and trans men who were
talking about looking at every aspect of Camp Trans and fig-
uring out how to make it an empowering experience for us.
That was extremely empowering to me.

I Had the Time of My Life

Two people—girls, trannyboys, genderqueers—I can't really tell in the
light, so bright it turns them into silhouettes, they are whirling across the
dusty makeshift dance floor doing a dance routine to a medley of songs from
the movie *Dirty Dancing*. Here is my proof that this gender-smashing revolution is a generational thing, when someone walks across the stage holding
a cardboard sign reading "Nobody puts Baby in a corner" and everyone
roars. I have no fucking idea what they are talking about. I was a moody
death rocker when *Dirty Dancing* came out. This was back before Hot
Topic stores in the malls, back when goth was a slightly dressier version of
punk and wearing black lipstick and ratting your hair into a tarantula was a
uniform which conveyed information such as "I am opposed to the dominant culture and movies such as *Dirty Dancing*." My little sister loved *Dirty
Dancing*, and I ragged her for it mercilessly. Patrick Swayze? Come on. But
I like watching these two spinning into each other, knocking each other
down, and crawling all over each other. At the very end of their act, after
dancing close, they draw apart and draw the audience in, and everyone
responds, they move into the brightness, becoming silhouettes that dance
and raise their hands into the light, and it's beautiful like a dark kaleido-
scope, all the bodies coming together under the light. My eyes well up with
tears again. Jesus. Chris asks me to dance, but I can't. I'm a mess. It's been
such an emotional day, and I'm spent. A trans man is straddling the lap of
a girl in a bright green dress, lap dancing her on the folding chair. Two
others are making out on the dance floor, and many booties are being
freaked. It's time for bed. I hike back to my tent, following the small spot of
light my flashlight tosses into the weeds.

Day Three
"I asked you to dance and you disappeared," Chris complains. We're on his patio. He's making real hot coffee on his camp stove, but I had to swear I would tell no one about this luxury, because he's almost out of gas. He starts talking about how confused he was about Camp Trans, how he thought it was a bunch of trans men trying to get into the women's festival, and he wasn't down with that. "You gain a few privileges, you lose a few," he laughs. "Go cry on your own damn shoulder. Get over yourself." Once he realized it was about getting trans women some women's-only privileges, he was down for the cause. He's glad he's here. "I'm so comfortable," he says, "My tree keeps getting closer." He means the tree he pees on. Maybe he saw *Sleepaway Camp II* as well and is scared of the portos, maybe he's lazy, or maybe it's just such a rarity to be a trans person who can take a piss in the woods without fear.

This Just In
Excerpted e-mail forwarded from Carolyn, received three days after returning from Camp Trans:

> Washington, D.C.
> In the past week, the Transgender community has been shaken by three shootings, two of which resulted in the deaths of the victims.
> On 8/16/03, Bella Evangelista (Elvys Perez) was murdered at Arkansas Avenue and Allison Street, N.W. Antoine Jacobs was immediately arrested and has been charged with first-degree murder while armed. The case has been classified by the Metropolitan Police Department as a suspected hate/bias-motivated crime (gender identity).
> In the evening hours of 8/20/03, a black male-to-female transgender individual was found near 3rd and I Streets, N.W. suffering from apparent gunshot wounds. The victim was transported to a local hospital, where she is in serious condition. The case has been classified as an assault with intent to kill.
> In the early morning hours of 8/21/03, Seventh District officers discovered the body of a black male-to-female trans-gender individual at 2nd Street and Malcolm X Avenue, S.E. The victim was unconscious and suffering from wounds by

unknown means. Since there was no sign of life, D.C. Fire/EMS did not transport the individual.

Camp Trans is unraveling before my eyes. Cars and trucks are rolling out of the parking lot, which is just another part of the field we've all been living in. People wave out of their windows as they pull onto the road. All day long the population shrinks. The planning meeting for Camp Trans 2004, which is happening beneath a tent, is repeatedly interrupted as vacating campers lavish good-bye hugs on their friends. I am sitting back and listening to participants raise their hands and offer compliments on what they felt went well at this year's gathering and what needs to be fine-tuned for next year. Everyone is generally pleased, and the renewed focus on trans women's needs and overturning the policy was a success. There are concerns about how white Camp Trans is, but no one is naïve about seeking out token people of color to make themselves feel better. Instead a resolution is made to make the event itself more welcoming to people of color, in the hope that the gathering will organically diversify. Geyl suggests travel scholarships for trans people who want to come but can't afford the time off work or the travel expenses out into The Middle of Nowhere, Michigan. People are happy about trans women being in charge, happy that there was essentially no rain in a region known for violent summer thunderstorms, and want greater accountability from women who say they are organizing within the festival gates. There will be greater fund-raising this coming year, though Camp Trans did come out financially ahead by $500. Incredible really, since at the start of the week ziplock baggies had been duct-taped inside the portos asking for spare change each time you took a whiz. It cost the camp eighty bucks each time those monsters got cleaned.

Over at the welcome tent, a few ladies from the festival have strolled in. They're older, in their fifties perhaps, from Utah. Probably they live for the festival and have never spoken to a transsexual in their lives, but they've come over, minds open, "to see what everybody's all 'ugh' about." Maybe because everyone at the welcome station is so burnt out on this, the last day, or maybe because I'm sitting closest to the two women, I wind up answering some of their questions, or rather, countering their concerns. Their concerns are the usual—penises and girlhoods. So many women have been traumatized by a penis, is it really fair to force them to glimpse one at their annual retreat? I tell them that women need to find a way to heal from their abuse without displacing responsibility for it onto the bodies of trans women, who are also likely to have been abused. That a roving, detached penis didn't abuse anyone but the man attached to it, and those men are not these women. I tell them that trans women did in fact have girlhoods, girlhoods as rough and confusing as any girl's. One tiny conversation, and I'm drained and frustrated. And this isn't even my life.

Everyone is called to help dismantle what's still standing of Camp Trans. Intimidated by the architecture of the tents and lean-tos that need to be torn down, I busy myself gently untying the neon plastic ribbons that have been knotted, for some reason, around a rusting cage which, for some reason, contains a stunted apple tree. Perhaps there's a hornet nest in the crook of its branches. A large swath of our field has been roped off all week with that same neon plastic, to keep everyone away from a burrowing hornet encampment. That's being torn down now, as well. I grab a trash bag and roam around the land, collecting debris. Part of what makes the Michigan Womyn's Music Festival is the land it takes place on. The trees are tall and cool, there's much grass, twining paths, the air smells fresh, it's nature: the real deal. And the women love it and care for it like a living thing, which it is. I try to arrange a similar mind-state about cleaning Camp Trans, but I don't feel connected to this rather lousy scrap of National Forest. Maybe if the event keeps occurring here for twenty-eight years, it will become imbued with the specialness and familiarity that haunts the woods across the road. I snatch the torn corner of a bag of Chex Mix from the ground, some empty water jugs, balls of toilet paper, bits of shredded trash bag that blew off one of the Fat-tastics' pom-poms. I pull from the ground tiki torches that had been guiding nighttime revelers to the porto-potties all week. I leave to decompose back into the land some carrots, some tofu dogs, some onion skins. There are bullet casings and smashed clay pigeons scattered throughout the weeds, left behind by whoever was here last.

Over by the portos is a structure made of tarps that all weekend I'd thought was someone's wicked punk-rock campsite. Tarps spray-painted with anti-policy slogans, tied and duct-taped to stakes driven into the ground. I'd had a brief fantasy that it was Geyl's squat-like queendom. But as I pass it, Chris sticks his head out from the plastic and asks, "Did you know there was a shower here?!" He is delighted. The shower is a little pump with a thin hose attached; it looks like the pesticide tank an exterminator lugs around. You pump the top like a keg, click a switch at the end of the hose, and a fine stream of water mists all around you. It looks like a feeble shower but a great way to cool off. Later I'll help Geyl and a person named Cassidy—butch girl? genderqueer?—tear the whole thing down, and have great fun squirting myself with all the leftover water in the little tank. I pull stakes from the ground and untangle knots of rope, listening to Cassidy tell the story of Blane, the man who rents out the portos we've been peeing in. Blane lives on five hundred acres of land and raises beefalo. Beefalo is a cross-breed of cow and buffalo, and Blane is proud that he has been able to breed out their horns. Beefalo is lower in cholesterol than regular beef, and after his doctor warned him that his cholesterol was shooting dangerously high, Blane took to farming the animal. He feeds them corn that he also grows on his land, and the corn is grown in compost made from the slurry in the porto-potties. All of our crap will be distributed throughout a nearby cornfield. It's incredible and slightly sickening.

"The birds of prey have come for us," Geyl points a long finger up to the sky, where some large birds are indeed circling. I've been trying to find a place to sit and read, but every patch of shade I see is inhabited by either creepy daddy longlegs or intimidating cliques of remaining campers. There's a girl doing yoga in a growth of weeds; her legs become visible, then her butt, her head, her legs. A car is flung open, all doors, the trunk, and people load their belongings. X's "White Girl" leaks from the stereo, soon to be overpowered by a car blaring Tiffany. I settle down in what's left of the dismantled welcome station and try to read, but I'm distracted by the heat, the mosquitoes, the loud sex noises howling out from the woods in front of me.

I hitch a ride into nearby Hart with a boy named Billy. Billy drives his big red truck into Hart every day three or four times to dump trash, redeem bottles, and fetch more water. It seems nuts that this duty has fallen solely on his shoulders, but he's a trooper about it. Especially considering how trashed the bed of the truck has become—gummy with spilled booze and moldy produce—and that he's been living in that same truck bed for the past seven months, traveling around the country. A lot of the campers at Camp Trans are part of what I've heard referred to as "travel culture" and "youth travel culture": the anarchist hitchhiker or the many groups of people who are not going home from here but traveling onward to distant states—New York, Chicago. Lots of people are heading to Tennessee, where a similar though less politically charged event will be taking place on a patch of land owned and inhabited by a group of pagan gay guys known as the Radical Faeries. Billy pulls in behind the nearest gas station, and I help him dump clanking bags of unredeemable glass, wobbly boxes heaped with vegetables gone bad. He grabs a bottle of whiskey, sucks the dregs, and tosses it empty into the Dumpster. Next Billy dumps me at a Mobil station while he fetches water, so I can call my boyfriend from a pay phone and grab some snacks. After a few days of nothing but tasteless nutrition bars, dry tuna, and cold canned chili, the weirdest snacks look appetizing. I buy a giant bottle of Coke, a pack of Pop-Tarts, and a bag of potato chips with a mysterious flavor—"Mustard and Onion 'Coney' Chips," the bag proclaims. They taste just like hot dogs. They're made by a guy called Uncle Ray, whose picture is on the back, posing with his wife Myrna and fluffy cocker spaniel Suki. Below that is a portrait of their three adult children, and beside it all is Chapter 29 of "The Life and Times of Uncle Ray," which I gather he is publishing, chapter by chapter, on the back of his various potato chip bags.

FROM "THE LIFE AND TIMES OF UNCLE RAY"

> I met Myrna on a city bus. (Read Chapter 14) We were married on March 25, 1961.
>
> Our first baby, Jennifer, was born nine years later. One day while Myrna was out shopping, Jennifer needed to be changed. I thought everything was OK until baby Jennifer stood up and the diaper fell off. There are many things God did not give me a talent for. Washing clothes and changing babies are but two of them. As for Myrna, she has many talents. She is a very good cook. (I taught her.) She can also sew, clean house, iron (use to), paint, cut grass, take care of our children, work outside of the home, and much more.
>
> Some people say that women should have equal rights. NO! Women should have preferred rights, because they have earned it.
>
> Genesis: 2:22—And the rib, which the LORD God had taken from man, made he a woman, and brought her unto the man.
>
> We know you have a choice when choosing potato chips and snacks.

Next is Dave's Party Store, where an affable, Pauley Shore–ish dude hands over $25 in exchange for a worn trash bag of sludgy bottles, and a literally rednecked white guy tells the cashier, in deep Ebonics, that he's going to join the traveling carnival. "That sounds like a great place for you," the woman says dryly. Back in the truck we listen to Lil' Kim and cruise to Camp Trans, past the music festival and its vast parking lot still stuffed with cars. There's Blane the porto-potty guy, vacuuming the ultimate grossness out from the portos, then loading the empty toilets onto his truck and driving them away. Now we'll all be peeing on trees. I use my rusty can opener to peel the lid off another can of vegetarian chili and wander over to Chris's van. I find him inside smoking pot with Andrew, a twenty-year-old trannyboy whose legend I'd already heard from Geyl last night at the dance. How he'd never met another tranny, ever, until arriving at Camp Trans yesterday. How he learned he was trans from watching the film *Boys Don't Cry*, for which the actress Hilary Swank won an Oscar for portraying the young trans man Brandon Teena, who was raped, then murdered when the boys he'd been hanging out with learned of his situation. Andrew lives in Lansing, caught a ride down to Camp Trans—which he'd just found out about—from a couple of anti–Camp Trans ladies on their way to the festival. They'd already stopped by earlier to inform him curtly that they were staying at their festival a little longer to hang out and catch the last concerts. "I don't want to go back with them at all," Andrew says, and soon he has arranged to catch a ride home with the nomadic Chris, who plans to continue meandering through the country in his surfer van for a few more months. Andrew is cute, he's got the buzz cut of a young recruit and eyes that shift icily between the palest blue and green. He is stroking the soft skin of his jaw tenderly. "Do I have a bruise?" he asks, half an honest question, half to brag. I don't see any marks, but soon we're hearing about the wrestling match he was part of last night. He tells us how someone walked right up to him and said, "Can I kiss you?" He'd never been approached so bluntly by an admirer, and he's surprised that it didn't make him feel weird, threatened, or unsafe. He felt like he could say a friendly "No," and the person would have backed off. But since he felt so safe, he said "Yes." Andrew has a girlfriend who is on her own vacation and who sounds familiar with the heightened sex vibes of queer gatherings. When she heard he was off to Camp Trans, she said, "Don't even try to be monogamous— you'll be miserable." "What a great girlfriend," I compliment, impressed. Andrew is satisfied with last night's kisses and wrestling and is anxious to get back to Lansing and be with his very modern paramour.

ADVENTURE
Jess is complaining that she needs an adventure, now on this last night of Camp Trans, when all who remain are part of the camp's core organizers— Sadie's fled back to D.C.—a few people procrastinating over their long drives home, Chris, and me. I have found an adventure, but Jess does not approve. In fact, Camp Trans does not approve. It is their policy to ask their campers please not to sneak onto the Michigan Womyn's Music Festival, but it is this that I am setting out to do. To be fair, it's not exactly sneaking.

260 * Michelle Tea

Some exiting festies tore their rubbery blue bracelets from their wrists and gave them away. I've got one; so does Calwell. Geyl has one, handed over to her by a woman who tearfully said, "You deserve to be in there." True enough, but Geyl isn't going to risk it. She lends the bracelet to a girl named Kelly, whose T-shirt reads "King Shit of Fuck Mountain." "We really don't want anyone going over there," Jess says earnestly. She is wearing a black slip and has a fake blue rose in her orange bob. Last year Camp Trans was accused of allowing, if not encouraging, bunches of campers to sneak into the gates. MWMF insist this is true because the amount of food eaten was higher than it should have been. "I don't know why they just didn't figure people were eating a lot," Jess shrugs. So far this year, no one has snuck over. Since we plan to do nothing but stroll through the woods, maybe find a party rumored to be going on at "the dump," it doesn't seem like a drag on anyone's resources. Off we go.

Excerpt from "Welcome to the Festival!"

> Those Security Gals: The womyn in tasteful orange vests are here to answer questions, keep things orderly and promote safety. Unfortunately, it has also become an increasing part of their job to deal with the girls who decide to try to sneak into the Festival in various places along the route. Please help in their effort to ensure everyone takes that basic first step and purchases a ticket to the festival.

We enter the festival perimeter by strolling through an unmanned (unwomanned?) checkpoint. The lean-to is there, the chair, draped with a security vest, but no worker. Calwell especially likes feeling that we are being sneaky, even though we've got the bracelets. Kelly is hoping to stay the night, maybe find a lady with a tent to get lucky in. Calwell wants to find the party at the dump, and I just want something to do. So we look for the dump. We do not find it. We find, instead, the RV campsite, where bunches of women are hanging out in luxury. Winnebagos and campers, patios set up with tables and mosquito netting, someone even brought a bird cage containing a live bird. Other women have set up mannequins on their front lawn or strung Christmas lights over their vehicle. No one is naked, but some women are topless. Hard as it is for some, the campers at Camp Trans are required to cover nipples and pubic hair at all times, the land being National Forest and all. Which means lots of topless people with patches of duct tape—ow!—slapped on their nipples. We find the acoustic stage quite

Transmissions from Camp Trans

by accident. It is filled with women, hundreds of them lined up on the cool grass before an elegant wood stage holding a white grand piano and a set of chairs, empty. It feels so strange to be on the inside of this compound we've been locked into opposition with all week. It feels a little scary actually, which is odd, because I've been on this land before and I don't really believe anything will happen to us, even if someone found out we half-snuck in. It's hard not to have an affection for these women, comfortable, all hanging out with each other on a hillside. It's also hard not to be wary of them, to feel conflicted. I think of Geyl, Sadie, Carolyn, all the trans women I've met this weekend. You can call it unjust that they can't come in, call it wrong, unfair, but really, more than anything, it just seems absurd. We march out from the acoustic stage and down some roads. We get royally lost in the woods, the sky darkening around us. Good thing I brought my trusty flashlight. The three of us crunch along paths that wind through real wilderness; we find ourselves in the infamous Twilight Zone, where the women who practice SM sex camp. We pass a campsite that is a collection of tarps stretched out and tied together, enclosing a large area. I can see a campfire burning inside the plastic barrier, a butch women moving around, a bunch of chains rigged up to a tree. But that's all. It wasn't that long ago that the SM women weren't welcome at MWMF. Their presence was protested, boycotted, until this space on the outskirts of the festival was created for them, so they could whip each other in peace without "triggering" the women who feel like it's just more of the patriarchy seeping in. The SM controversy perhaps peaked when the dyke punk band Tribe 8 were invited to play and were picketed by women holding signs accusing the performers of everything from domestic abuse to violence against children. I've heard a lot of people suggest that trans women be allowed to camp here, among the bondage practitioners and heavy partiers. At least they'd be in the gate, but what if a trans woman doesn't want to camp amidst such heavy sex play? I camped in the Twilight Zone my first year at the festival and, like those around me, was drunk pretty much around the clock. There was puke in our neighboring bushes; beer cans, cigarette butts, and latex sex supplies littered the grass outside our tents, and we almost got kicked out for lighting off fireworks. More than once, while stumbling around in search of a place to pee, I walked smack into the middle of a pretty intense sex scene. And each morning we were all awakened by the exaggerated sex cries of a woman camped down the path. To require anyone to camp in such an environment seems downright abusive.

It's calming to be off Camp Trans. To be in such a political, tense environment for an extended period of time does some wear and tear on your head. Me and Calwell talk about being afraid of being judged, feeling like you could say the wrong thing and wind up ostracized and alienated. It's kept him quieter than normal. Same for me. "I'd like a safe space to fuck up," I say, and we laugh. A space where everyone recognizes that everyone is trying their best, imperfectly struggling, human. But perhaps that's not possible. Activism is, famously, by any means necessary. People on both sides of this debate like to compare their stance to the struggle against racism, but it is true that, camping at Camp Trans these few days, I feel like I'm in the midst of the first swell of a new civil rights movement.

The Fire, Last Time

Back at Camp Trans, the final campfire roars, with Cassidy—somehow an expert on the various ways wood can grow—strategically loading branches into the flames. Chris is burning marshmallows on a long stick, Simon is shaving pieces of potato and garlic into an aluminum foil pouch to be roasted. Someone passes around cold pizza, someone else passes around a bottle of Boone's Farm. It's the first time alcohol has been visible all week, though many revelers have been visibly under its influence. Another of the National Forest laws. Max, a trans man who is part of the posse responsible for reviving Camp Trans in 1999, is telling the story of the lesbian curse. Actually he is acting it out, with the help of others who stand in as various characters—trans campers and angry lesbians, mostly. Geyl acts as "rain," hovering over them and flicking her fingers. It is the story of how Max awoke in his tent to find a coven of festie women flashing mirrors at their campsite. They were angry witches putting a spell on Camp Trans and they did succeed in scaring the crap out of Max. Simon tells a story of his first Camp Trans experience, and the action he undertook with a trans man named Tony, a sixteen-year-old trans girl named Cat, and the transsexual author and activist Riki Ann Wilchins.

Simon's First Festival

> First Tony went on the land to put the womyn-born-womyn policy to the test. He identified as a post-op trans man with bottom surgery (I forget the kind). He was saying that his dick was made out of the skin on his arm—I think that's a rhinoplasty??—anyway, he said, "Hey, if my trans women friends are still men because they were assigned male at birth, then I must still be a woman." So he went into the fest and took a shower.

He asked consent of the women showering, telling them what kind of body he had. They said okay, but because the showers were public, new folks came in and freaked. By the time the ticket-buying action happened the next morning, the rumor was that something like six non-op trans women flashed their erect penises at the girls' camp. Gross, eh?

The ticket-buying action: at noon on Saturday, Riki led a ticket-buying action at the fest. A bunch of the avengers [Lesbian Avengers—lesbian direct-action group that has prioritized fighting for the rights of trans women], myself included, bought tickets to the fest. The young trans woman who was with us also bought a ticket, though at the time she could have been "read" other than a womyn-born-womyn. This was a great victory for us, and there were certainly tears. Then the trouble began. A woman started walking in front of us, shouting, "Man on the Land!"

We did have some support from festie-goers who walked with us. We got to the main area, and it was very overwhelming. We were asked if we wanted to have a mediated discussion in the kitchen tent. Before that discussion, women were just coming at us from all over, some to be supportive, some to yell at us, and some to stare. There was very little middle ground, and it was very hostile. So we started this "mediated" discussion, and the setup was such: we (us avengers, maybe four of us, and Riki) were sitting on folding tables in the front, while seven rows of angry lesbians yelled at us, audience-style. I kid you not. People called us rapists, woman-haters, said we were destroying their space by just walking on it, that we had no respect for women, that we had no respect for rape survivors, et cetera. Three hours this lasted, and the mediation was so one-sided, we didn't get out of there with any confidence that anyone heard what we had to say. That was my first festival.

I don't want to leave the circle 'cause I know this is it. In the morning I will ride into Grand Rapids with a girl named Katina, a festie-goer who has spent basically all her time over at Camp Trans, much to the dismay of the girls she's camping with. "You know how every time you leave Michigan, you think, I'm coming back next year?" she asks. "Well this year it wasn't like that. I know I can't come back next year." Katina's got hair that's bound up in bunches of braids, the ends secured with brightly colored elastics in different colors. She lives and works in Brooklyn, where she supplements her income selling Strawberry Shortcake dolls on eBay. Her trick is to search for the dolls right there on eBay, but to search for sellers who have misspelled the name of the toys, therefore getting less bids and selling their wares cheaper. After securing the dolls, Katina puts them back up on the site with the proper spelling and doubles her money. She's a smart cookie. Camp Trans is lucky to have her. All week she's been offering her cell phone, offering hummus and wine, and now she's driving me to the airport. I give her a big hug as I climb out of her car. We used to see each other at MWMF, hug each other good-bye, say "See you next year." And now we say it again.

A Final E-Mail
Posted to the Michigan Womyn's Music festival message board:

> The last performer of the Michigan Womyn's Music Festival, comedian Elvira Kurt, made a gently humorous but very eloquent statement. She pointed out the wisdom that comes around age 28 and suggested that MWMF skip the stuff it is going through, let go of fear and just jump ahead to trans inclusion. The audience erupted into applause and shouts of approval. If anyone did not agree, they were pretty much drowned out. THAT was the note on which this year's festival's performances ended and anyone who was there knows this.

> From Elvira's glances off-stage right when recognizing Lisa's efforts in putting on the festival, I am pretty sure that Lisa Vogel was right there and heard it with her own ears.

> When not some unknown upstart, but the one and only Elvira, this year's "Woman Behind the Curtain and Voice of Michigan" makes a challenge like that to the festival community and gets the response she did, it is a truly momentous event.

> I doubt that ignoring it will make it go away. It seems to me that the time of debate has passed. Turning the clock back will be difficult to impossible, just as when lesbians made their entry into mainstream feminism or SM became an undeniable part of MWMF culture.

Sexsville: Outtakes

"The individual cannot help his age; he can only express that it is doomed."

—Søren Kierkegaard

The Great Rubber Failure, by Iva Child
A Girl's Anxiety, by R. U. Cumming
  (Also attributed to Mr. Period)
The Sheik's Demand, by Mustapha Boy
At the Twelfth Time, by John Henry Bent
The Contented Wife, by John Thomas Everhard
Limitation of Offspring, by Dr. Kutcha Kockoff

For a long time, the story goes, we supported a Victorian regime, and we continue even today. Thus the image of the imperial prude is emblazoned on our restrained, mute and hypocritical sexuality.

—Michel Foucault

The kid hands it over. It's a mangled sepia-toned photograph of a naked woman fellating a horse. Her back is turned to the camera. The forbidden knowledge. Seeing what was actually beneath all the stiff stuffing women in the '50s wore. Another kid takes us home—his parents are somewhere else—and plugs in the 8-mm projector. In torn, fractured, shattered, degraded film we see fucking, the act we've imagined as an abstraction, like those wall charts in grade school of the body as a factory. But this image is confusing as well as arousing. Marching orders. We're the guys, the new recruits, we're the ones who have permission to watch. Usually you never get to see the face of the phallic Übermensch. He's just a cock, a piston, an industrial pump going in and out of someone's cunt or mouth.

> *"If there's ATOMIC WARFARE this book may save your life!"*
> —How to Survive an Atomic Bomb, *by Richard Gerstell,*
> *Consultant, Civil Defense Office,*
> *National Security Resources Board*
> *(New York: Bantam, 1950)*

Smut's generationally and historically determined, existing to create and disturb, yet call into focus hypocrisy and incoherent lust for conquest and being conquered. Power rules, rocks, &tc.—and yet, how is one's role in the fantasy created, insinuated? For Berman and Alexander's generation, the truly transgressive was a deep underground exchange system of fragments of the acts in still photos, stag loops, or in endless "girlie" mags of the '50s with red-eared titles like *Whisper, Titter, Confidential, Wink: A Whirl of Girls* (titles alluding to sex as a covert mystery), *Eyeful: Glorifying the American Girl, Flirt,* where women in underwear provided the provocation for jism's jump-for-joy. Every woman was enclosed in her concealment and containment. Industrial bras, shimmery panties, garter belts, high heels, usually black nylons; deeply lipsticked mouths à la Betty Page. Models, exotic dancers, burlesque queens, like Zorita, the Snake Dancer, Rebel Randall, Lilly Christine ("you get a feeling she's a feline"), Evelyn ("The Treasure Chest") West, and in the first issue of *Playboy,* December 1953, naked Marilyn Monroe stretching on red satin. In the '40s, nudist magazines ("sunlight is the greatest factor in promoting and retaining Radiant Health") published photographs of nudists with airbrushed or whited-out pubes. These magazines stressed their "clean and wholesome" intent. Some nudist magazine showed families. Adding to the health image, all pictures were taken outdoors.

(Poet Judson Crews printed his chapbooks inserting pages from nudist magazines in between poems. Berman and Alexander were on his mailing list.) "Physical culture" mags celebrated male bodybuilders in loincloths and muscles aglow smeared with olive oil or Crisco or who knows?

> *Now this was just prior to the end of the war and just after the*
> *end of the war. . . . A lot of men were gone, so a lot of people*
> *were adventuring, seeking out places. I remember being*
> *stopped by the police, and I had a joint in my pocket. They*
> *searched me, and they saw it, and they didn't know what the*
> *hell it was [laughter]. During those days there was a lot of*
> *hustling, a lot of pimps, a lot of dope dealers, a lot of gangsters.*

*Los Angeles, I guess, like any other town, was kind of wide
open because it was during the war; a lot of people coming in
from the South, going into defense plants. There was new
money. People hadn't had that kind of money before. They
were spending it. . . . There were people that were kind of
adventurous seekers. And there always are a group of people
like that, and they just kinda found the music. Found out
where the musicians were. There was never a lack of an audience, if you were in the right place. Especially after it [bebop]
got started around '45, '46.*

—Sonny Criss

The hipster milieu was trying to score beyond the veil, that is, get past
the past, yet nevertheless affirm male centrality. It was like other modernist "sexual revolutions," from the nineteenth-century *La Vie de
Bohème* Europe via Paris, London, Berlin, to stuck-in-the-mud U.S. of A.
via Manhattan, Chicago, San Francisco, a bogus equality. Men ruled;
they were the geniuses, artists, Promethean channels whose work super-
seded any other work. Heroic, elevated, women were there to serve the
men, and rarely was the equation reversed or made equal. The same riff
recalled from pre– and post–World War I days in Greenwich Village. No
matter how the men waxed rebellious against traditional sexual formats,
inevitably the woman (as artist, writer, composer, or equal intelligence)
wound up washing dishes, bearing and raising children, while the great
man worked in solitary splendor. While "equality" was the buzz, it was
rarely the reality. While men felt free to roam and take on "mistresses,"
whenever one of their women asserted that same right, the bellowing of
the wounded creator was opera on overdrive. This was often the case in
the postwar arts culture too. Women as equals were again theoretical but
abstract like Aristotle. Men were the primary makers, while the "old
ladies" and "muses" were receptacles, handmaidens freeze-framed in conflicting roles of what was permissible across a limited map of male assumptions: mother/slut; whore/madonna—old-timey, deeply inscribed cultural
certainties.

The cult of the female form divine, as manifested by their
outsize bosoms and interminable legs, had reached heights
undreamed of by the ancient Greeks in their gaudiest rites.
Again, like the Greeks, we have our modern goddesses.

Sexsville: Outtakes

With names like Jane Russell and Marilyn Monroe, they cast ever-lengthening if shapely shadows from coast to coast. And in their images a million secondhand, standardized glamour girls are at us from every side.

They saturate our atmosphere, infesting movies, "comic" books, newspapers, newsreels and calendars. They turn up on men's ties, cocktail napkins, cereal boxes and fishing tackle; they line the walls of our beer halls and barracks. . . . We're completely hemmed in by sex—in print, film and songs. Flee the crowded city and it still pursues you in the pure open spaces. Take off for the stratosphere—and you'll find one of the goddesses outlined on the fuselage of your Army bomber. . . . This earnest and exclusive dedication to sex is tiresome. It's about as interesting as a 24-hour diet of caviar. But that's not the worst of it. I'm sick of Super-Sex because it's having an appalling effect on my friends and associates. It's creating super-headaches for men and women alike, forcing impossible yardsticks on both of them, and obliterating what was the spontaneous joy of boy-meets-girl.

—Ted Berkman, *The Cult of Super-Sex*
(Coronet, June 1955)

Boys' Town in a Peter Pan panoply of blitzed guys from the war who had nothing but improvisation as their defense against great deep offense to their beliefs. I remember record producer Jim Dickinson telling me about being in the first wave of Hell's Angels. They were mainly vets who returned to comatose suburbs and a culture erasing any kind of individuality. Middle-class life more and more rationalized and conformist in the terror panic of extinction by A-bombs. After so much unbelievable killing and horrific slaughter, Ozzie and Harriet were not who they fought for. Like Holocaust survivors, they found it impossible and improbable to adjust to the status quo.

In both world wars, men left home (the female) to homosocial dalliances with the impossible: shrapnel and mustard gas, disemboweled guts in trenches, khaki lacquered G.I. Joes became ducks in a row gunned down on beachheads, in jungles, in ancient cities, while on the home front, women were fitting easily into jobs their drafted boyfriends and husbands occupied before the war. The world turned upside down echoing the utopia of Revelation. But without a safety net, just a snood.

Sexsville: Outtakes

Horoscope: You want to be part of the greater whole yet remain as an outsider.

Whenever a taboo is broken, something vitalizing happens, another step towards greater truth and honesty and openness.
—Henry Miller

The imaginary is our delight or terror, depending on who we depend on, fetishize, who we seek or who seeks us.

Temptingly Beautiful girls in unretouched individual photos. No composites.

BE POPULAR! In Any Company Anywhere . . . These books will tell you how
    45. The Art of Kissing . . . . . . 75¢
    46. The Love Guide . . . . 75¢

IF YOU LIKE 'EM BUXOM maybe you'll like my photos.

EXOTIC BEAUTIES: ALL RACES.
    Catalog, 10 Special Combination Set of Sepia, Oriental and White Beauties, $2.00.

BIZARRE Book Service
We secure rare, out-of-print esoterica . . .

MENTAL DYNAMITE . . . Reach into the minds of men and women, CONTROL their THOUGHTS and ACTIONS and BEND THEM to your will.
           —From *Lowdown*, 1957 (an issue devoted to James Dean's posthumous revels)

Always active, imagination is also inevitably proactive. One imagines what isn't from what is, from what could or should be. Fantasies retaliate and relate to and against authority.

As power is hierarchical, starting from some unimaginable beyond, working its way down into the basement of being, so is the erotic and sexual production of icons and tropes that trigger some sense of brief triumph in

Sexsville: Outtakes

voluntary submission—a brief self-serving (servicing) autonomy the masturbator has control over.

> Fear not only of unwanted pregnancies but of "VD" and "sex fiends" and "drug fiends."
>
> Many cases come from carnal contact as the use of a recently soiled drinking cup or cigarette; in receiving services from diseased nursemaids, barber or beauty shop operators . . .
>
> All too often we lose sight of the fact that the homosexual (the communist, the lesbian) is a seducer of the young of both sexes, and that he presents a social problem because he is not content with being degenerate himself; he must have degenerate companions and is forever seeking his younger victims.
>
> —Dr Paul de Rider, *The Sexual Criminal* (1949)

A fear-based lexicon of consequences connected with immorality, vice, prostitution versus "good clean fun." Treatment for venereal diseases was punishment: sixty or more weekly visits to the clinic for painful injections in alternating courses of arsenicals and heavy metals.

VD produces human wrecks, incompetents, criminals.

Fiend—hated person, enemy, the devil.

Accosted, molested, men in shadows of movie houses, predators moving into the sanctified innocence of childhood, "degenerate sex offenders."

"Should wild beasts break out of circus cages, a whole city would be instantly mobilized. But depraved human beings, more savage than beasts, are free to rove American almost at will," wrote J. Edgar Hoover in 1947. The cross-dressing White Knight.

> Even one sex pervert in a government agency tends to have a corrosive influence upon his fellow employees. These perverts will frequently attempt to entice normal individuals to engage in pervert practices. This is particularly true in the case of young impressionable people who might come under the influence of a pervert. . . . One homosexual can pollute a government office.
>
> —Government Task Force paper, 1950

In any oppositional subculture (an oxymoron), there has to be the presence

and limit of what's being challenged. The resistance begins with the acceptance of being a part of that which is rejected.

"Nothing is more essentially transmitted by a social process of learning than
sexual behavior," writes Mary Douglas. Georges Bataille says, "In search of
any object outside himself . . . [he] answers the innerness of desire."

In the daze of those days, smoking weed was a real crime—as was being
queer—at the open-air newsstand on Western and Hollywood Boulevard I
worked at, I remember a gay customer telling me how the LAPD entrapped
gay men in public restrooms by "coming on" to them. The drugs were
always a bigger risk than the pornographic. Illegality is seductive; the anxiety of trafficking in the "forbidden," a dangerous game made sexier by risk.

In the book accompanying Berman's first major retrospective in Amsterdam, crypto-titled *Support the Revolution: Wallace Berman*, a big-
breasted naked fake blond with penciled-in eyebrows is on view before
one gets to the title page. Throughout this important catalog of Berman
drawings, collages, paintings, assemblages, and movie stills is the para-
doxical challenge of the Aleph in dialogue with the pornographized
female. The pornographic male imagination is often based on doubt and
fear and embedded gynophobia.

Okay, what was the sex vibe in those times? Foreshadowing our present
dead end, we could say it was repressed, hysterical, frustrated, itchy, clueless. In the presence of desire, overwhelming restraints.

Let's run through some shadowy tropes in loops and pics and magazines:
babysitters, nuns, schoolgirls, maids, high heels, corsets, nurse, police, soldiers
and sailors, Nazis, Japanese prison guards, white women enraptured by the
mythic mighty black dong, plantation slave-master bopathons as porno minstrel
display of anxious, intimidated, white male anxiety, extra terrestrial schlongs,
ubiquitous Betty Page, nudist and physical culture mags for that special homoerotic tingle, Asian submissives with secret arcane incense and geisha gaga for
round-eyed Yankee cocks oozing up from sloppy manicured lawns, the
fetishized yen for otherness in the suburban familiar and terror of crabgrass.

Fear ruled: political, nuclear, spies, communists, outer-space aliens, inner-
space neuroses, but if there was anything truly covert in the '50s, it was sex.
My smudged lens wants to focus on how the repressed expressed itself.
The '50s sex culture was dominated by the new ruling class—the middle

Sexsville: Outtakes

class—heirs of the Victorian girdle and muzzle—it was most overt in terms of conspicuous consumption but still, in the dark furrows of Victorianism, held to its covert and out-of-control sex visions and fantasies.

De Sade wrote in *Juliette*: "Can't you go to bed with a woman without loving her, and can't you love her without going to bed with her?" Sex separated from love. "Sexuality"—a nineteenth-century word—a new discrete phenomenon that trickled down into weird and obvious mutations of '50s striated layers of sexuality reinforced and re-repressed by biological terrorism. No matter how ithyphallic the free-spirited artist imagined himself, between his partner and his own disowning, seed splatted egg and resultant pregnancy had multitiered darkness shades of despair and too often tragedy. It's a cliché, a trope, the young '50s (gulp) guy going into a pharmacy to buy an Almond Joy, a pack of Old Golds, and, uh, rubbers; his girlfriend unsure about fucking's mystery—wanting it, not wanting it—all the consequences of such a brief unknowing encounter. The horror stories of botched abortions.

Foucault: How is it that in a society such as ours, sexuality is not simply that which permits us to reproduce the species, the family, and the individual? Not simply something which procures pleasure and enjoyment? How is it that sexuality has been considered the privileged place where our deepest "truth" is read and expressed? For this is the essential fact: that since Christianity, Western civilization has not stopped saying, "To know who you are, know what your sexuality is about." Sex has always been the center where our "truth" of the human subject has been tied up along with the development of our species.

In the '50s, males and females wanted to go "all the way" but also wanted not to go anywhere, wanted not to want. Immense tensions between the outer postwar satins, silks, and unknown new fabrics, those double-bind layers of barrier and allure women wore to challenge.

My mistake in this advanced age is to think that the '50s were more repressive than now. They were certainly less expressive—sexual dissidence was deeply coded but expressed between the lines in fetish magazines (*Bizarre, Exotique*), the "girlie" magazines, and the immensely brave gay and lesbian journals (*One* and *The Ladder*) which became the first wave celebrating an alternative sexual culture and had to deal with all hysterical government invasions and post office censorship and local police harassment.

Sexsville: Outtakes

The "pervert" was constructed as another form of "communist," a polluter of the pure body politic. The heterosex "girlie" magazines (*Wink, Titter* [Girls, Giggles, Gags], *Whisper, Eyeful*) celebrated the great mysteries of underwear, tactile silken utopias where fumbling hands hoped to get into and beyond in the struggle of backseat "making out." Black bras on very white lithe bodies; black nylons grasping and shaping long legs whose feet are lodged into patent-leather spiked heels. The garments, the vestments, all charged with ritual significance of an event most could only imagine. Finger fucking was beyond belief and as if it never happened even while it was happening. To gain entry into her whose sex was so industrialized in those sex manuals and schematics. Kinsey's *Sexual Behavior in the Human Male* allowed discourse above and below in the "objective and numeric" summary of his troupe's challenging data of longing. Kinsey, a closet kinkster in fantasy sex rites of S/M debauch and purge, broke through the lanolin lens to suggest that sex was complex and an urgent pleasure—forget drudge procreation—sex was a creative amazement, whether done with a partner or partners or solo in the deep imaginal digress of invention.

One wanted to fuck, to find out, to get past the mystery into the mystery. Instead, the misery entrapped unknowing kids into perpetuating uncertainty and anxiety.

"Rampant technology eliminates luxury, but not by declaring privilege a human right; rather, it does so by both raising the general standard of living and cutting off the possibility of fulfillment," wrote Theodor Adorno in exile in Hollywood in 1945.

Whatever "sex" was was an immense and tangled mystery that the available books overilluminated in terms of the mechanical particulars, except the overly complicated yet ecstatic Van de Velde's *Ideal Marriage* (1941), which insisted on mutual pleasure as the operating principle. The other so-called "sex manuals" were like engineering textbooks and none of them made sense to those, like me, groping in the heat of desire but clueless to the actuality. Kinsey's first report on male sexual behavior in 1948, followed in 1953 by the study on female sexual behavior, rationalized and legitimized sex, an ongoing and ordinary and extraordinary activity expressed or repressed in multiple variations and preoccupations. Kinsey made it seem okay with columns of statistics that made it "scientific," quantifiable, and therefore legit. Masturbation, homosexuality, and bisexuality were diagnosed as

Sexsville: Outtakes

quotidian, which for many middle-class guilt-damaged ones was a vindication and a supportive argument to confound the mixed-signal pinheads monitoring morality. Kinsey created a new discourse on sexuality, and its extraordinary ordinariness opened up the public discussion of private passions.

It was homosocial and homoerotic; it wanted the woman to be beyond the woman; her power, its mystery, became a challenge for their transgressions—all of this undetachable from the sexual Via Dolorosa paving the Victorian and early modernist screech into reactionary conservatism as a way of guarding the proprietary realms of male power, i.e., the female body—its difference, unknowability, cultural terror of what could not be seen—controlled. The pornographic was always about male control and power over the female body's willing submission to a fantasy of male empowerment, entitlement.

HOW WOMEN HURT MEN ["By being cruel witty, maliciously 'honest'—or just thoughtless—a wife can crush her husband's ego and imperil their marriage . . ."]

Pornographic texts and images were produced initially for the swells, the upper class, the gents with bucks, like today, power's privilege obviates doubt. But technologies invented new ways to produce the forbidden affordable images and texts for the masses.

How difficult it is to outline the completely "other" fear of (and yearning for) sex and sexuality in those days; that daze of fear, of unwanted pregnancies, lethal and humiliating abortions, and a phantasmagoria of subsets of fetishistic and male-hysteric stag movies, Tijuana Bibles (whose radicality deserves reconsideration), smudgy illegal photographs of all the variants of the carnal chronicle of absurdity, carbon-copy manuscripts of fuckbooks writ to order, loops and tropes for the one-eyed male.

> Wallace told me that he had been a pimp in E LA in the late '40s, that it went along with being hip, with dope, with the jazz, the scene, post-WWII. I've had Wally's revelations about just that, the desolation on a young (Jewish) man's consciousness, etc.—and that there was this moment, he actually told me, when he realized that he could not be an artist if he was a pimp, that he could not be an artist if he did not love. This was spring 1969, 20 years after the pimp/revelation time he was telling me about. Every time I've tried to tell this, I run up against mine

Sexsville: Outtakes

and others' disbelief, their hee-hawing that he was coming on to me . . . he saw who I was, was just smart enough to go there with me. . . . I don't have that journal here, though I have some things, maybe even a floppy, I will look for it tonight, and read the whole of your letter (funny, again last night the same thing, I get so into it, I don't get to the end, I fall too into the cave).

Do you remember Jim Gill? He was living next door to Wallace in Topanga. Talk about the male predatory stuff, and how it was the art. Maybe what you're writing, the difficulty is just the assignment, but maybe it's like the incredible spelunk I've taken myself with such essays about gender. Ouch, the most difficult, the most painful.

—Sharon Doubiago, e-mail communiqué

Yes, a lot of background in yr HD book essay was a revelation to me—WB may have been a junior pimp in those days as part of his masque of hipster, hepcat, reefer-toking, Central Avenue habitué—but I wd never dismiss his claims nor his profound insight on love as the real revolution—Wally was a lovely mishmash of trickster, hipster, and pure heart even though he loved the smirch—as most "guys" of that extended gang did—the more I search and re/search, the more (duh) obvious it becomes how the sexual repression and oppression of those born in WB's February framed a lot of their art—whereas anyone born after the Pill has a much looser and less burdened concept of sex and sexuality—more important, I see how oppression and repression provoke expression—it's ongoing—forever and ever—keeps us dancing—

You mention Jim Gill, whose work exemplified (like Ben Talbert's) transgressive recombining of the sad-sack pornographic culture soon to be uplifted from the margins into the art mainstream—Jack ran into Jim recently and Gill's become a Jehovah's Witness, has a *Father Knows Best* family and sees the errors or eros of his ways—

The prevailing U.S. assumptions of male privilege and license to predate (despite all that's been contested from the '60s on) sustains its one-dimensional covert or overt notions of power—phallocratic pathos—"power" over, or with?—the keyword is how we (you and me on the breadline of unified field hands) understand or describe "power"—Wally understood and

Sexsville: Outtakes

embodied the process that yields "Art Is Love Is God," an amazing mantra and meditation—just like his right-on "Fuck Nationalism"—

as poets entranced and devoted to the word, each of WB's mantras can keep us busy for many moons—

—Love

Whatever is now called "hard core" was always in circulation since the invention of photography and cinema. Technology limited the availability of manuscript smut, and carbon copies of typewritten texts were circulated at great expense, whereas "loops" or "blue" movies circulated within the same kind of underground economy pot smokers understood. It was against the Law, which gave it more charge and heat. Men in "smokers" watched incoherent loops of fucking and sucking done to and by awkward guys in socks and women in odd unflattering positions of arousal.

During the war and those years after, overground mass culture shifted—I was already a deep reader of comic books and paperback-filled racks at the candy store. I was reading Eisner's *The Spirit* and Jack Cole's *Plastic Man*, *Classics Illustrated*, *Weird Science*, Faulkner, Farrell, Celine, and all of it was coherent, as was the sudden discovery of the girlie magazines and the hint and taste of a deeper subversive stream not present in the aboveboard dream of an unspoiled life. Sex was the spoiler. It all changed in 1960 when the Pill arrived. The cultural shock of that freedom was revolutionary despite the usual repressive recoil and guilt industry working overtime to abolish pleasure as a principle.

I was seventeen when I first met the Bermans. I was sexually awake but still a virgin. My three girlfriends, May, Peggy, and Arlene (not all at once), were also virgins, and we all wanted not to be. Our sex was hot but not complete. I knew I was supposed to push through the mysterious hymen, which we tried to many times but never got it right.

Peggy and I used to go to the Coronet Louvre on La Cienega Boulevard, Raymond Rohauer's repertory cinema oasis. There we saw Eisenstein, James Broughton, Jean Cocteau, Maya Deren, and Stan Brakhage (Brakhage was also, at the time, Rohauer's janitor); we saw the premiere of Kenneth Anger's *Inauguration of the Pleasure Dome* with artist-poet Cameron as the Whore of Babylon.

Across the street was Norman Rose's bookstore—another oasis of avant-garde literature and seductive weirdness whose back room, covered by a curtain, emitted fumes of herbal awakenings. That's where the Bermans entered and exited en route to the movies. I've already described how remarkable Wallace and Shirley were as appearances; their singular style of dress, Shirley's Left Bank extreme kohl eye shadow and lyrical cool defined and challenged any suburban tendency to be nice or safe. They were in a newly minted zone, as were their comrades. Amazing visages announcing a new way of seeing and being.

"How Women Hurt Men," by John Kord Lagemann (*Coronet*, May 1959):
1. Present a united front to the world. Settle differences privately.
2. Accept your husband as he is. Don't try too hard to improve him. Try not to compare him unfavorably with other men.
3. Never make fun of his job, his hobby, his earning power, his physique, or his sexual abilities.
4. Enter marital relationships in a positive, wholehearted way. Do not use sex as a weapon or as a means of driving a hard bargain. Make an effort to be sexually attractive to him. He cannot please you unless you please him. When he pleases you, tell him. For the male, nothing succeeds like success.

The anger and anxiety of the male in control out of control in between wars and their topsy-turvy aftermaths reflected in comic strips like *Maggie and Jiggs, Blondie and Dagwood, Hi and Lois*—Philip Wylie's screed against Mom as castrator in *Generation of Vipers*—a panorama of henpecked hubbies, nebbishy wimpoids neutralized by the very institutions the culture advocated and in male control.

Foucault: For a long time they tried to pin women to their sexuality. They were told for centuries: "You are nothing other than your sex." And this sex, doctors added, is fragile, almost always sick and always indicating sickness. "You are the sickness of man." And toward the eighteenth century this very ancient movement quickened and ended up as the pathologization of woman: the female body became the medical object par excellence.

The spew and pump of sperm's brief glory dissipates into a kind of uric acid if not wiped away. What does this say to the uneasy lumberjack Abexers and, as Charles Brittin distinguishes, the poetic metaphysical types of low muscle mass, androgynous drifting dreamers lost on a reed, a reef of reefer cosmology?

True hipster communication was about breath—rooted and routed in inhale—but the amazed expression was exhale, the "whew" of insight beyond words.

Digging deeper into the "girlie magazine" culture of the '50s I see a mainstreaming of fetishism as an option. Men, who are the primary consumers of pornography, not only want to inhabit the female body but, via S&M fetishistic humiliation (read: "feminization") want to become the women they subject in order to be subjected by them. Resonates in Genet's *The Balcony* (reiterated by Xaviera Hollander's "Happy Hooker" observation that "slaves" are primarily "superior" CEOs and similar ilk who need shame to eroticize and justify their domination over "inferiors"). Sex as power as power play; as deception and reinvention; as imagination and utopic subjugation and chaos; confusion rocks the roost and, too often, the all-out debris, damage, is too achingly mundane.

"Power," like "technology," is neutral, an energy to be shaped in agreement with desire and will—

Difference is difference that claims its sameness as difference.

Stuck in a rut, Mutt.

Sisters, Saints, and Sibyls: Women and the Beat

*If you want to understand Beat women, call us transitional—
a bridge to the next generation, who in the 1960s, when a
young woman's right to leave home was no longer an issue,
would question every assumption that limited women's lives
and begin the long, never-to-be-completed work of trans-
forming relationships with men.*

—Joyce Johnson

THIS BOOK CAME ABOUT AFTER a modern poetry class I took from the ven-
erable Michael Krasny, an informed and inspiring teacher if ever there was
one. I looked forward to that class every Wednesday night because it was so
lively. When we came to the Beats, lively sometimes meant heated. I saw
how, even after all these years, Beat writing could set off sparks and had
such power to move people. When, sadly, the term ended, I hungered for
more Beat writing, the energy and raw passion, and soon discovered a
mother lode of writing I had never seen in bookstores and curriculums
before—Beat women! And thus this book was born with a desire to share
the wealth of brilliance and beauty of these women.

The fifties had a choke hold on consciousness, the Industrial Age at its
most insidiously rote and conformist. The Beats were the only game in town
or, as journalist Bruce Cook says, "the only revolution going on at the time."
The women of the Beat Generation, with rare exception, escaped the eye
of the camera; they stayed underground, writing. They were instrumental
in the literary legacy of the Beat Generation, however, and continue to be
some of its most prolific writers.

This book is a collection of women who participated in a revolution that
forever changed the landscape of American literature. Before the late forties
and early fifties, poetry was buttoned up tight. The Beats helped make literature a democracy, a game with no rules. All you needed, they believed,
was passion and a love of the written word. As the movement spread, the
Prufrockian ennui and Weltschmerz of Eliot gave way to Beat vision and
word jazz, and the literary world was never the same.

Beat was first coined when Times Square hustler and writer Herbert

Huncke picked up the phrase from carnies, small-time crooks, and jazz musicians in Chicago, who used it to describe the "beaten" condition of worn-out travelers for whom home was the road. Huncke used it to explain his "exalted exhaustion" of a life lived beyond the edge. Jack Kerouac took it one step further, saying, "I guess you might say we're a Beat Generation," when talking to his friend, writer John Clellon Holmes, who included the quote in an article for the *New York Times Magazine*. Kerouac and Allen Ginsberg further refined the concept as "beatific" and containing a spiritual aspect, invoking Catholicism, William Blake, and Buddhism, respectively. Toward the end of his life, Kerouac explained that he was really just a Catholic mystic all along.

Beat was a countercultural phenomenon, a splash of cold water in the face of a complacent society, that radiated out from certain places in America, primarily New York City and San Francisco, and consisted of many people, not all of whom received the attention of the mass media. Diane di Prima, considered by many to be the archetypal Beat woman, started her own press rather than wait for a publisher to come knocking. When a major house finally did pursue her, it was for erotica—*Memoirs of a Beatnik*—not her poetry. Elise Cowen, who typed *Kaddish* for Allen Ginsberg, was in her own right a strong and prolific poet whose work has never been published until now.

The women included in this anthology run the gamut from the famous—Carolyn Cassady and Jan Kerouac—to the as-yet undiscovered—Mary Fabilli and Helen Adam. The art, prose, and poetry selected represent the range and development of their work, from pre-Beat to, in many cases, new work that has never before been published. For those readers who want a fuller experience of these talented females, I have also included a list of collected works of each woman in the appendix of this book.

To place their accomplishments in context, it is important to understand why, in the seemingly idealized fifties' America of comfort and capital, anyone, man or woman, would choose to live marginally, to struggle and oppose. Postwar America was the richest, most powerful nation in the world, bustling with industry, pride, and the Puritan obsession with work and perfection. Or so it seemed. As it turns out, not everyone in America shared this swaggering posture. The Beats were simply the first to very vocally and artistically decry American materialism and conformity. Toward the end of the decade, after years of struggling in obscurity, perseverance and timing conjoined to catapult the Beats into the public eye, where they caught the attention of millions who were similarly disenchanted with the

American myth. In a very real sense, the Beats helped the Silent Generation find a voice and paved the way for the explosion of the sixties.

Women of the fifties in particular were supposed to conform like Jell-O to a mold. There was only one option: to be a housewife and mother. For the women profiled here, being Beat was far more attractive than staying chained to a brand-new kitchen appliance. For the most part, the liberal arts educations these young women were given created a natural predilection for art and poetry, for living a life of creativity instead of confining it to the occasional hour at the symphony. Nothing could be more romantic than joining this chorus of individuality and freedom, leaving behind boredom, safety, and conformity.

The women in this anthology were talented rebels with enough courage and creative spirit to turn their backs on "the good life" the fifties promised and forge their way to San Francisco and Greenwich Village. Long before the second wave of feminism, they dared to attempt to create lives of their own. From Sister Mary Norbert Korte, who left the convent to be a Beat poet under the tutelage of Denise Levertov, to Helen Adam and Madeline Gleason, co-founders of the San Francisco Poetry Festival, these women made their own way.

In many ways, women of the Beat were cut from the same cloth as the men: fearless, angry, high-risk, too smart, restless, highly irregular. They took chances, made mistakes, made poetry, made love, made history. Women of the Beat weren't afraid to get dirty. They were compassionate, careless, charismatic, marching to a different drummer, out of step. Muses who birthed a poetry so raw and new and full of power that it changed the world. Writers whose words weave spells, whose stories bind, whose vision blinds. Artists for whom curing the disease of art kills.

Such nonconformity was not easy. To be unmarried, a poet, an artist, to bear biracial children, to go on the road was doubly shocking for a woman, and social condemnation was high. Joyce Johnson and Elise Cowen fled respectable homes and parental expectations. Others married and raised families, but in an utterly unorthodox manner. Joan Vollmer Adams's common-law marriage to William Burroughs, for example, was shocking to their wealthy, upper-class families. Diane di Prima raised five children, taking them with her to ashrams, to Timothy Leary's psychedelic community in Millbrook, and on the road in a VW van for a cross-country reading tour. Hettie Jones's biracial marriage and children were a scandal even in New York's Greenwich Village, causing irrevocable rifts with her parents.

Sisters, Saints, and Sibyls: Women and the Beat

Their iconoclastic lifestyle matched their literary work. But though they were revolutionary, Beat poetry, art, and prose didn't spontaneously generate—although many literary precursors would not dare lay claim to it. The Beats themselves are quick to name their inspiration, and several names come up consistently: HD (Hilda Doolittle), Ezra Pound, William Carlos Williams, Walt Whitman, Gertrude Stein, and Emily Dickinson. In particular, the Imagist poets—HD and Ezra Pound—changed the course of poetry from strict formalism, loosened the corsets, so to speak, and freed the form. Immediately prior to the raw, unvarnished confessional writing of the Beats was a different breed of poet, a liberated artist, albeit embraced by academia, but prophetic in the cryptic, blunted free verse and experimentalism with style from haiku to rant. William Carlos Williams and the Imagists were, like the Beats, unrepentantly individual and beyond the ken of their peers. Like the Beats to come, they were very concerned with encouraging other poets, especially younger writers, and often found themselves in trouble for unpopular politics, poetics, and lifestyles.

The Black Mountain College in North Carolina was founded in the wake of this "liberated arts" movement by a group of brilliant individuals and boasted a world-class faculty—Charles Olson, Merce Cunningham, artist Robert Rauschenberg, and musician John Cage. Poet Charles Olson went to Black Mountain after the eminently successful publication of his Melville study, *Call Me Ishmael*. There, Olson, Robert Creeley, and Robert Duncan took an antiacademic stance on poetry and literature, propounding the belief that the energy the poet transfers to the writing is more important than form, content, or the judgment of critics. This stance attracted legions of young artists to the Black Mountain oeuvre, including a cadre that would soon be known as the Beats.

A few years after the antiacademy movement emerged, the New York art-and-poetry scene erupted—as depicted here in the memoirs of Hettie Jones, Diane di Prima, and Joyce Johnson—with constant readings, showings, performances, salons, plays, parties, and happenings, providing one of the two poles for the Black Mountain diaspora upon the demise of Black Mountain College. Robert Duncan went to San Francisco, where he encountered and encouraged such mavericks as Helen Adam and Madeline Gleason, with whom he kick-started the poetry movement known as the San Francisco Renaissance. Meanwhile Creeley and the others went to New York, often to be found at the Cedar Tavern, a favorite Beat gathering place. Although the writing and philosophy of these Beat progenitors is very different from that of the Beats, what they all have in common is a reaction to and a rebellion against rigidity.

Jack Kerouac would be the first to tell you that the mainstream and the media were the death of the Beat Generation. Sensationalism and mass success, by their very nature, negate that which is Beat. Beat is underground, raw, unedited, pure, shocking. Beat can't be refined, sanitized, second-guessed, premeditated; it must be immediate. Beat is an expulsion, a vomiting of vision. To pretty it up for the cameras and papers is to snuff the very essence of Beat. Ironically, because the women in the movement have, to a certain degree, been ignored and marginalized, they represent the precious little of that which remains truly Beat.

Why is it that the fascination with the Beats, far from dying down, continues to grow? Each of these women offers her own answer to this question, but all agree that, in a time of skyrocketing rents, mass layoffs, and the cultural desert of the sixty-hour work week, the Beat credo has much to offer in the way of courage and the creative identity of the individual.

The women of the Beat are the epitome of cool. They were the black-stockinged hipsters, renegade artists, intellectual muses, and gypsy poets who helped change our culture forever. They were feminist before the word was coined, and their work stands beside that of the men. To the Beat men, these women are sisters, saints, and sibyls. Jack Kerouac, who had many women in his life, once said, "The truth of the matter is we don't understand our women; we blame them and it's all our fault."

Women of the Beat Generation is an opportunity finally to understand these women as important figures in our literature, our history, and our culture and as some of the best minds of the Beat Generation.

Sisters, Saints, and Sibyls: Women and the Beat

V. Vale and Andrea Juno

Modern Primitives

MODERN: 1. Being at this time; now existing. 2. Of or pertaining to the present and recent times, as distinguished from the remote past; pertaining to or originating in the current age or period. 3. Characteristic of the present and recent times; new-fashioned; not antiquated or obsolete. 4. Everyday, ordinary, commonplace.

PRIMITIVE: 1. Of or belonging to the first age, period, or stage: pertaining to early times; earliest, original, ancient. At the beginning; anciently; originally in time, at first. 2. With the purity, simplicity, or rudeness of early times. 3. Original, as opposed to derivative; primary, as opposed to secondary; radical. 4. Math., etc. Applied to a line or figure from which some construction or reckoning begins; or to a curve, surface, magnitude, equation, operation, etc., from which another is in some way derived. 6. Of colors: Primary. 7. Anything from which something else is derived.

PRIMITIVIST: A primitivist is a person who prefers a way of life which, when judged by one or more of the standards prevailing in his own society, would be considered less "advanced" or less "civilized." The primitivist finds the model for his preferred way of life in a culture that existed or is reputed to have existed at some time in the past; in the culture of the less sophisticated classes within his society, or of primitive peoples that exist elsewhere in the world; in the experiences of his childhood or youth; in a psychologically elemental (sub-rational or even subconscious) level of existence; or in some combination of these. Primitivistic themes appear in almost all literatures: they are found in classical and medieval literature; in the last Renaissance. Montaigne, in his essay Des Cannibales, praises the happy and virtuous life of savages living close to nature; Pope envies the untutored

Indian; 18th century interest in p. receives its fullest expression in Rousseau's pietistic doctrine of the children of nature; Wordsworth attributes superior wisdom to sheep-herders and children; Thoreau tells us that "we do not ride on the railroad: it rides upon us"; the poetry of Rimbaud is a record of defiance of Europe and dogmatic Christianity in favor of an Oriental "fatherland" . . . D. H. Lawrence makes a similar condemnation of Western civilization and advocates a return to an older mode of living based on a recognition of man's "blood nature." Primitivists have differed widely on the nature of the evils and weaknesses of civilized life, the causes of these evils, the positive values of the primitive life, and the degree to which a regression to the primitive is possible.

—Princeton Encyclopedia of Poetry and Poetics

Modern Primitives examines a vivid contemporary *enigma:* the growing revival of highly visual (and sometimes shocking) "primitive" body modification practices—tattooing, multiple piercing, and scarification. Perhaps Nietzsche has an explanation:

> One of the things that may drive thinkers to despair is the recognition of the fact that the *illogical* is necessary for man and that out of the illogical comes much that is good. It is so firmly rooted in the passions, in language, in art, in religion and generally in everything that gives value to life, that it cannot be withdrawn without thereby injuring all these beautiful things. It is only the all-too-naïve person who can believe that the nature of man can be changed into a purely logical one.

Civilization, with its emphasis on logic, may be stifling and life-thwarting, yet a cliché-ridden illusion as to what is "primitive" provides no solution to the *problem:* How do we achieve an integration of the poetic and scientific imagination in our lives? There are pitfalls on both sides, and what is absolutely not intended is any romanticization of "nature" or "primitive society." After all, advances in science and technology have eliminated much mind-numbing, repetitive labor, and inventions such as the inexpensive microcomputer have opened up unprecedented possibilities for individual creative expression.

Modern Primitives

Obviously, it is impossible to return to an authentic "primitive" society. Those such as the Tasaday in the Philippines and the Dayaks in Borneo are irrevocably contaminated. Besides having been dubiously idealized and only partially understood in the first place, under scrutiny many "primitive" societies reveal forms of repression and coercion (such as the Yanomamo, who ritually bash each other's heads in, and African groups who practice clitoridectomy—removal of the clitoris) which would be unbearable to emancipated individuals of today. What is implied by the revival of "modern primitive" activities is the desire for and the dream of a *more ideal society*.

Amidst an almost universal feeling of powerlessness to "change the world," individuals are changing what they *do* have power over: *their own bodies*. That shadowy zone between the physical and the psychic is being probed for whatever insight and freedoms may be reclaimed. By giving visible bodily expression to unknown desires and latent obsessions welling up from within, individuals can provoke change—however inexplicable—in the external world of the social, besides freeing up a creative part of themselves; some part of their essence. (However, generalized proselytization has no place here—some people should definitely *not* get tattoos. Having a piercing is no infallible indication of advanced consciousness; as Anton LaVey remarked, "I've known plenty of people who have had tattooing and all kinds of modifications to their bodies—who are really screwed up!")

Art has always mirrored the Zeitgeist of the time. In this postmodern epoch in which all the art of the past has been assimilated, consumerized, advertised, and replicated, the last artistic territory resisting co-optation and commodification by museum and gallery remains the human body. For a tattoo is more than a painting on skin; its meaning and reverberations cannot be comprehended without a knowledge of the history and mythology of its bearer. Thus it is a true poetic creation and is always more than meets the eye. As a tattoo is grounded on living skin, so its essence emotes a poignancy unique to the mortal human condition. Likewise, no two piercings can be identical, because no two faces, bodies, or genitalia are alike.

These body modifications perform a vital function identical with art: they "genuinely stimulate passion and spring directly from the original sources of emotion, and are not something tapped from the cultural reservoir" (Roger Cardinal). Here that neglected function of art: *to stimulate the mind*, is unmistakably *alive*. And all of these modifications bear witness to personal pain endured which cannot be *simulated*. Although . . . society's machinery of co-optation gets faster and faster: a recent issue of *New York Woman* reported the marketing of *nonpiercing* nipple rings ranging from $26.50 to $10,000! No doubt further attempts at commercialization lie just around the corner. . . .

This book presents a wide range of rationales, ranging from the functional ("The *ampallang* makes sex *much* better!") to the extravagantly poetic and metaphysical. The archetypes have been investigated; nevertheless, numerous practitioners are absent—it was simply not possible to interview everyone of relevance. Many of the subjects started their experiments as children: before he was twelve, Ed Hardy had begun coloring "tattoos" on his peers; Fakir Musafar was enacting various primitive rituals borrowed from *National Geographic* by the age of fourteen. All share in common a *creative imperative* to which they have yielded in a kind of ultimate commitment: they have granted their *own bodies* as the artistic medium of expression.

Increasingly, the necessity to prove to the self the authenticity of unique, thoroughly private sensation becomes a threshold more difficult to surmount. Today, something as basic as sex itself is inextricably intertwined with a flood of alien images and cues implanted from media programming and advertising. But one thing remains fairly certain: *pain* is a uniquely personal experience; it remains loaded with tangible shock value. The most extreme practitioners of S-M probe the psychic territory of pain in search of an "ultimate," mystical proof that in their relationship (between the "S" and the "M"), the meaning of "trust" has been explored to its final limits, stopping just short of the infliction/experiencing of death itself.

The central, pivotal change in the world of the twentieth century—the wholesale deindividualization of man and society—has been accomplished by an inundation of millions of mass-produced images that, acting on humans, bypass any "logical" barriers of resistance, colonizing the memory cells of any receptive viewer within range. Almost unnoticed, firsthand "experience" and unself-conscious creative activities (hobbies such as whittling or quilt making) have been shunted aside in favor of a passive intake of images which the brain finds "pleasurable" and "relaxing": watching TV. The result: people all over the world share a common image bank of spurious memories and experiences, gestures, role models—even nuances of various linguistic styles, ranging from that of Peewee Herman to JFK to the latest commercial.

Our minds are colonized by images. Images are a virus. How does a virus work?

> Viruses are not cells; they are made up merely of *genetic material*—DNA or RNA. But once inside a host cell, the virus insinuates itself into the cell's replicative processes by attaching to its DNA or RNA, and tricks the cell into producing more viruses through the same mechanisms the cell uses to copy its own genes. Thus sabotaged, the cell not only fails to perform its intended function, but also is forced to help the enemy multiply.
> —Robin M. Henig, *Vogue*, March 1988

In the absence of truly unique, first-person experience in one's own RNA-coded memory cells, how can one feel confident about one's basic "identity"? And by extension, how can one, lacking unique experiences, create something truly eccentric? Virtually every experience possible in the world today—from touring Disneyland to trucking on photo safaris in Africa—has already been registered in the brain through *images* from a movie or TV *program*—an apt word indeed. (We are programmed, but for what? Where does the image end and reality begin?) It is cynically appropriate that the word *faux* (a pop correlative of the academic signifier "simulation") has comfortably settled into the working vocabulary of the eighties.

All the "modern primitive" practices being revived—so-called "permanent" tattooing, piercing, and scarification—underscore the realization that death itself, the Grim Reaper, must be stared straight in the face, unflinchingly, as part of the continuing struggle to free ourselves from our complexes, to get to know our hidden instincts, to work out unaccountable aggressions and satisfy devious urges. Death remains the standard whereby the authenticity and depth of all activities may be judged. And (complex) eroticism has always been the one implacable enemy of death. It is necessary to uncover the mass of repressed desires lying within the unconscious so that a *new eroticism* embracing the common identity of pain and pleasure, delirium and reason, and founded on a *full knowledge* of evil and perversion, may arise to inspire radically improved social relations.

All sensual experience functions to free us from "normal" social restraints, to awaken our deadened bodies to life. All such activity points toward a goal: the creation of the "complete" or "integrated" man and woman, and in this we are yet prisoners digging an imaginary tunnel to freedom. Our most inestimable resource, the unfettered imagination, continues to be grounded in the only truly precious possession we can ever have and know, and which is *ours* to do with what we will: *the human body*.

Fly

From *Peops: Stories and Portraits of People*

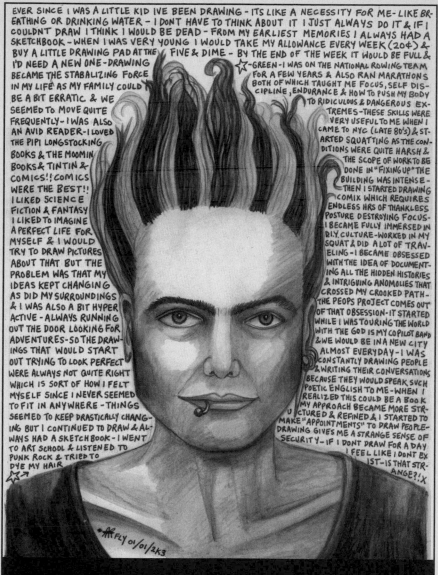

EVER SINCE I WAS A LITTLE KID IVE BEEN DRAWING - ITS LIKE A NECESSITY FOR ME- LIKE BREATHING OR DRINKING WATER - I DONT HAVE TO THINK ABOUT IT I JUST ALWAYS DO IT & IF I COULDNT DRAW I THINK I WOULD BE DEAD - FROM MY EARLIEST MEMORIES I ALWAYS HAD A SKETCHBOOK - WHEN I WAS VERY YOUNG I WOULD TAKE MY ALLOWANCE EVERY WEEK (20¢) & BUY A LITTLE DRAWING PAD AT THE FIVE & DIME - BY THE END OF THE WEEK IT WOULD BE FULL &

I'D NEED A NEW ONE - DRAWING BECAME THE STABALIZING FORCE IN MY LIFE AS MY FAMILY COULD BE A BIT ERRATIC & WE SEEMED TO MOVE QUITE FREQUENTLY - I WAS ALSO AN AVID READER - I LOVED THE PIPI LONGSTOCKING BOOKS & THE MOOMIN BOOKS & TINTIN & COMICS!! COMICS WERE THE BEST!! I LIKED SCIENCE FICTION & FANTASY I LIKED TO IMAGINE A PERFECT LIFE FOR MYSELF & I WOULD TRY TO DRAW PICTURES ABOUT THAT BUT THE PROBLEM WAS THAT MY IDEAS KEPT CHANGING AS DID MY SURROUNDINGS & I WAS ALSO A BIT HYPER ACTIVE - ALWAYS RUNNING OUT THE DOOR LOOKING FOR ADVENTURES - SO THE DRAWINGS THAT WOULD START OUT TRYING TO LOOK PERFECT WERE ALWAYS NOT QUITE RIGHT WHICH IS SORT OF HOW I FELT MYSELF SINCE I NEVER SEEMED TO FIT IN ANYWHERE - THINGS SEEMED TO KEEP DRASTICALLY CHANGING BUT I CONTINUED TO DRAW & ALWAYS HAD A SKETCH BOOK - I WENT TO ART SCHOOL & LISTENED TO PUNK ROCK & TRIED TO DYE MY HAIR

☆↗

★↗ -GREEN - I WAS ON THE NATIONAL ROWING TEAM FOR A FEW YEARS & ALSO RAN MARATHONS BOTH OF WHICH TAUGHT ME FOCUS, SELF DISCIPLINE, ENDURANCE & HOW TO PUSH MY BODY TO RIDICULOUS & DANGEROUS EXTREMES - THESE SKILLS WERE VERY USEFUL TO ME WHEN I CAME TO NYC (LATE 80's) & STARTED SQUATTING AS THE CONDITIONS WERE QUITE HARSH & THE SCOPE OF WORK TO BE DONE IN "FIXING UP" THE BUILDING WAS INTENSE - THEN I STARTED DRAWING COMIX WHICH REQUIRES ENDLESS HRS OF THANKLESS POSTURE DESTROYING FOCUS - I BECAME FULLY IMMERSED IN D.I.Y. CULTURE - WORKED IN MY SQUAT & DID A LOT OF TRAVELING - I BECAME OBSESSED WITH THE IDEA OF DOCUMENTING ALL THE HIDDEN HISTORIES & INTRIGUING ANOMOLIES THAT CROSSED MY CROOKED PATH - THE PEOPS PROJECT COMES OUT OF THAT OBSESSION - IT STARTED WHILE I WAS TOURING THE WORLD WITH THE GOD IS MY COPILOT BAND & WE WOULD BE IN A NEW CITY ALMOST EVERYDAY - I WAS CONSTANTLY DRAWING PEOPLE & WRITING THEIR CONVERSATIONS BECAUSE THEY WOULD SPEAK SUCH POETIC ENGLISH TO ME - WHEN I REALIZED THIS COULD BE A BOOK MY APPROACH BECAME MORE STRUCTURED & REFINED & I STARTED TO MAKE "APPOINTMENTS" TO DRAW PEOPLE - DRAWING GIVES ME A STRANGE SENSE OF SECURITY - IF I DONT DRAW FOR A DAY I FEEL LIKE I DONT EXIST - IS THAT STRANGE?! X

*AK FLY 01/01/2K3

FLY – 01/01/2K3 – LOISAIDA – NYC

PEOPS IS A COLLECTION OF PORTRAITS & STORIES — EACH PAGE CONTAINS A NEW FACE SURROUNDED BY WORDS — A STORY THAT THE PERSON TELLS ME — THE CONVERSATION WE HAVE AS I M DRAWING THEM — I M AMAZED AT HOW CO OPERATIVE PEOPLE WERE IN THIS PROJECT — IF SOMEONE SAT ME DOWN & TOLD ME THEY WERE GOING TO DRAW ME & WRITE DOWN WHAT I SAID I M NOT SO SURE THAT I WOULD WANT TO GO ALONG WITH THAT — & ALL THESE PEOPLE WITH THEIR INDIVIDUAL STORIES ADD UP TO MORE THAN WHAT IS REMEMBERED AS OFFICIAL HISTORY — EVERYONE IS & HAS AN INCREDIBLE STORY & EVERYONE DESERVES A VOICE — EVERYONE DESERVES TO BE LISTENED TO — WWW.BWAY.NET/~FLY — FLY@BYWAY.NET

From *Peops*

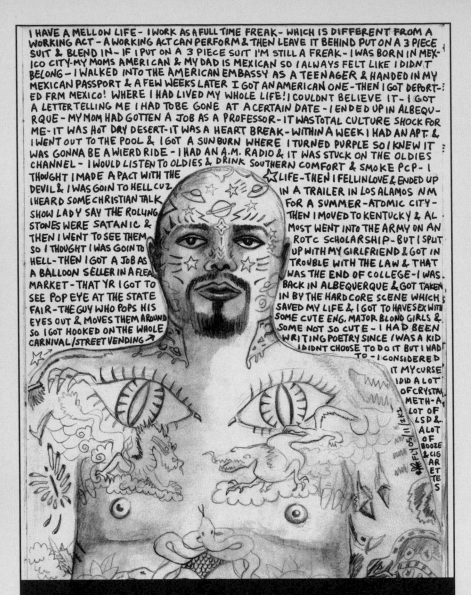

I HAVE A MELLOW LIFE - I WORK AS A FULL TIME FREAK - WHICH IS DIFFERENT FROM A WORKING ACT - A WORKING ACT CAN PERFORM & THEN LEAVE IT BEHIND PUT ON A 3 PIECE SUIT & BLEND IN - IF I PUT ON A 3 PIECE SUIT I'M STILL A FREAK - I WAS BORN IN MEXICO CITY - MY MOMS AMERICAN & MY DAD IS MEXICAN SO I ALWAYS FELT LIKE I DIDN'T BELONG - I WALKED INTO THE AMERICAN EMBASSY AS A TEENAGER & HANDED IN MY MEXICAN PASSPORT & A FEW WEEKS LATER I GOT AN AMERICAN ONE - THEN I GOT DEPORTED FRM MEXICO! WHERE I HAD LIVED MY WHOLE LIFE! I COULDNT BELIEVE IT - I GOT A LETTER TELLING ME I HAD TO BE GONE AT A CERTAIN DATE - I ENDED UP IN ALBEQURQUE - MY MOM HAD GOTTEN A JOB AS A PROFESSOR - IT WAS TOTAL CULTURE SHOCK FOR ME - IT WAS HOT DRY DESERT - IT WAS A HEART BREAK - WITHIN A WEEK I HAD AN APT. & I WENT OUT TO THE POOL & I GOT A SUNBURN WHERE I TURNED PURPLE SO I KNEW IT WAS GONNA BE A WIERD RIDE - I HAD AN A.M. RADIO & IT WAS STUCK ON THE OLDIES CHANNEL - I WOULD LISTEN TO OLDIES & DRINK SOUTHERN COMFORT & SMOKE PCP - I THOUGHT I MADE A PACT WITH THE DEVIL & I WAS GOIN TO HELL CUZ I HEARD SOME CHRISTIAN TALK SHOW LADY SAY THE ROLLING STONES WERE SATANIC & THEN I WENT TO SEE THEM SO I THOUGHT I WAS GOIN TO HELL - THEN I GOT A JOB AS A BALLOON SELLER IN A FLEA MARKET - THAT YR I GOT TO SEE POP EYE AT THE STATE FAIR - THE GUY WHO POPS HIS EYES OUT & MOVES THEM AROUND SO I GOT HOOKED ON THE WHOLE CARNIVAL/STREET VENDING →

☆ LIFE - THEN I FELL IN LOVE & ENDED UP IN A TRAILER IN LOS ALAMOS NM FOR A SUMMER - ATOMIC CITY - THEN I MOVED TO KENTUCKY & ALMOST WENT INTO THE ARMY ON AN ROTC SCHOLARSHIP - BUT I SPLIT UP WITH MY GIRLFRIEND & GOT IN TROUBLE WITH THE LAW & THAT WAS THE END OF COLLEGE - I WAS BACK IN ALBEQUERQUE & GOT TAKEN IN BY THE HARDCORE SCENE WHICH SAVED MY LIFE & I GOT TO HAVE SEX WITH SOME CUTE ENG. MAJOR BLOND GIRLS & SOME NOT SO CUTE - I HAD BEEN WRITING POETRY SINCE I WAS A KID I DIDNT CHOOSE TO DO IT BUT I HAD TO - I CONSIDERED IT MY CURSE I DID A LOT OF CRYSTAL METH - A LOT OF LSD & A LOT OF BOOZE & CIGARETTES

EAK — 05/11/2K1 — LOWER EAST SIDE — NYC

WHEN I FIRST MET EAK I DON'T THINK HE HAD ANY TATTOOS — AT LEAST I CANT REMEMBER IF HE DID OR NOT SO IF HE DID THEY WERENT THAT NOTICEABLE — EAK WAS IN A BAND & HE DID THE VOCALS — WHEN HE PERFORMED IT WAS LIKE HE WAS POSSESSED — HE WOULD BE TOTALLY OUT OF CONTROL — TRULY FREAKISH TO BEHOLD — THEN HE STARTED WORKING AT THE FREAK SHOW ON CONEY ISLAND & EVERYTIME I SAW HIM HE WOULD BE MORE INKED — BEING COVERED IN TATTOOS SEEMS TO HAVE MADE HIM MORE VISUALLY EXTROVERTED BUT HIS WHOLE SPIRIT SEEMS TO BE CALMER & MORE INTROVERTED — A TRUE FREAK — ARROCHAEAK@AOL.COM

From *Peops*

I HAVE NO IDEA I ONLY HAVE SAD STORIES THESE DAYS-I WROTE A LETTER TO A FRIEND TODAY THAT CRASHED-SAD STORY #1 - IT DETAILED ALL THE GOOD THINGS THAT HAPPENED TO ME THIS SEASON- NYC WINTERS ARE HARD THEY GET LONELY BUT THE GOOD THINGS ARE #1 THAT I GOT A JOB (HEY GIRLS! I WANT YOU TO REMEMBER THAT THERE ARE PEOPLE WHO LIVE DOWNSTAIRS! NADIA DO YOU REMEMBER WHAT IT WAS LIKE TO LIVE HERE? REMEMBER JENNIFER WOULD FREAK WHEN SHE HEARD NOISE FRM UPSTAIRS? NOW WITH THAT IN MIND YOU CAN GO BACK TO YR DRUM JAM) - I WANT YOU TO PUT THESE INTERSECTIONS IN - THIS IS MY LIFE - PICTURE 4 GIRLS WITH WHISTLES DRUMS TRAMPOLINES & MORACAS - DONT FORGET THE MORACAS! - OK - BASICALLY I TEACH PUSSY DOCTORS HOW TO EXAMINE PUSSIES & HOW TO TREAT THE WO-MEN WHO THOSE PUSSIES BELONG TO WHILE THEIR UP ON THE EXAM TABLE (NOT QUITE SO LOUD GIRLS! - ITS AFTER 10!) ALSO - I WANT TO GO TO ACUPUNCTURE SCHOOL - I WENT TO INTERVIEW A SCHOOL LAST NIGHT ITS PRETTY INTIMIDATING BUT I REALLY WANT IT - ITS A 4 YR COMMITMENT AS A FULL TIME STUDENT & 45000$! YEAH $45000!! THATS A LOGISTICAL PROBLEM BUT AS MY FRIEND SHEILA SAYS I HAVE TO PUT THE PUNK BACK INTO ACUPUNCTURE! $45000 IS NOT PUNK - ITS SO NOT PUNK - ITS MEDICAL SCHOOL - I WONDER IF MEDICAL SCHOOL IS PUNK? - ANOTHER GOOD THING THIS YR IS THAT THE STREET MEDICS IN THE N/E GOT REALLY TIGHT - WE FOUN-DED AN ASSOCIATION WITH BYLAWS, NON PROF-IT STATUS, CONFERENCES, ADVANCED TRAINING ETC WE HAVE A CONFER-ENCE THIS WEEK-END IN PHILLY WHERE I'M DO-ING AN HERB-AL FIRST AID TRAIN-ING ☆

I LOOK LIKE A TURTLE!

FAMOUS — MARCH 2K1 — NYC

WEEELLLLL — I KNEW HER BEFORE SHE WAS FAMOUS — BACK IN THE DAY — SHE S ALWAYS BEEN ONE OF THE COOLEST PEOPLE I KNOW & I HAVE TO APOLOGIZE FOR THE DRAWING BECAUSE IT REALLY ISNT AS BEAUTIFUL AS SHE IS — FAE IS A BADASS SQUATTER BABE — SUPERMOM — STREET MEDIC SUPREME — HERBAL GODDESS — GOURMET — CONSTURCTION QUEEN — & I VE SEEN HER DO SOME AMAZING COREOG-RAPHY WITH CHICKEN WIRE IN THE BASEMENT — SHE IS STRAIGHT UP GET SHIT DONE DO IT RIGHT THEN KICK BACK & HAVE FUN!! — SHE KNOWS HOW TO MAKE A HOUSE A HOME

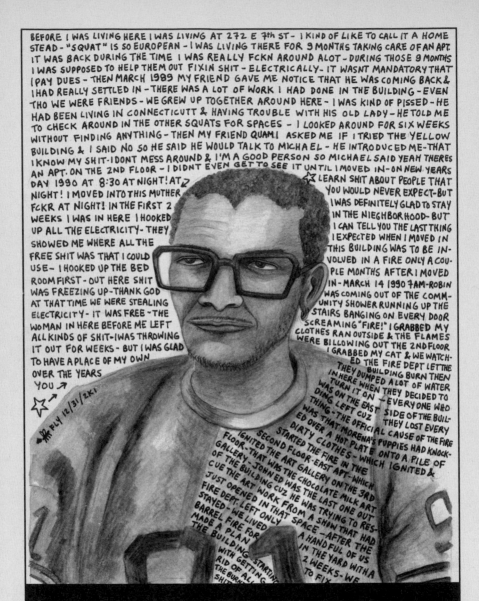

BEFORE I WAS LIVING HERE I WAS LIVING AT 272 E 7th ST – I KIND OF LIKE TO CALL IT A HOME STEAD – "SQUAT" IS SO EUROPEAN – I WAS LIVING THERE FOR 9 MONTHS TAKING CARE OF AN APT. IT WAS BACK DURING THE TIME I WAS REALLY FCKN AROUND ALOT – DURING THOSE 9 MONTHS I WAS SUPPOSED TO HELP THEM OUT FIXIN SHIT – ELECTRICALLY – IT WASNT MANDATORY THAT I PAY DUES – THEN MARCH 1989 MY FRIEND GAVE ME NOTICE THAT HE WAS COMING BACK & I HAD REALLY SETTLED IN – THERE WAS A LOT OF WORK I HAD DONE IN THE BUILDING – EVEN THO WE WERE FRIENDS – WE GREW UP TOGETHER AROUND HERE – I WAS KIND OF PISSED – HE HAD BEEN LIVING IN CONNECTICUTT & HAVING TROUBLE WITH HIS OLD LADY – HE TOLD ME TO CHECK AROUND IN THE OTHER SQUATS FOR SPACES – I LOOKED AROUND FOR SIX WEEKS WITHOUT FINDING ANYTHING – THEN MY FRIEND QUAMI ASKED ME IF I TRIED THE YELLOW BUILDING & I SAID NO SO HE SAID HE WOULD TALK TO MICHAEL – HE INTRODUCED ME – THAT I KNOW MY SHIT – I DONT MESS AROUND & I'M A GOOD PERSON SO MICHAEL SAID YEAH THERES AN APT. ON THE 2ND FLOOR – I DIDNT EVEN GET TO SEE IT UNTIL I MOVED IN – ON NEW YEARS DAY 1990 AT 8:30 AT NIGHT! AT NIGHT! I MOVED INTO THIS MUTHER FCKR AT NIGHT! IN THE FIRST 2 WEEKS I WAS IN HERE I HOOKED UP ALL THE ELECTRICITY – THEY SHOWED ME WHERE ALL THE FREE SHIT WAS THAT I COULD USE – I HOOKED UP THE BED ROOM FIRST – OUT HERE SHIT WAS FREEZING UP – THANK GOD AT THAT TIME WE WERE STEALING ELECTRICITY – IT WAS FREE – THE WOMAN IN HERE BEFORE ME LEFT ALL KINDS OF SHIT – I WAS THROWING IT OUT FOR WEEKS – BUT I WAS GLAD TO HAVE A PLACE OF MY OWN OVER THE YEARS YOU

FLY 12/31/2K1

LEARN SHIT ABOUT PEOPLE THAT YOU WOULD NEVER EXPECT – BUT I WAS DEFINITELY GLAD TO STAY IN THE NIEGHBORHOOD – BUT I CAN TELL YOU THE LAST THING I EXPECTED WHEN I MOVED IN THIS BUILDING WAS TO BE IN- VOLVED IN A FIRE ONLY A COU- PLE MONTHS AFTER I MOVED IN – MARCH 14 1990 7AM – ROBIN WAS COMING OUT OF THE COMM- UNITY SHOWER RUNNING UP THE STAIRS BANGING ON EVERY DOOR SCREAMING "FIRE!" I GRABBED MY CLOTHES RAN OUTSIDE & THE FLAMES WERE BILLOWING OUT THE 2ND FLOOR I GRABBED MY CAT & WE WATCH- ED THE FIRE DEPT LET THE BUILDING BURN THEN THEY DUMPED A LOT OF WATER IN HERE WHEN THEY DECIDED TO TURN IT ON – EVERYONE WHO WAS ON THE EAST SIDE OF THE BUIL- DING LEFT CUZ THEY LOST EVERY THING – THE OFFICIAL CAUSE OF THE FIRE WAS THAT MORENA'S PUPPIES HAD KNOCK- ED OVER A HOT PLATE ONTO A PILE OF DIRTY CLOTHES – WHICH IGNITED & STARTED THE FIRE IN THE SECOND FLOOR EAST APT – WHICH IGNITED THE ART GALLERY ON THE 3RD FLOOR – THAT WAS THE CHOCOLATE MILK ART GALLERY – JOHN ED WAS THE LAST ONE OUT OF THE BUILDING CUZ HE WAS TRYING TO RES- CUE THE ART WORK FROM A SHOW THAT HAD JUST OPENED IN THAT SPACE – AFTER THE FIRE DEPT. LEFT ONLY A HANDFUL OF US STAYED – WE LIVED IN THE YARD WITH A BARREL FIRE FOR 2 WEEKS – WE MADE A PLAN TO FIX THE BUILDING STARTING WITH GETTING RID OF ALL THE BURNT SHIT...

MAXIE MARSHALL – 12/31/2K1 – LOWER EAST SIDE – NYC
MAXIE ALSO LIVES IN MY BUILDING & IS ONE OF THE ORIGINAL SQUATTERS – I MET MAX IN THE SUMMER OF 92 WHEN I STARTED DOING WORK DAYS AT 209 – HE WAS ALWAYS NICE TO ME BUT LOOK OUT IF YOURE NOT SUPPOSED TO BE HERE – & ANY MEMBER OF THE BUILDING WHO MAYBE LOST THEIR KEY TO THE FRONT DOOR & NEEDS A NEW ONE HAS TO GO SEE MAXIE & LET ME TELL YOU IT WON T BE EASY – KEYS ARE A VERY SENSITIVE ISSUE SINCE LOST KEYS CAN ALWAYS BE FOUND BY THE WRONG PEOPLE – WELL – IT MIGHT BE EASIER IF YOU HAVE A LITTLE EXTRA CHANGE – BUT DONT FCK WITH MAX MAAAAAAN DON T *MAKE* HIM HAVE TO COME TO YOUR HOUSE & DEAL WITH YOU – SHIIIITT

From *Peops*

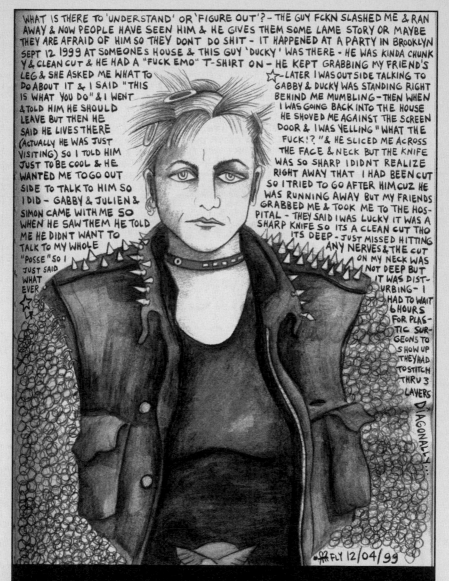

WHAT IS THERE TO 'UNDERSTAND' OR 'FIGURE OUT'? - THE GUY FCKN SLASHED ME & RAN AWAY & NOW PEOPLE HAVE SEEN HIM & HE GIVES THEM SOME LAME STORY OR MAYBE THEY ARE AFRAID OF HIM SO THEY DONT DO SHIT - IT HAPPENED AT A PARTY IN BROOKLYN SEPT 12 1999 AT SOMEONES HOUSE & THIS GUY 'DUCKY' WAS THERE - HE WAS KINDA CHUNKY & CLEAN CUT & HE HAD A "FUCK EMO" T-SHIRT ON - HE KEPT GRABBING MY FRIEND'S LEG & SHE ASKED ME WHAT TO DO ABOUT IT & I SAID "THIS IS WHAT YOU DO" & I WENT & TOLD HIM HE SHOULD LEAVE BUT THEN HE SAID HE LIVES THERE (ACTUALLY HE WAS JUST VISITING) SO I TOLD HIM JUST TO BE COOL & HE WANTED ME TO GO OUT SIDE TO TALK TO HIM SO I DID - GABBY & JULIEN & SIMON CAME WITH ME SO WHEN HE SAW THEM HE TOLD ME HE DIDN'T WANT TO TALK TO MY WHOLE "POSSE" SO I JUST SAID WHAT EVER

☆ - LATER I WAS OUTSIDE TALKING TO GABBY & DUCKY WAS STANDING RIGHT BEHIND ME MUMBLING - THEN WHEN I WAS GOING BACK INTO THE HOUSE HE SHOVED ME AGAINST THE SCREEN DOOR & I WAS YELLING "WHAT THE FUCK!? " & HE SLICED ME ACROSS THE FACE & NECK BUT THE KNIFE WAS SO SHARP I DIDNT REALIZE RIGHT AWAY THAT I HAD BEEN CUT SO I TRIED TO GO AFTER HIM CUZ HE WAS RUNNING AWAY BUT MY FRIENDS GRABBED ME & TOOK ME TO THE HOSPITAL - THEY SAID I WAS LUCKY IT WAS A SHARP KNIFE SO ITS A CLEAN CUT THO ITS DEEP - JUST MISSED HITTING ANY NERVES & THE CUT ON MY NECK WAS NOT DEEP BUT IT WAS DISTURBING - I HAD TO WAIT 6 HOURS FOR PLASTIC SURGEONS TO SHOW UP THEY HAD TO STITCH THRU 3 LAYERS DIAGONALLY...

FLY 12/04/99

AMYL NITRATE – 12/04/1999 – NYC
I FIRST MET AMYL ON MARKET ST. IN SF HANGIN OUT ON THE SIDEWALK WITH ALL THE PUNKS — SHE INTRODUCED ME TO FRANKS DEPRESSION WHO WAS SITTING THERE LOOKING LIKE AN ALIEN — AMYL WAS THE LEAD SINGER OF THE AWESOME BAND THE SPIDER CUNTS — DO NOT FUCK WITH AMYL SHE WILL PUNCH YOU BUT SHE IS SWEET TO ALL HER FRIENDS — I DREW THIS A LITTLE WHILE AFTER SHE SAID SHE HAD BEEN SLASHED IN THE FACE BY A GUY CALLED DUCKY WHO HAS STILL NOT ANSWERED FOR THIS BULLSHIT WWW.COMMUNICHAOS.COM

WHEN WE FIRST CAME TO NEW YORK WE LIVED IN BROOKLYN FOR 3 WEEKS - WE EVEN HAD A LEASE - AFTER MOHAMMED HAD BOUNCED THE BASKETBALL OFF OUR WINDOW FOR 10 DAYS WE HAD TO LEAVE - THE BASKETBALL WAS LIKE A REPRESENTATION OF SUBURBIA & WE DIDNT WANT SUBURBIA - THE DOG DIDNT LIKE IT EITHER - HE KEPT GETTING ATTACKED BY THE ATTACK CAT AT THE END OF THE BLOCK WHO WOULD ATTACK DOGS BY JUMPING ON THIER BACKS - WE MOVED TO BROOME ST - THERE WAS NICE FLOORING THERE BUT SOME AREAS WERE ALL PLYWOOD & THATS BECAUSE THE FORMER OWNERS WIFE HAD HEARD HER HUSBAND HAD BURIED $100,000$ THERE SO SHE HAD STARTED TO TEAR UP THE FLOORS - HER HUSBAND HAD BEEN A DENTIST & SHE GOT A HUGE FINE FOR DUMPING HIS STUFF CUZ IT HAD MERCURY VIALS IN IT - HIS SON HAD TO HAVE HIS JAW REWIRED & WORKED ON CUZ HE HAD X-RAYED IT SO MUCH - THAT TAKES CARE OF BROOME ST (KEITH HARING LIVED ABOVE US) - THEN WE MOVED TO THE BOWERY - A BIG SPACE - MY MOST LASTING MEMORY WAS THE CHINESE BAKERY THAT BUILT A PIPE THAT BLEW INTO OUR BACK WINDOW - IT WAS SUPPOSED TO BE BUILT TO THE ROOF - IT WAS NOISY - WE COMPLAINED TO THE EPA FOR ABOUT A YEAR & THEY FINALLY BUILT IT UP TO WHERE IT WAS SUPPOSED TO BE ⟶

THATS ENOUGH ABOUT THE BOWERY - I'LL TELL YOU ABOUT 9-11 - A FRIEND OF OURS PHONED US & SAID THERE HAD BEEN AN ACCIDENT AT THE WORLD TRADE CENTER SO WE WENT DOWN THERE IMMEDIATELY & GOT INTO THE AREA BEFORE THE POLICE SHUT IT DOWN - WE WENT EAST AS QUICKLY AS POSSIBLE AS EVERYONE ELSE WAS GOING WEST - WE ENDED UP ON THE WEST SIDE HIGHWAY POLICE WERE HERDING EVERYONE AROUND - WE DIDNT EVEN REALIZE A SECOND PLANE HAD HIT BECAUSE THAT HAPPENED WHILE WE WERE ON THE SUBWAY - WE NEVER THOUGHT THE BUILDINGS WOULD COLLAPSE NO ONE DID ☆↗

✦ - WE WERE TOLD TO LEAVE THE AREA SO WE STARTED HEADING NORTH ON THE WEST SIDE HIGHWAY - WE HAD BEEN VIDEOTAPING THIS WHOLE TIME - 26 MIN. WE SAW PEOPLE JUMPING OUT OF THE BUILDING - WE WERE A BLOCK AWAY - IT SEEMED TO TAKE THEM A LONG TIME TO FALL - IT WAS 110 STORIES - ONE OF THEM WAS WEARING WHAT LOOKED LIKE A 12 ft LONG SAFFRON SCARF. WE WERE WATCHING A HELICOPTOR NEAR THE TOP OF THE BUILDING & WE STARTED HEARING THIS CREAKING SOUND - & THEN TINKLING - LIKE WIND CHIMES - BUT IT WAS GLASS BREAKING & THE BUILDING STARTING TO FALL DOWN - THEN THERE WAS SO MUCH NOISE YOU COULDNT EVEN HEAR IT - EVEN THE CAMERA COULDNT HEAR THAT LOUD - IT WASNT LIKE T.V. - I WAS PUSHED - FELL ON MY FACE ON THE CAMERA BROKE THE CAMERA & GOT A CONCUSSION.

☀ FLY 12/11/2K1

ELSA RENSAA – 12/11/2K1 – LOWER EAST SIDE – NYC

I DON T THINK I WAS EVER FORMALLY INTRODUCED TO ELSA — SHE WAS JUST ALWAYS AROUND VIDEOTAPING WITH CLAYTON — DOCUMENTING ALL THE INSANITY OF THE LOWER EAST SIDE DURING THE WAR TORN DAYS BEFORE GENTRIFICATION HAD FULLY TAKEN OVER — ELSA & CLAYTON WOULD BE THERE FOR THE DEMOS OR THE RIOTS OR THE IMPROPTU PERFORMANCES OR THE SPEAK OUTS OR WHENEVER SHIT WAS JUST GOIN DOWN — THIS IS A TOTALLY HIDDEN HISTORY THAT THEY HAVE BEEN DOCUMENTING FOR DECADES NOW — ESSENTIAL & IMPORTANT WORK THAT DOESNT USUALLY GET THE RECOGNITION IT DESERVES

From *Peops*

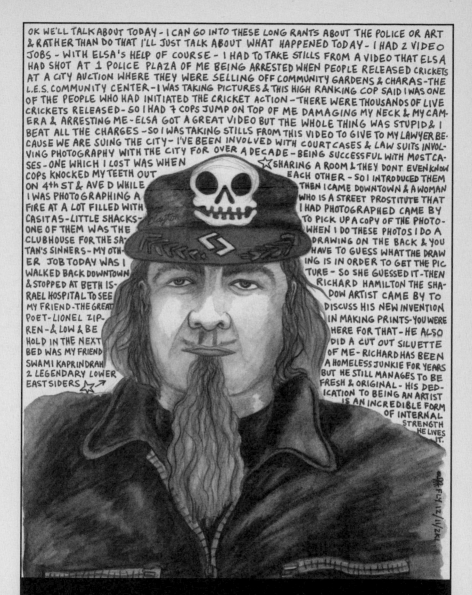

OK WE'LL TALK ABOUT TODAY - I CAN GO INTO THESE LONG RANTS ABOUT THE POLICE OR ART & RATHER THAN DO THAT I'LL JUST TALK ABOUT WHAT HAPPENED TODAY - I HAD 2 VIDEO JOBS - WITH ELSA'S HELP OF COURSE - I HAD TO TAKE STILLS FROM A VIDEO THAT ELSA HAD SHOT AT 1 POLICE PLAZA OF ME BEING ARRESTED WHEN PEOPLE RELEASED CRICKETS AT A CITY AUCTION WHERE THEY WERE SELLING OFF COMMUNITY GARDENS & CHARAS - THE L.E.S. COMMUNITY CENTER - I WAS TAKING PICTURES & THIS HIGH RANKING COP SAID I WAS ONE OF THE PEOPLE WHO HAD INITIATED THE CRICKET ACTION - THERE WERE THOUSANDS OF LIVE CRICKETS RELEASED - SO I HAD 7 COPS JUMP ON TOP OF ME DAMAGING MY NECK & MY CAMERA & ARRESTING ME - ELSA GOT A GREAT VIDEO BUT THE WHOLE THING WAS STUPID & I BEAT ALL THE CHARGES - SO I WAS TAKING STILLS FROM THIS VIDEO TO GIVE TO MY LAWYER BECAUSE WE ARE SUING THE CITY - I'VE BEEN INVOLVED WITH COURT CASES & LAW SUITS INVOLVING PHOTOGRAPHY WITH THE CITY FOR OVER A DECADE - BEING SUCCESSFUL WITH MOST CASES - ONE WHICH I LOST WAS WHEN COPS KNOCKED MY TEETH OUT ON 4th ST & AVE D WHILE I WAS PHOTOGRAPHING A FIRE AT A LOT FILLED WITH CASITAS - LITTLE SHACKS - ONE OF THEM WAS THE CLUBHOUSE FOR THE SATAN'S SINNERS - MY OTHER JOB TODAY WAS I WALKED BACK DOWNTOWN & STOPPED AT BETH ISRAEL HOSPITAL TO SEE MY FRIEND - THE GREAT POET - LIONEL ZIPREN - & LOW & BEHOLD IN THE NEXT BED WAS MY FRIEND SWAMI KAPRINDRAH 2 LEGENDARY LOWER EAST SIDERS ☆↗

SHARING A ROOM & THEY DON'T EVEN KNOW EACH OTHER - SO I INTRODUCED THEM THEN I CAME DOWNTOWN & A WOMAN WHO IS A STREET PROSTITUTE THAT I HAD PHOTOGRAPHED CAME BY TO PICK UP A COPY OF THE PHOTO - WHEN I DO THESE PHOTOS I DO A DRAWING ON THE BACK & YOU HAVE TO GUESS WHAT THE DRAWING IS IN ORDER TO GET THE PICTURE - SO SHE GUESSED IT - THEN RICHARD HAMILTON THE SHADOW ARTIST CAME BY TO DISCUSS HIS NEW INVENTION IN MAKING PRINTS - YOU WERE HERE FOR THAT - HE ALSO DID A CUT OUT SILUETTE OF ME - RICHARD HAS BEEN A HOMELESS JUNKIE FOR YEARS BUT HE STILL MANAGES TO BE FRESH & ORIGINAL - HIS DEDICATION TO BEING AN ARTIST IS AN INCREDIBLE FORM OF INTERNAL STRENGTH HE LIVES IT.

CLAYTON PATTERSON – 12/11/2K1 – LOWER EAST SIDE – NYC

SAME AS WITH ELSA I DON'T THINK I WAS EVER REALLY INTRODUCED TO CLAYTON – THE FIRST I KNEW OF HIM WAS WHEN I WALKED BY HIS STOREFRONT ON ESSEX SOME TIME IN THE LATE 80s & SAW HIS AMAZING HATS! – BEAUTIFUL COLORFULLY EMBROIDERED BLACK HATS – THEN I WOULD SEE CLAYTON & ELSA EVERYWHERE WITH THEIR CAMERAS DOCUMENTING THE EVOLUTION OF LOWER EAST SIDE CULTURE – THIS IS LIKE A LIFE'S WORK – CLAYTON BECAME "FAMOUS" AFTER THE 1988 TOMPKINS SQUARE PARK POLICE RIOT WHEN HE TAPED COPS BRUTALLY BEATING UP INNOCENT BYSTANDERS – THE COPS DIDNT LIKE HIM TOO MUCH AFTER THAT ONE

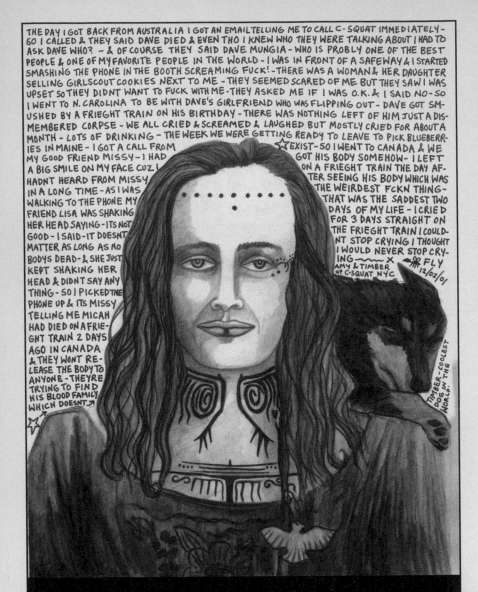

THE DAY I GOT BACK FROM AUSTRALIA I GOT AN EMAIL TELLING ME TO CALL C-SQUAT IMMEDIATELY - SO I CALLED & THEY SAID DAVE DIED & EVEN THO I KNEW WHO THEY WERE TALKING ABOUT I HAD TO ASK DAVE WHO? - & OF COURSE THEY SAID DAVE MUNGIA - WHO IS PROBLY ONE OF THE BEST PEOPLE & ONE OF MY FAVORITE PEOPLE IN THE WORLD - I WAS IN FRONT OF A SAFEWAY & I STARTED SMASHING THE PHONE IN THE BOOTH SCREAMING FUCK! - THERE WAS A WOMAN & HER DAUGHTER SELLING GIRLSCOUT COOKIES NEXT TO ME - THEY SEEMED SCARED OF ME BUT THEY SAW I WAS UPSET SO THEY DIDNT WANT TO FUCK WITH ME - THEY ASKED ME IF I WAS O.K. & I SAID NO - SO I WENT TO N. CAROLINA TO BE WITH DAVE'S GIRLFRIEND WHO WAS FLIPPING OUT - DAVE GOT SMUSHED BY A FRIEGHT TRAIN ON HIS BIRTHDAY - THERE WAS NOTHING LEFT OF HIM JUST A DISMEMBERED CORPSE - WE ALL CRIED & SCREAMED & LAUGHED BUT MOSTLY CRIED FOR ABOUT A MONTH - LOTS OF DRINKING - THE WEEK WE WERE GETTING READY TO LEAVE TO PICK BLUEBERRIES IN MAINE - I GOT A CALL FROM MY GOOD FRIEND MISSY - I HAD A BIG SMILE ON MY FACE CUZ I HADNT HEARD FROM MISSY IN A LONG TIME - AS I WAS WALKING TO THE PHONE MY FRIEND LISA WAS SHAKING HER HEAD SAYING - ITS NOT GOOD - I SAID - IT DOESNT MATTER AS LONG AS NOBODYS DEAD - & SHE JUST KEPT SHAKING HER HEAD & DIDNT SAY ANY THING - SO I PICKED THE PHONE UP & ITS MISSY TELLING ME MICAH HAD DIED ON A FRIEGHT TRAIN 2 DAYS AGO IN CANADA & THEY WONT RELEASE THE BODY TO ANYONE - THEYRE TRYING TO FIND HIS BLOOD FAMILY WHICH DOESNT ☆ EXIST - SO I WENT TO CANADA & WE GOT HIS BODY SOMEHOW - I LEFT ON A FRIEGHT TRAIN THE DAY AFTER SEEING HIS BODY WHICH WAS THE WEIRDEST FCKN THING - THAT WAS THE SADDEST TWO DAYS OF MY LIFE - I CRIED FOR 3 DAYS STRAIGHT ON THE FRIEGHT TRAIN I COULDNT STOP CRYING I THOUGHT I WOULD NEVER STOP CRYING ~~~ X ✳ FLY
AMY & TIMBER
at C-SQUAT NYC   12/02/01

TIMBER - COOLEST DOG IN THE WORLD

AMY & TIMBER – 12/02/2K1 – C SQUAT – NYC

I MET AMY IN THE EARLY 90s – SHE WAS ONE OF THE BADDEST GIRLS IN THE LOWER EAST SIDE – LIVING AT C SQUAT WITH HER DOG TIMBER WHO WAS THE COOLEST DOG I HAVE EVER MET & HE WAS REALLY SMART – WOULDNT BE PUT ON A LEASH – AMY & TIMBER WOULD TRAVEL A LOT AROUND THE US HOPPING TRAINS OR CATCHING RIDES – WHEN I WAS DRAWING THIS AT C SQUAT AMY WAS PLANNING TO GO TO NEW ORLEANS THE NEXT DAY WITH SOME OTHER FOLKS & SHE WAS TELLING ME HOW SHE WAS WORKING AS A DANCER DOWN THERE & MAKING GOOD MONEY – THE SAD THING IS THAT IN THE SPRING OF 2K2 TIMBER WAS KILLED – RUN OVER BY A TRACTOR – ITS REALLY FCKN SAD

From *Peops*

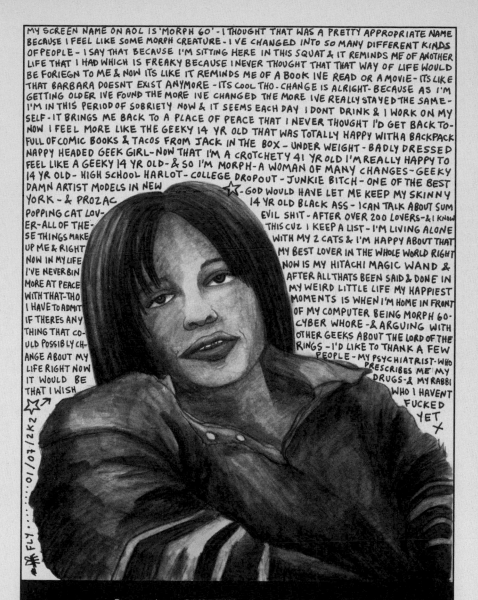

MY SCREEN NAME ON AOL IS 'MORPH 60'- I THOUGHT THAT WAS A PRETTY APPROPRIATE NAME BECAUSE I FEEL LIKE SOME MORPH CREATURE- I'VE CHANGED INTO SO MANY DIFFERENT KINDS OF PEOPLE - I SAY THAT BECAUSE I'M SITTING HERE IN THIS SQUAT & IT REMINDS ME OF ANOTHER LIFE THAT I HAD WHICH IS FREAKY BECAUSE I NEVER THOUGHT THAT THAT WAY OF LIFE WOULD BE FORIEGN TO ME & NOW ITS LIKE IT REMINDS ME OF A BOOK I'VE READ OR A MOVIE- ITS LIKE THAT BARBARA DOESNT EXIST ANYMORE - ITS COOL THO- CHANGE IS ALRIGHT- BECAUSE AS I'M GETTING OLDER I'VE FOUND THE MORE I'VE CHANGED THE MORE I'VE REALLY STAYED THE SAME- I'M IN THIS PERIOD OF SOBRIETY NOW & IT SEEMS EACH DAY I DONT DRINK & I WORK ON MY SELF - IT BRINGS ME BACK TO A PLACE OF PEACE THAT I NEVER THOUGHT I'D GET BACK TO- NOW I FEEL MORE LIKE THE GEEKY 14 YR OLD THAT WAS TOTALLY HAPPY WITH A BACKPACK FULL OF COMIC BOOKS & TACOS FROM JACK IN THE BOX - UNDER WEIGHT - BADLY DRESSED NAPPY HEADED GEEK GIRL- NOW THAT I'M A CROTCHETY 41 YR OLD I'M REALLY HAPPY TO FEEL LIKE A GEEKY 14 YR OLD - & SO I'M MORPH- A WOMAN OF MANY CHANGES- GEEKY 14 YR OLD- HIGH SCHOOL HARLOT- COLLEGE DROPOUT - JUNKIE BITCH - ONE OF THE BEST DAMN ARTIST MODELS IN NEW YORK - & PROZAC POPPING CAT LOVER - ALL OF THESE THINGS MAKE UP ME & RIGHT NOW IN MY LIFE I'VE NEVER BIN MORE AT PEACE WITH THAT- THO I HAVE TO ADMIT IF THERES ANY THING THAT COULD POSSIBLY CHANGE ABOUT MY LIFE RIGHT NOW IT WOULD BE THAT I WISH GOD WOULD HAVE LET ME KEEP MY SKINNY 14 YR OLD BLACK ASS - I CAN TALK ABOUT SUM EVIL SHIT - AFTER OVER 200 LOVERS - & I KNOW THIS CUZ I KEEP A LIST - I'M LIVING ALONE WITH MY 2 CATS & I'M HAPPY ABOUT THAT MY BEST LOVER IN THE WHOLE WORLD RIGHT NOW IS MY HITACHI MAGIC WAND & AFTER ALL THATS BEEN SAID & DONE IN MY WEIRD LITTLE LIFE MY HAPPIEST MOMENTS IS WHEN I'M HOME IN FRONT OF MY COMPUTER BEING MORPH 60- CYBER WHORE - & ARGUING WITH OTHER GEEKS ABOUT THE LORD OF THE RINGS - I'D LIKE TO THANK A FEW PEOPLE - MY PSYCHIATRIST- WHO PRESCRIBES ME MY DRUGS - & MY RABBI WHO I HAVENT FUCKED YET

FLY ·········· 01/07/2K2

BARBARA LEE – 01/07/2K2 – LOWER EAST SIDE – NYC

WHEN I FIRST MET BARBARA LEE I THINK I WAS A LITTLE INTIMIDATED – SHE WAS ALWAYS REALLY SWEET TO ME BUT SHE WAS SUCH A TOUGH GIRL – I CAN REMEMBER IN THE EARLY & MID 90S WE'D ALL BE OUT ON THE STREET AT SOME DEMO OR POLICE RIOT OR SOMETHING & BARBARA WOULD HAVE NO FEAR – SHE WOULD JUST BE GETTING RIGHT UP IN THE COPS FACES – & ANYONE WHO FUCKED WITH HER WOULD BE IN SERIOUS PHYSICAL DANGER – BUT LIKE I SAID – SHE HAS ALWAYS BEEN REALLY SWEET TO ME – I DON'T SEE HER AROUND MUCH ANYMORE CUZ NOW SHE LIVES IN BROOKLYN WHERE SHE ENJOYS HER SOBRIETY & EXPLORING ALL AVENUES OF HER SPIRITUALITY – MORPH60@AOL.COM

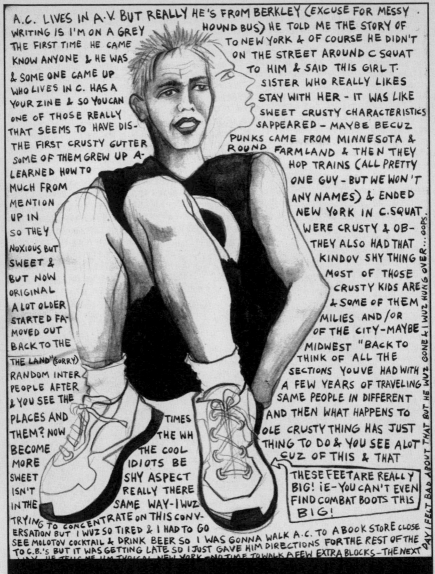

A.C. LIVES IN A.V. BUT REALLY HE'S FROM BERKLEY (EXCUSE FOR MESSY WRITING IS I'M ON A GREY HOUND BUS) HE TOLD ME THE STORY OF THE FIRST TIME HE CAME TO NEW YORK & OF COURSE HE DIDN'T KNOW ANYONE & HE WAS ON THE STREET AROUND C SQUAT & SOME ONE CAME UP TO HIM & SAID THIS GIRL T. WHO LIVES IN C. HAS A SISTER WHO REALLY LIKES YOUR ZINE & SO YOU CAN STAY WITH HER - IT WAS LIKE ONE OF THOSE REALLY SWEET CRUSTY CHARACTERISTICS THAT SEEMS TO HAVE DIS- SAPPEARED - MAYBE BECUZ THE FIRST CRUSTY GUTTER PUNKS CAME FROM MINNESOTA & SOME OF THEM GREW UP A- ROUND FARMLAND & THEN THEY LEARNED HOW TO HOP TRAINS (ALL PRETTY MUCH FROM ONE GUY - BUT WE WON'T MENTION ANY NAMES) & ENDED UP IN NEW YORK IN C.SQUAT. SO THEY WERE CRUSTY & OB- NOXIOUS BUT THEY ALSO HAD THAT SWEET & KINDOV SHY THING BUT NOW MOST OF THOSE ORIGINAL CRUSTY KIDS ARE A LOT OLDER & SOME OF THEM STARTED FA- MILIES AND/OR MOVED OUT OF THE CITY-MAYBE BACK TO THE MIDWEST "BACK TO THE LAND"(SORRY) THINK OF ALL THE RANDOM INTER SECTIONS YOUVE HAD WITH PEOPLE AFTER A FEW YEARS OF TRAVELING & YOU SEE THE SAME PEOPLE IN DIFFERENT PLACES AND AND THEN WHAT HAPPENS TO THEM? NOW OLE CRUSTY THING HAS JUST BECOME THING TO DO & YOU SEE A LOT MORE CUZ OF THIS & THAT SWEET ISN'T IN THE TIMES THE WH THE COOL IDIOTS BE SHY ASPECT REALLY THERE SAME WAY-I WUZ TRYING TO CONCENTRATE ON THIS CONV- ERSATION BUT I WUZ SO TIRED & I HAD TO GO SEE MOLOTOV COCKTAIL & DRINK BEER SO I WAS GONNA WALK A.C. TO A BOOK STORE CLOSE TO C.B.'S BUT IT WAS GETTING LATE SO I JUST GAVE HIM DIRECTIONS FOR THE REST OF THE

THESE FEET ARE REALLY BIG! iE- YOU CAN'T EVEN FIND COMBAT BOOTS THIS BIG!

DAY I FELT BAD ABOUT THAT BUT HE WUZ GONE & I WUZ HUNG OVER...OOPS.

WALK A FEW EXTRA BLOCKS-THE NEXT

AARON COMETBUS — JULY 1999 — LOUISAIDA — NYC

I HAD BEEN READING AARONS ZINE COMETBUS FOR YEARS BEFORE I MET HIM — AT SOME POINT I SENT HIM ONE OF MY FLY POSTCARDS & HE WROTE ME BACK — I THINK HE THOUGHT I WAS A LITTLE NUTTY AT THAT POINT — EVENTUALLY I MET HIM IN CHICAGO WHILE I WAS ON TOUR WITH GOD IS MY CO-PILOT & HE WAS ON TOUR WITH GREEN DAY — I DREW THIS PAGE AFTER AARON & COREY (FRM AUS ROTTEN) HAD A BONDING MOMENT SOAPING UP THEIR HAIRS TOGETHER — IT WAS SO SWEET — AARON WOULDNT LET ME WRITE ANYTHING DOWN WHILE WE WERE TALKING SO I MADE UP ALL THE WORDS WEEKS LATER AS I WAS RIDING A GREYHOUND TO PITTSBURGH TO VISIT THE ROTTENS

WE CANT TALK ABOUT PERSONAL SHIT CUZ WHO KNOWS WHO WILL BE READING THIS - TOR-
TILLA CHIPS ARE BULLSHIT- ITS ALL ABOUT POTATOE CHIPS - LATELY IVE BEEN GETTING
INTO CHEDDAR CHEESE - I USED TO EAT POTATOE CHIPS AS A KID - I WOULD EAT A ONE
POUND BAG IN ONE SITTING - THAT WAS BACK WHEN A POUND WAS A POUND- CAN YOU
BELIEVE A 2×4 IS ACTUALLY... (HA HA HA) MODERN WORLD - EVERYTIME I OPEN MY MO-
UTH I GET INTO MORE TROUBLE - I'M SO TIRED OF PEOPLE USING THE INFORMATION I GIVE
THEM TO BEAT ME OVER THE HEAD - WHY CANT THEY THINK FOR THEMSELVES- PICK UP THIER
OWN WEAPONS- DON'T USE MINE - IVE BEEN HAVING THE WIERDEST MEMORY FLASH-
BACKS SINCE 9-11 - I REMEMBER SWIMMING IN A POOL - NO I WASNT SWIMMING - I WAS
DROWNING - I MUST HAVE BEEN ABOUT 7 OR 8 YRS OLD & I DIDNT REALLY KNOW HOW
TO SWIM BUT I JUMPED INTO THE DEEP PART OF THE POOL AT SOME HOTEL IN MEXICO
& I STARTED SINKING - YOU KNOW HOW YOU DO THE DOG PADDLE TO STAY UP - I WAS GRAB
BING HANDFULS OF WATER & I WAS
TRYING TO YELL BUT MY MOUTH
WAS FILLING WITH WATER SO
IT WAS LIKE GURGLE GURG-
LE - AS I WAS GOING DOWN
FOR THE LAST TIME I LOOKT
OVER TO THE SIDE OF THE
POOL & THE LAST IMAGE
I REMEMBER IS THIS BL-
URRY PICTURE OF MY BRO-
THER STANDING BY THE
POOL WITH HIS HANDS
IN HIS POCKETS WATCH-
ING ME DROWN - I AL-
WAYS THOUGHT HE WAS

☆ TAKING THE CHANGE OUT OF
HIS POCKETS GETTING READY
TO JUMP IN - BUT NOW I HAVE
MY DOUBTS- THEN AN ARM
GRABBED ME & PULLED ME
OUT WITH UNBELIEVABLE
FORCE - JUST SOME STRAN-
GER WHO WAS IN THE POOL
I COULD TELL YOU ANOTHER
NEAR DEATH EXPERIENCE
ON A BIKE GETTING SQUEE-
ZED BETWEEN A CAR & A
BUS - OR DRIVING A CAR IN
NEW ORLEANS THAT I DIDNT
KNOW HOW TO DRIVE - I COULD
TELL YOU ABOUT A UFO EXPER-
IENCE

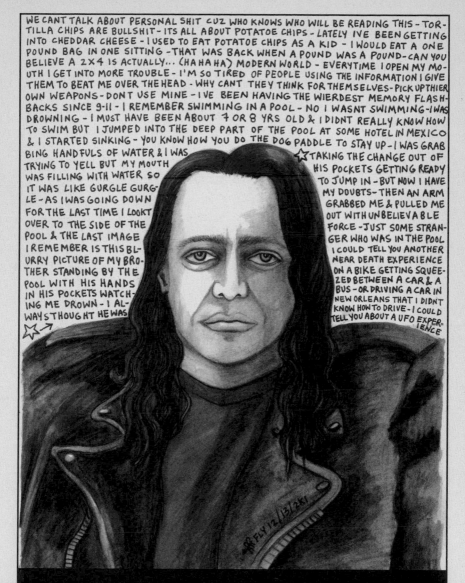

JOHN ZORN — 12/13/2K1 — LOWER EAST SIDE — NYC

ZORN LIVES ACROSS THE STREET FROM ME & I SEE HIM ALL THE TIME RUNNING TO GIGS OR JUMPING IN
A CAB TO GO THE AIRPORT TO GO TO JAPAN — ZORN IS FAMOUS FOR MAKING INSANE SOUNDS ON A SAX
& ALSO FOR TOTALLY SHAKING UP THE JAZZ WORLD — I REALLY DON'T KNOW TOO MUCH ABOUT JAZZ
BUT I KNOW THAT ZORN'S MUSIC CAN REALLY TWIST MY HEAD — HE'S PRODUCED A LOT OF CD'S ON HIS
LABEL — TZADIK — WHENEVER I SEE HIM HE ALWAYS HAS A BIG SMILE — ONE TIME LAW & ORDER WAS
FILMING ON OUR STREET & THEY WERE TRYING TO MAKE EVERYONE BE QUIET & ZORN WAS ACROSS THE
STREET FROM ME & WE BOTH JUST STARTED YELLING & RUINED THE WHOLE TAKE — HA!

From Peops

Meeting Mose T

MR. MOSE TOLLIVER LIVES ON SAYRE STREET in Montgomery, Alabama. If anyone is interested in buying his work, it is possible to go to his house without an appointment, knock on the door, and introduce yourself. However, you will need to go to his house early. Eight o'clock in the morning is a good time to go there. Sometimes, his daughter Mildred will answer the door. If you're are lucky, his grandson, James, also a painter, will be standing near by and know immediately who you are looking for and direct you to the right house. James may also show you his own work, plus some paintings done by Mose's daughter, Annie T, James's mother. Since I arrived at two o'clock in the afternoon, it was too late for me to meet Mose.

During my encounter with James, he showed me three pictures while we stood in the front yard. One painting was done by Mose, another by James, and a third by Annie T. James made me an offer I thought was reasonable, I paid cash, and suddenly I owned paintings by three generations of painters. Finished with our dealings, James entered the house, and I walked in behind him. Sitting in a large cloth-covered armchair was another of Mose's daughters, Mildred. She was talking on the telephone. Two great-grandchildren were sitting on a couch talking, looking at me. After James introduced me to Mildred, he gave me his phone number and address, then left.

I glanced around the rooms. The walls in the front room were covered with pictures. Some of them were cut out from magazines, reproductions of Rembrandt's paintings beside children's drawings. Mildred paused from talking on the phone and told me I could look around the rest of the house. I walked into the next room, a kind of combination bedroom/painting studio. A large fireplace was located on my left beneath a mirror. From a shelf above the fireplace, five small paintings were hung. One picture was of a painted snake, another of a strange rodent, and one was of a rat. The wall above the bed was covered with pictures: a self-portrait, a black Christ, a watermelon painting, and three or four pictures painted by Tommy, one of Mose's grandchildren. A fourth generation. Soon Mildred got off the phone and mentioned to me that all the pictures on the walls were for sale.

I walked into the kitchen area, adjacent to a hallway. The walls were bare. I walked back into the living room. By now, the grandchildren were gone. Mildred told me about a dealer who had come the day before and brought every painting hanging on the walls in the hallway.

I was beginning to get the idea that Mildred was Mose's official salesperson, and my idea was reinforced as I began to ask about a picture hanging in the bedroom, a very interesting self-portrait of Mose. Mildred named a price, but I was put off. I liked a painting of a snake hanging over the fireplace, but I didn't ask her about the price. Instead, I began to look at one of Mose's watermelon paintings. Mose is famous for his watermelon paintings. These pictures are larger and more rectangular, showing large red slices containing black, painted seeds. The picture I liked was a small, square picture painted on a piece of plywood. The melon was round and not rectangular. It was closer to a rattlesnake melon, since the meat was a dark red, and not like a yellow-meat melon. Mildred told me the price, and I bought it.

I then asked if her father was here, and she said no; he had gone to the store for some beer, then to visit his girlfriend. Because of the big sale the day before, Mose was doing a little celebrating at his girlfriend's house. He was expected back in about two to three hours. I was disappointed. Since I had other plans for the evening, I would not be coming back, and my plane was leaving the next morning at eleven thirty.

I explained my situation, and Mildred suggested if I came by at eight o'clock the next morning, Mose would be in. I asked Mildred if she painted, and she said no. I was glad since I only had $30 cash left on me and I still needed to pay for my hotel room. I thanked her and left, walking to my hotel, half a mile away in downtown Montgomery.

The following morning I woke up at six A.M., had breakfast and called my usual cab driver, Walter, at seven o'clock. He drives for Young's Limo Service and works as a disc jockey at a nightclub on the weekends.

We drove to Mose's house. I got out of the car, telling Walter I would only be about twenty minutes. I walked up to the house, rang the bell, and got no answer.

I rang it twice more and waited. I walked out of the yard and started back toward the car, when I heard Mildred's voice from inside the house telling me to wait there. Five minutes later, she opened the door, and I went in. Mose was sitting on the bed in his studio, painting.

I introduce myself, and he looked up, smiled, and kept painting. I asked if I could take some pictures, and he said, "Sure, I don't mind."

Meeting Mose T

"When did you start painting?"
MT: "1965."
"Did you know Bill Traylor? [an outsider artist from Montgomery, Alabama, now dead]
MT: "Sure."
"What was he like?"
MT: "He was okay."
"What kind of paint do you use."
MT: "House paint."
"Do you thin it?"
MT: "Sure. You have to or you couldn't paint with it. It would dry up."

Mose was painting the edges of the picture. It was the figure of a person or child.

"I don't paint. It's too difficult."
MT: "If you don't have the patience, it's no use. You got to take to it."
"You have two generations of painters, James and Annie T."
MT: "More than that."
"Do you paint every day?"
MT: "Sometimes."
What artists do you like?"
MT: "Artists who like good work."

It was now nine o'clock, and I had about five minutes left until I had to leave for the airport. I was also beginning to wonder if Walter was still parked outside. I was looking at the pictures hanging over the fireplace and eyeballing the snake painting. It was two feet long and six inches narrow, painted in gray on a white background with a red border. The self-portrait hanging over the bed was gone. I was disappointed. Mose told me someone bought it.

"How much for this snake picture?"
Mose named a price, and I bought it.

"Do you take traveler's checks?
MT: "Traveler's checks? I don't take checks."
"It's not a personal check"
MT: "That's okay."

I signed the check and handed it to him.

MT: "Thank you. I'm glad you found something you like. You can have that chair in the corner."

It was a straight-back wooden chair completely covered with Mose's work, painted in pink and white, very nice.

"I don't think I can get it on the plane."
MT: "Carry it. Put it in some cardboard."
"I don't think I can carry it."
MT: "okay."

We shook hands, and I promised to send him copies of the photographs I took.

It was five minutes after nine o'clock. I walked out of the house to Walter's van, and we drove to the airport. After Walter dropped me off, I carried all my bags and pictures to a nearby bank of chairs. I was two hours early. Of course, I regretted not buying the chair as soon as I got to the airport.

All of Mose's paintings have a metal pop-top tacked onto the back of the picture so you can hang it on the wall. He only paints on plywood.

Currently, there is only one book, *Mose T's Slapout Family Album*, containing twenty paintings by Mose to accompany the poems of a local Montgomery lawyer/poet, Robert Ely. This book was published in 1996 by the Black Belt Press. It is currently out of print, but I found a copy for sale from a book dealer by searching for it on the Internet. The town of Slapout in the title is a small Alabama town consisting of a few stores. According to the following story, the town was so named because whenever a customer entered the dry goods store to buy a particular item, the owner would slap the counter top with the palm of his hand and proclaim, "We're slapout of that!" It stuck.

The only other publication containing a fair amount of Mose's work is *Raw Vision*, issue no. 12. It is a magazine devoted solely to the work of outsider artists. Mose's work is also on the cover of this particular issue. Mose's pictures are charming. And in terms of their value, his work is in the Museum of American Folk Art (New York) and a number of museums, which you can research for yourself.

Mose is eighty-one years old. In Japan, he would be considered a living national treasure. If you do go to visit this artist at his home, you might also meet a visiting art dealer doing business with Mildred.

Meeting Mose T

"Paul Simon" from *Noise of the World*

I DIDN'T DO "EL CONDOR PASA" because I knew it would become a standard. I didn't know it would be a standard. I just did it because I was interested in it. It just happened that in those times there was more acceptance of what was unusual or nonmainstream music. Now we're in a more primitive phase. I think I was fortunate in those days that radio and audiences were open to listen to that kind of music. Now I think it's more difficult to reach that kind of an audience.

The experience with Urubamba was great, too. This was an entire album that was one song. Similar experiences, because, again, learning about another culture, interacting with other musicians, is very liberating for a musician. You get a lot of information that you wouldn't otherwise get.

I hope I'll be able tell you something about what was a tremendous adventure for me, both musically and on a personal level. This project began quite by accident when a friend of mine gave me a cassette of an album called *Gumboots: Accordion Jive Volume Two*. That was in the summer of 1984. I listened to the album all summer. It was an instrumental album—accordion, guitar, drums—and as the summer went on, I was scat singing, improvising melodies over these tracks. I didn't have any intention of recording. I hadn't even thought about that.

I was just driving along and playing a cassette and singing along with it. But toward the end of the summer, I began to think that maybe I could record with this group, except that I really didn't know anything about them, where they came from, who they recorded for, because what I had was a copy of a copy of a cassette—I'm sure the recording industry would be pleased to hear that. Basically, I learned all of this from a bootleg tape.

I went to track down this recording, and it turned out it came from South Africa and in fact it was township jive, mbaqanga, music of Soweto and the black townships of South Africa. My first thought when I heard that was it's too bad this is not the music of Zimbabwe or Nigeria or Zaire, because life would be much more simple if that were the case. But then I began to think, this is the music of South Africa, and it's extraordinarily beautiful. So I began to pursue this musical train of thought, and I was put in touch with a man named Hilton Rosenthal, who produced a group called Jaluka. Jaluka was well known in South Africa because they were the first racially integrated band to play there. They have since disbanded, but they had quite a significant success there, and they had records released here, which are not very well known here, except among members of the music community.

Anyway, Hilton Rosenthal was the producer, and asked me, "When did you begin to get interested in South African music?" I told him that I didn't really know that much about it at all. This is my first experience with it, this township jive record. So he asked if I would like to hear more music, and of course I said I would. He sent me about twenty albums of different styles of music and different groups and different tribes. The more I listened to the music, the more fascinated I became with it. I began to wonder if it would be possible to go and record with these groups. So, again I called Hilton and I asked, "Is there any restriction against me recording with these groups? Can I travel freely there? Can the groups record with me? Is there any problem with that?"

He said, "No, I'd have to check with record companies, I'd have to check with management. If it's okay with those people, then it's entirely possible for you to do this."

In fact, that's what happened. We set it up, I traveled.

Early in 1985 I went with Roy Haley, my old friend and the engineer who recorded all the Simon and Garfunkel records, and we flew to Johannesburg. The first night I was there, we went to a reception at Hilton Rosenthal's house that they had for me and for Roy, and most of the music community was there. It was an integrated group, it was a mixed group, and the discussion was pretty open. Mostly about music, but also about politics. They wanted to know what the American people felt about politics in South Africa, and I told them that the country was absolutely unified in a sense of moral outrage and frustrated as to just what could be done about it. There was a divergence of viewpoints: that the Reagan administration was in favor of constructive engagement and many people felt that stronger measures should be taken.

As the discussion got further into politics, and our views were clearly shared, they told me—several of the guys there were well-known producers and musicians—that the black musicians union had voted prior to me coming there as to whether they wanted me to come. I was unaware of this vote. What they decided was that it would be beneficial to the music community there to let me record, because they felt what they were experiencing was a form of double apartheid. They were living under a repressive government, and when they tried to exploit their music and have their music played to the outside world, the music was often rejected on the grounds that it was South African. What they were experiencing was being blocked on all fronts. There was tremendous frustration, because the musical scene is very rich and very much modern. This also could be said for the other artistic fields: playwrights and poets also had a lot of trouble getting their work heard or seen. So they thought, since I was an artist whose work was popular internationally, I would be a good vehicle for them to show their music, an album of South African music.

Obviously I'm not South African. I went to make an album of my music and the music of the musicians that I hoped to interact with. I didn't know when I first went out there whether I would be able to achieve this, because I didn't know the musicians, I didn't know the conditions I would be working under, and I hadn't written songs. I was just going to see if I could create the structure of songs and then later on write it. I had done this occasionally in the past. Songs like "Late in the Evening" and a few other songs of mine were written that way, where I cut the track first and then wrote the song.

In this particular case, I intended to do all of the recording and all of my writing that way, cutting the tracks, then writing the song. How I went about doing that was, with the various musicians and groups that came in, we'd sit in the studio, I wouldn't play, because I wanted the musical backing to be what they played, so what I would do was sing into a microphone and improvise melody and meaningless words, phrases so I could hook them on to a melody and try to form the structure of a song. In my mind I thought later on I would actually write the song about a subject matter that I didn't know at the time it was recorded.

I became friends with a lot of musicians. I had a chance to go to Soweto, I had a chance to hear many different groups that I was unaware of when I went there. I knew of three groups when I went over. When I was there, more and more groups would come forward and say they'd like to play, and since we had block studio time, it was kind of possible to just bring people in and see what kind of music we could make.

Eventually I found a rhythm section that I really liked working with. They are extraordinary musicians and they're all Soweto guys. They are English-speaking, they are thoroughly familiar with American music. They knew who I was, knew my music. In that sense they were different from the groups I went to record with originally, who really didn't know who I was, who didn't speak English—we had to communicate through an inter-preter—and essentially they didn't know what I was doing, and since I myself didn't exactly know what I was doing, I couldn't explain it.

All of these songs where I used elements of music or thoughts that orig-inated from these records or thoughts that came out of these sessions that

Paul Simon

were not my own thoughts, on all of those compositions, I consider that we were co-writers. So this is the first album that I've ever done where over half the songs are co-written.

Joseph Shabalala is the lead singer and composer for Ladysmith Black Mambazo, which is a very well-known group in South Africa. I had first heard of the group and seen the group a few years ago on a BBC documentary called *Rhythm of Resistance: Music of South Africa*. When I was over there on this trip, Joseph came by the studio to visit, and we met for the first time. I wanted to find a way of singing with Ladysmith, but it actually took me several months to get up the nerve to ask if he would consider doing it. I was very much in awe of the group. I was intimidated to ask whether they'd want to sing with me.

I'm pleased to say that they said yes they would, so now the question was how to write a song that would fit Ladysmith Black Mambazo style and also was a Paul Simon song. That took me a couple of more months to figure out what that song would be. I had to listen to Ladysmith recordings and eventually I wrote the melody to "Homeless," the English words and the melody, and I sent them over on a demo to Joseph. I said change any words you want, change the harmony, add words in Zulu, continue the story, feel free to just take this as a sketch.

We met in Abbey Road Studios, of Beatles fame, in October of 1985, and Joseph had added considerably more to the song in Zulu, then we wrote one of the verses together in English.

They are known for each of the albums having a particular ending for each of the songs. I chose one of the endings that I liked and that I was able to phonetically sing, and we decided that that would be the very end of the music. When we got finished with the "Homeless" section, it was going so well that we decided to enlarge the piece, and basing the next section on another Ladysmith song, I made up English words that led into that vocal riff, and that actually led into their song, and when that finished, we went back to the English and then put the ending on. That was our first day of work in the studio.

On the second day, Joseph said that the group had been working until late into the night on an introduction that was a traditional Zulu song, and they changed the words to fit into the story of "Homeless" and all that it implied.

I didn't pick Joseph because we're the same size. I picked him because I liked Ladysmith.

Paul Simon

"Miriam Makeba" from *Noise of the World*

WHEN I CAME HERE, I was something completely new, because I sang my songs. I sang my "clicking songs," so it was something completely different. It opened the way for many South African artists, including Hugh Masekela, Dollar Brand, what's his name now? Abdullah Ibrahim. At home he was Dollar Brand. He was best known at home as Dollar Brand. Everyone is in. Paul Simon has opened it even wider.

With Harry Belafonte, I had another vehicle, because when I was performing with him, I was reaching more people. His audience was wide, so is Paul's. So when I'm with him, I'm reaching different people. It is an audience that we might never have reached on our own. Paul's audience is completely different. And they like it, when we came on stage, even those who had never heard us before, they were happy to discover and hear. And people left happy: they came backstage and said they liked our music.

I think artists should be like that, should help each other. I've always liked to perform with other artists, because I think I'm contributing something to them as well as they're contributing something to me. Paul's record was big, but in the show, all of us contributed something to make the show the success that it was. I'm very grateful to him, because I feel, through his show, I was able to come back here and renew my old friendships and fans. People are quite happy that I'm here.

Even though Paul Simon used South African township musicians and South African township music, he has a style all his own, and his style and my style are completely different. I don't want to measure anything I do against what Paul Simon does, or any other artist for that matter. I think that is the spirit of competition that I never was used to and will never get used to. I always feel that I am going to do what I'm doing. If it works, it works. If it doesn't, it doesn't, but I'm not going to measure myself according to so and so.

My door was open before I sang with Paul Simon, before Paul Simon did anything. With his style and his mixing of our music with his style, it worked for him. It was very good. Maybe more young people are talking about South African music because of Paul Simon.

That doesn't mean that it opened my door, because my door was opened before that. I never sold millions, but my first performance in this country was on the first of November 1959, on Steve Allen's show, which was viewed by 60 million people. Then I opened at the Village Vanguard the next day. I' stayed here for the next ten years, when in fact I was only supposed to stay for four weeks. So my little door was there, because I came from nowhere to stay for four weeks, and I wound up staying for ten years and working everywhere.

I've never sold records like Paul Simon has, because it's not the same thing. That's why I don't like the comparison. I cannot dispute the younger people, simply because I was not here from 1969 until I came back with Paul Simon. I was completely off the scene in this country. So children who are the age of my grandson, who is twenty-one, most of them do not know Miriam Makeba, except for children who have parents who are my fans, who heard the music in their homes. That was not because of anything else except the fact that I was not here. And coming back with Paul Simon in 1987 was very good for me, because I came back then, and coming back in a show like his was just wonderful for me. I hope that I will not be erased again.

"Pata Pata" is the song that really took off for me in the sixties. I wasn't very happy about it. Like, man, let me move away from "Pata Pata." But they say, "Hey, people like 'Pata Pata.'" You have to do what people like.

I remember, I did an interview with Al Jackson on the radio in New York, and when "Pata Pata" played, the phones were blinking and blinking because people were calling. There is a friend of mine, Duma, who said, "You see, when 'Pata Pata' plays, all the phones light up." I always say to him, "Get me away from 'Pata Pata,'" and he says, "You can't do anything about it, because that's the song that became big for you, and because the people like it. You've got to keep singing it."

It's the language. Many of my compatriots say they're from South Africa, they hear, "Can you click like Miriam Makeba?" It's like this language is mine. It's not, but they heard it first from me. It's like the short haircut. Some people would ask me, "Why do you wear your hair natural?" and I said, "You want me to wear my hair unnatural? You answered yourself. It's natural."

One cannot just stay in one place. You have to grow, you have to change, without changing your basic style. I think if I completely changed my style and went to sing jazz or something else, people would be shocked, maybe, unless I put just one song of a different type within my usual type of singing. Then it wouldn't be too much of a shock. We're always afraid to do

Miriam Makeba

that, because you don't know the reaction you're going to get from the press, from your fans, from everybody else. I think working with Sipho Mabuse brought something a little bit new from the younger generation in South Africa, because he is still in South Africa, and he came from there to Brussels to work with me on the album.

I always wanted to leave home. I never knew they were going to stop me from coming back. Maybe, if I knew, I never would have left. It is kind of painful to be away from everything that you've ever known. Nobody will know the pain of exile until you are in exile. No matter where you go, there are times when people show you kindness and love, and there are times when they make you know that you are with them but not of them. That's when it hurts.

I was banned from going home. I am still banned, but in the past year, I got phone calls from home from people saying that the government said I could come home if I want to and I apply for a visa, just like anybody else, because I'm not South African any more. I told the newspaper guy who called me, "Well, you can tell them that I consider myself South African, always South African." If I have any other travel document that I am using, it is an honorary one, because I never renounced my citizenship of birth, and second, we have leaders who are in prison; we have a state of emergency that keeps our people in prison. If they say we can come home, then lift the state of emergency, release all our people from prison, and let all our exiles come back home and be free, to come back home and vote for whomever we want to vote for. We might surprise them. We might vote for one of them. They don't know that. They should give us at least that opportunity. For me to just be told I can go home, why was I told that I couldn't go home in the first place. I never understood that.

I must say I was the first person to come over and let people discover a little of our culture, not only of South Africa, but of Africa. That's why they call me Mama Africa. I always knew that it was possible. All I needed to do was be here. I'm very confident about that because I know I have something different and special to give. There aren't too many Makebas.

Miriam Makeba

Love as the Practice of Freedom

IN THIS SOCIETY, THERE IS no powerful discourse on love emerging either from politically progressive radicals or from the left. The absence of a sustained focus on love in progressive circles arises from a collective failure to acknowledge the needs of the spirit and an overdetermined emphasis on material concerns. Without love, our efforts to liberate ourselves and our world community from oppression and exploitation are doomed. As long as we refuse to address fully the place of love in struggles for liberation, we will not be able to create a culture of conversion where there is a mass turning away from an ethic of domination.

Without an ethic of love shaping the direction of our political vision and our radical aspirations, we are often seduced, in one way or the other, into continued allegiance to systems of domination—imperialism, sexism, racism, classism. It has always puzzled me that women and men who spend a lifetime working to resist and oppose one form of domination can be systematically supporting another. I have been puzzled by powerful visionary black male leaders who can speak and act passionately in resistance to racial domination and accept and embrace sexist domination of women, by feminist white women who work daily to eradicate sexism but who have major blind spots when it comes to acknowledging and resisting racism and white-supremacist domination of the planet. Critically examining these blind spots, I conclude that many of us are motivated to move against domination solely when we feel our self-interest directly threatened. Often, then, the longing is not for a collective transformation of society, an end to politics of dominations, but rather simply for an end to what we feel is hurting us. This is why we desperately need an ethic of love to intervene in our self-centered longing for change. Fundamentally, if we are committed only to an improvement in that politic of domination that we feel leads directly to our individual exploitation or oppression, we not only remain attached to the status quo but act in complicity with it, nurturing and maintaining those very systems of domination. Until we are all able to accept the interlocking, interdependent nature of systems of domination and recognize specific ways each system is maintained, we will continue to act in ways that undermine our individual quest for freedom and collective liberation struggle.

The ability to acknowledge blind spots can emerge only as we expand our concern about politics of domination and our capacity to care about the oppression and exploitation of others. A love ethic makes this expansion possible. The civil rights movement transformed society in the United States because it was fundamentally rooted in a love ethic. No leader has emphasized this ethic more than Martin Luther King Jr. He had the prophetic insight to recognize that a revolution built on any other foundation would fail. Again and again, King testified that he had "decided to love" because he believed deeply that if we are "seeking the highest good," we "find it through love," because this is "the key that unlocks the door to the meaning of ultimate reality." And the point of being in touch with a transcendent reality is that we struggle for justice, all the while realizing that we are always more than our race, class, or sex. When I look back at the civil rights movement, which was in many ways limited because it was a reformist effort, I see that it had the power to move masses of people to act in the interest of racial justice—and because it was profoundly rooted in a love ethic.

The sixties black power movement shifted away from that love ethic. The emphasis was now more on power. And it is not surprising that the sexism that had always undermined the black liberation struggle intensified, that a misogynist approach to women became central as the equation of freedom with patriarchal manhood became a norm among black political leaders, almost all of whom were male. Indeed, the new militancy of masculinist black power equated love with weakness, announcing that the quintessential expression of freedom would be the willingness to coerce, do violence, terrorize, indeed, utilize the weapons of domination. This was the crudest embodiment of Malcolm X's bold credo "by any means necessary."

On the positive side, the Black Power movement shifted the focus of black liberation struggle from reform to revolution. This was an important political development, bringing with it a stronger anti-imperialist, global perspective. However, masculinist sexist biases in leadership led to the suppression of the love ethic. Hence progress was made even as something valuable was lost. While King had focused on loving our enemies, Malcolm called us back to ourselves, acknowledging that taking care of blackness was our central responsibility. Even though King talked about the importance of black self-love, he talked more about loving our enemies. Ultimately,

Love as the Practice of Freedom

neither he nor Malcolm lived long enough to fully integrate the love ethic into a vision of political decolonization that would provide a blueprint for the eradication of black self-hatred.

Black folks entering the realm of racially integrated American life because of the success of the civil rights and black power movements suddenly found we were grappling with an intensification of internalized racism. The deaths of these important leaders (as well as liberal white leaders who were major allies in the struggle for racial equality) ushered in tremendous feelings of hopelessness, powerlessness, and despair. Wounded in that space where we would know love, black people collectively experienced intense pain and anguish about our future. The absence of public spaces where that pain could be articulated, expressed, shared meant that it was held in—festering, suppressing the possibility that this collective grief would be reconciled in community even as ways to move beyond it and continue resistance struggle would be envisioned. Feeling as though "the world had really come to an end," in the sense that a hope had died that racial justice would become the norm, a life-threatening despair took hold in black life. We will never know to what extent the black masculinist focus on hardness and toughness served as a barrier preventing sustained public acknowledgment of the enormous grief and pain in black life. In *World as Lover, World as Self*, Joanna Macy emphasizes in her chapter on "Despair Work" that:

> the refusal to feel takes a heavy toll. Not only is there an impoverishment of our emotional and sensory life . . . but this psychic numbing also impedes our capacity to process and respond to information. The energy expended in pushing down despair is diverted from more creative uses, depleting the resilience and imagination needed for fresh visions and strategies.

If black folks are to move forward in our struggle for liberation, we must confront the legacy of this unreconciled grief, for it has been the breeding ground for profound nihilistic despair. We must collectively return to a radical political vision of social change rooted in a love ethic and seek once again to convert masses of people, black and nonblack.

A culture of domination is anti-love. It requires violence to sustain itself. To choose love is to go against the prevailing values of the culture. Many people feel unable to love either themselves or others because they do not know what love is. Contemporary songs like Tina Turner's "What's Love Got to Do with It" advocate a system of exchange around desire, mirroring the economics of capitalism: the idea that love is important is mocked. In his essay "Love and Need: Is Love a Package or a Message?" Thomas Merton argues that we are taught within the framework of competitive consumer capitalism to see love as a business deal: "This concept of love assumes that the machinery of buying and selling of needs is what makes everything run. It regards life as a market and love as a variation on free enterprise." Though many folks recognize and critique the commercialization of love, they see no alternative. Not knowing how to love or even what love is, many people feel emotionally lost; others search for definitions, for ways to sustain a love ethic in a culture that negates human value and valorizes materialism.

The sales of books focusing on recovery, books that seek to teach folks ways to improve self-esteem, self-love, and our ability to be intimate in relationships, affirm that there is public awareness of a lack in most people's lives. M. Scott Peck's self-help book *The Road Less Traveled* is enormously popular because it addresses that lack.

Peck offers a working definition for love that is useful for those of us who would like to make a love ethic the core of all human interaction. He defines love as "the will to extend one's self for the purpose of nurturing one's own or another's spiritual growth." Commenting on prevailing cultural attitudes about love, Peck writes:

> Everyone in our culture desires to some extent to be loving,
> yet many are in fact not loving. I therefore conclude that the
> desire to love is not itself love. Love is as love does. Love is an
> act of will—namely both an intention and an action. Will also
> implies choice. We do not have to love. We choose to love.

His words echo Martin Luther King's declaration, "I have decided to love," which also emphasizes choice. King believed that love is "ultimately the only answer" to the problems facing this nation and the entire planet. I share that belief and the conviction that it is in choosing love and beginning with love as the ethical foundation for politics that we are best positioned to transform society in ways that enhance the collective good.

It is truly amazing that King had the courage to speak as much as he did about the transformative power of love in a culture where such talk is often seen as merely sentimental. In progressive political circles, to speak

Love as the Practice of Freedom

of love is to guarantee that one will be dismissed or considered naïve. But outside those circles there are many people who openly acknowledge that they are consumed by feelings of self-hatred, who feel worthless, who want a way out. Often they are too trapped by paralyzing despair to be able to engage effectively in any movement for social change. However, if the leaders of such movements refuse to address the anguish and pain of their lives, they will never be motivated to consider personal and political recovery. Any political movement that can effectively address these needs of the spirit in the context of liberation struggle will succeed.

In the past, most folks both learned about and tended the needs of the spirit in the context of religious experience. The institutionalization and commercialization of the Church have undermined the power of religious community to transform souls, to intervene politically. Commenting on the collective sense of spiritual loss in modern society, Cornel West asserts:

> There is a pervasive impoverishment of the spirit in American society, and especially among black people. Historically, there have been cultural forces and traditions, like the Church, that held cold-heartedness and mean-spiritedness at bay. However, today's impoverishment of the spirit means that this coldness and meanness is becoming more and more pervasive. The Church kept these forces at bay by promoting a sense of respect for others, a sense of solidarity, a sense of meaning and value which would usher in the strength to battle against evil.

Life-sustaining political communities can provide a similar space for the renewal of the spirit. That can happen only if we address the needs of the spirit in progressive political theory and practice.

Often when Cornel West and I speak with large groups of black folks about the impoverishment of spirit in black life, the lovelessness, sharing that we can collectively recover ourselves in love, the response is overwhelming. Folks want to know how to begin the practice of loving. For me, that is where education for critical consciousness has to enter. When I look at my life, searching it for a blueprint that aided me in the process of decolonization, of personal and political self-recovery, I know that it was learning the truth about how systems of domination operate that helped, learning to look both inward and outward with a critical eye. Awareness is central to the process of love as the practice of freedom. Whenever those of us who are members of exploited and oppressed groups dare critically to interrogate our locations, the identities and allegiances that inform how we live our lives, we begin the process of decolonization. If we discover in ourselves self-hatred, low self-esteem, or internalized white-supremacist thinking and we face it, we can begin to heal. Acknowledging the truth of our reality, both individual and collective, is a necessary stage for personal and political growth. This is usually the most painful stage in the process of learning to love—the one many of us seek to avoid. Again, once we choose love, we instinctively possess the inner resources to confront that pain. Moving through the pain to the other side, we find the joy, the freedom of spirit that a love ethic brings.

Choosing love, we also choose to live in community, and that means that we do not have to change by ourselves. We can count on critical affirmation and dialogue with comrades walking a similar path. African-American theologian Howard Thurman believed that we best learn love as the practice of freedom in the context of community. Commenting on this aspect of his work in the essay "Spirituality out on the Deep," Luther Smith reminds us that Thurman felt the United States was given to diverse groups of people by the universal life force as a location for the building of community. Paraphrasing Thurman, he writes: "Truth becomes true in community. The social order hungers for a center (i.e., spirit, soul) that gives it identity, power, and purpose. America, and all cultural entities, are in search of a soul." Working within community, whether it be sharing a project with another person or with a larger group, we are able to experience joy in struggle. That joy needs to be documented. For if we focus only on the pain, the difficulties, which are surely real in any process of transformation, we only show a partial picture.

A love ethic emphasizes the importance of service to others. Within the value system of the United States any task or job that is related to "service" is devalued. Service strengthens our capacity to know compassion and deepens our insight. To serve another I cannot see them as an object, I must see their subjecthood. Sharing the teaching of Shambala warriors, Buddhist Joanna Macy writes that we need weapons of compassion and insight.

> You have to have compassion because it gives you the juice,
> the power, the passion to move. When you open to the pain
> of the world you move, you act. But that weapon is not

enough. It can burn you out, so you need the other—you need insight into the radical interdependence of all phenomena. With that wisdom you know that it is not a battle between good guys and bad guys, but that the line between good and evil runs through the landscape of every human heart. With insight into our profound interrelatedness, you know that actions undertaken with pure intent have repercussions throughout the web of life, beyond what you can measure or discern.

Macy shares that compassion and insight can "sustain us as agents of wholesome change" for they are "gifts for us to claim now in the healing of our world." In part, we learn to love by giving service. This is, again, a dimension of what Peck means when he speaks of extending ourselves for another.

The civil rights movement had the power to transform society because the individuals who struggle alone and in community for freedom and justice wanted those gifts to be for all, not just the suffering and the oppressed. Visionary black leaders such as Septima Clark, Fannie Lou Hamer, Martin Luther King Jr., and Howard Thurman warned against isolationism. They encouraged black people to look beyond our own circumstances and assume responsibility for the planet. This call for communion with a world beyond the self, the tribe, the race, the nation, was a constant invitation for personal expansion and growth. When masses of black folks starting thinking solely in terms of "us and them," internalizing the value system of white-supremacist capitalist patriarchy, blind spots developed, the capacity for empathy needed for the building of community was diminished. To heal our wounded body politic we must reaffirm our commitment to a vision of what King referred to in the essay "Facing the Challenge of a New Age" as a genuine commitment to "freedom and justice for all." My heart is uplifted when I read King's essay; I am reminded where true liberation leads us. It leads us beyond resistance to transformation. King tells us that "the end is reconciliation, the end is redemption, the end is the creation of the beloved community." The moment we choose to love, we begin to move against domination, against oppression. The moment we choose to love, we begin to move towards freedom, to act in ways that liberate ourselves and others. That action is the testimony of love as the practice of freedom.

Contributors

Robert Beck was born Robert Lee Maupin on August 4, 1918. Assuming the name Robert Beck, he briefly studied at the famed Tuskegee Institute before embarking upon a criminal career. Beck started to pimp at age eighteen in Chicago and in time acquired yet another name, one that became legend among fellow pimps and criminals: Iceberg Slim. In 1960, while serving a prison stretch, his third, at the Cook County House of Corrections, Beck decided to leave the street life and try his hand at writing. The resulting book, *Pimp*, based on his personal experiences, was a sensation when it appeared, and pioneered a genre of self-revelatory street-wise black confessional that, in turn, opened the door for writers, filmmakers, and even social activists. Today, *Pimp* is widely recognized as a literary classic. Beck's other books include *The Naked Soul of Iceberg Slim*, *Mama Black Widow*, *Trick Baby*, *Death Wish*, *Airtight Willie & Me*, and *Long White Con*. He died on April 28, 1992. His books continue to be published by Holloway House, which first brought them out, and are still ushered into print by the legendary editor Bentley Morriss, who gave Robert Beck his start.

Author, editor, performer, educator, and one of the nation's leading commentators on matters of sex, **Susie Bright** was born on March 25, 1958, in Arlington, Virginia, and grew up in California and Canada. She received a BA in Community Studies from the University of California at Santa Cruz in 1981 and has lived in the Bay Area since 1980. She has one daughter, Aretha, born in 1990. Bright has served as series editor for *The Best American Erotica* since 1993 and is the author of numerous books, including *Susie Bright's Sexual Reality: A Virtual Sex World Reader*, *Mommy's Little Girl: Susie Bright on Sex, Motherhood, Pornography, and Cherry Pie*, and *The Sexual State of the Union*.

In 1991, Bright was featured in V. Vale's now legendary "Angry Women" issue of *Re/Search* and she was one of the first lesbian sex gurus to appear in the pages of *Rolling Stone*. Her lectures, video presentations, and safe sex demos pack theaters in the United States, Canada, and Europe.

Hank Bordowitz is one of the first music journalists to take World Music seriously and has been writing on the subject for nearly four decades. His books include *Turning Points of Rock and Roll, Every Little Thing Is Gonna Be Allright—The Bob Marley Reader*, and *The Bruce Springsteen Scrapbook*.

William Seward Burroughs was born in St. Louis, Missouri, on February 5, 1914, to a wealthy family, heirs of the Burroughs Adding Machine fortune. Raised in conditions of relative ease, he studied medicine, English, and anthropology at Harvard, where he graduated in 1936. However, Burroughs was clearly not destined for a leisurely life. By the 1940s, he was struggling with full-blown heroin addiction in the seedier precincts of New York City, leading a life of (then) illegal homosexuality while consorting with dangerous professional criminals and hustlers of all sorts. He was also committing crimes. During this time he met the young Jack Kerouac and Allen Ginsberg. Impressed with the older, more experienced outlaw, they formed with Burroughs a unique literary association that in time grew to become the Beat Generation. Arrested for drug possession, Burroughs fled to Mexico where, in 1951, he accidentally killed his wife, Joan Burroughs, while attempting, drunk, to shoot an apple off her head. Carl Solomon, the friend to whom Allen Ginsberg dedicated his famed poem *HOWL*, worked as an editor at his uncle's publishing house, Ace Books, and with Ginsberg's encouragement published Burroughs's first novel as an inexpensive paperback. *Junky* appeared in 1953 under the pseudonym Bill Lee and was a modest financial success. Other books followed, including *Naked Lunch* (1959), which led to a Supreme Court battle; *The Soft Machine* (1961), *The Ticket That Exploded* (1962), and *Nova Express* (1964). By then, Burroughs was a countercultural idol, a world-famous writer, widely read and translated into many languages. His other works include *The Adding Machine* (1986), *The Burroughs File* (1984), *Place of Dead Roads* (1983), and *The Western Lands* (1987). Burroughs died in 1997 at age 83.

Ray Charles was born on September 23, 1930, in Albany, Georgia, and was raised in Florida. Afflicted with glaucoma, and by the age of seven completely blind, Charles attended the Saint Augustine School of the Blind and Deaf, where he studied music. Orphaned by the age of seventeen, he began working as a traveling musician throughout Florida, and later Washington State, traveling with country-western and jazz bands, singing and playing the piano. In 1950 he moved to Los Angeles, and in 1954 had his first major hit, with Atlantic Records, "I Got a Woman." The recording brought Charles fame and marked the beginning of a new genre, "soul." In 1962 he released *Genius + Soul = Jazz*, and a number of very popular country albums, including *Modern Sounds in Country and Western* (Vol. 1 and 2), which included such major hits as "I Can't Stop Loving You," "Born To Lose," and "Busted." In the mid-1960s an arrest for drug possession precipitated a long-overdue recovery from heroin addiction. There followed hits with a number of Beatles covers, and the song "Crying Time." His output during the 1970s and 1980s included work with the singers Randy Newman and Stevie Wonder and frequent television appearances. In 1992 President Bill Clinton awarded him the National Medal of Arts. Ray Charles died on June 10, 2004.

Eldridge Cleaver, the celebrated author of *Soul on Ice* and the former information minister of the Black Panther Party, became a fugitive from justice in late 1968, at the height of the domestic unrest. After years in Cuba, Algeria, and France, Cleaver surrendered to U.S. authorities, returned to California, and announced his conversion to Christianity. He died in 1998.

Sue Coe is our modern-day Goya, the greatest illustration artist working in the world today. Born in Britain, Sue Coe moved to the United States in 1972 and immediately began work for the op-ed page of the *New York Times*. Her drawings have since been included in *The New Yorker, Time, Newsweek, Rolling Stone, Mother Jones, National Lampoon,* and *Artforum,* among other publications. Coe has an unerring instinct for anticipating significant issues. Her book *How to Commit Suicide in South Africa* (1983) — about the death of Stephen Biko and other student organizers in South African prisons — became an anti-apartheid organizing tool used on college campuses to persuade investors to divest themselves of South African stock. Similarly, her 1986 book *X (The Life and Times of Malcolm X)* prefigured the resurgence of popular interest in the black leader. Since 1986, Coe has devoted her energies, more and more exclusively, to the defense of animals in industry, from factory farming to medical research and genetic engineering.

Her dedication to animal rights began early; she grew up in a house adjacent to a slaughterhouse, with all of its associated sights and smells. From 1986 to 1992, Coe visited slaughterhouses in the United States, Canada, and England. Through associates who worked in the meat industry, she gained access to stockyard operations in Arizona, California, Missouri, Minnesota, Texas, and Montreal; a meatpacking plant in Los Angeles; a free-range cattle ranch in Utah; dairies in New Mexico; egg factories in North Carolina and Pennsylvania; and kosher and Muslim slaughterhouses in New Jersey. Although cameras and videos were forbidden, Coe's sketchbook was usually considered harmless. When she was not allowed to sketch she made notes. Her research resulted in a series she calls *Porkopolis*, after the slang term for Cincinnati, the first centralized meat processing center in the United States. Published in 1996 under the title *Dead Meat*, the series provides a detailed look at the American meat industry. Many of the images are gruesome and difficult to look at, depicting as they do practices employed in factory farms and slaughterhouses, practices that in many cases are unthinkable and well hidden in modern society. Other images—such as "Modern Man Followed by the Ghosts of his Meat" and "Scientists Find a Cure for Empathy"—use satire, sarcasm, or humor to inform. The victimization of animals in *Porkopolis* is related to other issues, other situations of social and political oppression. The meat industry exploits its workers and pollutes the environment; its abuse of animals is a variation on the theme of the exploitation of the weak by the strong. In the words of Theodor Adorno, "Auschwitz begins whenever someone looks at a slaughterhouse and thinks: they're only animals." Sue Coe's other books include *Pit's Letter* and *Bully! Master of the Global Merry-Go-Round* (with Judith Brody).

Fly has been squatting since 1990 on the Lower East Side of Manhattan, where she paints and draws comics and illustrations. Her work has been published in the *New York Press*, *Village Voice*, San Francisco *Bay Guardian*, *Raygun*, *Bikini*, *World War III Illustrated*, *Punk Planet*, *Maximumrocknroll*, *Slug & Lettuce*, and numerous other publications. Fly toured the world playing bass in the band God Is My Co-pilot. Fly's first book, *CHRON!IC!RIOTS!PA!SM!* was published by Autonomedia in 1998. Fly has also produced countless 'zines and comics over the past two decades.

Ben Fong-Torres, one of rock's most celebrated journalists and a real-life character in *Almost Famous*, the 2000 film by Cameron Crowe, was born in Alameda, California, in 1945, and raised in Oakland's Chinatown, where his parents owned a restaurant. After attending San Francisco State College (now University), he began writing for *Rolling Stone* magazine in 1968 in its eighth issue, and in May 1969 became its news editor. His interviews included some of the most important subjects in contemporary American music: Bob Dylan, the Rolling Stones, Ray Charles, Paul McCartney, Elton John, Stevie Wonder, Bonnie Raitt, the Jackson 5, Linda Ronstadt, Neil Diamond, Diana Ross, Marvin Gaye, the Grateful Dead, and Ike & Tina Turner. The Ray Charles interview won the Deems Taylor Award for Magazine Writing in 1974. Fong-Torres has also DJ'd and hosted extensively for Bay Area radio and television, and since his departure from *Rolling Stone* has written for dozens of magazines, including *Esquire, GQ, Parade, Playboy, Sports Illustrated, Travel & Leisure, American Film, TV Guide, Harper's Bazaar,* and the *San Francisco Chronicle.* He is the author of several acclaimed books, including *The Rice Room: From Number Two Son to Rock and Roll; Hickory Wind: The Life and Times of Gram Parsons,* which was nominated for the Ralph J. Gleason Book Award; and *Not Fade Away: A Backstage Pass to 20 Years of Rock & Roll.*

Allen Ginsberg was born in 1926 and raised in Paterson, New Jersey, an upbringing marred by his mother's declining mental health. He attended Columbia University, where he met on campus, and around Times Square, an odd assemblage of bohemian literary aspirants that included students, life drop-outs, heroin addicts, and petty criminals, among them Jack Kerouac, William Burroughs, Herbert Huncke, John Clellan Holmes, and Neal Cassady. Their views and experimental literary productions would make them famous as the Beat Generation—a movement that virtually changed the course of American history. As a poet, Ginsberg is best known for two extraordinary full length poems: *HOWL* and *Kaddish,* the one a devastating critique of American capitalism, the other a heartrending reminiscence of his mother's descent into insanity. But Ginsberg's fame extends, as well, to his brilliant helmsmanship of countercultural activism over the decades, from the early days of the *HOWL* obscenity trial to the 1960s, when he seemed to be everywhere on the front lines of youth protest—demonstrating against the Pentagon, outside the 1968 Democratic Convention, investigating links between the CIA, drugs and Latin American dictatorships, placing his body in harm's way to prevent nuclear proliferation. He was above all a friend to fellow poets and writers, both famous and unknown, and extended a willing assist whenever called upon, to donate poems to a new small magazine, write an intro for a first chapbook of poems, make a small loan, or just lend a place to crash. He was a member of the Academy of Arts and Letters, was awarded France's medal Le Chevalier de l'Ordre des Arts et Lettres, and was a cofounder of the Jack Kerouac School of Disembodied Poets at Naropa Institute, the first accredited Buddhist college in the Western world. His passing in 1997 was mourned throughout the world.

Mike Golden is the editor and publisher of *Smoke Signals* and was the founder of the infamous Club 86'ed. He is a poet, journalist, novelist, filmmaker, and award-winning playwright and screenwriter. Through his book *The Buddhist Third Class Junkmail Oracle: the art and poetry of d. a. levy*, Golden has done more then any other person to preserve the legacy of d.a. levy and to garner for the Cleveland poet the admiration that he assuredly deserves. His essay first appeared in a different version in *New York Writer*, in 1989. The version in this volume appeared in 1994 in *BEET*, Joe Maynard's legendary underground 'zine. It was scanned for printing by Bart Plantenga, printed out on Dave Mandl's printer and photocopied, staple-bound and enclosed in an issue of *BEET*.

Scarlot Harlot (a.k.a. Carol Leigh) or "Big Red" as she is sometimes known, is a self-described "unrepentant whore, activist and artist" who first coined the term "sex work" in the late seventies. She has written, performed, and produced work in a variety of genres on women's issues and on her experiences in the sex industry and has appeared on *Nightline, Donahue, Court TV, Access America, The Late Show, The Roseanne Show*, and *Geraldo*. Her one-woman play *The Adventures of Scarlot Harlot* was featured at the National Festival of Women's Theater. She is a founding member of ACT UP in San Francisco and has served on the San Francisco Board of Supervisor's Task Force on prostitution, representing San Francisco's Commission on the Status of Women. She has also received numerous awards for her video documentaries and co-directed Annie Sprinkle's *Herstory of Porn*. She directs and curates the San Francisco Sex Workers' Film and Video Festival and teaches multimedia production in San Francisco. Scarlot Harlot lectures at universities and colleges around the world.

Jack Hirschman, a writer and the current Poet Laureate of San Francisco and is regarded by some as the greatest living poet in America. He was born on December 13, 1933, in New York City. Hirschman received his Bachelor of Arts degree from City College of New York in 1955, and earned both his MA and PhD from Indiana University in 1957 and 1961, respectively. He is a member of the Union of Street Poets, the Union of Left Writers, the Roque Dalton Cultural Brigade, and the Jacques Roumain Cultural Brigade. In his career Hirschman has worked as a poet of Dartmouth College (1952); instructor and assistant professor of English at the University of California at Los Angeles (1959–61; 1961–66); painter and collagist, with exhibitions in

Los Angeles and Venice, California; and translator of over twenty-five books from the original German, French, Spanish, Italian, Russian, Albanian, and Greek. He has taken the free exchange of poetry and politics into the streets and uses his skills to help awaken the American people to homelessness as an expression of a system that can no longer take care of its people. He has written more than fifty volumes of poetry and essays.

From slam to hip-hop, from performance poetry to spoken word, **Bob Holman** has been a central figure in the reemergence of poetry. Dubbed a member of the "Poetry Pantheon" by the *New York Times Magazine* and featured in a Henry Louis Gates Jr. profile in *The New Yorker*, Holman has previously been crowned "Ringmaster of the Spoken Word" (New York *Daily News*), "Poetry Czar" (*Village Voice*), "Dean of the Scene" (*Seventeen*), and "the best poetry MC in the world," (San Francisco's *Poetry Flash*). His latest collection of poems, a collaboration with Chuck Close, *A Couple of Ways of Doing Something*, was first exhibited at the Peggy Guggenheim Museum during the Venice Biennale and published by Aperture. The TV series he produced for PBS, "The United States of Poetry," won the INPUT, International Public Television Award; he founded Mouth Almighty/Mercury Records, the first-ever major spoken word label, in 1995; and ran the infamous poetry slams at the Nuyorican Poets Café from 1988 to 1996. He is currently Visiting Professor of Writing at the Columbia School of the Arts, founder/proprietor of the Bowery Poetry Club, and artistic director of Study Abroad on the Bowery, a certificate program in applied poetics.

bell hooks, one of the most admired and controversial thinkers in the United States today, is a self-described "Black woman intellectual, revolutionary activist." She was born Gloria Jean Watkins on September 25, 1952, in Hopkinsville, Kentucky. For her books, Watkins adopted the pseudonym bell hooks, after one of her great-grandmothers, a Native American. She is Distinguished Professor of English at City College of New York and the author of many books, including *Breaking Bread: Insurgent Black Intellectual Life* (with Cornel West), *Sisters of the Yam: Black Women and Self-Recovery, Teaching to Transgress: Education as the Practice of Freedom*, and *Outlaw Culture*.

Brenda Knight's landmark anthology *Women of the Beat Generation* unearthed a well-concealed vein of Beat Generation history: the significant contribution made by the women writers, lovers, and participants who staked their futures on the new, radical modes of Beat lifestyle and creativity, and in so doing risked the disapprobation of both their culture and their families. Knight's book has become a sensational seller and has opened new doors of scholarship as well as providing vital examples for today's women and their ongoing quest for personal freedom. Knight won the American Book Award in 1997 for *Women of the Beat Generation*. A scholar of medieval literature and modern poetry and former editor of *Etc.* magazine, her books include *Sheroes: Bold, Brash (and Absolutely Unabashed) Superwomen* and *Wild Women and Books*. She is a senior editor at RedWheel/Weiser Books and lives in San Francisco, where she is an advocate—by example and activism—for cutting-edge art and literature and for radical social and cultural change.

Paul Krassner cut his teeth as a journalist at *MAD* magazine, served time as Lenny Bruce's "obscenity coach," and together with Abbie Hoffman and Jerry Rubin founded the Yippies. In 1958 he decided that what the world needed was a satirical magazine for adults and he has written and published *The Realist* discontinuously ever since. *People* magazine calls him the "father of the underground press." Krassner has appeared on such national television shows as *Late Night with Conan O'Brien* and *Politically Incorrect with Bill Maher*. His writing has appeared in *Rolling Stone, Spin, High Times, New York, National Lampoon,* the *Village Voice, Whole Earth Review, Playboy* and *The Nation*. His autobiography, *Confessions of a Raving, Unconfined Nut: Misadventures in the Counter-Culture,* was published in 1994. *We Have Ways of Making You Laugh,* his new compact disc, is available from Mercury Records. He is the author of *One Hand Jerking: Reports from an Investigative Journalist* and publishes "The Disneyland Memorial Orgy" at paulkrassner.com. He lives in Venice, California, with his wife Nancy.

Erik La Prade, a poet, journalist, and photographer, was born in New York City on January 27, 1951. His parents were highly cultured and inculcated La Prade in a taste for art and literature. He grew up in the tougher precincts of the Bronx and Manhattan, attending public schools. His father was acquainted with the poet James Wright, whom La Prade met. Also, in these years, he traveled to Europe and absorbed continental influences. He graduated from City College of New York in 1978 with a BA in English, and in his early thirties began to write. In 1990 Laprade received his MA in comparative literature from City College. His first book of poems, *Things Maps Don't Show*, was published in 1995, and a second collection, *Figure Studies*, appeared in 1999. His poems, articles, and photographs have run in numerous publicatons, including the *New York Times, Fish Drum, Night* magazine, *The Louisiana Review, Long Shot, Witness, The Brooklyn Rail, HOWL: San Francisco Poetry News; New York Arts, The Reading Room,* and *The Hat*. He is anthologized in *Captured: A History of Film and Video on the Lower East Side*.

Timothy "Speed" Levitch was born in 1970 in New York City. While attending college he served a brief internship as a proofreader for *Penthouse*, and after he and graduated in 1992 he got a tour guide's license and a position with the New York City bus tour operator, Apple Tours. When an aspiring amateur documentary filmmaker named Bennet Miller filmed Levitch holding forth from the deck of a tour bus, and then followed him around town with a camera, recording Levitch's nonstop street commentary on the history and meaning of Manhattan, the result was an instant cult film classic: *The Cruise*. In his review of *The Cruise* in the *New York Times*, Stephen Holden called Levitch "a loquacious New York City tourbus guide, sidewalk philosopher and one-man almanac of urban lore," while *Rolling Stone* magazine has dubbed Levitch as "a one-man counterculture." Since then, Levitch has appeared in several independent films, performed his works on stage to musical accompaniment in clubs across the country and is a pivotal figure in the "Burning Man" scene. He is the author of *Speedology: Speed on New York on Speed* and travels frequently between New York and San Francisco.

Miriam Makeba was born in 1932 in South Africa. After a stint as a featured vocalist with the Manhattan Brothers, she left to record with her all-woman group, the Skylarks. During this time she toured South Africa with Alf Herberts' African Jazz and Variety. In 1959, Makeba sang the lead female role in the show *King Kong*, a Broadway-inspired South African musical. She was invited to sing at a celebration of President Kennedy's birthday and subsquently worked in New York with Harry Belafonte. In 1963 Makeba testfied on apartheid before the United Nations, and as a result the South African government revoked her citizenship. Thus began a long period of exile. She remained in the United States and married Stokely Carmichael, a Black Nationalist leader but was forced, due to harassment by US authorities, to flee America for Guinea. Makeba returned to world prominence when she performed with Paul Simon on the Graceland tour. In the late 1980's she returned to her homeland as a free South African.

Born in 1937 in Rochester, New York, **David Meltzer**, a poet, jazz aficionado, and anthologist, spent some of his youth as a rock musician in Boston and, in the late 1960s, in California. An integral figure in the California Beat scene and later, the small press scene of the 1960s and 1970s, Meltzer has published most of his books through large houses and small presses alike, including Penguin Books, City Lights, Black Sparrow, Mercury House, Unicorn Press, and Robert Hawley's Oyez Press—over fifty books in little more than twenty-five years. Meltzer has edited a number of anthologies and the significant collection of interviews *The San Francisco Poets* (1971). The book consists of interviews, poetry, and bibliographies of Lawrence Ferlinghetti, Kenneth Rexroth, Lew Welch, Michael McClure, Richard Brautigan, and William Everson. His titles include *The Selected Poems of David Meltzer, Beat Thing, The Selected Garden: Anthology in the Kabbalah* and *Arrows: Selected Poetry, 1957–1992*. He teaches at New College in San Francisco and lives in Berkeley, California.

Eileen Myles has written thousands of poems since she gave her first reading at CBGB's in 1974. *Bust* magazine calls her "the rock star of modern poetry" and the *New York Times* says she's "a cult figure to a generation of post-punk females forming their own literary avant-garde." *Publishers Weekly* declares that, in her new book *Skies*, she is "the native informant of living life punkily on the streets," but also "having the best of both worlds, as working-class Bostonian and New York aesthete." Eileen headed to New York after college (the University of Massachusetts, Boston), quickly gaining the friendship of Allen Ginsberg, working for the poet James Schuyler, becoming a habitué of the household of Ted Berrigan and Alice Notley, and generally being a notable part of the turbulent punk and art scene that animated Manhattan's East Village. From 1977 to 1979 she edited a poetry magazine, *dodgems*. From 1984 to 1986 she was artistic director of St. Mark's Poetry Project. She also wrote, acted in, and directed plays at St. Mark's and PS 122: *Joan of Arc*: a spiritual entertainment; *Patriarchy*, a play, *Feeling Blue, Pts. 1, 2 & 3; Modern Art; My Sor Juana Inez de la Cruz*; and a solo performance piece, *Leaving New York*. She has been a virtuoso performer of her own work, reading to audiences at colleges, performance spaces, and bookstores across the country as well as in Europe,

Iceland, and Russia. In 1992 she conducted a write-in campaign for President of the United States. In 1997 Eileen toured with Sister Spit's Ramblin' Road Show. Her books include *Skies* (2001), *on my way* (2001), *Cool for You* (a novel, 2000), *School of Fish* (1997), *Maxfield Parrish* (1995), *Not Me* (1991), and *Chelsea Girls* (stories, 1994). In 1995, with Liz Kotz, she edited *The New Fuck You/Adventures in Lesbian Reading*. She's a frequent contributor to *Book Forum*, *Art in America*, the *Village Voice*, the *Nation*, the *Stranger*, *Index*, and *Nest*.

Born in Minnesota in 1942, **Dotson Rader** has served as editor and contributing editor at *New Politics*, *Esquire*, and *Parade*. He has also been a consultant to the National Committee for Literary Arts at Lincoln Center. Rader won the Odyssey Institute Award for Journalism in 1982 and is the author of several books, including the memoir *I Ain't Marchin' Anymore!*

In 1951 **Barney Rosset** bought a fledgling literary publishing company, Grove Press, named after the Greenwich Village street where it began. For the next thirty-three years he ran it from various locations in the same neighborhood, developing Grove into a critical part of the downtown New York firmament and one of the most influential publishers of its day. Writers came to Grove because it championed their work in an otherwise often hostile environment. In the fifties, Rosset published D. H. Lawrence's *Lady Chatterly's Lover* and Henry Miller's *Tropic of Cancer*, defending the books and others in courts when they were attacked. Over the years Grove took on hundreds of lawsuits, in the process expanding the range of public discourse. Following his strong personal tastes, Rosset developed an impressive list of authors. His journal, *Evergreen Review*, published by Grove Press and edited with Fred Jordan and Donald Allen, was one of the leading avant-garde journals of its day, featuring many of Grove's authors in its pages. Indeed, many Grove writers, who were considered iconoclasts in their day, are now regarded as central figures in our culture, such as: Samuel Beckett, William S. Burroughs, Frantz Fanon, Octavia Paz, Pablo Neruda, Alain Robbe-Grillet, Marguerite Duras, Jean Genet, Eugene Ionesco, Harold Pinter, Tom Stoppard, Hubert Selby Jr., Kensaburo Oe, Kathy Acker, and David Mamet. In 1988 the PEN American Center presented Rosset with its Publisher Citation for "distinctive and continuous service to international letters, to the freedom and dignity of writers, and for the free transmission of the printed word across the barriers of poverty, ignorance, censorship, and repression." Rosset turned eighty-four in 2006 and continues, with Astrid Meyers, to issue *Evergreen Review* online (http://www.evergreenreview.com) and to publish groundbreaking novels, plays, and memoirs, as well as CDs, DVDs, videos, and ebooks by emerging and renowned authors through his imprint Foxrock Books (http://www.foxrock.com).

Hubert Selby Jr., arguably the most significant American novelist of the postwar era, was born in Brooklyn in 1928 and went to sea as a merchant mariner while still in his teens. After a decade of hospitalizations for lung disease, he was sent home to die. Deciding instead to live, but having no way to make a living, he came to a realization that would change the course of literature: "I knew the alphabet. Maybe I could be a writer." Drawing from the landscape of his Brooklyn neighborhood, he wrote *Last Exit to Brooklyn* (1964), a novel that Allen Ginsberg predicted would "explode like a rusty hellish bombshell over America and still be eagerly read in a hundred years."

In 1989 *Last Exit to Brooklyn* was made into a film by the German director Uli Edel; Selby himself made a cameo appearance. In 2000, *Requiem For a Dream* became a widely acclaimed motion picture. In 1997 Selby, who toured frequently with Henry Rollins, recorded the whole of *Last Exit To Brooklyn* as a multi-CD boxed set for 2.13.61, Rollins's label. Rollins also worked with Selby on the 1990 CD *Our Fathers Who Aren't in Heaven* and in 1995 released Selby's *Live in Europe 1989*. Selby's work has appeared through the years in *Yugen, Black Mountain Review, Evergreen Review, Provincetown Review, Kulchur, New Directions Annual, Swank, Open City*, and other publications. His other books include *The Room, The Demon, Song of the Silent Snow, Waiting Period*, and *The Willow Tree*. Selby died of chronic pulmonary disease in Los Angeles in 2004. Nick Tosches has written: "To begin to define Selby's brilliance and power, you have to go back to the rhythms of Homer, Hesiod, and Sappho; back to the dark and light and beauty of Dante; and back to what lay beyond and beneath that sign on the Belt Parkway from which he took the title of his first novel. Everything that Herman Melville, that other great ex-seaman, and no stranger to Brooklyn, is held up to be in the pantheon of American literature, Hubert Selby Jr. is. What *Moby Dick* was to Melville's century, *Last Exit to Brooklyn* is to ours, and between the two, Selby's is the better book. If that be called heresy, know that it be called so only by those of the same dead mind as they who allowed Melville to die unknown."

In the winter of 1957, two sixteen-year-olds from Queens, New York, calling themselves "Tom and Jerry" cut a single that hit the charts: "Hey School-girl." Later, they sang duo under their real names. Simon and Garfunkel became one of the greatest folk-rock groups of all times. The release of "The Sounds of Silence" as a single in 1965 launched them, and for the next five years, **Paul Simon** wrote the songs, and sang them with Art Gar-funkel, creating numerous hit singles and albums. In 1970, after the release of their most popular album, *Bridge Over Troubled Water,* the two split up and Simon continued as a solo performer, releasing a number of albums that have sold millions of copies, including the reggae-flavored Top Ten single "Mother and Child Reunion." This was followed by "There Goes Rhymin," and a live album, *Still Crazy After All These Years,* which won the Grammy for Album of the Year. Simon's experiments with South African music resulted in *Graceland* in 1986, which became his biggest-selling solo album, won him another Album of the Year Grammy, and established Simon as one of the earliest pioneers of World Music. His latest album release is *Surprise.*

John Sinclair was born on October 2, 1941, in Flint, Michigan. In February 1967 Sinclair organized (with his partner and now wife Leni Arndt Sinclair and the artist Gary Grimshaw) a "total cooperative tribal living and working commune," Trans-Love Energies Unlimited, as an attempt to con-solidate the energies of the developing counterculture. Trans-Love pro-duced dance concerts, rock and roll, light shows, books, pamphlets, posters, and the *Warren-Forest Sun* newspaper and served as a cooperative booking agency for the rock groups the MC-5, the Stooges, and Billy C. and the Sunshine. Deeply influenced by the Black Panther leaders Huey Newton and Eldridge Cleaver, Sinclair (with Pun Plamondon), founded the White Panther Party in November 1968, serving first as its minister of information and later as chairman. The ten-point program of the White Panther Party demanded economic and cultural freedom. "Everything free for every-body!" and a total "assault" on the culture by any means necessary were the essence of the White Panther program. The White Panther Party soon had affiliated chapters established nationwide. In July 1969 Sinclair was sen-tenced to prison for nine and a half to ten years for possession of two mar-ijuana cigarettes. While in prison he assembled and wrote *Guitar Army* and published another collection of writings, *Music & Politics,* coauthored by Robert Levin. Two and a half years of legal and political battles culminated at Crisler Arena in Ann Arbor on December 10, 1971, with 15,000 people attending the Free John Now Rally headlined by John Lennon and Yoko Ono. Just three days later, the Michigan Supreme Court, on its own motion, ordered Sinclair released, and later overturned his conviction, upholding his contention that Michigan's marijuana statutes were unconstitutional and void.

Sparrow is a substitute teacher, palindrome scholar, poet, and theologian who lives above a children's clothing store in Phoenicia, New York, with his wife, Violet Snow, their daughter, Sylvia, and rabbit, Bananacake. He is the first person to be published in *The New Yorker* as a result of protesting against it. With a group of his cronies known as The Unbearables he demonstrated against the magazine on Pearl Harbor Day, 1993. While his comrades filibustered in the *New Yorker* offices, Sparrow quickly wrote eighteen poems. Alice Quinn, the poetry editor, rejected the poems with a warm note, and Sparrow continued to submit to the magazine. He has now had four poems accepted by the *New Yorker*. His work has also appeared in the *Village Voice*, the *Daily News*, *Verses That Hurt, Aloud: Poetry from the Nuyorican Poets Café*, *The Outlaw Bible of American Poetry*, and *The Exquisite Corpse Reader*, and is featured in the PBS documentary *The United States of Poetry*. Sparrow ran for president in 1992 with the Pajama Party and was the first candidate in history to beg his supporters not to vote for him. [This biographical note is culled from "The One Hundred Thousand Biographical Notes of Sparrow."]

Annie Sprinkle was born Ellen F. Steinberg on July 23, 1954, in Philadelphia. A self-styled "Post-Porn Modernist," she had her art denounced on the floor of the U.S. Senate by the conservative Senator Jesse Helms of North Carolina as pornography. She is undoubtedly the first porn star to earn a PhD in human sexuality (Institute for Advanced Study of Human Sexuality, San Francisco). Her work, spanning three decades, is studied in universities nationwide. In her best-known theater/performance art piece, *Public Cervix Announcement*, she invites the audience to "celebrate the female body" by viewing her cervix with a speculum and flashlight. She has appeared in over two hundred films: XXX, X, B movies, loops, numerous documentaries, four HBO Reel Sex programs, and produced, directed, and starred in several of her own films, including *Annie Sprinkle's Herstory of Porn*. Her books include *Pees on Earth, Xxxooo 2: Love and Kisses from Annie Sprinkle, Dr. Sprinkle's Spectacular Sex*, and *Post Porn Modernist*.

James Sullivan was a pop culture critic at the *San Francisco Chronicle* for seven years. He is the author of *Jeans: A Cultural History of an American Icon*. He has also written for the *Boston Globe, Rolling Stone, Entertainment Weekly*, and *Book*. He lives in Massachusetts.

Michelle Tea of San Francisco is one of the most prolific and gifted young writers in America today. She is also much admired for her innovative arts organizing, including Sister Spit, the all-girl open-mic event that won a *San Francisco Bay Guardian* "Best of the Bay" Award. Tea's first novel, *The Passionate Mistakes and Intricate Corruption of One Girl in America*, garnered lengthy, positive reviews in the *Village Voice* and the *Nation*. *Valencia*, her second work, received the 2000 Lambda Literary Award for Best Lesbian Fiction, was selected by the *Voice Literary Supplement* as one of the top twenty-five books of the year, and earned Tea both a *San Francisco Bay Guardian* "Goldie Award" for Literature and a prestigious award from the Rona Jaffe Foundation for female writers at the start of their careers. Tea's third book, *The Chelsea Whistle*, was nominated for a Lambda Literary Award in the autobiography category, and was selected by the *San Francisco Chronicle* as one of the Top 100 books of 2002. Her most recent books include *Rent Girl* and *Rose of No Man's Land*.

With a few hundred dollars given to him by Beat founders Lawrence Ferlinghetti and Allen Ginsberg, **V. Vale** began publishing out of San Francisco *Search & Destroy*, an independent publication devoted to the Punk movement. Building upon the success of *Search & Destroy*, Vale started RE/Search publications with the aim of exploring the dark side of culture. Large-format books with innovative layouts and original graphics, and presenting urban anthropological investigations into the new subversive underground, RE/Search books have managed to carve out a place entirely their own in the cultural landscape, including volumes—half-manifesto/half-freakish encyclopedia—on William Burroughs and Bryon Gysin, Mark Pauline and the Survival Reseach Lab, J. G. Ballard, *The Atrocity Exhibition, Octave Mirbeaus, The Torture Garden, The Confessions of Wanda von Sacher-Masoch, Infamous Pranks, Modern Primitives and Angry Women*. They remain, to this day, without precedent, irreplacable alternatives to "official culture"—a deeply countercultural dark-side narrative of American society. **Andrea Juno** is an author, editor, and the publisher of Juno Books. She has collaborated on many landmark RE/Search publications, including *Ten Angry Women* and *Angry Women in Rock*.

Kurt Vonnegut Jr., was born on November 11, 1922, in Indianapolis. In 1940 Vonnegut studied at Cornell. In 1943 he volunteered for military service. When his mother committed suicide in 1944, Vonnegut returned home briefly and then shipped back to Europe, where he served in the Battle of the Bulge as a battalion scout. He was taken prisoner and transported to Dresden, Germany. Between February 13 and 14, the Royal Air Force and United States Air Force made heavy raids on Dresden, and Vonnegut, imprisoned in a meatlocker under a slaughterhouse, was among the few people to survive the total destruction. He portrayed his experience in the acclaimed novel *Slaughterhouse Five* (1969). Considered our best living satirist, he is the author of numerous books, including *Breakfast of Champions, Cat's Cradle, Mother Night,* and *Welcome to the Monkey House.* His works continue to enjoy a broad following, particularly among the young. Vonnegut has served as vice president of P.E.N. American Center and was elected to the American Academy of Arts and Letters. He is Distinguished Professor of English Prose at City University of New York and has been awarded an honorary Doctorate of Literature by Hobart and William Smith College.

Tennessee Williams was born Thomas Lanier Williams in Columbus, Mississippi, on March 26, 1911. After a struggling start, what many consider to be his finest play, *The Glass Menagerie,* came to Broadway and won the New York Drama Critics' Circle award as the best play of the season. Williams was thirty-four. Over the next eight years his plays, *A Streetcar Named Desire, Summer and Smoke, The Rose Tattoo,* and *Camino Real,* appeared on Broadway. He received his first Pulitzer Prize in 1948 for *Streetcar,* and world-wide fame arrived in 1950 and 1951 when *The Glass Menagerie* and *A Streetcar Named Desire* were made into motion pictures. Over the next thirty years, he divided his time between homes in Key West, New Orleans, and New York. His reputation continued to grow and he saw many more of his works produced on Broadway and made into films, including *Cat on a Hot Tin Roof* (for which he earned a second Pulitzer Prize in 1955), *Orpheus Descending,* and *The Night of the Iguana.* Williams died on February 24, 1983, in New York City.

Permissions

Alan Kaufman's novel *Matches* was published in the fall of 2005. David Mamet has called *Matches* "an extraordinary war novel," and Dave Eggers has written that "there is more passion here than you see in twenty other books combined." Kaufman's critically acclaimed memoir *Jew Boy* has appeared in three editions, hardcover and paperback, in the United States and Great Britain. He is the award-winning editor of several anthologies, the most recent of which, *The Outlaw Bible of American Literature*, was reviewed on the cover of the *New York Times Book Review*. He has taught in the graduate and undergraduate schools of the Academy of Art University and in writing workshops in San Francisco. His work has appeared in *Salon*, the *Los Angeles Times*, the *San Francisco Chronicle*, *Partisan Review*, and the *San Francisco Examiner*. Kaufman has been widely anthologized, most recently in *Nothing Makes You Free: Writings From Descendents of Holocaust Survivors*.